SRI LANKA HANDBOOK

with The Maldives

Editors **Robert & Roma Bradnock**
Maps by **Sebastian Ballard**

Beside Adam's Peak at an infinite depth and distance lay the flat blue sea, in between a thousand mountains, broad valleys, narrow ravines, rivers and waterfalls, in countless folds, the whole mountainous island on which legend places paradise.

Herman Hesse 1911

TRADE & TRAVEL *Handbooks*

Trade & Travel Publications Ltd
6 Riverside Court, Lower Bristol Road, Bath BA2 3DZ, England
Telephone 01225 469141 Fax 01225 469461
Email 100660.1250@compuserve.com

ISBN 0 900751 71 1

CIP DATA: A catalogue record for this book is available from the British Library

In North America, published and distributed by

PASSPORT BOOKS
a division of *NTC Publishing Group*

4255 West Touhy Avenue, Lincolnwood (Chicago), Illinois 60646-1975, USA
Telephone 708-679-5500 Fax 708-679-2494 Email NTCPUB2@AOL.COM

ISBN 0-8442-4902-5

Library of Congress Catalog Card Number 95-71560

IMPORTANT: While every endeavour is made to ensure that the facts printed in this book are correct at the time of going to press, travellers are cautioned to obtain authoritative advice from consulates, airlines, etc, concerning current travel and visa requirements and conditions before embarking. The publishers cannot accept legal responsibility for errors, however caused, that are printed in this book.

Cover illustration by Suzanne Evans

Printed and bound in Great Britain by Clays Ltd., Bungay, Suffolk

CONTENTS

MAP SYMBOLS 4

MAP INDEX 5

THE EDITORS 6

INTRODUCTION 7

PLANNING A ROUTE 10

INFORMATION FOR VISITORS 15
- Before travelling 15
- Getting there 18
- On arrival 19
- Where to stay 24
- Food and drink 26
- Getting around 30
- Communications 32
- Entertainment 32
- Holidays and festivals 32
- Further reading 36

ACKNOWLEDGEMENTS 39

HEALTH INFORMATION 40
- Before travelling 40
- Common problems 42
- Returning home 45
- Further information 45

SRI LANKA: LAND, CULTURE AND HISTORY 47
- Land and life 47
- Religion 53
- Culture 72
- History 81
- Modern Sri Lanka 88

COLOMBO 93
- The Centre and North 95
- The South 98
- Excursions 98
- Museums 99
- Parks and zoos 100
- Tours 101
- Local information 101
- Short excursions 108

THE WESTERN AND SOUTHERN PROVINCES 111
- Colombo to the Ruhunu-Yala National Park: the coastal route 112
- Colombo to Ratnapura and Bandarawela 141
- Colombo to Kandy 149
- Colombo to Kurunegala and Anuradhapura: the western route 154
- Colombo to Negombo, Puttalam and the Wilpattu National Park 157

KANDY, THE CENTRAL, NORTH AND UVA PROVINCES 167
- Kandy 170
- Kandy to Nuwara Eliya and Horton Plains 183
- Kandy to Nuwara Eliya via Hatton and Talawakele 192
- Kandy to the cultural triangle 198
- Anuradhapura and Mihintale 202
- Sigiriya 214
- Polonnaruwa 219

THE EASTERN PROVINCE 228
- Eastern province (north) 229
- Eastern province (south) 235

JAFFNA AND THE NORTHERN PROVINCE 239
- Jaffna 240

MALDIVES 241

GLOSSARIES 275

INDEX 278

MAP SYMBOLS

Administration

- State / Province Border
- Neighbouring state
- Towns

Roads and travel

- Main Roads (National Highways) — A62
- Other Roads
- Jeepable Roads, Tracks
- Railway
- Railway under construction

Water features

- River — *Mahaweli Gangai*
- Lakes, Reservoirs, Tanks
- Seasonal Marshlands
- Sand Banks, Beaches
- Ocean
- Waterfall
- Canals
- Ferry

Topographical features

- Contours (approx), Rock Outcrops
- Mountains
- Palm trees
- Deciduous /fir trees

Cities and towns

- Built Up Areas
- Main through routes
- Main streets
- Minor Streets
- National Parks, Gardens, Stadiums
- Fortified Walls
- Airport
- Banks
- Bus Stations (named in key)
- Hospitals
- Market
- Police station
- Post Office
- Telegraphic Office
- Tourist Office
- Key Numbers — 1 2 3 4 5
- Bridges
- Stupa
- Hindu temple
- Mosque
- Cathedral, church

National parks, trekking areas

- National Parks and Bird Sanctuaries
- Camp site
- Refuge
- Motorable track
- Walking track

Other symbols

- Archaeological Sites
- Places of Interest
- Viewing point

SRI_SYM

MAP INDEX

Anuradhapura 203
Ari Atoll 266
Central, N Central and Uva provinces 169
Colombo 94
Bambalapitiya 103
Fort and Pettah 97
Galle Face and Beira Lake area 99
Kollupitiya 102
Dambulla 199
Eastern Province (south) 235
Galle 121
Hambantota to Tissamaharama and Kataragama 136-137
Hambantota 134
Hikkaduwa area 117
beach 118
Kaafu Atoll 266
Kandy 172-173
Kurunegala area 155
Kurunegala 154
Mahiyangana 226
Maldives 260
Male 260
Matara and Polhena 129
Mihintale sacred centre 211
Mihintale 210
Mount Lavinia 112
Negombo Town 158
Negombo Beach 160
Northern provinces 240
Nuwara Eliya 185
Peradeniya Botanical Gardens 151
Polonnaruwa 220
The quadrangle 222
Pottuvil and Arugam Bay 237
Ratnapura 143
Sigiriya 215
Southern Highlands 190
Sri Lanka 9
200 million years ago 48
administrative districts 89
coconut, rubber, spices, tea 91
main destinations 11
mean annual rainfall 49
mean annual temperatures 50
National Parks and Sanctuaries 52
population density 90
relief and drainage 49
Tangalla 129
Trincomalee area 232
Trincomalee 230
Unawatuna 126
Weligama 127
Western and Southern provinces 110-111

THE EDITORS

Robert Bradnock

Born in India in 1943, Robert Bradnock went to India overland in 1966 as a research student at Cambridge, and made the first of his visits to Sri Lanka in the same year. That journey was the first of many research visits living and working throughout South Asia. Since joining the School of Oriental and African Studies in 1968, where he is now a Senior Lecturer in Geography with special reference to South Asia, he has carried out and supervised research in all of the countries of the region. He edits the India Handbook. Research for this book has been carried out in successive visits from 1992 to 1995.

An international authority on South Asia, Robert Bradnock broadcasts frequently on TV and radio about South Asian current affairs for the BBC and many other networks across the world. He was Editor of the Royal Geographical Society's *Geographical Journal* from 1992-1995, and he lectures extensively on South Asia in Britain and Europe.

Roma (Das) Bradnock

A Bengali by birth, Roma was brought up in Calcutta where she graduated before working with the British Council Library. An extended leave abroad brought her to England which subsequently became her home. When her daughters were growing up she began teaching English to Asian adults, an interest she has retained.

Roma has travelled extensively in India and returns there at least once a year to research for the India Handbook which she helps to edit. She also visited Sri Lanka in 1995 and travelled across the island to prepare the present Handbook.

The Handbooks have provided a new interest but still allows her time to enjoy gardening and music.

INTRODUCTION

For generations of travellers Sri Lanka has conjured up almost dream like images. Of glistening white dagobas, perfectly curving towards the sky-ward pointing finial, islands of peace, watched over in permanent silence by the stone-carved Buddha. Of the shattering sound of trumpets as the white stillness of a temple is emblazoned with coloured light. Of shadowy figures weaving their sinuous way between elephants and packed crowds, trying to get a glimpse of the casket enshrining the Buddha's tooth. Of Kandy's Perahera, when the powers of the universe are focused for an instant on Sri Lankan Buddhism's unique religious identity.

Such dreams are still lived today, yet they also summon up the past. A past when European explorers thought they had chanced – 'serendipitously' – on paradise. The English, with their Indian Empire taking shape across the water, determined to bring order, 'enlightenment' and trade to the island's shores. Just inland from the palm-fringed coast English eyes rose slowly to the great forest-covered hills beyond. They saw more than just the remnants of a great Sinhalese civilization struggling for survival in the mountain fastnesses of Kandy, or the ruins of an irrigation system which, hundreds of years before, had brought life to the parched lands of the N and E. They saw the opportunity to create new sources of wealth, previously undreamed of. Coffee. Rubber. Coconuts. And tea – above all, tea. Today, in your own mind's eye, if you tear yourself away from that sliver of silver sand that surrounds the often rocky coast, you see the pale mist which envelops the ever-wet highlands with its green gold.

The British were only the most recent of foreign intruders. Surely that is a hint of Dutch power shown in coastal canals and the distinctive church gable? And all those Catholic churches, dotted among the coastal villages between Negombo and Chilaw – they suggest a Portuguese past. It was the cinnamon which particularly drew the Dutch, while twisting pepper vines, ground hugging cardamom and hot ginger had given the Portuguese hope of a spice trade offering unparalleled wealth.

But the imagination is drawn even further back. From any of the idyllic beaches which fringe Sri Lanka or the Maldivian atolls you can see sails drifting languorously past – an Arab dhow? It's not so far fetched, for the Arabs had been trading for over 1,000 years before the Portuguese first opened up their route. Indeed, before the Arabs themselves adopted the new faith of Islam. For them the islands – Sri Lanka and the Maldives – offered a convenient staging post on their journey E. But so much more. Conch shells from the Maldives and spices from Sri Lanka entered the trade routes of the world. The Arabs converted that promise into reality – a reality of multi-coloured gems and much-demanded spice. In golden topped mosques and Muslim fishing communities they too left an indelible mark.

Still earlier Roman merchants had discovered that the island was full of heavily scented promise. Ptolemy wrote that the island's elephants were larger and nobler than those elsewhere and its yield of pepper "wonderful in abundance". Yet nearly 250 years before the birth of Christ, long before Ptolemy wrote, missionaries of the great Indian Buddhist emperor Asoka brought a message of peace and right living to the Sri Lankan King Devanampiya Tissa.

Anuradhapura, the capital he built and which dominated Sri Lanka's political life for a millennium, remains. It is home to a sapling culled from the sacred Bo tree under which the Buddha himself attained enlightenment, watched over every day for more than 2,000 years by specially appointed guardians.

And today? The beautiful landscapes of Sri Lanka and the Maldivian atolls, surrounded by coral reefs and scattered like islets of silver dust in the translucent ocean, so invitingly lined with pure white sand, are no mirage. Diving, snorkelling, or just soaking up the seemingly endless warmth and sun are reward in themselves. But in Sri Lanka, beyond the silver beaches and their waving coconut palms is so much more to explore. From the modern Sri Lankan capital of Colombo roads radiate to S, E and N. To the Central Highlands with their crisply cool nights and tea estates, still interspersed by stands of mountain forest. To Kandy, with its temple enshrining the Buddha Tooth Relic, but also lying at the centre of a region of extraordinary animal, plant and bird life. To the Horton Plains where a short trek reveals a totally unexpected high altitude wilderness. To the historic triangle at the heart of much of Sri Lanka's history, where the remains of the former capitals Anuradhapura and Polonnaruwa bear witness to the vibrant traditions of Sri Lankan Buddhism. To the great new irrigation and settlement projects E of the Central Highlands. And to the dry, hot SE, once a third major centre of political power and home to one of Sri Lanka's most important pilgrimage centres at Kataragama.

Yet like so many other parts of the world, not all is peace and harmony. In the last 15 years conflict in Jaffna and the far N and E has brought tragedy to thousands, a conflict which, though restricted to a relatively small part of the island, continues to leave deep scars on its political and social life. Travel outside the far N and E is as safe as anywhere in South Asia, but as you move inland you become increasingly aware of the complexities of the island's inheritance. Sri Lanka is not just a museum piece or a tourist brochure cut out, it is a living island, rich in cultural and political diversity yet facing daunting economic and political challenges in the modern world. The Maldivian atolls or the beach resorts of Sri Lanka still offer a wonderful chance to 'get away from it all'. But Sri Lanka's interior offers more – an insight into the islanders' response to the challenge of interweaving of past and present.

SRI LANKA
001
Delhi
Calcutta
Bombay
Madras
Colombo
N
Kankesanturai
Point Pedro
Jaffna
Kayts
Champiyanpattu
Chundikkulum Bird Sanctuary
Delft
Elephant Pass
Paranthan
Mullaittivu
Adams Bridge
Talaimannar
Kokkila Bird Sanctuary
Mannar Sanctuary
Mankulam
Pulmoddai
Mannar
Giant's Tank
Murunkan
Bay of Bengal
Vavuniya
Kuchchaveli
Paraiyanalankulam
Nilaveli
Uppuveli
Trincomalee
Medawachchiya
Naval Head Sanctuary
Foul Point
Wilpattu NP
Rambewa
Anuradhapura
Kantalai
Mihintale
Kalpitiya
Somawathie Sanctuary
Karaitivu
Talawa
Vakarai
Habarana
Kekirawa
Puttalam
Polonnaruwa
Kalkuda
Sigiriya
Dambulla
Wasgomuwa Reserve
Maho
Udappawa
Batticaloa
Battulu-Oya
Pandeniya
Chilaw
Maha Oya
Kurunegala
Matale
Madampe
Kalmunai
Hasalaka
Kallodai
Marawila
Polgahawela
Kandy
Gal Oya NP
Negombo
Kegalla
Inginiyagala
Katunayake
Pidurutalagala 2524 m
Bibile
Akkairaipattu
Pasyala
Komariya
Nuwara Eliya
Badulla
Pottuvil
COLOMBO
Watawala
Ella
Arugam Bay
Mt. Lavinia
Adam's Pk. 2260 m
Lahugala
Hanwella
Moneragala
Moratuwa
Haputale
Panawa
Panadura
Ratnapura
Wellawaya
Okanda
Kalutara
Balangoda
Uda Walawa NP
Ruhuna (Yala) NP
Kumana Bird Sanctuary
Beruwela
Kataragama
Bentota
Rakwana
Yala
Ambalangoda
Wirawila
Indian Ocean
Kirinda
Hikkaduwa
Hambantota
Bundala
Kalametiya
Galle
Ambalantota
0
50
km
Matara
Tangalla
Unawatuna
Weligama
Dondra

PLANNING A ROUTE

Despite its small scale there are several alternative ways of seeing the island's great variety of scenery and its historically and culturally fascinating sites. Because all international flights now arrive in Colombo the city is the natural starting point for any trip. However, an excellent alternative can be to take the train to Kandy and then to take buses or to hire a car for visiting the Central Highlands and the cultural triangle. Even if you are based at a beach hotel on the SW or S coasts it is easy to get up to Kandy and to make that a base for further exploration.

This book is based on alternative routes which you can take round and across the island. The routes outlined below suggest a few major itineraries offering different options for seeing some of the most interesting places conveniently and simply in between 1 and 3 weeks.

Route 1

Colombo to Anuradhapura, Mihintale, Sigiriya, Polonnaruwa, Kandy and Colombo (4-6 days). From Colombo this route takes you straight to the heart of the 'cultural triangle'. It is easy to go either by train to Anuradhapura or by bus or car. Hiring a car in Colombo allows you greater flexibility in your timetable and gives you a chance to choose the order in which you visit sites.

Day 1 It is approximately a 6 hrs drive from Colombo to Anuradhapura, the most ancient settlement in Sri Lanka and its most important early capital. There is comfortable time to visit some of the fascinating religious monuments in the afternoon, and plenty of options of comfortable accommodation in either Anuradhapura itself or at Mihintale 11 km away, where there is an excellent *Government Hotel*.

Day 2 The second day can be spent sightseeing in Aunradhapura and Mihintale. The famous stupas which are

SERENDIPITY – THE ISLAND OF THE LION

Sri Lanka has had many different names in its long history. To the Greeks and Romans it was Taprobane, a word derived from Pali and Sanskrit names, Tambavanna, Tambrapani and Tambapanni. In the form of Tamraparni it remains the name today of the major river of Tirunelveli District in Tamil Nadu, across the Palk Straits. Other names were derived from the Pali word for lion, ***Sihalam***. Thus Salai, Siele, Sielidiba, Sielendiba and Serendip have all been used at one time or another. Serendip could have evolved from 'Swarandwip' (golden isle) and hence 'Sarandip'. Serendib gave English the word serendipity, coined by the writer Horace Walpole, to describe the gift of making happy and unexpected discoveries purely by accident. From 1802, when the Island became a British Crown Colony, until 1972, when the island took its present name of Sri Lanka (the 'hallowed island') it was known as Ceylon. This too had a number of forms – among them Ceilan, Ceyllan, Sailan and Zeilan. Lanka itself had the early form of Lankadipa, and the more recent Lankava. It was a name that crossed the straits to India, for the Tamils knew the island not only as Eelam or Ilanare but as Elankai, in which form it figured in a wide range of Hindu myths.

scattered across the Anuradhapura township, the most holy of Buddhist shrines at the sacred Bo tree, and the meeting place of Mahinda, Asoka's son and Buddhist missionary who met the Sri Lankan king at a grove in Mihintale, can comfortably be visited in the course of a day. The second night could also be in Anuradhapura, or 50 km S at Habarana or Sigiriya.

Day 3 Sigiriya – the magnificent rock palace of Sigiriya is quiet, empty, cool and

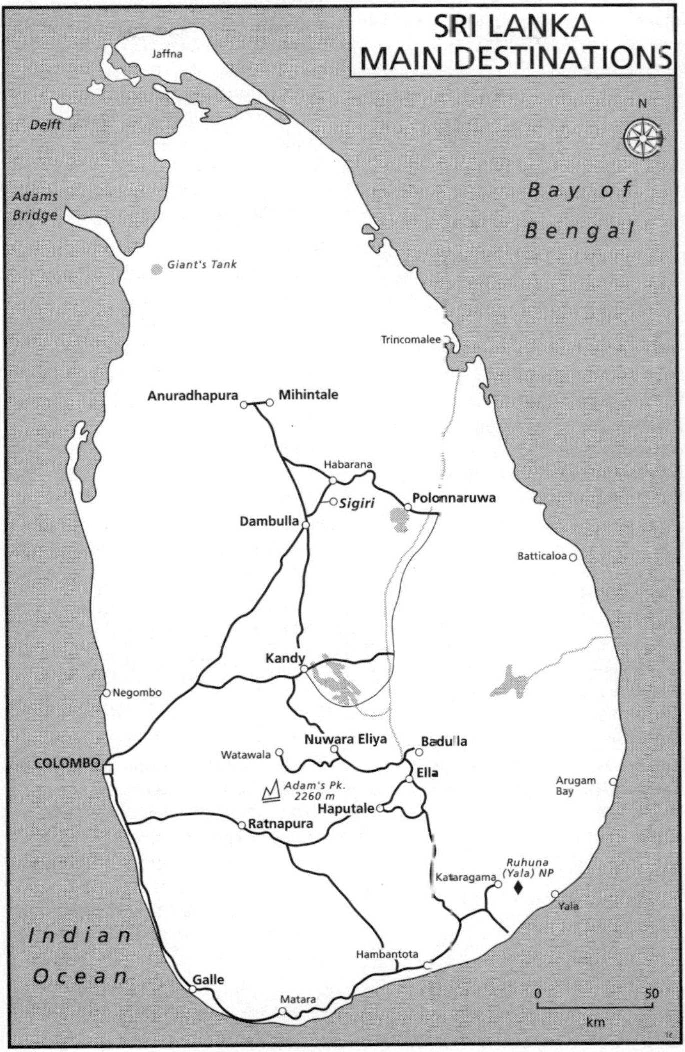

at its most magical early in the morning, but if you choose to stay the day you might also feel like climbing half way up the rock again to see the superb mural paintings in the late afternoon sunlight, particularly if you want to take photos. Return to Habarana for the night, or continue to hotels at Minneriya – Giritale, within easy distance of Polonnaruwa.

Day 4 Polonnaruwa – the second ancient capital is the site of remarkable Buddhist sculptures, remains of the last great medieval Sri Lankan kingdom, and the huge artificial lake known as Parakrama Samudra, built by the king Parakrama Bahu I in the 13th Century. If you leave Polonnaruwa after lunch it is perfectly possible to continue to Kandy the same day. The fastest route takes the new road across the great Mahaweli Ganga colonisation scheme to Mahiyangana, then climbs into the Central Highlands.

Day 5 Kandy – the capital of the Kandyan Kingdom and the last stronghold of independent Sinhalese power, Kandy is an attractive small town. Famous for its Temple of the Tooth and its great Perahera procession each Jul, Kandy is an excellent base for further trips into the Central Highlands. Nearby are the Botanic Gardens at Peradeniya and there is always a chance to see elephants bathing at Pinnewela. The journey back to Colombo takes no more than 4 hrs.

Route 2

Kandy, Matale, Dambulla, Sigiriya, Anuradhapura, Mihintale, Polonnaruwa, Mahiyangana and Kandy (3-5 days).

Day 1 Taking the train up to Kandy from Colombo is a beautifully relaxing and scenic way to reach the gateway to the Central Highlands. This suggested route goes N to the cultural triangle, passing through the spice gardens near Kandy and the temples of Matale and Dambulla to Sigiriya. Overnight at Sigiriya.

Day 2 Continue up to Anuradhapura and Mihintale. From here you follow the same route as that outlined in Route 1 (above).

Route 3

Kandy to Hatton, Adam's Peak, Nuwara Eliya, and Kandy (3-4 days). Kandy is the northwestern gateway to the tea estates of the Central Highlands, and to the highest mountains in Sri Lanka. Although Adam's Peak is not the highest it is the most popular and the most sacred of Sri Lanka's peaks. The most popular way to climb is by moonlight, arriving at the peak at dawn. The most popular path to the top starts at Dalhousie, about 6 hrs drive from Kandy.

Day 1 If you intend to climb Adam's Peak you can leave Kandy after lunch, travelling via the beautiful Ginigathena Pass to Hatton, and on to Dalhousie, where the night walk starts. There is some modest accommodation here as well as restaurants. Although Hatton is one of the major centres of the tea estates there is little accommodation, so if you do not want to climb Adam's Peak it is better to leave Kandy in the morning and drive through the estates to Nuwara Eliya.

Day 2 Nuwara Eliya – there are plenty of opportunities to relax in this attractive hill resort, ranging from gentle walks to a day on the golf course. The nearby Hakgala Botanic gardens are well-maintained and richly varied.

Day 3 The drive back from Nuwara Eliya to Kandy passes through beautiful hill scenery of tea estates and temperate montane forest.

Route 4

Kandy to Nuwara Eliya, Badulla, Ella, Haputale, Horton Plains and Kandy (2-3 days).

Day 1 The direct route to Nuwara Eliya, Sri Lanka's main hill station gives a cross-section of Central Highland scenery, from the lush lower altitude vegetation around kandy itself to the crisp fresh air of the tea estates surrounding Nuwara Eliya itself. A comfortable 4 hrs drive, there is a wide range of accommodation in Nuwara Eliya, from small guest houses to the colonial-style *Grand Hotel*.

Day 2 Badulla and Ella are two of the most romantic spots in Sri Lanka. Badulla, a smaller hill station than Nuwara Eliya and the end of the railway line from Colombo, is no more than a 3 hrs drive from Nuwara Eliya, and it is easily possible to take in the Hakgala Botanic Gardens on the way. After lunch you can drive back to Ella, one of Sri Lanka's favourite 'honeymoon' Rest Houses, for the second night – though you have to book in advance. It has superb views to the E over the plains.

Day 3 From Ella it is a short drive down to Haputale, another small town with commanding views over the plains to the SW. From Haputale you can drive up to the Horton Plains via Bragala. Popular for day treks or for overnight stays,the Horton Plains are surprisingly bleak and isolated. The route back to Nuwara Eliya follows the winding road past the peak of Totapola through Pattipola and Ambiwela. You can either stay overnight again in Nuwara Eliya or continue back to Kandy.

Route 5

Kandy to Yala, the S Coast and Colombo (4-6 days). This longer excursion offers an exciting range of Sri Lanka's most varied landscapes. After passing through the highest areas of the Central Highlands you drop down to the heat of the SE plains and the Yala National Park, and then round the S coast to Colombo.

Day 1 An early start from Kandy would allow you to reach Ella at lunch time. After a break you can drive down the hill road to the plains at Wellawaya and through the edge of Ruhunu-Yala National Park to Tissamaharama. Alternatively you could take 2 days over the journey, stopping to see more of the Central Highlands on the way.

Day 2 Tissamaharama is the natural base from which to explore Ruhunu-Yala National Park and the remarkable temple town of Kataragama.

Day 3 A drive along the coast road takes you through Hambantota, surrounded by extraordinary, glistening white salt pans. The are several striking and scarcely discivered beaches as you drive W through the Dry Zone, and there are several possible stopping places – Tangalla, Dikwella, Matara, Weligama or Galle. You could reach Galle comfortably in 1 day, but you might wish to take four or five.

Day 4 Galle – exploring the old fort town and its neighbourhood provides plenty to see and do in a comfortably relaxed way.

Day 5 You can follow the coast road up through many of the most famous beach resorts of Sri Lanka. You might like to take a short diversion inland to small villages such as Baddegama, near Hikkaduwa, or much closer to Colombo but inland a bit, the country estate of Horana.

Day 6 After relaxing on the beach or exploring something of the interior you can take the short drive in through Mount Lavinia to Colombo.

Route 6

The SW Coast resorts to the Central Highlands via Sinharaja Forest Reserve and Ratnapura. From any of the beach resorts of the SW coast you can easily travel inland to see one of Sri Lanka's best forest reserves and the gem capital of South Asia, before heading into the cool interior of the Central Highlands.

Day 1 Roads go inland to the Sinharaja Forest reserve from half a dozen places on the coast between Colombo and Hambantota, so it is easily acccessible by car from any of the major resorts. You can approach it from entrances in either the N or the S, and should allow 2 nights to explore.

Day 2 Exploring the forest reserve. You can either stay the second night or go on to Ratnapura, about 40 km from the northern entrance to the Park.

Day 3 Ratnapura, the 'city of gems', is world famous for its precious and semi-precious stones, and there are plenty of opportunities to buy – if you trust yor judgement and advice – or to look. After a morning in Ratnapura you can take the very attractive road which skirts the southern edge of the Central Highlands as far as Belihul Oya, an attractive and popular Government Rest House – an excellent place to stay if you do not mind the roar of rushing water from the river next door.

Day 4 Continuing of the same road you can pass from the humid lowlands to the tea estates and fresh air of the Central Highlands in half a day. Haputale and Ella both offer superb views on the way as well as the chance of refreshment, and Nuwara Eliya makes for an attractive and comfortable night halt.

Day 5 Several alternative routes lead to Kandy. If you take the shortest you will have a chance to spend the afternoon in the town itself, visiting the most interesting of the religious and historical sites, including the Temple of the Tooth.

Day 6 A morning spent in Kandy can be followed either by a return to Colombo or back to the SW coast resort from which you started.

INFORMATION FOR VISITORS

Contents

Before travelling 15
- **Entry requirements** 15
- **When to go** 16
- **Money** 16
- **What to take** 17

Getting there 18
Air; Sea; Customs

On arrival 19
Documentation and tax; Transport into town; Essential information; Women travellers

Where to stay 24

Food and drink 26

Getting around 30
Air; Train; Road; Travelling with children

Communications 32
Postal services; Telephone services

Entertainment 32
Newspapers; Radio and television

Holidays and festivals 32

Further reading 36

Before travelling

Entry requirements

• Visas and permits

Nationals of the following countries as tourists require a valid passport but do not need a visa for a period of 30 days: Australia, Austria, Bahrain, Bangladesh, Belgium, Britain, Bangladesh, Bahrain, Canada, Denmark, Eire, Finland, France, Germany, Indonesia, Italy, Japan, Kuwait, Luxembourg, Malaysia, the Maldives, Nepal, Netherlands, New Zealand, Norway, Oman, Pakistan, Philippines, Qatar, Saudi Arabia, Singapore, S Korea, Spain, Sweden, Switzerland, Thailand, UAE, USA and Yugoslavia. **NB** All tourists should have a valid visa for the country that is their next destination if that country requires a visa. Nationals of all other countries require a visa. Check with your nearest Sri Lankan representative.

Extensions Extensions are available beyond 1 month provided you have US$30 to spend per day, a valid passport and an onward or return ticket. Proof of daily spending US$30 during the first month may be required. Apply to Department of Immigration and Emigration, Galle Buck Rd, Colombo 1, T 29851.

Visitors require sufficient funds to maintain themselves and a return (or onward) ticket or foreign exchange to buy a ticket.

Registration Tourists from non-Commonwealth countries granted an extension of their tourist visa must register at the Aliens Bureau, Grd Flr, New Secretariat Bldg, Colombo 1.

Work permits All foreigners intending to work require work permits. Apply to the Sri Lankan Representative in your country of origin.

Representation overseas

Australia, 35 Empire Circuit, Forrest, Canberra ACT 2603; **Belgium**, 21-22 Ave des Arts (4e étage), 1040 Brussels, T 513 98 92; **Canada**, 102-104, 85 Range Rd, Ottawa, Ontario K1M 8J6; **France**, 15 Rue d'Astorg, 75008 Paris, T 266-35-01, open 0900-1200, 1400-1700, Mon-Fri; **Germany**, Rolandstrasse 52, 5300 Bonn 2; **India**, 27 Kautilya Marg, Chanakyapuri, New Delhi 110021; **Indonesia**, 70 Jalan Diponegoro, Jakarta;

Singapore, 1207-1212 Goldhill Plaza, Singapore 11; **Thailand**, Lailart Bldg, 87 Sukhumvit Rd, Bangkok; **Switzerland**, 56 Rue de Moillebeau, 1211, Geneva 19; **UK**, 13 Hyde Park Gardens, London W2 2LU, T 0171 262 5009, F 0171 262 7970; **USA**, 2148 Wyoming Av, NW, Washington DC 20008, T 483 4025, F 282 7181.

● Tourist offices overseas

Australia, 241 Abercrombie St, Chippendale NSW 2008, T 02 698 5226; **Canada**,Ontario M5B 1K2; **France**, 19, rue de Quatre Septembre, 75002 Paris, T 42 60 49 99; **Japan**, Dowa Bldg 7-2-22, Ginza Chuo-Ku, T 3289 0771, F 3289 0772; **Germany**, Allerheiligentor 2-4, D 6000 Frankfurt/Main 1, T 287734, F 288371; **Thailand**, PO Box 316, 1/8 Soi 10, Sukhumvit Rd, Bangkok, T 251 8062, F 662 2544820; **UK**, 13 Hyde Park Gardens, London W2 2LU, T 0171 262 5009, F 0171 262 7970.

● Specialist tour operators

The following tour companies (among others) operate from the UK – *Allegro Holidays*, T 01737 221323; *BA Worldwide*, T 01293 611611; *Coromandel*, T 0181 995 3642; *Explore Worldwide*, T 01252 319448; *Hayes & Jarvis*, T 0181 748 5050; *Kuoni*, T 01306 740500; *Paradise*, T 0171 2297686; *Sri Lanka Tours*, T 0171 434 3921; *Thomsons*, T 0171 431 2005; *Young World*, T 01273 203764. Also *Cosmos*, *Sri Lanka Tours*, *JBS Study Tours*, *Annis Travels* and *Eleanor Travels*.

When to go

● Best time to visit

The best times to visit Sri Lanka are between the main rainy seasons. Because the island lies just N of the Equator temperatures remain almost constant throughout the year. However, rainfall varies widely. In the SW and the Central Highlands the best period is from late Oct to early Mar, after the SW monsoon has finished. However, the N and E are affected by the NE monsoon during this period and are dry – but hot – during the summer months of Jun to Oct. The Central Highlands are much cooler throughout the year, but are very wet both during the SW monsoon (Jun to Oct) and the NE monsoon (Oct to Dec).

Money

● Currency

The Sri Lanka Rupee is made up of 100 cents. Notes in denominations of Rs 1,000, 500, 100, 50, 20, 10, 5, 2; coins of Rs 5, 2, and 1, and of 50, 25, 10, 5, 2, and 1c. Keep plenty of small change and low denomination notes as they can be difficult to find, and changing a large note can also be difficult.

● Exchange

Banking hours: 0900-1300 Mon and 0900-1330 Tues-Fri.

Bank of Ceylon, York St, Fort, is open 0800-2000 every day. It is easier to get cash using a Visa card in Sri Lanka than elsewhere in South Asia. The **Bank of Ceylon** may accept UK cheques backed by Visa cards.

The **Bank of America**, Head Branch, will give cash on a Visa card.

People's Bank, Foreign Branch, 27 MICH Bldg, Bristol St, Colombo 1, T 546409, weekdays, 0900-1330, except Mon till 1300. Night Branch, Sir CA Gardiner Maw, Colombo 2, Tues-Fri, 1530-1900, Sat 0900-1330, closed Sun, Mon.

Main branches stay open 0900-1600, accept TCs and sterling but not credit cards for cash. Colombo, Kandy, Galle, Kurunegala, Anuradhupura. Even in small branches, exchange facilities at correct rate – tourists are sometimes offered special treatment and the transaction can be completed quickly.

NB All foreign exchange transactions must be made through authorized banks and exchanges and entered on the Customs and Immigration form. Unspent rupees may be reconverted at time of departure at a commercial bank. Govt approved hotels and shops are allowed to deal in foreign currency. Keep the receipts when you change money. For visa extension you may need to show proof of spending US$30 a day during the first month.

● Cost of living

Sri Lankan costs of living remain well below those in the industrialized world, though significantly higher than in India. Most food, accommodation, and public transport, especially rail and bus, are exceptionally cheap by western standards. Even the most expensive hotels and restaurants in the major cities are less expensive than their counterparts in Europe, Japan or the United States. Budget travellers (sharing a room) can expect to spend about Rs 700-900 each (about US$14-16 or £9-11) a day to cover cost of accommodation, food and travel.

● Credit cards

Shops accept most major credit cards although some may try to add a surcharge which is not authorized. The **Hong Kong Bank**, 24 Sir Baron Jayatilleke Maw, Colombo, and the **Bank of America**, 324 Galle Rd, Colombo 3, allow Visa and Master Card holders to obtain cash and TCs. See note above on exchange transactions. However, American Express is not widely accepted.

● Transferring money to Sri Lanka

Thomas Cook and American Express can make instant transfers to their offices in Sri Lanka but charge about 8%. You can have a Bank Draft up to US$1,000 posted out personally (by Speedpost) for which normal charges are between 1.5% and 2%.

● Travellers' cheques (TCs)

Most TCs are accepted without difficulty, but some organizations only accept TCs from the biggest companies. It can be useful to have TCs from different companies, eg American Express and Thomas Cook, and in different currencies. TCs nearly always have to be exchanged in banks or hotels, and can only very rarely be used directly for payment. Identification documents, usually a passport, need to be shown. Except in hotels, encashing TCs can easily take up to 30 mins or longer, so it is worth taking larger denomination TCs and changing enough money to last for some days. Hotels will normally only cash TCs for resident guests, but the rate is often poorer than in banks. Most banks will accept US$ TCs but sterling and other major currency TCs are accepted nearly everywhere.

Warning If you use sterling, always make certain that you have not been given rupees at the dollar rate.

What to take

It is always best to keep luggage to a minimum. A travelpack, a hybrid backpack/suitcase, rather than a rigid suitcase, covers most eventualities and survives bus boot, roof rack and plane/ship hold with ease.

Light cotton clothes are useful at any time of year. It is a good idea to have some very lightweight long sleeve cottons and trousers for evenings, preferably light in colour, as they also give some protection against mosquitoes. It can be cool at night in the Central Highlands and some woollens are essential. Dress is usually informal, though one or two clubs and hotels expect guests to be formally dressed at evening meals. In Colombo short-sleeved shirts and ties are often worn for business. For travelling loose clothes are most comfortable. Some find open shoes or sandals best in hot weather, with or without light cotton socks, but it is also important to guard against blisters, cuts and bruises which are common problems with unprotected feet. Comfortable shoes or trainers are good options. Modest dress for women is advisable; also take a sunhat and headscarf.

● Checklist:
Air cushions for hard seating
Bumbag
Contact lens cleaning equipment – not readily available in parts of Sri Lanka
Earplugs
Eye mask
Insect repellent and/or mosquito net, electric mosquito mats, coils
Neck pillow
International driving licence
Photocopies of essential documents
Short wave radio (though most hotels now have satellite TV)
Socks: take a thick pair for visiting temples and mosques
Sun hat
Sun protection cream – factor 10 plus
Sunglasses
Swiss Army knife
Tissues/toilet paper
Torch and spare batteries
Umbrella (excellent protection from sun and unfriendly dogs)
Wipes (*Damp Ones* or equivalent)
Zip-lock bags

Those intending to stay in budget accommodation might also include:
Cotton sheet sleeping bag
Money belt
Padlock (for hotel room and pack)
Plastic sheet to protect against bed bugs on mattresses
Soap
Student card
Towel
Toilet paper
Universal bath plug

● Health kit:
Antiacid tablets
Anti-diarrhoea tablets
Anti-malaria tablets
Anti-infective ointment
Condoms/Contraceptives
Dusting powder for feet
First aid kit and disposable needles
Flea powder
Sachets of rehydration salts
Tampons
Travel sickness pills
Water sterilizing tablets

Getting there

Air

Air Lanka (the National airline) and several international carriers (with phone numbers in London) link airports around the world with Colombo. In London: Air France, T 0181 742 6600; Gulf Air T 0171 408 1717; Emirates T 0171 930 5356; KLM T 0181 750 9000; Kuwait Airways T 0171 412 0007; PIA T 0171 734 5544; Royal Jordanian T 0171 734 2557.

Indian Airlines also flies to Colombo daily from Madras and twice weekly from Trivandrum.

Air Lanka T Colombo 21161. In South Asia it flies to Bombay (Mon, Thur), Delhi (Wed, Sat, excellent Airbus service), Madras (daily), Trivandrum (Mon, Tues, Thur, Fri, Sat) Tiruchirappalli (Thur, Sun), Male and Karachi. Thiruvananthapuram (Trivandrum) is marginally cheaper than Tiruchirappalli. **NB** Flights need to be reconfirmed at least 72 hrs before the flight. Tickets booked overseas are likely to be deleted from computer record unless confirmed in person – which is not easy in some cities at weekends.

European destinations include Amsterdam, Frankfurt, Paris, Rome and London, which has two non-stop connections and two one-stop flights per week on its Airbus 340. Other destinations: in the Far East include Bangkok, Hong Kong, Kuala Lumpur, Tokyo; in Australia, Sydney and Melbourne; in the Middle East, Abu Dhabi, Bahrain, Dubai, Kuwait and Riyadh.

Overseas offices: Amsterdam T 717733; Bangkok T 2360159; Bombay T 223299; Frankfurt T 069 740941; Hong Kong T 5 252171; Karachi T 514421; London T 0171 930 2099; Madras T 867932; Male T 3459; New York

T 838 5120; Paris T 429 74344; Tokyo T 5734261; Trivandrum T 68767. Sri Lanka's modern International Airport at **Katunayake**, 35 km N of the capital, has several facilities, including a duty-free shop, bank and an expensive restaurant. The Bank of Ceylon exchange counter, airport restaurant, short-stay rooms and the tobacco counter are open 24 hrs. The Tourist Information Centre and the Tea Centre (behind Customs area) are open for flight arrivals and departures. Porter, left luggage and bond baggage service are available, as well as assistance with meeting passengers. **NB** The restaurant in the transit lounge will only accept hard currency – rupees are not accepted.

Sea

Although some cruise ships are still visiting Colombo it is almost impossible to travel to Sri Lanka by ship. It is occasionally possible to get a berth on a cargo or container ship from ports in the Gulf region or South East Asia, but impossible to book trips in advance. The most popular sea route to Sri Lanka for many years, from Rameswaram in Tamil Nadu to Talaimannar, has been stopped since the outbreak of Sri Lanka's civil war in 1983 and showed no sign of being resumed in 1996.

Customs

● Duty free allowances

You are permitted to bring in items for 'personal use' provided they are not intended for sale. You must declare all currency including TCs, drafts etc, precious metals and gem stones, firearms, weapons, drugs, narcotics and any goods in commercial quantities (see Prohibited and restricted items below). In addition to completing Part II of the Immigration Landing Card, a tourist may be asked by the Customs Officer to complete a Baggage Declaration Form.

200 cigarettes or 50 cigars or 375g of tobacco (or in combination). Two bottles of wine and 1.5 litres of spirits. A small quantity of perfume and 250 ml of toilet water. Travel souvenirs up to a max value of Rs 1,000. Customs should be satisfied that other articles will be re-exported on departure.

● Prohibited and restricted items

Export of the following without a permit is forbidden: precious metals (gold, platinum and silver), antiques (rare books, palm leaf manuscripts, rare anthropological material etc), ivory, precious and semi-precious stones (even when set in jewellery), narcotics, firearms, explosives, dangerous weapons, and fauna and flora. A max of Rs 250 in local currency, 3 kg of tea, and goods bought for personal use using foreign currency, can be exported. See 'Exchange' above for regulations on reconverting unspent rupees.

Import of all the items listed above and in addition, Indian and Pakistani currency, obscene and seditious literature or pictures is prohibited.

Warning It is illegal to buy items made from wild animals and reptiles.

● Currency regulations

Foreign currency in excess of US$5,000 must be declared on Exchange Control, Form D. Up to Rs 250 may be imported or exported. On departure Sri Lankan money must be changed back before Customs.

On arrival

Documentation and tax

Tourists must complete and hand in Part I of the Immigration Landing Card and present Part II for certification by the Customs officer. This should be retained and produced at the time of departure. However should you lose it, the Custom officer will merely make you write out fresh ones!

There are several banks at the airport. It is worth changing some money here as they are all quick and efficient with reasonable rates. It is worth buying the monthly guide *This month in Sri Lanka* at the airport bookshop when you arrive.

● Departure tax

Embarkation Tax of Rs 500 payable after check-in. Unlike India, Sri Lanka makes no concessions for departures to its neighbouring member countries of the South Asian Association for Regional Cooperation (SAARC).

Transport into town

● Bus

A/c coaches, minibuses and local buses are available for transfer to Colombo and Negombo. Tickets are for sale in the airport arrivals hall. Local bus Nos 187, 300 and 875 – often crowded, but the cheapest way. Tickets on the bus.

● Helicopter

There is now a helicopter service to the city centre.

● Taxis

Airport taxis (up to three passengers) charge according to distance; the price is fixed. **NB** The more expensive hotels may offer to meet you at the airport – expect to have about US$25 added to your hotel bill.

● Train

There are train services to the city at 0746, 0820, 1632 and 1720. Airport Express Enquiries, T 687037.

Essential information

● Conduct

Greeting "Ayubowan" (may you have long life) is the traditional welcome greeting among the Sinhalese, said with the hands folded upwards in front of the chest. The same gesture accompanies the word 'vanakkam' among Tamils.

Use your right hand for giving, taking, eating or shaking hands as the left is considered to be unclean. Women do not normally shake hands with men as this form of contact is not traditionally acceptable between acquaintances. It is best not to photograph women without permission.

Courtesy and appearance Cleanliness and modesty are appreciated even in informal situations. Nudity and topless bathing are prohibited; heavy fines can be imposed. Displays of intimacy are not considered suitable in public and will probably draw unwanted attention. Unaccompanied women may find problems of harrassment, though this is rare.

Visiting religious sites Visitors to Buddhist temples are welcome. Parts of Hindu temples are sometimes closed to non-Hindus. Visitors to both Buddhist and Hindu temples should be properly dressed (skirts or long trousers) – shorts and swim wear are not suitable. Shoes should be left at the entrance. (Best to visit early in the day and to take socks for protection against the hot stone.)

Do not attempt to shake hands or be photographed with Buddhist *bhikkus* (monks) or to pose for photos with statues of the Buddha or other deities and paintings. Remember that monks are not permitted to touch money so donations should be put in temple offering boxes. Monks renounce all material possessions and so live on offerings. (However, you are advised not to give to ordinary beggars.)

Mosques may be closed to non-Muslims shortly before prayers. In mosques women should be covered from head to ankle.

Visiting archaeological sites Tourist Information Centres will help with providing trained English speaking guides (and occasionally speaking a European language, Malay or Japanese). Fees are specified, usually about Rs 250 per day depending of size of group. Alternatively ask at hotel.

Tickets For the major archaeological sites, eg Polonnaruwa and Anuradhapura, the Entry ticket is US$12;

(children under 12 – half price (Rs 295); a similar student discount, with an ISIC card, is sometimes available); for Sigiriya US$7. **NB** Entry fees to ancient archaeological sites, museums etc are much higher for foreign visitors than for Sri Lankans.

The **Cultural Triangle Entry Permit**, US$30, covers entry and photography at the major archaeological sites of Anuradhapura, Polonnaruwa, Sigiriya and also Dambulla, Kandy and Nalanda. However,not all parts of these sites are included, eg there is a separate camera fee for the Kandy Dalada Maligawa (Temple of the Tooth), and also for entering Issurumuniya Museum and Sri Maha Bodhi at Anuradhapura. The permit is valid for 14 days starting from the first visit and permits the holder to take photographs (except where it is restricted). It is available from one of main site offices or from Colombo, Central Cultural Fund, 212 Bauddhaloka Maw, Colombo 7, T 500733, F 500731. It is worth getting one if you plan to visit all three principal sites.

The sites are usually open 0600-1800; the ticket office often only opens at 0700. If you are keen to miss the crowds and visit a site early in the day, buying the triangle permit in advance enables you to avoid having to wait for the ticket office to open. One traveller reported "student tickets could be bought at Sigiriya (with ISIC card), but were not available at Polonnaruwa".

NB When visiting sites with temples, eg Kandy and Dambulla, please wear a long skirt or trousers; otherwise visitors will be expected to hire a *lungi* (sarong).

● Hours of business

Banks: usually 0900-1300 Mon, 0900-1330 Tues-Fri. Closed on Sat, Sun, Poya days and National holidays. Main branches of Peoples Bank open 0900-1600 Mon-Fri, 1030-1230 Sat. Top hotels sometimes have 24-hr service. See page 16 and also Colombo Banks for details of others open on Sat mornings and for evening service.

Post Offices: 1000-1700, Mon-Fri; Sat mornings.

Government offices: 0930-1700, Mon-Fri; 0930-1300, Sat (some open on alternate Sat only).

Shops: 0830-1630 Mon-Fri. Some open on Sat 0830-1300. Shops often close for lunch from 1300-1400 on weekdays, most close on Sun. Sun street bazaars in some areas. **NB** *Poya* (Full moon) days are holidays.

● Official time

GMT + 5½ hrs. Conception of time is sometimes rather vague in South Asia. Unpunctuality is common so patience can be needed.

● Photography

For photography of museum exhibits at the ancient sites, in theory, you need a permit from the Department of Archaeology, Marcus Fernando Maw, Colombo 7, but in practice checks are rare. Filming permits are also obtainable from Cultural Triangle Office, 212 Bauddalaka Maw, Colombo 7. Individual site offices also issue permits with tickets from 0600-1800. Many monuments now charge a camera fee, often with much higher fees for video use.

Please ask before taking photographs of local people.

It is advisable to take rolls of films and any specialist camera batteries although colour and black and white films are available cheaply at major tourist centres (check expiry date and seal). **NB** Only buy films from a reputable shop. Hawkers and roadside stalls may pass off used film as new.

● Police

Even after taking all reasonable precautions people do have valuables stolen. This can cause great inconvenience. You can minimize this by keeping a record of vital documents, including your passport number and TC numbers in a completely separate place from the documents themselves. If you have items stolen, they should be reported to the police as soon as possible. Larger hotels will be able to assist in contacting and dealing with the police.

Warning Dealings with the police can be difficult. The paper work involved in reporting losses can be time consuming and irritating, and your own documentation (eg passport and visas) will normally be demanded. Tourists should not assume that if procedures move slowly they are automatically being expected to offer a bribe. If you face really serious problems, for example in connection with a driving accident, you should contact your consular office as quickly as possible.

● Safety

Confidence tricksters These are common where people are on the move, notably around railway stations or places where budget tourists gather. The demands are likely to increase sharply if sympathy is shown. A common plea is some sudden and desperate calamity; sometimes a letter will be produced in English to back up the claim.

Travel arrangements, especially for sight-seeing, should only be made through reputable companies; bogus agents operate in popular seaside resorts.

It is essential to take care that credit cards are not run off more than once when making a purchase. Gems offered for sale on the street or by some traders are often fake.

Personal security In general the threats to personal security for travellers in Sri Lanka are small. In most areas other than the N and E it is possible to travel without any risk of personal violence. However, care is necessary in some places, and basic common sense needs to be used with respect to looking after valuables.Both men and women travelling alone do report that they are sometimes harassed, and that it is much more pleasant to travel with a companion.

The N and E of Sri Lanka have been subject to political violence and civil war. Very few hotels are open and the army is deployed and on constant alert. Although the situation appeared to be easing in early 1995 the civil war resumed after the ceasefire between the LTTE and the Government broke down. In Nov 1995 the Sri Lankan army encircled Jaffna and the entire population of the town was reported to have fled. It was impossible for visitors to travel safely either to Jaffna or to much of the E coast.

NB It is often best to seek advice on security from your own consulate.

Theft is not uncommon, especially when travelling by train or crowded bus. It is essential to take good care of personal valuables both when you are carrying them, and when you have to leave them anywhere. **You cannot regard hotel rooms as automatically safe**. It is wise to use hotel safes for valuable items, though even they cannot guarantee security. It is best to keep TCs and passports with you at all times. Money belts **worn under clothing** are one of the safest options, although you should keep some cash easily accessible in a purse.

NB Travelling bags and cases should be made of tough material, if possible not easily cut, and external pockets (both on bags and on clothing) should never be used for carrying either money or important documents. Strong locks for travelling cases are invaluable. Use a leather strap around a case for extra securtiy. Pickpockets and other thieves do operate in Colombo and some of the resort centres. Crowded areas are particularly high risk. Keep valuables as close to the body as possible.

● Shopping

Batik, tea, spices, silverware, coir articles, leather goods, jewellery and gem stones are good buys. Govt *Laksala* shops in Colombo, Kandy, Galle, Nuwara Eliya, Matara, Kegalle, Kalutara, Kurunegala, Udagama, Batticaloa, Anuradhapura, Bentota, Hikkaduwa, Negombo, Ratnapura and Medawachchiya.

Bazars – the local markets – are often a great experience, but you must be prepared to bargain. It pays to look around first. Street hawkers often pass off fake precious semi-precious stones, coral etc as real. Taxi drivers and couriers sometimes insist on recommending certain shops where they expect a commission and prices are likely to be inflated. Export of certain items such as antiquities, ivory, furs and skins is controlled or banned, so it is essential to get a certificate of legitimate sale and permission for export. In some private shops and markets bargaining is normally essential.

● Tipping

A 10% Service Charge is now common in even the most basic hotels and restaurants in the tourist areas. This is levied whatever the quality of service.

In the largest hotels a tip of Rs 10 per piece of luggage carried would be appropriate. In restaurants 5% or rounding off the bill with small change is completely acceptable. Tour companies sometimes make recommendations for 'suitable tips' for coach drivers and guides. Some of the figures may seem modest by European standards but are very inflated if compared with normal earnings. Some group companies recommend a tip of Rs 50 per day for drivers and guides. This can safely be regarded as generous.

The more expensive hotels and restaurants frequently add a service charge to the bill. Otherwise 10% is the usual amount to leave in expensive hotels, less elsewhere. Taxi drivers do not expect to be tipped but a small extra amount over the fare is welcomed and particularly if a large amount of luggage is being carried.

When shopping outside Government emporia and the biggest hotels, expect to bargain hard.

● Voltage

230-240 volts, 50 cycles AC. The current is variable. Some top hotels have transformers to enable visitors to use their appliances. There may be pronounced variations in the voltage, and power cuts are common. Socket sizes vary so you are advised to take a universal adaptor (available at airports). **Note** Some hotels do not have electric razor sockets. It is difficult to obtain shaver adaptors for Sri Lankan sockets in shops outside Sri Lanka, so a battery operated shaver is recommended.

● Weights and measures

Sri Lanka uses the metric system for weights and measures.

Women travellers

Compared with many other countries it is relatively easy and safe for women to travel around Sri Lanka, even on their own, though most people find it an advantage to travel with at least one companion. There are some problems to watch out for and some simple precautions to take which make it possible to avoid both personal harassment and giving offence.

Modest dress for women is always advisable: loose-fitting, non see through clothes, covering the shoulders, and skirts, dresses or shorts (at least knee-length).

Unaccompanied women may find problems of harassment, though this is relatively rare. It is always best to be accompanied when travelling by rickshaw or taxi in towns.

Women do not normally shake hands with men as this form of contact is not traditionally acceptable between acquaintances.

Where to stay

Sri Lanka has a surprisingly uneven range of accommodation. You can stay safely and cheaply by western standards in Colombo, Kandy and the popular coastal areas of the S and SW. In Colombo, Kandy and among the several beach resorts there is a choice of high quality hotels, offering a full range of personal and business facilities (though their food can be bland and uninspired). In smaller centres even the best hotels are far more variable. In the peak season (Dec to Mar for much of the island) bookings can be extremely heavy. It is therefore desirable to reserve well in advance if you are making your own arrangements, and to arrive reasonably early in the day. If you travel out from Colombo or the major resorts it will often be necessary to accept much more modest accommodation.

Hotel Classifications

The first six categories used in this Handbook are based on prices of the best double rooms, in mid-1995. They are **not** star ratings, and individual facilities vary considerably. Normally the following facilities will be found as standard in the given classes. In mid-1995 most **AL** and some **A** category hotels charged all foreigners, except those working in India, a 'dollar price', about 50% more than the 'rupee price'. This policy may change in the next 12 months.

AL US$90+ – International class luxury hotels, usually found only in the regional capitals and the largest cities. All facilities for business and leisure travellers to the highest international standard.

A US$60-90 – International class. Central a/c, rooms with attached baths, telephone and TV with video channel, a business centre, multicuisine restaurants, bar, and all the usual facilities including 24 hr room service, shopping arcade, exchange, laundry, travel counter, swimming pool and often other sports such as tennis and squash. They often have hairdresser, beauty parlour and a health club, and accept credit cards.

B US$35-60 – Most of the facilities of **A** but perhaps not business centre, swimming pool and sports and lacking the feeling of luxury.

C Rs 800-1,500 – Often the best hotels available in medium and small towns, but not always the best value. The entrance and reception areas are usually more 'grand' than **D** and **E** price hotels, but the quality of the rooms is often no better despite the higher price. However, they often serve excellent value meals. Usually central a/c, comfortable, with restaurant, exchange facilities, travel agent and accept credit cards.

D Rs 450-800 – Many in this category will have a range of rooms, some at the bottom of the price range and a few at the top, sometimes a/c rooms with bath attached. Most have TV as standard. Restaurant and room service normally available. Most medium to large towns will have at least one hotel in this category.

Budget hotels – **NB** Many hotels which charge up to Rs 250 per night for a double room also have much cheaper accommodation.

E Rs 250-450 – Simple rm with fan (occasionally a/c), shower or bucket 'bath'. May have shared toilet facilities. Limited room service may include meals brought in when no restaurant is available. At the lower end of this scale, some may not provide top sheets, pillow cases and towels.

F Below Rs 250 – Very basic, usually with shared toilet facilities (often 'squat'), but sometimes very good value, especially in South India. May be in noisy or remote locations. Very variable cleanliness and hygiene. These often have rooms for under Rs 60 and dormitory beds for under Rs 20.

The Tourist Board issues a free 'Accommodation List' at the International Airport and at their office at 78 Steuart Pl, Galle Rd, Colombo; the list is not entirely comprehensive. From international class hotels in the capital with a full range of facilities and excellent 'Resort' style accommodation on beaches or near important cultural sites (min US$60), the choice ranges to moderately priced comfortable accommodation in the city or very simple guest houses in small coastal towns and villages or Wildlife Conservation Department bungalows in the parks (about Rs 250). Government *Rest Houses*, sometimes in converted colonial houses, some in superb locations (about Rs 800 for a double room) still often offer good accommodation at a reasonable price. It is also possible to book rooms in plantation estate bungalows or private homes in towns; this is a good alternative for those on a low budget.

Ceylon Hotels Corporation (the CHC), 63 Janadhipathi Maw, Colombo 1, T 320235, reservations T 323501, F 422732, are now responsible for management of several of the old Government *Rest Houses* across the island. Occasionally an individual Rest House may accept a direct telephone booking but not necessarily honour it. To avoid disappointment use Central Reservations in Colombo on T 323501, F 422732.

In 1995, prices charged by some *Rest Houses* on arrival varied from what was quoted on the phone and from the 'Official' typed rates showing the tariff across the island which only a few managers acknowledged existed.

NB Hotels close to temples can be very noisy, especially during festival times. Music blares from loudspeakers late at night and from very early in the morning, often making sleep impossible.

● Budget hotels

A special feature of the *Sri Lanka Handbook* is the budget category of hotels. Hotels in general are much more expensive than in neighbouring India and outside a few of the coastal resorts popular with backpackers it is much less easy to find a choice of good cheap accommodation. Some hotels in the **F** category have rooms for Rs 200 and under. These are always very basic, but can be clean and good value. Prices for luxury hotels are sometimes comparable with the West.

The price for each category is a guide to what you would pay for the best standard double room.

● Off-season rates

Large reductions are made by hotels in all categories out-of-season in many resort centres. Always ask if any is available.

In many areas outside the biggest cities there are government guest houses. Formerly these had an excellent reputation for cleanliness, service and good value. Today the standards in some of these rest houses have fallen badly, but a few remain excellent.

Unmarried people sharing hotel rooms usually causes no difficulties.

● Short stays

For people travelling off the beaten track there are several cheap options. Railway stations have *Retiring Rooms* or 'Rest Rooms'. These may be hired for periods of between 1 and 24 hrs. However, unlike India, railway retiring rooms are few (only seven in the whole country) and rather poor. Some are open to people without rail tickets, and can be useful in an emergency.

Air-conditioning Only the larger hotels have central a/c. Elsewhere a/c rooms are cooled by individual units and occasionally large 'air-coolers'.

Insects Mosquitoes may penetrate even the best hotels. In cheap hotels you need to be prepared for a wider range of insect life, including flies, cockroaches, spiders, ants, and harmless house lizards. Poisonous insects, including scorpions, are extremely rare. Hotel managements are nearly always prepared with insecticide sprays, and will come and spray rooms if asked. It is worth taking your own repellent creams. Remember to shut windows and doors after dusk. Electrical devices, used with insecticide pellets, are now widely available, as are 'mosquito coils' which burn slowly to emit a scented smoke. Many small hotels have mosquito nets. Dusk and early evening are the worst times for mosquitoes. Light-coloured trousers and long-sleeved shirts are advisable, especially out of doors. At night fans can be very effective in keeping mosquitoes off.

Leeches can be a problem in wet forest areas.

Toilet facilities Apart from the **AL** and **A** categories, 'baths' do not necessarily refer to bathrooms with Western bathtubs. Other hotels may provide a bathroom with a toilet, basin and a shower. In the lower priced hotels and outside large towns, a bucket and tap may replace the shower, and a 'squat' toilet instead of a Western WC. During the cold weather and in hill stations, hot water will be available at certain times during the day, sometimes in buckets. Even medium sized hotels which are clean and pleasant do not always provide towels, soap and toilet paper.

Food and drink

● Food

Rice and curry are the staple main course food of Sri Lanka, but that term conceals an enormous variety of subtle flavours. Coriander, chillies, mustard, cumin, pepper, cinnamon and garlic are just some of the common ingredients which add flavour to both sea food and meat curries. Fresh sea food – crab, lobster and prawn, as well as fish – is excellent, and meat is cheap. Rice forms the basis of many Sri Lankan sweet dishes, palm treacle being used as the main traditional sweetener. This is also served on curd as a delicious dessert. Sadly, it is not easy to get good Sri Lankan food in most hotels which concentrate on western dishes. A meal in a first class restaurant could cost as little as Rs 250.

Some foods that are common in Europe are both less readily available and of much lower quality in Sri Lanka. Cheese and chocolates are two. Bringing small quantities of such foods can help but you need to be certain of being able to keep them cool.

NB Vegetarian food is much less common in Sri Lanka than in India, and in places can be difficult to get.

Fruit Sri Lanka has a wide variety of tropical fruit throughout the year, pineapple, papaya and banana being particularly good. The extraordinarily rich jack (jak) fruit are also available all year. Seasonal fruit include mangosteen (no relation of mangos), passion fruit, custard apples, avocado pears, durian and rambutan from Jul-Oct. In addition to ordinary green coconuts, Sri Lanka is also home to the distinctive King Coconut (*thambili*). The milk is particularly sweet and nutritious.

Many spices are grown in the island and are widely available in the markets and shops. Cinnamon, nutmeg, cloves, cardamom and pepper are all grown, the Kandy region being a major centre of spice production. Many private spice gardens are open to the public.

● Drink

Soft drinks There is a huge variety of bottled soft drinks, including well known international brands (eg Sprite, Fanta, Coke at about Rs 11). The local Elephant brand mineral waters include Soda water (Rs 7), Ginger Beer (Rs 12) and others at about Rs 11 (Cream Soda, Lemonade, Necto, Orange barley). These are perfectly safe but always check the seal. One of the most popular drinks however is tender coconut, very widely available, always pure straight from the nut and refreshing. Sri Lanka has its own almost unique variety – the golden King Coconut, widely regarded as a particular delicacy.

Eating Out - Food And Menus

Pronounce ā as in car ī as in see
ō as in old

Note These marks to help with pronunciation do not appear in the main text.

Cooking in Sri Lanka, though similar in many ways to S India, remains distinctive in the frequent use of some ingredients, eg coconut in various forms, *umbalakada* the powdered dry Maldive fish used to flavour curries as well as the different ways in which rice is prepared eg *appa, pittu.*

Sri Lankan food is also influenced by Dutch and Portuguese cuisine from colonial times, as found in festive *lamprais* (see below) and *frikkadels* the small, crumbed and fried meat or fish balls. The influence is more obvious in confectionary and desserts using eggs, as in *breudher* the 'Christmas cake' or *wattapallam*, as well as flaky pastries like *foguete* or the cashew-filled *bolo folhado.*

A typical Sri Lankan '**rice and curry** meal' would expect to include a couple of different curries and sambols, some chutney and pickles, and would be eaten with the fingers of the right hand. Even in a simple restaurant, however, you may get a spoon to eat the meal. It is quite usual to ask for second helpings of whatever you fancy. For variety rice may be replaced by *hoppers, pittu* or *rotty* on occasions.

As a rough guide as to how hot the curry is - *Kiri* are fairly mild 'white' curry prepared with coconut milk; *Badun* prepared with freshly roasted spice are drier, 'black' and hotter; *Rathu* the 'red' curries are hottest, with plenty of dried red-chilli (*rathu miris*) powder added.

Spices which are grown locally and which attracted sea-faring traders to the island, are liberally used in the kitchen - cardamom (*enasal*), cinnamon (*kurundu*), cloves, fenugreek and pepper etc, as well as the typical cumin, coriander and turmeric.

Coconut is plentiful and appears in various forms or during cooking or serving - coconut oil, coconut 'milk' (strained infusion) to cook with or prepare a batter, grated coconut, small pieces of kernel - even the shell is used as a ladle. *Molee* are mild curries with a creamy coconut milk gravy.

As a drink, King Coconut water (*thambili*) is safe and refreshing. The unfermented palm sap produces *thelija,* the fermented *toddy* and the distilled *arrack.*

Basic vocabulary

	Sinhalese	**Tamil**
bread	*pān*	*rotti/ pān*
butter		*butter/ vennai*
(too much) chilli	*miris wadi*	*kāram*
drink	*bīma*	*kudi*
egg	*biththara*	*muttai*
fish	*malu*	*mīn*
fruit	*palathuru*	*palam*
food	*kama*	*unavu*
jaggery	*hakuru*	*sīni/ vellam*
juice	*isma*	*sāru*
meat	*mus*	*iraichchi*
oil	*thel*	*ennai*
pepper	*gammiris*	*milagu*
pulses (beans, lentils)	*parippu*	*thāniyam*
rice	*buth*	*arisi*
salt	*lunu*	*uppu*
savoury		*suvai*
spices	*kulubadu*	*milagu*
sweetmeats	*rasakevili*	*inippu pondangal*
treacle	*pani*	*pāni*

vegetables	*elawalu*	*kai kari vagaigal*
water	*wathura*	*thanneer*
Fruit		
avocado	*alkigetapera*	
banana	*keselkan*	*valaippalam*
cashew	*cadju*	*muruthivi*
coconut	*pol*	*thengali*
green coconut	*kurumba*	*pachcha niramulla thengai*
jackfruit	*(jak) kos ambul*	
mango	*amba*	*mangai*
orange	*dodam*	
papaya	*papol*	*pappa palam*
pineapple	*annasi*	*annasi*
Vegetables		
aubergine	*vambatu*	*kathirikai*
beans (green)	*bonchi*	*avarai*
cabbage	*gowa*	*muttaikosu*
gourd (green)	*pathola*	*pudalankai*
mushrooms		*kalān*
okra	*bandakka*	*vendikkai*
onion	*luunu*	*venkayam*
pea		*pattani*
pepper	*miris*	*kāram*
potato	*ala*	*uruka kilangu*
spinach	*niwithi*	*pasali*
tomato	*thakkali*	*thakkali*
Meat, fish and seafood		
chicken	*kukulmas*	*koli*
crab	*kakuluvo*	*nandu*
pork	*ōroomas*	*pantri*
prawns	*isso*	*irāl*

Ordering a meal in a restaurant (Sinhalese)

Please show the menu	*menu eka penwanna* (show)
No chillis please	*miris nathuwa*
....sugar/ milk/ice...	*..sīni/ kiri/ ice*
A bottle of mineral water please	*drink botalayak genna*
....do not open it	*arinna epa*
sweet/savoury	*sweet/ rolls*
spoon, fork, knife	*handa, garappuwak, pihiya*

Ordering a meal in a restaurant (Tamil)

Please show the menu	*thayavu seithu thinpandangal patti tharavum*
No chillis please	*kāram vendām*
....sugar/ milk/ice..	*sīni/ pāl/ ice.*
A bottle of mineral water please	*oru pothal soda panam tharavum*

SRI LANKAN SPECIALITIES

amblulthial sour fish curry

kaha buth *kaha* rice (yellow - cooked in coconut-milk with spices and saffron/turmeric colouring) *kiri* - similar, but white and unspiced, served with treacle, chilli or pickle)

biththara rotti rotti mixed with eggs

buriyani rice cooked in meat stock and pieces of spiced meat sometimes garnished with boiled egg slices

hoppers (*āppa*) cupped pancakes made of fermented rice flour, coconut milk and yeast, eaten with savoury curry(or sweet) *lamprai* rice cooked in stock, parcelled in banana leaf with dry meat and vegetables curries, fried meat and fish balls, and baked gently

mellung boiled, shredded vegetables cooked with spice and coconut

pittu rice-flour and grated coconut steamed in bamboo moulds; eaten with coconut-milk and curry

polos pahi pieces of young jack fruit ('tree-lamb'!) replaces meat in this dry curry

rotty/ rotti flat, circular, unleavened bread cooked on a griddle

sambol hot and spicy accompaniment - usually made with onions, grated coconut, pepper (and sometimes dried fish)

sathai spicy meat pieces, baked on skewers (sometimes sweet-and-sour)

"short eats" a selection of meat and vegetable snacks (in pastry or crumbed and fried), charged as eaten

string hoppers *(indiāppa)* flat circles of steamed rice-flour noodles eaten ususally at breakfast with thin curry

thosai (dosai) large crisp pancake made with rice- and lentil-flour batter

vadai deep-fried savoury lentil 'dough-nut' rings.

Sweets *(rasakavilis)*

curd rich, creamy, buffalo-milk yoghurt, served with treacle or jaggery

gulab jamun dark fried spongy balls of milk-curd and flour soaked in syrup

halwa/ aluva fudge-like, made with reduced milk, nuts and fruit

kadju kordial fudge squares made with cashew nuts and jaggery

kaludodol dark, mil-based, semi solid sweet mixed with jaggery, cashew and spices (a moorish delicacy)

kavun **(oil cake)** fried, conical shaped flour-based, sweet (traditional Sinhalese delicacy)

rasgulla syrup-filled white spongy balls of milk-curd and flour

thalaguli balls formed after pounding roasted sesame seeds with jaggery

wattalapam set 'custard' of coconut milk, eggs and cashew, flavoured with spices and jaggery

Indian Cuisine

A typical meal in an Indian restaurant would include some 'bread' (*roti, chapāti* or *nān*) and/or rice (plain *chawal* or fragrant *pilau*), a vegetable and/or meat curry, lentils (*dāl,*) *raita* (yoghurt with shredded cucumber or some fruit) and *pāpadam* (deep- fried, pulse flour wafer rounds).

Some popular dishes

do piaza with onions (added twice during cooking)

dāl makhani lentils cooked with butter

dum aloo potato curry with a spicy yoghurt, tomato and onion sauce

kebab skewered (or minced and shaped) meat or fish; a dry spicy dish cooked on a fire

kīma mattar mince meat with peas

korma in fairly mild rich sauce using cream /yoghurt

matar panīr curd cheese cubes with peas and spices (and often tomatoes)

Mughlai rich N Indian style

murgh massallam chicken in rich creamy marinade of yoghurt, spices and herbs with nuts

rogan josh mutton/ beef pieces in rich creamy, red sauce

tandoori baked in a *tandoor* (special clay oven)

tikka marinated meat pieces, baked quite dry

NB Do not add ice cubes to drinks as the water from which the ice is made may not be pure.

Alcoholic drinks are widely available, though imported drinks (wines) are very expensive. Local beer (*Lion*, *Carlsberg* and *Three Coins Pilsner*) is acceptable but can be expensive (Rs 60-76), larger hotel restaurants charging about Rs 125. Spirits are available too, eg Mendis Special (Rs 190) and Double distilled (Rs 250). The local spirit *arrack* is distilled from palm toddy.

NB Alcohol is not sold on *Poya* (monthly full-moon) days. You can, however, usually order alcoholic drinks in your hotel.

Getting around

Warning As the civil war continued in the N and parts of the NE these areas remained dangerous and closed to visitors in 1995. Conditions for tourists returned to normal in the rest of the island and large numbers are visiting the island now. Government *Rest Houses* still often offer the best accommodation in the lower price range, though in Sri Lanka these are not as cheap as in India. However, some are outstanding value, in beautiful settings.

Air

All internal air services are unscheduled. Upali Travels and Air Taxi Ltd operate charter helicopter and fixed winged aircraft to destinations of tourist interest and to domestic airports from the Ratmalana Airport, Colombo. Details under Colombo. Also from Government Tourist Offices and Thomas Cook, 15 Sir Baron Jayatilleka Maw, Colombo 1, T 545971-4.

Train

Although the network is restricted there are train services to a number of major destinations, and journeys are comparatively short. There are three 'routes': a line N to Anuradhapura via Kurunegala (branch E to Polonnaruwa and Trincomalee and N to Jaffna in peacetime), a line E to Kandy and Badulla through the hills, including stops at Nanu Oya for Nuwara Eliya, Hatton, Ohiya for the Horton Plains and Ella; a line S along the coast to Galle and as far as Matara, connecting all the popular coastal resorts. Fares are low compared to the West, eg from Colombo to Polonnaruwa, Rs 45 (3rd class), Rs 123 (2nd), Rs 214 (1st); to Kandy, Rs 21 (3rd class), Rs 57 (2nd), Rs 100 (1st); to Galle, Rs 20 (3rd class), Rs 54 (2nd), Rs 94 (1st). Special a/c trains operate to Kandy and Hikkaduwa, and there is an inter-city express service (one class), Colombo-Kandy (Rs 60 or Rs 90 return within 10 days, for cash payment). The Colombo Matara line is now being extended and eventually will reach Kataragama. The first leg to Dikwella is expected to be operational by the end of 1995. There are now direct trains from Matara to Kandy and Anuradhapura, which saves the change which used to be necessary and a lot of hassle. 3rd class has hard seats, 1st is relatively comfortable.

Road

● Bus

The nationalized bus service (CTB) has competition from a range of private operators, especially minibuses. There are more comfortable than most of the CTB buses, which carry white signs for local routes and yellow signs for long distance routes. Long distance bus travel is very cheap but can be exhausting.

● Car

There are several self-drive car hire firms based in Colombo including some of the main international operators. An international driving permit is needed to obtain a temporary local licence. Contact Automobile Association of Sri Lanka. However, it may actually be cheaper (and more relaxing) to hire a car with driver, available through travel agents and tour operators for about US$50 a day. See 'Transport' under major towns.

● Taxis

Taxis have yellow tops with red numbers on white plates, and are available in most towns. Negotiate price for long journeys. Expect to pay about Rs 30 minimum and Rs 15 for each extra kilometre. See Colombo for details of taxis and auto rickshaws in the city.

Travel tips No distances are great, and roads are generally good, though they are slow. The train journey from Colombo to Kandy passes through spectacular scenery and is a more leisured way to travel than the road journey. This is also true for the journey S along the coast. Many foreigners find driving conditions difficult and dangerous. Pedestrians and animals often wander across the roads apparently aimlessly, and some buses drive very fast for the conditions.

Travelling with children

Children of all ages are widely welcomed, being greeted with a warmth in their own right which is often then extended to those accompanying them. In the big hotels there is no difficulty with obtaining safe baby foods, though disposable nappies are not readily available in many areas. To help young children to take anti-malarial tablets, one suggestion is to crush them between spoons and mix with a teaspoon of dessert chocolate (for cake-making) bought in a tube.

	Anuradhapura	Badulla	Batticaloa	Colombo	Dambulla	Galle	Habarana	Hambantota	Hikkaduwa	Kandy	Kurunegala	Negombo	Nuwara Eliya	Polonnaruwa	Ratnapura	Sigiriya	Tissamaharama
Badulla	272																
Batticaloa	196	167															
Colombo	206	230	303														
Dambulla	66	206	163	148													
Galle	322	256	381	116	264												
Habarana	57	199	139	173	23	290											
Hambantota	364	135	261	238	298	124	335										
Hikkaduwa	195	120	398	98	248	17	312	141									
Kandy	138	134	187	116	72	232	96	245	216								
Kurunegala	121	175	217	93	55	209	79	243	31	42							
Negombo	177	230	264	35	112	151	160	273	133	99	57						
Nuwara Eliya	216	56	224	180	150	290	173	167	133	77	119	176					
Polonnaruwa	101	233	95	216	68	332	45	323	317	140	122	179	217				
Ratnapura	240	129	296	101	174	150	214	124	133	142	119	136	148	241			
Sigiriya	67	215	162	169	24	286	21	322	269	96	72	129	166	67	190		
Tissamaharama	348	125	231	264	289	148	313	29	166	216	258	299	139	295	153	305	
Trincomalee	106	277	138	257	109	373	96	367	358	182	164	221	259	129	283	113	338

Sri Lanka distance chart (Km)

Extra care must be taken to protect children from the heat by creams, hats, umbrellas etc and by avoiding being out in the hottest part of the day. Cool showers or baths help if children get too hot. Dehydration may be counteracted with plenty of drinking water – bottled, boiled (furiously for 5 mins) or purified with tablets. Preparations such as 'Dioralyte' may be given if the child suffers from diarrhoea. Moisturizer, zinc and castor oil (for sore bottoms due to change of diet) are worth taking. Mosquito nets or electric insect repellents at night may be provided in hotel rooms which are not a/c, but insect repellent creams are a must. The biggest hotels provide babysitting facilities.

Communications

Postal services

Details of postal rates to other countries can be obtained from major hotels, or from the Inquiries Counter of the GPO in Janadhipathi Maw, Colombo 1. Poste Restante here will keep your mail (letters and packages) for 2 months. Information in Colombo T 26203. The GPO is open 24 hrs for the sale of stamps and for local telephone calls. DHL Worldwide Express Parcel Service, 130 Glennie St, Colombo 2, T 541285.

Telephone services

Calls within Sri Lanka incur a maximum of Rs 30 for 3 mins, the rate depending on distance; eg Nilaveli from Colombo is charged at Rs 20 per 3 mins. International phone calls can be made from the GPO between 0700 and 2100. Foreign cables also accepted at GPO. Directory Enquiries, T 161, International Calls, T 100, Trunk Calls, T 101. There is now a growing number of International Direct Dialling centres. In Colombo these operate at reasonably competitive international rates. Elsewhere and in hotels rates may be as much as three times as high. Phone cards can be bought from post offices. It is possible to dial abroad directly from card operated phones.

Entertainment

Newspapers

The Daily News and *The Island* are national daily newspapers published in English. In Colombo and some other hotels a wide range of international daily and periodical newspapers and magazines is available. The *Lanka Guardian* is a respected monthly.

Radio and television

Sri Lanka Broadcasting Corporation operates in nine languages, between 0530 and 2300. Two TV channels. *ITN* from 1830. News in English at 2200. *Rupavahini* – English newscast at 2130. Liberalisation has opened the door to several private channels and an ever growing number of private radio stations.

Sri Lanka's national radio and television network, broadcasts in Sinhalese and English. Many Sri Lankans now watch satellite TV, including the BBC World, CNN and others. Some international channels are currently relayed through the Star Network. BBC World Service radio has a large audience in both English and regional languages.

Holidays and festivals

Sat and Sun are always holidays. *Full Moon Poya* days of each month are also holidays. Buddhists visit temples with offering of flowers, to worship and remind themselves of the precepts. Certain temples hold special celebrations in connection with a particular full moon, eg *Esala* at Kandy. Accommodation may be difficult in certain places on Poya days, and public transport is crowded. No liquor is sold (you can, however, order drinks at your hotel, the day before) and all places of entertainment are closed. **NB** Some religious festivals (Buddhist, Muslim and Hindu)

Useful Sinhalese Words And Phrases

Pronounce ah is shown **ā** as in car
ee is shown **ī** as in see
oh is shown **ō** as in old

Note These marks to help with pronunciation do not appear in the main text.

Useful words and phrases

general greeting	*ayubowan*
Thank you/no thank you	*es-thu-thee/mata epa*
Excuse me, sorry	*samavenna*
Pardon?	*āh*
Yes/no	*ou/nā*
never mind/that's all right	*kamak na*
please	*karunakara*
What is your name?	*nama mokakda*
My name is	*mage nama..........*
How are you?	*kohamada?*
I am well, thanks	*mama hondin innava*
Not very well	*wadiya honda ne*
Do you speak English?	*Ingirisi kathakaranawatha*

Shopping

How much is this?	*mīka kīyada?*
That will be **20** rupees	*rupial* ***wissai***
Please make it a bit cheaper!	*karunakara gana adukaranna!*

The hotel

What is the room charge?	*kamarayakata gana kīyada*
May I see the room please?	*kamaraya karnakara penvanna?*
Is there an a/c room?	*a/c kamarayak thiyenawada?*
Is there hot water?	*unuwathura thiyenawada?*
.... a **fan/mosquito net**	***fan/maduru delak*** *(or m net)*
Please clean the room	*karnakara kamaraya suddakaranna*
This is OK	*meka hondai*
Bill please	*karunakara bila gaynna*

Travel

Where's the **railway station**?	*dumriyapola koheda?*
When does the **Colombo** bus leave?	*Colombata bus eka yanne kīyatada?*
How much is it to **Colombo**?	***Colombota*** *kīyada?*
Will you go for **10** rupees?	*rupiyal* ***dah****ayakata yanawada?*
left/right	*wamal dakuna*
straight on	*kelin yanna*
nearby	*langa*
Please wait here	*karunakara mehe enna*
Please come here at **8**	*karunakara mehata* ***atata*** *enna*
stop	*nawathinna*

Time and days

right now	*dang*
morning	*ude*
afternoon	*dawal*
evening	*sawasa*
night	*raya*
today	*atha*
tomorrow/yesterday	*heta/iye*
day	*dawasa*
week	*sathiya*
month	*masey*
Sunday	*irrida*
Monday	*sanduda*
Tuesday	*angaharuwada*
Wednesday	*badhada*
Thursday	*brahaspathinda*
Friday	*sikurada*
Saturday	*senasurada*

Numbers

1	*eka*	9	*namaya*
2	*deka*	10	*dahaya*
3	*thuna*	20	*wissai*
4	*hathara*	30	*thihai*
5	*paha*	40	*hathalihai*
6	*haya*	50	*panahai*
7	*hatha*	100/200	*sīayai/desīyai*
8	*ata*	1000/2000	*dāhai/dedāhai*

Basic vocabulary

Some English words are widely used, such as, airport, bathroom, bus, embassy, ferry, hospital, stamp, taxi, ticket, train (though often pronounced a little differently).

bank	*bankuwa*	hot (temp)	*rasnai*
café/food stall	*kamata kadyak*	hotel	*hōtalaya*
chemist	*beheth sappuwa*	open	*arala*
clean	*sudda*	police station	*policiya*
closed	*wahala*	restaurant	*kāmata hotalayak*
cold	*sīthai*	road	*pāra* (accent on ā)
dirty	*apirisidui*	room	*kamaraya*
doctor	*dosthara*	shop	*kade*
excellent	*hari honthai*	sick (ill)	*asaneepai*
ferry	*bottuwa*	station	*istashama*
food/to eat	*kanda/kāma*	this	*meka*
hospital	*rohala*	that	*araka*

Sri Lankan Tamil

Useful words and phrases

general greeting	*vanakkam*
Thank you/ no thank you	*nandri*
Excuse me, sorry, pardon	*mannikkavum*
Yes/ no	*ām/ illai*
never mind/ that's all right	*paruvai illai*
please	*thayavu seithu*
What is your name?	*ungaludaya peyr enna*
My name is	*ennudaya peyr..........*
How are you?	*nīngal eppadi irukkirīrgal?*
I am well, thanks	*nan nantraga irrukkirain*
Not very well	*paruvayillai*
Do you speak English?	*nīngal angilarn kathappirgala?*

Shopping

How much is this?	*ithan vilai enna?*
That will be 20 rupees	*athan vilai irupathu rupa*
Please make it a bit cheaper!	*thayavu seithu konjam kuraikavuam!*

The hotel

What is the room charge?	*arayin vilai enna?*
May I see the room please?	*thayavu seithu arayai parka mudiyama?*
Is there an a/c room?	*kulir sathana arai irukkatha?*
Is there hot water?	*sudu thanīr irukkuma?*
......**a bathroom?**	***oru kuliyal arai**........?*
... a **fan/mosquito net?**	***katotra sathanam/ kosu valai**......?*
Please clean the room	*thayavu seithu arayai suththap paduthavu*
This is OK	*ithuru seri*
Biil please	*bill tharavum*

Travel

Where's the **railway station**?	*station enge?*
When does the **Colombo** bus leave?	*eppa* ***Colombo*** *bus pogum?*
How much is it to **Kandy**?	***Kandy*** *poga evalavu?*
Will you go to Kandy for **10** rupees?	***paththu*** *rupavitku Kandy poga mudiyama?*
left/right	*idathu / valathu*
straight on	*naerakapogavum*
nearby	*arugil*
Please wait here	*thayavu seithu ingu nitkavum*
Please come here at **8**	*thayavu seithu ingu* ***ettu***
stop	*nivuthu*

Time and days

right now	*ippoh*
morning	*kalai*
afternoon	*pitpagal*
evening	*malai*
night	*iravu*
today	*indru*
tomorrow/ yesterday	*nalai/ naetru*
day	*thinam*
week	*vaaram*
month	*maatham*
Sunday	*gnatruk kilamai*
Monday	*thinkat kilamai*
Tuesday	*sevai kilamai*
Wednesday	*puthan kilamai*
Thursday	*viyalak kilamai*
Friday	*velli kilamai*
Saturday	*sanik kilamai*

Numbers

1	*ontru*
2	*erantru*
3	*moontru*
4	*nāngu*
5	*ainthu*
6	*āru*
7	*aelu*
8	*ettu*
9	*onpathu*
10	*pattu*
20	*erupathu*
30	*muppathu*
40	*natpathu*
50	*ompathu*
100/200	*nooru/ irunooru*
1000/2000	*āiyuram/ irandā iuram*

Basic vocabulary

Some English words are widely used, often alongside Tamil equivalents, such as, airport, bank, bathroom, bus, embassy, ferry, hospital, hotel, restaurant, station, stamp, taxi, ticket, train (though often pronounced a little differently).

airport	*āgaya vimana nilayam*
bank	*vungi*
bathroom	*kulikkum arai*
café/food stall	*unavu kadai*
chemist	*marunthu kadai*
clean	*suththam*
closed	*moodu*
cold	*kulir*
dirty	*alukku*
embassy	*thootharalayam*
excellent	*miga nallathu*
ferry	*padagu*
hospital	*āspathri*
hot (temp)	*ushnamana*
hotel/ restaurant	*sāpathu viduthi*
juice	*sāru*
open	*thira*
police station	*police ilaka*
road	*pathai*
room	*arai*
shop	*kadi*
sick (ill)	*viyathi*
stamp	*muththirai*
station	*nilayam*
this	*ithu*
that	*athu*
ticket	*anumati sītu*
train	*rayil*
water	*thannīr*
when?	*eppa?*
where?	*enge?*

are determined by the lunar calendar and therefore change from year to year. Please check at the Tourist Information Centre for exact dates.

Jan: *Duruthu Poya day* – Sri Lankan Buddhists believe that the Buddha visited the island and celebrate with Colombo's biggest annual festival at the Kelaniya Temple. *Tamil Thai Pongal* day observed by Hindus.

Feb: *National Day* (**4**) – processions, dances, parades. *Navam* Poya Day. A large celebration with elephant processions in Colombo. *Navam Poya* now marked by celebrations at Colombo's Gangaramaya Temple, with elephant processions around Beira Lake-Viharamahadevi Park area. *Id-ul-Fitr* marking the end of Ramazan, the Mulim month of fasting. **Feb/Mar**: *Maha Sivarathri* marks the night when Siva danced his celestial dance of destruction (*Tandava*) celebrated with feasting and fairs at Siva temples, preceded by a night of devotional readings and hymn singing.

Mar: *Medin Poya Day*.

Apr: *Bak Poya Day* – Good Friday with Passion Plays in Negombo, in particular on Duwa Island. **13-14**: Sinhala and Tamil *New Year Day* marked with celebrations, by closure of many shops and restaurants.

May: *May Day* (**1**). *Wesak Poya Day* and the day following. celebrating the key events in the Buddha's life: his birth, enlightenment and death. Clay oil-lamps are lit across the island; also folk theatre performances. Special celebrations at Anuradhapura, Kelaniya (Colombo) and Kandy. **22**: *National Heroes' Day*.

Jun: *Poson Poya Day*, marking Mahinda's arrival in Sri Lanka as the first Buddhist missionary; Mihintale and Anuradhapura hold special celebrations. *Id-ul-Zuha/Bakr-Id* Muslims commemorate Ibrahim's sacrifice of his son according to God's commandment. An animal (goat) is sacrificed and special meat and vermicelli dishes are prepared. *Bank Holiday* (**30**).

Jul (**early Aug**): *Esala Poya Day* – this is the most important Sri Lankan festival with a grand procession of elephants, dancers etc, honouring the Sacred Tooth of the Buddha in Kandy lasting 10 days. and elsewhere including Dewi Nuwara (Dondra). *Kataragama Festival* with purification rituals including firewalking. *Vel Festival* in Chilaw, and in Colombo from Sea St Hindu temple, procession to Bambalapitiya and Wellawatte.

Aug: *Nikini Poya Day* – celebrations at Bellanwila, Colombo.

Sep: *Binara Poya Day* – Perahera in Badulla.

Oct: *Wap Poya Day*. *Milad-un-Nabi*, Prophet Mohammad's birthday. **Oct/Nov**: *Deepavali*, Festival of Lights celebrated by Hindus with fireworks, commemorating Rama's return after his 14 years' exile in the forest when citizens lit his way with earthen oil lamps.

Nov: *Il Poya Day*.

Dec: *Unduwap Poya Day*, marking the arrival of Emperor Asoka's daughter, Sanghamitta, with a sapling of the Bodhi Tree from India. Special celebrations at Anuradhapura, Bentota and Colombo. **25**: *Christmas Day*. **31**: *Special Bank Holiday*.

Further Reading

● Art and architecture

Archer, WG & Paranavitana, S; *Ceylon, paintings from Temple Shrine and Rock*; Paris, New York Graphic Soc, 1958. Arumugam, S; *Ancient Hindu temples of Sri Lanka*; Colombo, 1982. Coomaraswamy, AK; *Medieval Sinhalese Art*; New York, Pantheon, 1956. Godakumbure, CE; *Architecture of Sri Lanka*; Colombo, Department of Cultural Affairs Monograph, 1963. Goonatilleke; *Masks and Mask Systems*.

● Current affairs and politics

Little, D; *Sri Lanka: the invention of enmity*; Washington: United States Institute of Peace Press, 1994; a recent attempt to provide a balanced interpetation of conflict in Sri Lanka. Moore, MP; *The State and Peasant Politics in Sri Lanka*; London, 1985; an academic account of contemporary Sri Lankan political development. McGowan, W; *Only man is vile: The Tragedy of Sri Lanka*; Picador, 1983; an account of the background to the 1983 Tamil-Sinhalese conflict.

● History: pre-history and early history

Deraniyagala, SU; *The Prehistory of Sri Lanka*; Colombo: Department of Archaeological Survey of Sri Lanka, 2 Vols, 1992; a superb detailed account of the current state of research into pre-historic Sri Lanka, available in Colombo and at the Anuradhapura Museum.

● History: medieval and modern

de Lanerolle, Nalini; *A Reign of Ten Kings*; Colombo, CTB, 1990. de Silva, KM; *A History of Sri Lanka*; London, OUP, 1981; arguably the most authoritative historical account of Sri Lanka. Geiger, W; *Culture of Ceylon in Mediaeval times*; Wiesbaden, Harrassowitz, 1960. Robinson, Francis (ed); *Cambridge Encyclopedia of India, Pakistan*; 1989, ed, Cambridge; excellent and readable introduction to many aspects of South Asian society.

● Language

Dissanayake, JB; *Say it in Sinhala*.

● Literature

Clarke, Arthur C; *View from Serendib* (among many others), New York, Random House, 1977; a personal view from the prolific author who has made Sri Lanka his home. Goonetileke, Hai; *Lanka, their Lanka*; New Delhi, Navrang, 1984; delightful cameos of Sri Lanka seen through the eyes of foreign travellers and writers. Gunesekhara, Ramesh; *Monkfish Moon*; Penguin; evocative collection of stories of an island paradise haunted by violent undercurrents. *Reef*; Penguin, 1994; the story of a young boy growing up in modern Sri Lanka. Obeyesekere, R & Fernando, C, Eds; *An anthology of modern writing from Sri Lanka*; Tucson, Arizona, 1981. Ondaatje, Michael; writing by modern novelist, including autobiographical *Running in the family*; Penguin, 1983. Reynolds, CHB, Ed; *An anthology of Sinhalese Literature of the 20th century*; London, 1987. Goonetilleke, DCRA, Ed; *The Penguin New Writing in Sri Lanka*; India, 1992.

● People and places

Cordiner, James; a description of Ceylon, an account of the country, inhabitants and natural productions, London, 1807, now reprinted by Colombo, Tisara Prakasakayo, 1983. Beny, Rolf; *Island Ceylon*; London, Thames & Hudson, 1971; large coffee-table book with some excellent photos and illustrative quotes. Brohier, RL; *Changing face of Colombo 1505-1972*; Lake House Colombo, Lake House, 1984; excellent history of Colombo. Maloney, Clarence; *Peoples of South Asia*, New York, Holt, Rheinhart & Winston, 1974; a wide ranging and authoritative review, perhaps over-emphasising the Dravidian connection with Sri Lanka.

● Religion

Malangoda, K; *Buddhism in Sinhalese Society, 1750-1900*; Berkeley, 1976. Perera, HR; *Buddhism in Ceylon, Past and Present*; Kandy, Buddhist Publication Soc, 1966. Qureshi, IH; *The Muslim Community of the Indo-Pakistan Sub-Continent 610-1947*; Karachi, OAP, 1977. Stutley, Margaret and James; *Dictionary of Hinduism*; London, Routledge Kegan Paul, 1977. *Dictionary of Buddhism*.

● Travel

American Women's Assoc; *Colombo Handbook*; 3rd ed, Colombo, AWA, 1981. *Handbook for the Ceylon Traveller*; 2nd ed, Studio Times, Colombo, 1983; a good collection of essays from many writers about people, places and everything Sri Lankan, now dated, but many interesting insights.

Hatt, John; *The tropical traveller: the essential guide to travel in hot countries*; 3rd ed 1992; excellent, wide ranging and clearly written common sense, based on extensive experience and research. Anderson, JG, ed; *Insight Guide to Sri Lanka*; 6th ed, APA, 1995; some excellent text articles and good photographs, some inaccuracies especially with updating since 1991. Rushbrook-Williams, LF; *A Handbook for travellers in India, Pakistan, Nepal, Bangladesh and Sri Lanka*; John Murray, 1982 (22nd edition); still a remarkable guide, rich in British historical material.

● Natural History

Bond, Thomas; *Wild Flowers to the Ceylon Hills*; OUP, 1953. Henry, GM; *Guide to the birds of Ceylon*; Kandy, De Silva & Sons, 1978. Munro, Ian; *Marine and Fresh water fishes of Ceylon*; Canberra, Austrailian Department of External Affairs, 1955. Woodcock, Martin; *Handguide to Birds of the Indian Sub-Continent*; Collins, London. Woodhouse, IGO; *Butterfly fauna of Ceylon*; Govt Press, 1942.

Maps

● Sri Lanka

The *Road Map of Sri Lanka*, Scale 1:500,000 (Rs 50), published by the Survey Department, is adequate for those planning to hire a car to see the principal sights around the island (partly revised in 1993 so does not include changes in the last few years). The small insets of places of tourist interest lack detail, however; these places are all covered in this Handbook in far greater detail. For greater detail their four large sheet maps cover the island, Scale 1:250,000, 1992, which is the best available. Many large scale maps are available for consultation at the Survey Department, Map Sales Branch, Kirula Rd, Narahenpita, T 585111, and a few at the Map Sales Centre, York St, Colombo 1, T 35328. Most large scale maps and town plans are not for sale for security reasons.

The *National Atlas of Sri Lanka*, 1988, also published by the Survey Department, is a superb large format colour atlas with excellent text and maps.

Ceylon Tourist Board, 78 Steuart Place, Colombo 3, T 437059, F 437953, and some of their offices abroad, give out a Sri Lanka itinerary map plus several city and site guides with sketch maps, free, but these are not particularly clear.

Nelles Verlag 1:450,000 *Sri Lanka*, is conventional with four city insets. The new Sarvodaya Vishva Lekha (41 Lumbini Ave, Ratmalana, T 722932, F 722932) is 1:500,000. It has four foldouts in a handy format with added advantage of an index, but does not include small towns everywhere.

● Colombo

Numerous single sheet maps are available. Two booklets are more useful: the *A to Z Atlas and Street Index*, 1:12,500, 1989, Rs 50, from the Survey Department is the most detailed and accurate; *A-Z Street Guide*, 1994, Rs 295, published by Arjuna, Dehiwala, includes Colombo surrounds plus Anuradhapura, Kandy, Nuwara Eliya and Polonnaruwa, but lacks the accuracy of the former.

ACKNOWLEDGEMENTS

We are particularly grateful to the following who have carried out research specifically for the Handbook. Rupert Linton travelled widely throughout Sri Lanka and Richard Smith reported extensively on the Central Highlands. Patrick Dawson also contributed important information from the Highlands, the ancient sites and the southern coast. Jeevan Thiagarajah gave a great deal of practical help, as well as providing advice on Tamil and Sinhala phrases. Toni de Laroque, the Maldives Lady, provided much up to date material on the Maldives.

A number of others have provided valuable information: OV Atulavamsa, Sigiriya; Linda Duthie and Oyvind Berg, Oslo, Norway; Benedikt J Fuchs, Eichenau, Germany; Mrs Julie Goulding, Ruislip, Middx, UK; Mrs K Kalyani, Anuradhapura; SG Sunil Peramaratna, Ankumbura, Kandy Amanda Purves, Woodbridge, Suffolk, UK; Roshan de Silva, *Sigiriya Village Hotel*; Dickson Charles de Silva, Colombo; Dolores Spessa, Torino, Italy; Thomas Schweiger, Vienna, Austria.

HEALTH INFORMATION

Contents

Before travelling	40
Common problems	42
Returning home	45
Further information	45

The following information has been compiled for us by Dr David Snashall, Senior Lecturer in Occupational Health, United Medical Schools of Guy's and St Thomas' Hospitals and Chief Medical Adviser, Foreign and Commonwealth Office, London.

The traveller to Sri Lanka is inevitably exposed to health risks not encountered in North America or Western Europe. Because much of the area is economically underdeveloped, infectious diseases are still found in a way in which they used to predominate in the West some decades ago. There is an obvious difference in health risks between the business traveller or tourist who tends to stay in international class hotels in large cities or resorts, and the backpacker trekking through the rural areas. There are no hard and fast rules to follow; you will often have to make your own judgements on the healthiness or otherwise of your surroundings.

There are many well qualified doctors in Sri Lanka, a large proportion of whom speak English. There are systems and traditions of medicine wholly different from the western model and you may be confronted with unusual modes of treatment such as herbal medicine and acupuncture, but you will always be within easy range of good western medical services too. Even so a certain amount of self medication may be helpful and you will find many of the drugs available have familiar names. However, always check the date stamping and buy from reputable pharmacies because the shelf life of some items, especially vaccines and antibiotics, is markedly reduced in hot conditions.

With the following precautions and advice, you should keep as healthy as usual.

Before travelling

Take out Medical Insurance. You should have a dental check up, obtain a spare glasses prescription and, if you suffer from a longstanding condition such as diabetes, high blood pressure, heart/lung disease or a nervous disorder, arrange for a check up with your doctor who can at the same time provide you with a letter explaining details of your disability. Check the current practice for malaria prophylaxis (prevention) as recommendations are constantly under review.

Vaccination & immunization

The following vaccinations are recommended:

Typhoid (monovalent): one dose followed by a booster in 1 month's time. Immunity from this course lasts 2-3 years. An oral preparation is currently being marketed in some countries.

Polio-myelitis: this is a live vaccine generally given orally and a full course consists of three doses with a booster in tropical regions every 3-5 years.

Tetanus: one dose should be given with a booster at 6 weeks and another at 6 months and 10 yearly boosters thereafter are recommended. Children should, in addition, be properly protected against diphtheria, whooping cough, mumps and measles. Teenage girls, if they have not had the disease, should be given rubella (German measles) vaccination. Consult your doctor for advice on BCG innoculation against tuberculosis; the disease is still common in the region.

Meningococcal Meningitis and Japanese B Encephalitis (JBE): immunization (effective in 10 days) gives protection for around 3 years. There is an extremely small risk, though it varies seasonally and from region to region. Consult a Travel Clinic or MASTA (see below for details).

Hepatitis A: the Havrix vaccine gives protection for 10 years after two injections (10 days to be effective). Alternatively, one gamma globulin injection to cover up to 6 months' travel is effective immediately. Regular travellers should have a blood test first to check whether they are already immune.

Rabies: pre-exposure vaccination gives anyone bitten by a suspect animal time to get treatment (so particularly helpful to those visiting remote areas) and also prepares the body to produce antibodies quickly; cost of vaccine can be shared by three receiving vaccination together.

Malaria: Prophylactic tablets are strongly advised for visitors to affected countries but since a particular course of treatment is recommended to a specific part of the world (which can change in time) seek up-to-date advice from the Malaria Reference Laboratory, T 0891 600 350 (recorded message, premium rate) or the Liverpool School of Tropical Medicine, T 051 708 9393. In the USA, try Centre for Disease Control, Atlanta, T 404 332 4555.

Small-pox, cholera and yellow fever vaccinations are not required. You may be asked for a certificate if you have been in a country affected by yellow fever immediately before travelling to Sri Lanka.

Infectious Hepatitis (jaundice)

This is common and can be caught by travellers. The main symptoms are stomach pains, lack of appetite, nausea, lassitude and yellowness of the eyes and skin. Medically speaking, there are two types: the less serious but more common is hepatitis A for which the best protection is careful preparation of food, the avoidance of contaminated drinking water and scrupulous attention to toilet hygiene. Human normal immunoglobulin (gamma globulin) confers considerable protection against the disease and is particularly useful in epidemics. It should be obtained from a reputable source and is certainly recommended for travellers who intend to live rough. The injection should be given as close as possible to your departure and, as the dose depends on the likely time you are to spend in potentially infected areas, the manufacturer's instructions should be followed.

The other, more serious, version is hepatitis B, which is acquired as a sexually transmitted disease, from a blood transfusion or an injection with an unclean needle or possibly by insect bites. The symptoms are the same as hepatitis A but the incubation period is much longer.

You may have had jaundice before or you may have had hepatitis of either type before without becoming jaundiced, in which case it is possible that you could be immune to either hepatitis A or B. This immunity can be tested for before you travel. If you are not immune to hepatitis B already, a vaccine is available (three shots over 6 months) and if you are not immune to hepatitis A already, then you should consider having gamma globulin.

AIDS

In Sri Lanka AIDS is still rare but is increasing in its prevalence as in most countries, but with a pattern closer to that of developing societies. Thus, it is not wholly confined to the well known high risk sections of the population, ie homosexual men, intravenous drug abusers, prostitutes and the children of infected mothers. Heterosexual transmission is probably now the dominant mode and so the main risk to travellers is from casual sex. The same precautions should be taken as when encountering any sexually transmitted disease. In some of the countries, almost the whole of the female prostitute population is HIV positive and in other parts, intravenous drug abuse is common. The AIDS virus (HIV) can be passed via unsterile needles which have been previously used to inject a HIV positive patient but the risk of this is very small indeed. It would, however, be sensible to check that needles have been properly sterilized or disposable needles used. The chance of picking up hepatitis B in this way is much more of a danger. Be wary of carrying disposable needles yourself; customs officials may find them suspicious. The risk of receiving a blood transfusion with blood infected with the HIV virus is greater than from dirty needles because of the amount of fluid exchanged. Supplies of blood for transfusion are now largely screened for HIV in all reputable hospitals, so the risk must be very small indeed. Catching the AIDS virus does not necessarily produce an illness in itself; the only way to be sure if you feel you have been put at risk is to have a blood test for HIV antibodies on your return to a place where there are reliable laboratory facilities. The test does not become positive for many weeks.

Common problems

Heat

Full acclimatization to high temperatures takes about 2 weeks and during this period, it is normal to feel relatively apathetic, especially if the relative humidity is high. Drink plenty of water (up to 15 litres a day are required when working physically hard in the tropics), use salt on your food and avoid extreme exertion. Tepid showers are more cooling than hot or cold ones. Large hats do not cool you down but prevent sunburn. Loose fitting cotton clothes are still the best for hot weather. Warm clothing and woollens are necessary after dark in the Central Highlands.

Insects

These can be a great nuisance. Some of course are carriers of serious diseases such as malaria, dengue fever or filariasis and various worm infections. The best way of keeping mosquitoes away at night is to sleep off the ground with a mosquito net and to burn mosquito coils containing Pyrethrum. Aerosol sprays or a 'flit' gun may be effective as are insecticidal tablets which are heated on a mat which is plugged into the wall socket (if taking your own, check the voltage of the area you are visiting so that you can take an appliance that will work. Similarly, check that your electrical adaptor is suitable for the repellent plug).

Or you can use personal insect repellent of which the best contain a high concentration of Diethyltoluamide. Liquid is best for arms and face (take care around eyes and make sure you do not dissolve the plastic of your spectacles). Aerosol spray on clothes and ankles deter mites and ticks. Liquid DEET suspended in water can be used to impregnate cotton clothes and mosquito nets. If you are bitten, itching may be relieved by cool baths and anti-histamine tablets (care with alcohol or driving), corticosteroid creams (great care – never use if any hint of sepsis) or by judicious scratching. Calamine lotion and cream have limited effectiveness and anti-histamine creams have a tendency to cause skin allergies and are, therefore, not generally recommended. Bites which become infected (commonly in the tropics) should be treated with a local antiseptic or antibiotic cream such as Cetrimide as should infected scratches. Skin infestations with body lice, crabs and scabies are unfortunately easy to pick up. Use Gamma benzene hexachloride for lice and Benzyl benzoate for scabies. Crotamiton cream alleviates itching and also kills a number of skin parasites. Malathion lotion 5% is good for lice but avoid the highly toxic full strength Malathion used as an agricultural insecticide.

Intestinal upsets

These are common, so be prepared. Most of the time, intestinal upsets are due to the insanitary preparation of food. Do not eat uncooked fish or vegetables or meat (especially pork), fruit with the skin on (always peel your fruit yourself) or food that is exposed to flies (especially salads). Tap water may be unsafe, especially in the monsoon and the same goes for stream water or well water. Filtered or bottled water is usually available and safe. If your hotel has a central hot water supply, this is safe to drink after cooling. Ice for drinks should be made from boiled water but rarely is, so stand your glass on the ice cubes, instead of putting them in the drink. Dirty water should first be strained through a filter bag (available from camping shops) and then boiled or treated. Bringing the water to a rolling boil at sea level is sufficient. Various sterilizing methods can be used and there are proprietary preparations containing chlorine or iodine compounds. Pasteurized or heat treated milk is now widely available, as is ice cream and yogurt produced by the same methods. Unpasteurized milk products, including cheese, are sources of tuberculosis, brucellosis, listeria and food poisoning germs. You can render fresh milk safe by heating it to 62°C for 30 mins, followed by rapid cooling or by boiling it. Matured or processed cheeses are safer than fresh varieties.

Diarrhoea is usually the result of food poisoning, occasionally from contaminated water. There are various causes – viruses, bacteria, protozoa (like amoeba), salmonella and cholera organisms. It may take one of several forms, coming on suddenly, or rather slowly. It may be accompanied by vomiting or by severe abdominal pain and the passage of blood or mucus when it is called dysentery. How do you know which type you have and how do you treat them? All kinds of diarrhoea, whether or not accompanied by vomiting respond favourably to the replacement of water and salts taken as frequent small sips of some kind of rehydration solution. There are proprietary preparations, consisting of sachets of powder which you dissolve in water, or you can make your own by adding half a teaspoonful of salt (3.5 grams) and 4 tablespoonfuls of sugar (40 grams) to a litre of boiled water.

- If you can time the onset of diarrhoea to the minute, then it is probably viral or bacterial and/or the onset of dysentery. The treatment, in addition to rehydration, is Ciprofloxacin 500 mgs every 12 hrs. The drug is now widely available.
- If the diarrhoea has come on slowly or intermittently, then it is more likely to be protozoal, ie caused by amoeba or giardia and antibiotics will have no effect. These cases are best treated by a doctor as should any diarrhoea continuing for more than 3 days. If there are severe stomach cramps, the following drugs may help: Loperamide (Imodium, Arret) and Diphenoxylate with Atropine (Lomotil).

Thus, the lynch pins of treatment for diarrhoea are rest, fluid and salt replacement, antibiotics such as Ciprofloxacin for the bacterial types and special diagnostic tests and medical treatment for amoeba and giardia infections. Salmonella infections and cholera can be devastating diseases and it would be wise to get to a hospital as soon as possible if these were suspected. Fasting, peculiar diets and the consumption of large quantities of yogurt have not been found useful in calming travellers' diarrhoea or in rehabilitating inflamed bowels.

Oral rehydration has, especially in children, been a lifesaving technique and as there is some evidence that alcohol and milk might prolong diarrhoea, they should probably be avoided during and immediately after an attack. There are ways of preventing travellers' diarrhoea for short periods of time when visiting these countries by taking antibiotics but these are ineffective against viruses and, to some extent, against protozoa, so this technique should not be used, other than in exceptional circumstances. Some preventives such as Entero-vioform can have serious side effects if taken for long periods.

Malaria

Malaria is prevalent in Sri Lanka. It remains a serious disease and you are advised to protect yourself against mosquito bites as above and to take prophylactic (preventive) drugs. Start taking the tablets a few days before exposure and continue to take them 6 weeks after leaving the malarial zone. Remember to give the drugs to babies and children and pregnant women also. The subject of malaria prevention is becoming more complex as the malaria parasite becomes immune to some of the older drugs. In particular, there has been an increase in the proportion of cases of falciparum malaria which is particularly dangerous. Some of the preventive drugs can cause side effects, especially if taken for long periods of time, so before you travel you must check with a reputable agency the likelihood and type of malaria in the countries which you intend to visit and take their advice on prophylaxis and be prepared to receive conflicting advice. Because of the rapidly changing situation in the area I have not included the names and dosage of the drugs. You can catch malaria even when taking prophylactic drugs, although it is unlikely. If you do develop symptoms (high fever, shivering, severe headache, sometimes diarrhoea) seek medical advice immediately. The risk of the disease is obviously greater the further you move from the cities into rural areas with primitive facilities and standing water.

Snake bites

If you are unlucky enough to be bitten by a venomous snake, spider, scorpion, centipede or sea creature try (within limits) to catch the animal for identification. The reactions to be expected are fright, swelling, pain and bruising around the bite, soreness of the regional lymph glands, nausea, vomiting and fever. If, in addition, any of the following symptoms supervene get the victim to a doctor without delay: numbness, tingling of the face, muscular spasm, convulsions, shortness of breath or haemorrhage. Commercial snake bite or scorpion sting kits may be available but are only useful for the specific type of snake or scorpion for which they are designed. The serum has to be given intravenously, so is not much good unless you have had some practice in making injections into veins. If the bite is on a limb, immobilize the limb and apply a tight bandage between the bite and the body, releasing it for 90 secs every 15 mins. Reassurance of the bitten person is very important because death from snake bite is, in fact, very rare. Do not slash the bite area and try to suck out the poison because this sort of heroism does more harm than good. Hospitals usually hold stocks of snake bite serum. Best precaution: do not walk in snake territory with bare feet, sandals or shorts.

If swimming in an area where there are poisonous fish such as stone or scorpion fish (also called by a variety of local names) or sea urchins on rocky coasts, tread carefully or wear plimsolls. The sting of such fish is intensely painful and this can be helped by immersing the stung part in water as hot as you can bear for as long as it remains painful. This is not always very practical and you must take care not to scald yourself, but it does work. Avoid spiders and scorpions by keeping your bed away from the wall, look under lavatory seats and inside your shoes in the morning. In the rare event of being bitten, consult a doctor.

Sunburn and heat stroke

The burning power of the tropical sun is phenomenal, especially at high altitude. Always wear a wide brimmed hat and use some form of sun cream or lotion on untanned skin. Normal temperate zone suntan lotions (protection factor up to 7) are not much good. You need to use the types designed specifically for the tropics or for mountaineers or skiers with a protection factor between 7 and 15. Glare from the sun can cause conjunctivitis so wear sunglasses, especially on the beaches.

There are several varieties of 'heat stroke'. The most common cause is severe dehydration. Avoid dehydration by drinking lots of non-alcoholic fluid.

Other afflictions

Remember that **rabies** is endemic so do not go near any wild animal or an unknown dog. If you are bitten by a domestic animal, try to have it captured for observation and see a doctor at once. Treatment with human diploid vaccine is now extremely effective and worth seeking out if the likelihood of having contracted rabies is high. A course of anti-rabies vaccine might be a good idea before you go.

Dengue fever is present. It is a virus disease, transmitted by mosquito bites, presenting with severe headache and body pains. Complicated types of dengue known as haemorrhagic fevers occur throughout Asia but usually in persons who have caught the disease a second time. Thus, although it is a very serious type, it is rarely caught by visitors. There is no treatment, you must just avoid mosquito bites.

Athlete's foot and other fungal infections are best treated by sunshine and a proprietary preparation such as Tolnaftate.

Influenza and **respiratory diseases** are common, perhaps made worse by polluted cities and rapid temperature and climatic changes.

Intestinal worms are common and the more serious ones, such as hook worm can be contracted by walking barefoot on infested earth or beaches.

Leishmaniasis – this can be a serious disease taking several forms and transmitted by sand flies. These should be avoided in the same way as mosquitoes.

Prickly heat A very common itchy rash is avoided by frequent washing and by wearing loose clothing. It is helped by the use of talcum powder to allow the skin to dry thoroughly after washing.

Returning home

Remember to take your anti-malaria tablets for 6 weeks. If you have had attacks of diarrhoea, it is worth having a stool specimen tested in case you have picked up amoebic dysentery. If you have been living rough, a blood test may be worthwhile to detect worms and other parasites.

Further information

The following organizations give information regarding well trained English speaking Physicians throughout the world: International Association for Medical Assistance to Travellers, 745 5th Ave, New York, 10022; Intermedic 777, Third Ave, New York, 10017.

Information regarding country by country malaria risk can be obtained from the World Health Organisation (WHO) or the Ross Institute, The London School of Hygiene and Tropical Medicine, Kepple St, London WC1E 7HT, which publishes a strongly recommended book entitled: *The Preservation of Personal Health in Warm Climates*.

The organization MASTA (Medical

Advisory Service for Travellers Abroad) also based at the London School of Hygiene and Tropical Medicine, Telephone 0171 631-4408 – Telex 895 3474) will provide country by country information on up to date health risks.

Further information on medical problems overseas can be obtained from the new edition of *Travellers' Health: How to Stay Healthy Abroad*, edited by Richard Dawood (Oxford University Press,1992). We strongly recommend this revised and updated edition, especially to the travellers who go to the more out-of-the-way places.

SRI LANKA: LAND, CULTURE AND HISTORY

LAND AND LIFE

CONTENTS

Geology and landscape	47
Climate	49
Vegetation, land and wildlife	51

Basics

OFFICIAL NAME: *Sri Lanka Prajatantrika Samajawadi Janarajaya* (Democratic Socialist Republic of Sri Lanka)

NATIONAL FLAG: On a dark red field, within a golden border, a golden lion passant holding a sword in its right paw, and a representation of a bo-leaf coming from each corner; to its right, two vertical saffron and green stripes (representing Hindu and Muslim minorities), also within a golden border.

CAPITAL: *Colombo*

NATIONAL ANTHEM: *Namo Namo Matha* (We all stand together)

KEY STATISTICS: *Population*: 18.1 million. *Annual growth rate*: 1.6%. *Crude birth rate*: 2.4%. *Crude death rate*: 0.8%. *Urban population*: 21%. *Life expectancy at birth* 72. *Infant mortality*: 2.9% of live births. *Adult Literary*: M 93%; F 84%. *Area*: 66,000 sq km. *Population density*: 256 per sq km. *GDP per capita*: US$620 (*UN real GDP per cap*: US$3,000). *Average Annual growth rate*: 1993-95 5.8%. *Main agricultural products*: 1994: tea 232,000 tonnes, rubber 108,000 tonnes, paddy 2.56 million tonnes, coconut 2.2 billion nuts. *Major exports*: textiles and garments US$1.41bn, tea US$413mn, petroleum products US$79mn, gems US$76mn, rubber US$64mn, coconuts US$58mn.

Geology and landscape

Location

Situated between 5°55′-9°51′N, Sri Lanka is at the heart of the Indian Ocean trading routes. After the opening of the route round the Cape of Good Hope by Vasco da Gama in 1498 the island was brought into direct contact with Western Europe. The opening of the Suez Canal in 1869 further strengthened the trading links with the West.

The origins of Sri Lanka's landscapes

Only 100 million years ago Sri Lanka was still attached to the great land mass of what geologists call 'Pangaea', of which South Africa, Antarctica and the Indian peninsula were a part. Indeed, geologically Sri Lanka is a continuation of the Indian Peninsula, from which it was separated less than 10,000 years ago by the 10m deep and 35 km wide **Palk Straits**. Its area of 65,525 sq km makes Sri Lanka a little smaller than Belgium and the Netherlands combined. It is 432 km long and at its broadest 224 km wide. Its 1,600 km of coastline is lined with fine sandy beaches, coral reefs and lagoons.

Many of the rocks which comprise over 90% of Sri Lanka and the Indian Peninsula were formed alongside their then neighbours in South Africa, South America, Australia and Antarctica. Generally crystalline, contorted and faulted, the **Archaean** rocks of Sri Lanka and the Indian Peninsula are some of the oldest in the world.

The fault line which severed India from Africa was marked by a N-S ridge of mountains. These run N from the Central Highlands of Sri Lanka through the Western Ghats, which form a spine running up the W coast of India. Both in Sri Lanka and India the hills are set back from the sea by a coastal plain which varies from 10 to over 80 km wide. In Sri Lanka and southern India the hills are over 2,500m high.

The oldest series are the Charnockites, intrusive rocks named after the founder of Calcutta and enthusiastic amateur geologist, Job Charnock. These are between 2,000 and 3,000 million years old. In India some of the most striking examples are found in the Nilgiri, Palani and Annamalai Hills in Tamil Nadu and Kerala. In Sri Lanka they run like a broad belt across the island's heart, important partly because they contain most of Sri Lanka's minerals, including gems, though these are found largely in the gravelly river deposits rather than in their original rocks.

Unlike the central Himalaya to their N, which did not begin to rise until about 35 million years ago the Highlands of Sri Lanka and the Western Ghats of India have been upland regions for several hundred million years. The island has never been completely covered by the sea, the only exception being in the far N where the Jaffna peninsula was submerged, allowing the distinctive Jaffna limestones to be deposited in shallow seas between 7 million and 26 million years ago.

Today the ancient crystalline rocks form an ancient highland massif rising to its highest points just S and SW of the geographical centre of the pear-shaped island. The highlands rise in three dissected steps to *Piduratalaga* (Sri Lanka's highest mountain at 2,524m) and the sacred *Adam's Peak* (2,260m). The steps are separated from each other by steep scarp slopes. Recent evidence suggests that the very early folding of the ancient rocks, followed by erosion at different speeds, formed the scarps and plateaus, often deeply cut by the rivers which radiate from the centre of the island. Even though the origin of these steps is not fully understood the steep scarps separating them have created some beautiful waterfalls and enormous hydro-electric power potential. Some of this has now been realized, notably through the huge Victoria Dam project on the Mahaweli Ganga, but in the process some of the most scenic waterfalls have been lost.

Rivers lakes and floods

By far the largest of the 103 river basins in Sri Lanka is that of the Mahaweli Ganga, which covers about 16% of the

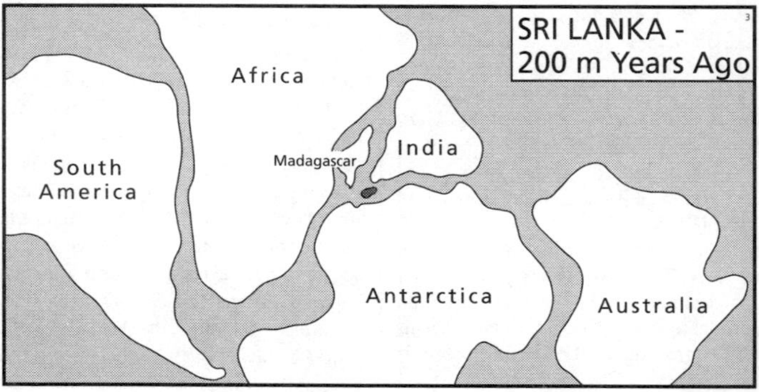

island's total area. The river itself has a winding course, rising about 50 km S of Kandy and flowing N then NE to the sea near Trincomalee, covering a distance of 320 km. It is the only perenniel river to cross the Dry Zone. Its name is a reference to the Ganga of N India, and in Sri Lanka all perenniel rivers are called Ganga, while seasonal streams are called Oya (in Sinhalese) or Aru (in Tamil). A number of the rivers have now been developed both for irrigation and power, the Victoria project on the Mahaweli Ganga being one of the biggest in Asia – and one of the most controversial. It has created Sri Lanka's largest lake, the Victoria Reservoir.

The short rivers of Sri Lanka's Wet Zone sometimes have severe floods, and the Kelani, which ultimately reaches the sea at Colombo, has had four catastrophic floods this century. Others can also be turbulent during the wet season, tumbling through steamy forests and cultuvated fields on their short courses to the sea.

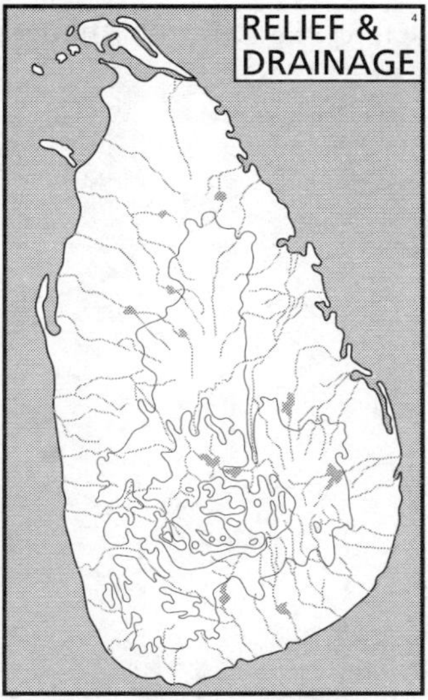

Climate

Sri Lanka's location just N of the Equator places it on the main track of the two monsoons which dominate South Asia's weather systems. An Arabic word meaning 'season', the term monsoon refers to the wind reversal which replaces the relatively cool, dry and stable northeasterlies, characteristic of winter and spring, with the very warm and wet southwesterlies of the summer. However, because Sri Lanka is so far S and the Northeasterlies, which originate in the arid interior of China, have crossed over 1,500 km of the Bay of Bengal by the time they reach Sri Lanka, even the NE monsoon brings rain, especially to the N and E of the island.

Rainfall Nearly three quarters of Sri Lanka lies in what is widely known as the 'Dry Zone', comprising the northern half and the whole of the E of the country. Average annual rainfall in this region is generally between 1,200-1,800 mm. In comparison with many parts of Europe this may not seem unduly dry, but like much of SE India, virtually all

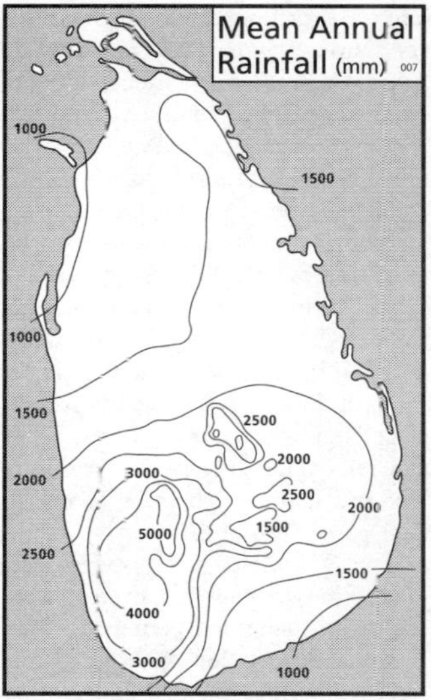

of the region's rain falls in the 3 months of the NE Monsoon between Oct and Dec. The rain often comes in relatively short but dramatic bursts. Habarana, for example, located in the Dry Zone between Polonnaruwa and Anuradhapura received 1,240 mm (nearly 50") of rain in the 3 days around Christmas in 1957. These rains caused catastrophic floods right across the Dry Zone.

The Wet Zone also receives some rain during this period, although the coastal regions of the SW are in the rain shadow of the Central Highlands, and are much drier than the NE between Nov and Jan. The SW corner of Sri Lanka, the Wet Zone, has its main wet season from May to Sep, when the SW Monsoon sweeps across the Arabian Sea like a massive wall of warm moist air, often over 10,000m thick. The higher slopes of the Central Highlands receive as much as 4,000 mm during this period, while even the coastal lowlands receive over 500 mm.

Agriculture in the N and E suffers badly during the SW Monsoon because the moisture bearing winds dry out as they descend over the Central Highlands, producing hot, drying and often very strong winds. Thus Jun, Jul and Aug are almost totally rainless throughout the Dry Zone. For much of the time a strong, hot wind, called *yal hulunga* by the Sinhalese peasantry and *kachchan* by the Tamils, dessicates the land.

From late Oct to Dec cyclonic storms often form over the Bay of Bengal, sometimes causing havoc from the southern coast of India northwards to Bangladesh. Sri Lanka is far enough S to miss many of the worst of these, but it occasionally suffers major cyclones. These generally come later in the season, in Dec and Jan and can cause enormous damage and loss of life.

The Wet Zone rarely experiences long periods without rain. Even between the major moonsoon periods, in Mar-Apr and in Oct-Nov, widespread rain can occur. Convectional thunderstorms bring extensive rain to the S and SW in the first period, and depressions tracking across the Bay of Bengal can bring heavy rain in Oct-Nov.

Temperatures
Lowland Sri Lanka is always relatively hot and humid. On the plains temperature reflects the degree of cloud cover. Colombo has minimum of 25°C in Dec and a maximum of 28°C in May. At Nuwara Eliya, over 2,000m up in the Central Highlands, the average daytime temperatures hover around 16°C, but you need to be prepared for the chill in the evenings. Only the NE occasionally experiences temperatures of above 38°C.

Humidity
The coastal regions have humidity levels above 70% for most of the year. In the SW it is rare for levels to fall below 80%, which can be very uncomfortable. However, sea breezes often bring some relief on the coast itself.

Warning In the monsoon travelling by road, especially off the National Highways, can be hazardous. Roads

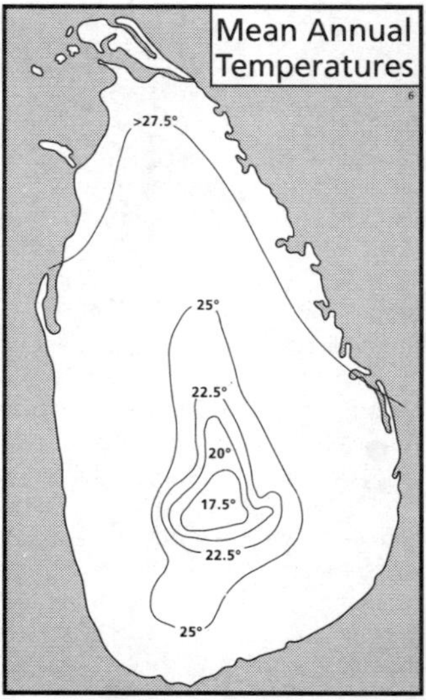

can become impassable and occasionally bridges are washed away. Railway timetables can also be unpredictably disrupted.

Vegetation, land and wildlife

Vegetation

Considering the relatively small size of Sri Lanka it has a surprisingly wide range of natural vegetation types, ranging from tropical Thorn Forest in the driest regions of the SE and NW, generally with a rainfall of less than 1,200 mm, through the Montane Temperate forest of the Central Highlands to the Mangroves of some stretches of the coast. Today these are restricted almost exclusively to a stretch of the W coast N of Puttalam and of the SE coast E of Hambantota.

None of the original forest cover has been unaffected by human activity, and much has now been either converted to cultivated land, or given over to a range of tree cash crops, notably coconut and rubber at low altitudes and tea at higher levels. Indeed most of the forest cover is now restricted to the Dry Zone. Here dry evergreen forest, with trees generally less than 12m in height, and moist deciduous forest, whose canopy level is usually up to 20 or 25m, provide an excellent habitat for wildlife, and continue to cover extensive tracts of land. Even here the original forest has been much altered, most having re-colonized land which was extensively cultivated until 500 years ago. Sri Lanka also has four different types of grassland, all the result of human activity.

Wildlife

Sri Lanka's 24 wildlife sanctuaries are home to a wide range of native species, eg elephants, leopard, sloth bear, the unique loris, a variety of deer, the purple-faced leaf monkey, the endangered wild boar, porcupines and ant-eaters. Reptiles include vipers and the marsh and estuarine crocodiles. Among the 16 amphibians unique to the island are the Nanophrys frogs in the hills. Most of the fish are river or marsh dwelling – the trout, introduced by the British, being found in the cool streams of the Horton Plains.

HOLY BUT NOT WHOLLY EFFICACIOUS!

The *sal* tree is one of the most widespread and abundant trees in the tropical and sub-tropical Ganges plains and Himalayan foothills; it was the tree under which Guatama Buddha was born. Like the *pipal* (*Ficus religiosa*), under which the Buddha was enlightened, the *sal* is greatly revered in Sri Lanka. It is often planted near temples, for example on the lawn close to the Temple of the Tooth Relic in Kandy. However, the *sal* in Sri Lanka is very different to the one found in northern South Asia, and the difference has been known to have serious consequences since extracts from the tree are widely used for medicinal preparations. The *sal* tree proper is *Shorea robusta* (Dipterocarpaceae), whereas the *sal* of Sri Lanka is the tree known all over the tropics as the Cannon Ball Tree (*Couroupita surenamensis*). Unfortunately, the difference is not widely known and it is not unknown for Auyurvedic medicinal preparations using the Sri Lankan *sal* but following recipes of Indian origin, to have been taken without any positive effect!

The distinctive shape of the flowers on *C. surenamensis* which appear at the end of extraordinarily long stems which cascade down the full length of the trunk is of special significance. These stems are large and have a hooded structure which overhangs the reproductive organs of the flowers in a form reminiscent of the way the cobra is depicted as having protected the Buddha when he resided in the forest alone.

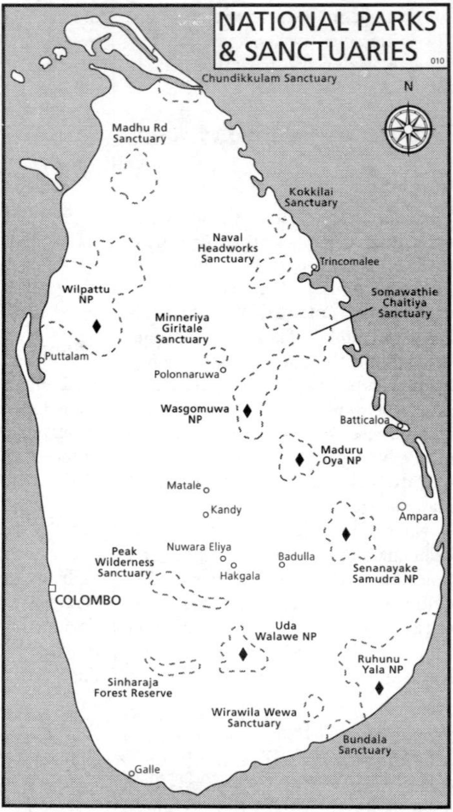

The three largest sanctuaries are the National Parks at **Ruhunu-Yala**, **Wilpattu** and **Gal Oya**. The elephants of Lahugala and Gal Oya are famous as while Wilpattu still harbours a sizeable number of leopards.

The indigenous 240 (of the total of 440) species of butterflies are seen below 1,000m and Mar/Apr is the period of seasonal migration. Sri Lanka is also an ornithologist's paradise with over 250 resident species, mostly found in the Wet Zone, including the Grackle, whistling thrush, yellow-eared Bulbul, Malkoha and brown-capped Babbler. The winter migrants come from distant Siberia and W Europe, the reservoirs attracting vast numbers of waterbirds (stilts, sandpipers, terns and plover, as well as herons, egrets and storks). The forests attract species of warblers, thrushes, cuckoo and many others. The **Kumana** sanctuary in the E, and **Bundala** (famed for flamingoes), **Kalametiya** and **Wirawila** sanctuaries between Tissemaharama and Hambantota in the S, all with lagoons, are the principal bird sanctuaries.

The off-shore coral reefs also harbour rich marine life, making snorkelling and diving particularly popular along the SE coast.

The **Sinharaja Biosphere Reserve** (World Heritage Site) and the highland **Peak Wilderness Sanctuary** near Adam's Peak and **Udawattekele** near Kandy, are famous. The Wildlife Conservation programme is undertaken by the government with an office in Colombo at Chaitiya Rd, Marine Drive, Fort, T 25248, F 580721.

See also Wildlife colour section in the centre.

RELIGION

Contents

Buddhism	53
Hinduism	59
Islam	67
Christianity	69

Buddhism

In Sri Lanka Buddhism is the most widespread religion of the majority Sinhalese community. Although India was the original home of Buddhism, today it is practised largely on the margins of the sub-continent, and is widely followed in Ladakh, Nepal and Bhutan as well as Sri Lanka.

The Buddha's life

Siddharta Gautama, who came to be given the title of the Buddha – the Enlightened One – was born a prince into the warrior caste in about 563 BC. He was married at the age of 16 and his wife had a son. When he reached the age of 29 he left home and wandered as a beggar and ascetic. After about 6 years he spent some time in Bodh Gaya. Sitting under the Bo tree, meditating, he was tempted by the demon Mara, with all the desires of the world. Resisting these temptations, he received enlightenment.

These scenes are common motifs of Buddhist art. The next landmark was the preaching of his first sermon on 'The Foundation of Righteousness' in the deer park near Benaras. By the time he died the Buddha had established a small band of monks and nuns known as the Sangha, and had followers across N India. His body was cremated, and the ashes, regarded as precious relics, were divided up among the peoples to whom he had preached. Some have been discovered as far W as Peshawar, in the NW frontier of Pakistan, and at Piprawa, close to his birthplace.

After the Buddha's death

From the Buddha's death – or Parinirvana (Parinibbana) – to the destruction of Nalanda (the last Buddhist stronghold in India) in 1197 AD, Buddhism in India went through three phases. These are often referred to as Hinayana, Mahayana and Vajrayana, though they were not mutually exclusive, being followed simultaneously in different regions.

Hinayana

The Hinayana, or Little Way, insists on a monastic way of life as the only path to achieving nirvana (see box page 54). Divided into many schools, the only surviving Hinayana tradition is the Theravada Buddhism (from *thera*, meaning wise man or sage), which was taken to Sri Lanka by Mahinda, either the son or possibly the brother of the Indian Emperor Asoka. It became the state religion under King Dutthagamenu in the 1st century AD.

Mahayana

In contrast to the Hinayana schools, the followers of the Mahayana school (the Great Way) believed in the possibility of salvation for all. They practised a far more devotional form of meditation, and new figures came to play a prominent part in their beliefs and their worship – the **Bodhisattvas**, saints who were predestined to reach the state of enlightenment through thousands of rebirths. They aspired to Buddhahood, however, not for their own sake but for the sake of all living things. The Buddha is believed to have passed through numerous existences in preparation for his final mission. One of the most notable

The Buddha's Four Noble Truths

The Buddha preached Four Noble Truths: that life is painful; that suffering is caused by ignorance and desire; that beyond the suffering of life there is a state which cannot be described but which he termed nirvana; and that nirvana can be reached by following an eightfold path.

The concept of nirvana is often understood in the W in an entirely negative sense – that of 'non-being'. The word has the rough meaning of 'blow out' or 'extinguish', meaning to blow out the fires of greed, lust and desire. In a more positive sense it has been described by one Buddhist scholar as 'the state of absolute illumination, supreme bliss, infinite love and compassion, unshakeable serenity, and unrestricted spiritual freedom'. The essential elements of the eightfold path are the perfection of wisdom, morality and meditation.

Mahayana philosophers was the 2nd or 3rd century saint, Nagarjuna. Mahayana Buddhism became dominant over most of South Asia, and its influence is evidenced in Buddhist art from Sigiriya in Sri Lanka to Ajanta in central India and as far as Gandhara in northern Pakistan.

Vajrayana

The Diamond Way resembles magic and yoga in some of its beliefs. The ideal of Vajrayana Buddhists is to be 'so fully in harmony with the cosmos as to be able to manipulate the cosmic forces within and outside himself'. It had developed in the N of India by the 7th century AD, matching the parallel growth of Hindu Tantrism, and periodically also exercised some influence in Sri Lanka.

Buddhism's decline in India

The decline of Buddhism in India probably stemmed as much from the growing similarity in the practice of Hinduism and Buddhism as from direct attacks. Mahayana Buddhism, with its reverence for Bodhisattvas and its devotional character, was more and more difficult to distinguish from the revivalist Hinduism characteristic of several parts of N India from the 7th to the 12th centuries AD. In S India the Chola Empire contributed to the final extinction of

The Buddha in Bhumisparcamudra – calling the earth goddess to witness.

The Buddha in Dhyanamudra – meditation.

ZSR 201

Buddhism in the southern Peninsula, while the Muslim conquest of northern India dealt the final death blow, being accompanied by the large scale slaughter of monks and the destruction of monasteries. Without their institutional support Buddhism in India gradually faded away, retreating to the regions peripheral to mainland India. The nature of Buddhism's decline on mainland India may well have contributed to the powerful sense in Sri Lanka that militant Hindu expansionism was a major threat to the security of Sri Lanka's Buddhists.

India still has many sites of great significance for Buddhists around the world. Some say that the Buddha himself spoke of the four places his followers should visit. **Lumbini**, the Buddha's birthplace, is in the Nepali foothills, near the present border with India. **Bodh Gaya**, where he attained what Buddhists term his 'supreme enlightenment', is about 80 km S of the modern Indian city of Patna; the deer park at **Sarnath**, where he preached his first sermon and set in motion the Wheel of the Law, is just outside Varanasi; and **Kushinagara**, where he died at the age of 80, is 50 km E of Gorakhpur. In addition there are remarkable monuments, sculptures and works of art, from Gandhara in modern Pakistan to Sanchi and Ajanta in central India, to the treasures in ancient sites in Sri Lanka where it is still possible to see the vivid evidence of the flowering of Buddhist culture in South Asia.

Sri Lankan Buddhism

The recent history of Sri Lanka's Theravada Buddhism may conceal the importance of the cultural and historical links between Sri Lanka and India in the early stages of Sri Lankan Buddhism's development. The first great stupas in Anuradhapura were built when Buddhism was still a religious force to be reckoned with in mainland India, and as some of the sculptures from Sigiriya suggest there were important contacts with Amaravati, another major centre of Buddhist art and thought, up to the 5th century AC

The origins of Sri Lankan Buddhism are explained in a legend which tells how King **Devanampiya Tissa** (d 207 BC) was converted by Mahinda, widely believed to have been Asoka's son, who was sent to Sri Lanka specifically to bring the faith to the Island's people. He established the Mahavihara monastery. Successors repeatedly struggled to preserve Sri Lankan Buddhism's distinct identity from that of neighbouring Hinduism and Tantrism. It was also constantly struggling with Mahayana Buddhism, which gained the periodic support of successive royal patrons. King Mahasena (AD 276-303) and his son Sri Meghavarna, who received the famous 'tooth of the Buddha' when it was brought to the island from Kalinga in the 4th century AC, both advocated Mahayana forms of the faith. Even then Sri Lanka's Buddhism is not strictly orthodox, for the personal character of the Buddha is emphasized, as was the virtue of being a disciple of the Buddha. *Maitreya*, the 'future' Buddha, is recognized as the only *Bodhisattva*, and it has been a feature of Buddhism in the island for kings to identify themselves with this incarnation of the Buddha.

The Sinhalese see themselves as guardians of the original Buddhist faith. They believe that Pali scripture was first written down by King **Vattagamani Abhaya** in the 1st century BC. The *Pali canon* of scripture is referred to as three 'baskets', because the palm leaf texts on which they were written were stored in baskets. They are '**conduct**' (*vinaya*), or rules; '**sermon**' (*sutta*), the largest and most important of the three; and '**metaphysics**' (*Abhidhamma*). There are also several works that lack the full authority of the canon but are nonetheless important. Basham suggests that the main propositions of the literature are psychological rather than metaphysical. Suffering, sorrow and dissatisfaction are the nature of ordinary life, and can only be eliminated by giving up desire. In turn, desire is a result of the misplaced belief in the reality of individual existence. In its Theravada form, Hinayana Buddhism taught that there is no soul and ultimately no god. Nirvana was a state of rest beyond the universe, once found never lost.

The cosmology

Although the Buddha discouraged the development of cosmologies, the Hinayana Buddhists produced a cyclical view of the universe, evolving through four time periods.

Period 1 Man slowly declines until everything is destroyed except the highest heaven. The good go to this heaven, the remainder to various hells.

Period 2 A quiescent phase.

Period 3 Evolution begins again. However, 'the good *karma* of beings in the highest heaven' now begins to fail, and a lower heaven evolves, a *world of form*. During this period a great being in the higher heaven dies, and is re-born in the world of form as Brahma. Feeling lonely, he wishes that others were with him. Soon other beings from the higher heaven die and are reborn in this world. Brahma interprets these people as his own creation, and himself as The Creator.

Period 4 The first men, who initially had supernatural qualities, deteriorate and become earthbound, and the period fluctuates between advance and deterioration.

The four-period cycles continue for eternity, alternating between 'Buddha cycles' – one of which we live in today – and 'empty cycles'. It is believed that in the present cycle four Buddhas – *Krakucchanda*, *Kanakamuni*, *Kasyapa*, and *Sakyamuni* – have already taught, and one, *Maitreya*, is still to come.

In Sri Lanka the scriptures came to be attributed with almost magical powers. Close ties developed between Buddhist belief and Sinhalese nationalism. The Sinhalese scholar *Buddhaghosa* translated Sinhalese texts into Pali in the 5th century AD. At the beginning of the 11th century Sri Lankan missionaries were responsible for the conversion of Thailand, Burma, Cambodia and Laos to Theravadin Buddhism. Subsequently, in the face of continued threats to their continued survival, Sri Lanka's Buddhist monks had to be re-ordained into the valid line of Theravadin lineage by monks from SE Asia. Buddhist links with Thailand remain close.

Buddhist practice

By the time Buddhism was brought to Sri Lanka there was a well developed religious organization which had strong links with secular authorities. Developments in Buddhist thought and belief had made it possible for peasants and lay people to share in the religious beliefs of the faith. As it developed in Sri Lanka the main outlines of practice became clearly defined. The king and the orders of monks became interdependent; a monastic hierarchy was established; most monks were learning and teaching, rather than practising withdrawal from the world. Most important, Buddhism accepted a much wider range of goals for living than simply the release from permanent rebirth.

The most important of these were 'good rebirth', the prevention of misfortune and the increase in good fortune during the present life. These additions to original Buddhist thought led to a number of contradictions and tensions, summarized by Tambiah as: the Buddha as a unique individual, rather than a type of person (*Bodhisattva*) coming into the world periodically to help achieve release from *samsara* (rebirth), or rebirth into a better life; Buddhism as a path to salvation for all, or as a particular, nationalist religion; Buddhism as renunciation of the world and all its obligations, in contrast with playing a positive social role; and finally, whether monasteries should be run by the monks themselves, or with the support and involvement of secular authorities. These tensions are reflected in many aspects of Buddhism in Sri Lanka today, as in debates between monks who argue for political action as against withdrawal from the world.

Until the 16th century Buddhism in Sri Lanka enjoyed the active support of the state. It remained longest in Kandy, but was withdrawn steadily after the British took control in 1815. The 18th century revival of Buddhism in the Wet Zone was sponsored by the landowning village headmen, not by royalty, and castes such as the Goyigama and Salagama played a prominent role. Through the 19th century they became the dominant influence on Buddhist thought, while the remaining traditional Buddhist authority in Kandy, the *Siyam Nikaya*, suffered permanent loss of influence.

The Siyam Nikaya, one of the three sects of Sri Lankan Buddhism today, originated in the 18th mission of the Kandyan kings to Ayuthya in Thailand (Siam) to re-validate the Buddhist clergy. By a royal order admission to the sect's two branches was restricted to high caste Sinhalese. Today their monks are distinguished by carrying umbrellas and wearing their robe over one shoulder only. The exclusion of lower castes from this sect however bred resentment, and in 1803 a new sect, the *Amarapura Nikaya* was established to be open to all castes, while in 1835 the third contemporary sect, the *Ramanya Nikaya*, was set up in protest at the supposedly excessive materialism of the other two. Both these sects wear robes which cover both shoulders, but while the Amarapura sect carry umbrellas the Ramanya carries a traditional shade.

This new, independent Buddhism, became active and militant. It entered into direct competition with Christians in proselytising, and in setting up schools, special associations and social work. After Independence, political forces converged to encourage State support for Buddhism. The lay leadership pressed the government to protect Buddhists from competition with other religious groups. The Sinhalese political parties saw benefits in emphazising the role of Buddhism in society.

Buddhist worship

The Buddha himself refuted all ideas of a personal God and of worshipping a deity, but subsequent trends in Buddhism have often found a place for popular worship. Even in the relatively orthodox Theravada Buddhism of Sri Lanka personal devotion and worship are common, focused on key elements of the faith. Temple complexes (*pansalas*) commonly have several features which can serve as foci for individual devotion. Stupas or dagobas, which enshrine personal relics of the Buddha, are the most prominent, but Bodhi or Bo trees and images of the Buddha also act as objects of veneration.

Sri Lankan Buddhists place particular emphasis on the sanctity of the relics of the Buddha which are believed to have been brought to the Island. The two most important are the sacred **Bo tree** and the tooth of the Buddha. The Bo tree at Anuradhapura is believed to be a cutting from the Bo tree under which the Buddha himself achieved enlightenment at Bodh Gaya in modern Bihar. The Emperor Asoka is recorded as having entrusted the cutting to Mahinda's sister Sanghamitta to be carried to Sri Lanka on their mission of taking Buddhism to the island. As the original Bo tree in Bodh Gaya was cut down, this is the only tree in the world believed to come directly from the original tree under which the Buddha sat, and is visited by Buddhists from all over the world. Many other Bo trees in Sri Lanka have been grown from cuttings of the Anuradhapura Bo tree.

The tooth of the Buddha, now enshrined at the Dalada Maligawa in Kandy, was not brought to Sri Lanka until the 4th century AC. The Portuguese reported that they had captured and destroyed the original tooth in their attempt to wipe out all evidence of other religious faiths, but the Sinhalese claimed to have hidden it and allowed a replica to have been stolen. Today pilgrims flock from all over the island, queuing for days on special occasions when special access is granted to the casket holding the tooth in the Dalada Maligawa.

In ordinary daily life many Buddhists will visit temples at least once a week on *poya* days, which correspond with the four quarters of the moon. Full moon day, a national holiday, is a particularly important festival day. It is also an opportunity for the worship of non-Buddhist deities who have become a part of popular Buddhist religion. Some have their origins explicitly in Hinduism. The four Guardian Deities seen as future Buddhas, include Natha, Vishnu, Skanda and Saman. **Skanda**, described below, the Hindu god of war, is worshipped as Kataragama, and **Vishnu** is seen as the island's protector. It is not surprising, therefore, to see the Hindu deities in Buddhist temples. Other deities have come from the Mahayana branch of Buddhism, such as **Natha**, or *Maitreya*, the future Buddha. Thus in worship as in many other aspects of daily life, Sinhalese Buddhism shares much in commmon with Hindu belief and practice with which it has lived side by side for over 2,000 years.

A final feature of Buddhist worship which is held in common with Hindu worship is its individualism. Congregational worship is entirely absent, and individuals will normally visit the temple, sometimes soliciting the help of a bhikku in making an offering or saying special prayers. One of the chief aims of the Buddhist is to earn merit (*punya karma*), for this is the path to achieving nirvana. Merit can be earned by selfless giving, often of donations in the temple, or by gifts to bhikkus, who make regular house calls early in the morning seeking alms. In addition merit can be gained by right living, and especially by propagating the faith both by speech and listening.

Caste in Sri Lankan Buddhism

Some elements of the caste system were probably present in pre-Buddhist Sri Lanka, with both the priestly caste of Brahmins and a range of low caste groups such as scavengers. Although Buddhism encouraged its followers to eradicate distinctions based on caste, the system clearly survived and became a universal feature of social structures among Buddhists and subsequently Christians, despite their beliefs which explicitly condemn such social stratification. However, the complexities and some of the harsh exclusiveness of the caste system as practised in India was modified in Sri Lanka.

Sinhalese Buddhism has no Brahmin or Kshatriya caste, although some groups claim a warrior lineage. The caste enjoying highest social status and the greatest numbers is the *Goyigama*, a caste of cultivators and landowners who are widely seen as roughly equivalent to the *Vellala* caste among Jaffna Tamils. The *Bandaras* and the *Radalas* comprise a sub-caste of the Goyigamas who for generations have formed a recognisable aristocracy. Among many other castes lower down the social hierarchy come fishermen (*Karavas*), washermen (*Hena*), and toddy tappers (*Durava*).

Some caste groups, such as the Karava, have achieved significant changes in their status. Ryan suggests for example that the original Karava community came from S India and converted to Buddhism and began to speak Sinhalese while retaining their fishing livelihoods. Subsequently many converted to Roman Catholicism, located as they were in the heart of the coastal region just N of modern Colombo controlled by the Portuguese. Through their conversion many Karavas received priveleges reserved by the Portuguese for Christians, enabling them to climb up the social ladder. Thus today, unlike the fishing communities of Tamil Nadu who remain among the lowest castes, the Karava are now among Sri Lanka's upper caste communities.

Hinduism

Hinduism in N Sri Lanka was brought over by successive Tamil kings and their followers. It has always been easier to define Hinduism by what it is not than by what it is. Indeed, the name Hinduism was given by foreigners to the peoples of the sub-continent who did not profess the other major faiths, such as Muslims, Christians or Buddhists. The beliefs and practices of modern Hinduism began to take shape in the centuries on either side of the birth of Christ. But while some aspects of modern Hinduism can be traced back more than 2,000 years before that, other features are recent. Hinduism has undergone major changes both in belief and practice. Such changes came from outside as well as from within. As early as the 6th century BC the Buddhists and Jains had tried to reform the religion of Vedism (or Brahmanism) which had been dominant in some parts of South Asia for 500 years.

Modern Hinduism

A number of ideas run like a thread through intellectual and popular Hinduism, some being shared with Buddhism. Some Hindu scholars and philosophers talk of Hinduism as one religious and cultural tradition, in which the enormous variety of belief and practice can ultimately be interpreted as interwoven in a common view of the world. Yet there is no Hindu organization, like a church, with the authority to define belief or establish official practice. Although

The Four Stages Of Life

It is widely believed that an ideal life has four stages: that of the student, the householder, the forest dweller and the wandering dependent or beggar (sannyasi). These stages represent the phases through which an individual learns of life's goals and of the means of achieving them, in which he 'carries out his duties and raises sons', and then retires to meditate alone; and then finally when he gives up all possessions and depends on the gifts of others. It is an ideal pattern which some still try to follow.

One of the most striking sights is that of the saffron clad sannyasi (*sadhu*), or wandering beggar, seeking gifts of food and money to support himself in the final stage of his life. There may have been sadhus even before the Aryans arrived. Today, most of these wanderers, who have cast off all the moral requirements of their surrounding cultures, are devotees of popular Hindu beliefs. Most give up material possessions, carrying only a strip of cloth, a staff (*danda*), a crutch to support the chin during meditation (*achal*), prayer beads, a fan to ward off evil spirits, a water pot, a drinking vessel, which may be a human skull, and a begging bowl. You may well see one, almost naked, covered only in ashes, on a city street.

The age in which we live is seen by Hindu philosophers as a dark age, the *kaliyuga*. The most important behaviour enjoined on Hindus for this period was that of fulfilling the obligations of the householder. However, each of the stages is still recognized as a valid pattern for individuals.

the Vedas are still regarded as sacred by most Hindus, virtually no modern Hindu either shares the beliefs of the Vedic writers or their practices, such as sacrifice, which died out 1,500 years ago. Not all Hindu groups believe in a single supreme God. In view of these characteristics, many authorities argue that it is misleading to think of Hinduism as a religion at all.

Be that as it may, the evidence of the living importance of Hinduism is visible among Hindu communities in Sri Lanka as well as in India. Hindu philosophy and practice has also touched many of those who belong to other religious traditions, particularly in terms of social institutions such as caste.

The four human goals

For many Hindus there are four major human goals; material prosperity (*artha*), the satisfaction of desires (*kama*), and performing the duties laid down according to your position in life (*dharma*). Beyond those is the goal of achieving liberation from the endless cycle of rebirths into which everyone is locked (*moksha*). It is to the search for liberation that the major schools of Indian philosophy have devoted most attention. Together with dharma, it is basic to Hindu thought.

Dharma

Dharma (written of as dhamma by Buddhists) represents the order inherent in human life. It is essentially secular rather than religious, for it doesn'T depend on any revelation or command of God but rather has 10 'embodiments': good name, truth, self-control, cleanness of mind and body, simplicity, endurance, resoluteness of character, giving and sharing, austerities and continence. In *dharmic* thinking these are inseparable from five patterns of behaviour: non-violence, an attitude of equality, peace and tranquillity, lack of aggression and cruelty, and absence of envy.

Karma

The idea of *karma* 'the effect of former actions' – is central to achieving liberation. It is believed that "Every act has its appointed effect, whether the act be thought, word or deed. If water is exposed to the sun, it cannot avoid being dried up. The effect automatically follows. It is the same with everything. The cause holds the effect, so to say, in its womb. If we reflect deeply and objectively, the entire world will be found to obey unalterable laws. That is the doctrine of karma".

Rebirth

The belief in the transmigration of souls (samsara) in a never-ending cycle of rebirth has been Hinduism's most distinctive and important contribution to the culture of India and Sri Lanka. The earliest reference to the belief is found in one of the Upanishads, around the

KARMA – AN EYE TO THE FUTURE

According to karma, every person, animal or god has a being or self which has existed without beginning. Every action, except those that are done without any consideration of the results, leaves an indelible mark on that self. This is carried forward into the next life, and the overall character of the imprint on each person's 'self' determines three features of the next life. It controls the nature of his next birth (animal, human or god) and the kind of family he will be born into if human. It determines the length of the next life. Finally, it controls the good or bad experiences that the self will experience. However, it does not imply a fatalistic belief that the nature of action in this life is unimportant. Rather, it suggests that the path followed by the individual in the present life is vital to the nature of its next life, and ultimately to the chance of gaining release from this world.

7th century BC, at about the same time as the doctrine of karma made its first appearance. By the late Upanishads it was universally accepted, and in Buddhism there is never any questioning of the belief.

Ahimsa

AL Basham pointed out that belief in transmigration must have encouraged a further distinctive doctrine, that of non-violence or non-injury – *ahimsa*. Buddhism campaigned particularly vigorously against the then-existing practice of animal sacrifice. The belief in rebirth meant that all living things and creatures of the spirit – people, devils, gods, animals, even worms – possessed the same essential soul.

Hindu philosophy

It is common now to talk of six major schools of Hindu philosophy. The best known are yoga and vedanta. Yoga is concerned with systems of meditation that can lead ultimately to release from the cycle of rebirth. It can be traced back as a system of thought to at least the 3rd century AC. It is just one part of the wider system known as Vedanta, literally the final parts of the Vedantic literature, the Upanishads. The basic texts also include the Brahmasutra of Badrayana, written about the 1st century AC, and the most important of all, the Bhagavadgita, which is a part of the epic the Mahabharata.

Hindu worship

The sacred in nature Some Hindus believe in one all-powerful God who created all the lesser gods and the universe. The Hindu gods include many whose origins lie in the Vedic deities of the early Aryans. These were often associated with the forces of nature, and Hindus have always revered many natural objects. Mountain tops, trees, rocks and above all rivers, are regarded as sites of special religious significance. They all have their own guardian spirits. You can see the signs of the continuing lively belief in these gods and demons wherever you travel. Thus trees for example are often painted with vertical red and white stripes and will have a small shrine at their base. Occasionally branches of trees will have numerous pieces of thread or strips of coloured cloth tied to them – placed there by devotees with the prayer for fulfilmemt of a favour. Hill tops will frequently have a shrine of some kind at the highest point, dedicated to a particularly powerful god. Pilgrimage to some important Hindu shrines is often undertaken by Buddhists as well as Hindus.

Puja

For most Hindus today worship (often referred to as 'performing puja') is an integral part of their faith. The great majority of Hindu homes will have a

How Sarasvati Turned Brahma's Head

Masson-Oursel recounts one myth that explains how Brahma came to have five heads. "Brahma first formed woman from his own immaculate substance, and she was known as Sarasvati, Savitri, Gayatri or Brahmani. When he saw this lovely girl emerge from his own body Brahma fell in love with her. Sarasvati moved to his right to avoid his gaze, but a head immediately sprang up from the god. And when Sarasvati turned to the left and then behind him, two new heads emerged. She darted towards heaven, and a fifth head was formed. Brahma then said to his daughter, 'Let us beget all kinds of living things, men, Suras and Asuras'. Hearing these words Sarasvati returned to earth, Brahma wedded her and they retired to a secret place where they remained together for a hundred (divine) years."

The Duty Of Tolerance

One of the reasons why the Hindu faith is often confusing to the outsider is that as a whole it has many elements which appear mutually self-contradictory but which are reconciled by Hindus as different facets of the ultimate truth. S Radhakrishnan suggests that for a Hindu "tolerance is a duty, not a mere concession. In pursuance of this duty Hinduism has accepted within its fold almost all varieties of belief and doctrine and accepted them as authentic expressions of the spiritual endeavour." Such a tolerance is particularly evident in the attitude of Hindus to the nature of God and of divinity. C Rajagopalachari writes that there is a distinction that marks Hinduism sharply from the other monotheistic faiths such as Christianity or Islam. This is that "the philosophy of Hinduism has taught and trained the Hindu devotee to see and worship the Supreme Being in all the idols that are worshipped, with a clarity of understanding and an intensity of vision that would surprise the people of other faiths. The Divine Mind governing the Universe, be it as Mother or Father, has infinite aspects, and the devotee approaches him or her, or both, in any of the many aspects as he may be led to do according to the mood and the psychological need of the hour."

shrine to one of the gods of the Hindu pantheon. Individuals and families will often visit shrines or temples, and on special occasions will travel long distances to particularly holy places such as Kataragama or Puri in India. Such sites may have temples dedicated to a major deity but will always have numerous other shrines in the vicinity dedicated to other favourite gods.

Acts of devotion are often aimed at the granting of favours and the meeting of urgent needs for this life – good health, finding a suitable wife or husband, the birth of a son, prosperity and good fortune. In this respect the popular devotion of simple pilgrims of all faiths in South Asia is remarkably similar when they visit shrines, whether Hindu, Buddhist or Jain temples, the tombs of Muslim saints or even churches.

Performing puja involves making an offering to God, and darshana – having a view of the deity. Although there are devotional movements among Hindus in which singing and praying is practised in groups, Hindu worship is generally an act performed by individuals. Thus Hindu temples may be little more than a shrine in the middle of the street, housing an image of the deity which will be tended by a priest and visited at special times when a darshan of the resident God can be obtained. When it has been consecrated, the image, if exactly made, becomes the channel for the godhead to work.

Images

The image of the deity may be in one of many forms. Temples may be dedicated to Vishnu or Siva, for example, or to any one of their other representations. Parvati, the wife of Siva, and Lakshmi, the wife of Vishnu, are the focus of many temple shrines. The image of the deity becomes the object of worship and the centre of the temple's rituals. These often follow through the cycle of day and night, as well as yearly lifecycles. The priests may wake the deity from sleep, bathe, clothe and feed it. Worshippers will be invited to share in this process by bringing offerings of clothes and food. Gifts of money will usually be made, and in some temples there is a charge levied for taking up positions in front of the deity in order to obtain a darshan at the appropriate times.

VISHNU'S TEN INCARNATIONS

Name	Form	Story
1. *Matsya*	Fish	The earth was covered in a flood. Vishnu took the form of a fish to rescue Manu (the first man), his family and the Vedas. The story is similar to that of Noah's ark.
2. *Kurma*	Tortoise	Vishnu became a tortoise to rescue all the treasures that were lost in the flood. These included the divine nectar (ambrosia or Amrita) with which the gods preserved their youth. The gods put a mountain (*Mount Kailasa*) on the tortoise's back, and when he reached the bottom of the ocean they twisted the divine snake round the mountain. They then churned the ocean with the mountain by pulling the snake. The ambrosia rose to the top of the churning waters along with other treasures, and the Goddess *Lakshmi*, Vishnu's consort.
3. *Varaha*	Boar	Vishnu appeared again to raise the earth from the ocean's floor where it had been thrown by a demon, Hiranyaksa. The story probably developed from a non-Aryan cult of a sacred pig, incorporated into the Vishnu myth. The boar incarnation was an important focus of worship in the 4th century AD.
4. *Narasimha*	Half man half lion	The demon *Hiranyakasipu* had persuaded Brahma to guarantee that he could not be killed either by day or night, by god, man or beast. He then terrorized everybody. When the gods pleaded for help, Vishnu burst out from a pillar in the demon's palace at sunset, when it was neither day nor night, in the form of a half man and half lion and killed Hiranyakasipu.
5. *Vamana*	A dwarf	Bali, another demon, achieved enormous supernatural power by following a course of asceticism. To protect the world Vishnu appeared before him in the form of a dwarf and asked him a favour. Bali agreed, and Vishnu asked for as much land as he could cover in three strides. Once granted, Vishnu became a giant, covering the earth in three strides. He left only hell to the demon.
6. *Parasurama*	Rama with the axe	Vishnu took human form as the son of a brahman, Jamadagni. *Parasurama*, killed the wicked king for robbing his father. The king's sons then killed Jamadagni, and in revenge Parasurama destroyed all male *kshatriyas*, twenty one times in succession.
7. *Rama*	The Prince of Ayodhya	In this form he came to the world to rescue it from the dark demon, *Ravana*. His story, told in the *Ramayana*, is seen by his devotees as one of long suffering and patience, shown particularly by his faithful wife Sita. This epic also saw the creation of Hanuman, the monkey-faced god who is the model of a strong and faithful servant, and who remains one of the most widely worshipped minor deities across India.
8. *Krishna*	The charioteer for Arjuna. Many forms	The stories of his incarnations, childhood and youth, in the words of A.L. Basham "meet almost every human need. As the divine child he satisfies the warm maternal drives of Indian womanhood. As the divine lover, he provides romantic wish-fulfilment in a society still tightly controlled by ancient norms of behaviour which give little scope for freedom of expression in sexual relations. As charioteer of the hero Arjuna on the battlefield of Kurukshetra, he is the helper of all those who turn to him, even saving them from evil rebirths, if he has sufficient faith in the Lord."
9. *The Buddha*		Probably incorporated into the Hindu pantheon in order to discredit the Buddhists, the dominant religious group in some parts of India until the 6th century AD. One of the earliest Hindu interpretations however suggests that Vishnu took incarnation as Buddha in order to show compassion for animals and to end sacrifice.
10. *Kalki*	Riding on a horse	Vishnu's arrival will accompany the final destruction of this present world, judging the wicked and rewarding the good.

Hindu sects

Today three Gods are widely seen as all-powerful: Brahma, Vishnu and Siva. Their functions and character are not readily separated. While Brahma is regarded as the ultimate source of creation, Siva also has a creative role alongside his function as destroyer. Vishnu in contrast is seen as the preserver or protector of the universe. There are very few images and sculptures of Brahma, but Vishnu and Siva are far more widely represented and have come to be seen as the most powerful and important. Their followers are referred to as Vaishnavite and Saivites respectively, the majority in Sri Lanka today being Saivites.

Sarasvati

Seen by some Hindus as the 'active power' of Brahma and popularly thought of as his consort, Sarasvati has survived into the modern Hindu world as a far more important figure than Brahma himself. In popular worship

Vishnu, preserver of the Universe

Krishna, eighth and most popular incarnation of Vishnu

Sarasvati represents the goddess of education and learning, worshipped in schools and colleges with gifts of fruit, flowers and incense. She represents 'the word', which began to be deified as part of the process of the writing of the Vedas, which ascribed magical power to words themselves. Unlike Brahma Sarasvati plays an important part in modern Hindu worship. Normally shown as white coloured and riding on a swan, she usually carries a book, and is often shown playing a vina.

Vishnu

Vishnu is seen as the God with the human face. From the 2nd century a new and passionate devotional worship of Vishnu's incarnation as Krishna developed in S India. For Vaishnavites, God took 10 different forms in order to save the world from impending disaster. These include **Rama and Krishna**, in which he was believed to take recognizable human form. In the earliest stories about Rama he was not regarded as divine. Although he is now seen as an earlier incarnation of Vishnu than Krishna, he was added to the pantheon very late, probably after the Muslim invasions of India in the 12th century AD. The story has become part of the cultures of SE Asia. Krishna is worshipped extremely widely as perhaps the most human of the gods. His advice on the battlefield of the Mahabharata is one of the major sources of guidance for the rules of daily living for many Hindus today.

In Sri Lanka, Vishnu appears in Buddhist temples since he is considered to be one of the four 'Guardian Deities', destined to become a future Buddha. He is seen as the protector of Buddhism on the island.

Lakshmi Commonly represented as Vishnu's wife, Lakshmi is widely worshipped as the goddess of wealth.

Hanuman is the faithful monkey who helped Rama search of Sita. The Ramayana tells how he went at the head of his monkey army in search of the abducted Sita across India and finally into the demon Ravana's forest home of Lanka. He used his powers to jump the sea channel separating India from Sri Lanka and managed after a series of heroic and magical feats to find and rescue his master's wife. Whatever form he is shown in he remains almost instantly recognizable.

Siva

Siva is interpreted as both creator and destroyer, the power through whom the universe evolves. He lives on Mount Kailasa with his wife **Parvati** (also known as Uma, Sati, **Kali** and **Durga**) and two sons, the elephant-headed Ganesh and the 6-headed Karttikeya, known in Sri Lanka and S India as Subrahmanya, Kataragama or Skanda. To many contemporary Hindus Siva and Parvati and their sons form a model of sorts for family life. In sculptural representations Siva is normally accompanied by his 'vehicle', the bull (*nandi or nandin*).

Siva is also represented in Shaivite temples by the linga, literally meaning 'sign' or 'mark', but referring in this context to the sign of gender or phallus and *yoni*. On the one hand a symbol of energy, fertility and potency, as Siva's symbol it

Siva as Nataraj, Lord of the Dance

Ganesh, bringer of prosperity

also represents the yogic power of sexual abstinence and penance. The linga has become the most important symbol of the cult of Siva. **Nandin** Siva's vehicle, the bull, is one of the most widespread of sacred symbols of the ancient world. Strength and virility are key attributes, and pilgrims to Siva temples will often touch the nandin's testicles on their way into the shrine. **Ganesh** is one of Hinduism's most popular gods. He is seen as the great clearer of obstacles. Shown at gateways and on door lintels with his elephant head and pot belly, his image is revered among Hindu communities across the world. Meetings, functions and special family gatherings will often start with prayers to Ganesh.

Skanda (**Kataragama**) The name Skanda means 'attacker', and he is seen as the God of War. Kataragama, one of the sons of Siva and Parvati, is one of Sri Lankan Hinduism's most important deities. One legend suggests that he was conceived by the Goddess Ganga from Siva's seed, and he is seen as the bringer of disease and the robber of good health. Different aspects of Kataragama are worshipped in several major Hindu temples on the island. His vehicle is the cock which was sacrificed to him In Sri Lanka Kataragama carries the trident, known as the *vel*, in India the weapon of Siva himself, and he is the presiding deity at the great Kataragama Festival.

Kataragama is one of the four Guardian Deities who appear in Buddhist art as future Buddhas, and is hence a figure venerated by Buddhists. His power is associated with the fight by the Sinhalese in ancient times, against Hindu Tamil dominance. His colour is red.

Hindu society

Caste

One of the defining characteristics of South Asian societies, caste has helped to shape the social life of most religious communities in South Asia. Although the word caste (meaning 'unmixed' or 'pure') was given by the Portuguese in the 15th century AC, the main features of the system emerged at the end of the Vedic period. Two terms – *varna* and *jati* – are used in India itself, and have come to be used interchangeably and confusingly with the word caste. In Sri Lanka the Tamils of Jaffna have a modified form of the caste social structure typical of neighbouring Tamil Nadu.

Varna, which literally means colour, had a fourfold division. By 600 BC this had become a standard means of classifying the population. The fair-skinned Aryans distinguished themselves from the darker skinned earlier inhabitants. The 4th century 'Laws of Nanu' suggested that the priestly varna, the Brahmins, were seen as coming from the mouth of Brahma; the Kshatriyas (or Rajputs as they are commonly called in NW India) were warriors, coming from Brahma's arms; the Vaishyas, a trading community, came from Brahma's thighs, and the Sudras, classified as agriculturalists, from his feet. Relegated beyond the pale of civilized Hindu society were the untouchables or outcastes, who were left with the jobs which were regarded as impure, usually associated with dealing with the dead (human or animal) or with excrement.

Jati The great majority of Sri Lankan Hindus (and Indians) do not put themselves into one of the four varna categories, but into a jati group. All are part of local or regional hierarchies, not organized in any institutional sense, and traditionally with no formal record of caste status. While individuals found it impossible to change caste or to move up the social scale, groups would sometimes try to gain recognition as higher caste by adopting practices of the Brahmins such as becoming vegetarians. Many used to be identified with particular activities, and occupations used to be hereditary. Caste membership is decided simply by birth. Although you can be evicted from your caste by your fellow members, usually for disobedience to caste rules such as over marriage, you cannot join another caste, and technically you become an outcaste.

Among Jaffna Tamils Brahmins occupy the same priestly position that they hold in India, and have also played an important role in education. Beneath them in ritual hierarchy but occupying a dominant social and political position, until recent times at least, were the cultivating and landlord caste known as the *vellalas*. Below them in rank was a range of low and outcaste groups, filling such occupations as washermen, sweepers and barbers,such as the Pallas and Nallavas. The tea plantation workers are all regarded as low caste.

Jaffna was subject to Christian missionary work, especially through education, from the early 19th century. It produced a Hindu response, and a Hindu renaissance took place in the late 19th century under the leadership of *Arumuga Navalar*. Setting up an extensive network of schools, he was anxious to strengthen orthodox Saivism, on the one hand through restoring temples and on the other by publishing religious texts.

Virtually all Hindu temples in Sri Lanka were destroyed by the Portuguese and the Dutch. Those that have been rebuilt never had the resources available to compare with those in India, not having had their lands restored in the post colonial period, so they are generally small. However, they play a prominent part in Hindu life. De Silva suggests that Arumuga Navalar's failure to argue for social reform meant that caste – and untouchability – were virtually untouched. The high caste **Vellalas**, a small minority of the total Hindu population, maintained their power unchallenged until after Independence. Removal of caste disabilities started in the 1950s. The civil war over the demand for a separate Tamil state, Tamil Eelam, during which the Liberation Tigers of Tamil Eelam (LTTE) have taken complete control of social and political life in Jaffna and the N, may have changed the whole basis of caste far more thoroughly than any programme of social reform. Such changes will only be open to scrutiny when peace has returned.

Islam

Islam was brought to Sri Lanka by Arab traders. Long before the followers of the Prophet Mohammed spread the new religion of Islam Arabs had been trading across the Indian Ocean with SW India, the Maldives, Sri Lanka and South East Asia. When the Arab world became Muslim so the newly-converted Arab traders brought Islam with them, and existing communities of Arab origin adopted the new faith. However, numbers were also swelled by conversion from both Buddhists and Hindus, and by immigrant Muslims from S India who fled the Portuguese along the W coast of India. The great majority of the present Muslim population of Sri Lanka is Tamil speaking, although there are also Muslims of Malay origin. Both in Kandy and the coastal districts Muslims have generally lived side by side with Buddhists, often sharing common interests against the colonial powers. However, one of the means by which Muslims maintained their identity was to refuse to be drawn into colonial education. As a result, by the end of the 19th century the Muslims were among the least educated groups. A Muslim lawyer, *Siadi Lebbe*, helped to change attitudes and encourage participation by Muslims.

In 1915 there were major Sinhalese-Muslim riots, and Muslims began a period of active collaboration with the British, joining other minorities led by the Tamils in the search for security and protection of their rights against the Sinhalese. The Muslims have been particularly anxious to maintain Muslim family law, and to gain concessions on education. One of the chief of these is the teaching of Arabic in government schools to Muslim children. Until 1974 Muslims were unique among minorities in having the right to choose which of three languages – Sinhala, Tamil or English – would be their medium of instruction. Since then a new category of Muslim schools has been set up, allowing them to distance themselves from the Tamil Hindu community, whose language most of them speak.

Muslim beliefs

The beliefs of Islam (which means 'submission to God') could apparently scarcely be more different from those of Buddhism or Hinduism. Islam has a fundamental creed; 'There is no God but God; and Mohammad is the Prophet of God' (*La Illaha illa 'llah Mohammad Rasulu 'llah*). One book, the Qur'an, is the supreme authority on Islamic teaching and faith. Islam preaches the belief in bodily resurrection after death, and in the reality of heaven and hell.

Ramadan

For Muslims many aspects of life are significantly altered during Ramadan. They do not eat between sunrise and sunset, and food and drink are not publicly available in Muslim states. For the next 10 years Ramadan falls in the winter. The date for the start of Ramadan in 1996 is towards the end of Jan. The exact date is determined by the appearance of the new moon.

The idea of heaven as paradise is pre-Islamic. Alexander the Great is believed to have brought the word paradise into Greek from Persia, where he used it to describe the walled Persian gardens that were found even 3 centuries before the birth of Christ. For Muslims, Paradise is believed to be filled with sensuous delights and pleasures, while hell is a place of eternal terror and torture, which is the certain fate of all who deny the unity of God.

Islam has no priesthood. The authority of Imams derives from social custom, and from their authority to interpret the scriptures, rather than from a defined status within the Islamic community. Islam also prohibits any distinction on the basis of race or colour, and there is a strong antipathy to the representation of the human figure. It is often thought, inaccurately, that this ban stems from the Qur'an itself. In fact it probably has its origins in the belief of Mohammad that images were likely to be turned into idols.

Muslim Sects

During the first century of its existence Islam split in two sects which were divided on political and religious grounds, the Shi'is and Sunni's. The religious basis for the division lay in the interpretation of verses in the Qur'an and of traditional sayings of Mohammad, the Hadis. Both sects venerate the Qur'an but have different *Hadis*. They also have different views as to Mohammad's successor.

The Sunnis – always the majority in South Asia – believe that Mohammad did not appoint a successor, and that Abu Bak'r, Omar and Othman were the first three caliphs (or vice-regents) after Mohammad's death. Ali, whom the Sunni's count as the fourth Caliph, is regarded as the first legitimate Caliph by the Shi'is, who consider Abu Bak'r and Omar to be usurpers. While the Sunni's believe in the principle of election of Caliphs, Shi'is believe that although Mohammad is the last prophet there is a continuing need for intermediaries between God and man. Such intermediaries are termed Imams, and they base both their law and religious practice on the teaching of the Imams.

The two major divisions are marked by further sub-divisions. The Sunni Muslims in South Asia have followers of the Hanafi, Shafei, Maliki and Hanbali groups, named after their leaders.

From the Mughal emperors in India, who enjoyed an unparalleled degree of political power, down to the poorest fishermen in Sri Lanka, Muslims in South Asia have found different ways of adjusting to their Hindu or Buddhist environment. Some have reacted by accepting or even incorporating features of Hindu belief and practice in their own. Akbar, the most eclectic of Mughal emperors, went as far as banning activities like cow

Calculating The Hijra Year

Murray's Handbook for travellers in India gave a wonderfully precise method of calculating the current date in the Christian year from the AH date: "To correlate the Hijra year with the Christian year, express the former in years and decimals of a year, multiply by .970225, add 621.54, and the total will correspond exactly with the Christian year."

The Five Pillars Of Islam

In addition to the belief that there is one God and that Allah is his prophet, there are four further obligatory requirements imposed on Muslims. Daily prayers are prescribed at daybreak, noon, afternoon, sunset and nightfall. Muslims must give alms to the poor. They must observe a strict fast during the month of ***Ramadan***. They must not eat or drink between sunrise and sunset. Lastly, they should attempt the pilgrimage to the Ka'aba in Mecca, known as the Hajj. Those who have done so are entitled to the prefix Hajji before their name.

Islamic rules differ from Hindu practice in several other aspects of daily life. Muslims are strictly forbidden to drink alcohol (though some suggest that this prohibition is restricted to the use of fermented grape juice, that is wine, it is commonly accepted to apply to all alcohol). Eating pork, or any meat from an animal not killed by draining its blood while alive, is also prohibited. Meat prepared in the appropriate way is called Halal. Finally usury (charging interest on loans) and games of chance are forbidden.

slaughter which were offensive to Hindus and celebrating Hindu festivals in court.

The Mughal prince Dara Shikoh, who died in 1659, even argued that the study of Hindu scriptures was necessary to obtain a complete understanding of the Qur'an. The 16th century Bengali poet Sayyed Sultan wrote an epic in which the main Hindu gods were shown as prophets who preceded Adam, Noah, Abraham, Moses, Jesus and Mohammad, and the idea of prophet was matched to the Hindu concept of *avatar*, or incarnation.

The Muslim year

The first day of the **Muslim calendar** is 16 July 622 AD. This was the date of the Prophet's migration from Mecca to Medina, the Hijra, from which the date's name is taken (AH = Anno Hijrae).

The Muslim year is divided into 12 lunar months, alternating between 29 and 30 days. The first month of the year is *Moharram*, followed by *Safar*, *Rabi-ul-Awwal*, *Rabi-ul-Sani*, *Jumada-ul-Awwal*, *Jumada-ul-Sani*, *Rajab*, *Shaban*, *Ramadan*, *Shawwal*, *Ziquad* and *Zilhaj*.

Significant dates First day of *Moharram* – New Year's Day; 9th and 10th of *Moharram* – Anniversary of the killing of the Prophet's grandson Hussain, commemorated by Shi'i Muslims; 12th of *Rabi-ul-Awwal* – Birthday of the Prophet (Milad-ul-Nabi); 1st of *Ramadan* – Start of the fasting month; 21st of *Ramadan* – Night of prayer (Shab-e-Qadr); 1st of *Shawwal: Eid-ul-Fitr* – 3-day festival to mark the end of Ramadan; 10th of *Zilhaj: Eid-ul-Ajha* – 2-day festival commemorating the sacrifice of Ismail; the main time of pilgrimage to Mecca (the Haj).

Christianity

Christianity was introduced by the Portuguese. Unlike India, where Christian missionary work from the late 18th century was often carried out in spite of colonial government rather than with its active support, in Sri Lanka missionary activity enjoyed various forms of state backing. One Sinhalese king, Dharmapala, was converted, endowing the church, and even some high caste families became Christian. When the Dutch evicted the Portuguese they tried to suppress Roman Catholicism, and the Dutch Reformed Church found some converts. Other Protestant denominations followed the arrival of the British, though not always with official support or encouragement. Many of the churches remained dependent on outside support. Between the two World Wars Christian influence in government was radically reduced. Denominational schools lost their protection and special status, and since the 1960s have had to come to terms with a completely different role in Sri Lanka.

Christian beliefs

Christian theology had its roots in Judaism, with its belief in one eternal God, the Creator of the universe. Judaism saw the Jewish people as the vehicle for God's salvation, the 'chosen people of God', and pointed to a time when God would send his Saviour, or Messiah. Jesus, whom Christians believe was 'the Christ' or Messiah, was born in the village of Bethlehem, some 20 km S of Jerusalem. Very little is known of his early life except that he was brought up in a devout Jewish family. At the age of 29 or 30 he gathered a small group of followers and began to preach in the region between the Dead Sea and the Sea of Galilee. 2 years later he was crucified in Jerusalem by the authorities on the charge of blasphemy – that he claimed to be the son of God.

Christians believe that all people live in a state of sin, in the sense that they are separated from God and fail to do his will. They believe that God is personal, 'like a father'. As God's son, Jesus accepted the cost of that separation and sinfulness himself through his death on the cross. Christians believe that Jesus was raised from the dead on the third day after he was crucified, and that he appeared to his closest followers. They believe that his spirit continues to live today, and that he makes it possible for people to come back to God.

The New Testament of the Bible, which, alongside the Old Testament, is the text to which Christians refer as the ultimate scriptural authority, consists of four 'Gospels' (meaning 'good news'), and a series of letters by several early Christians referring to the nature of the Christian life.

Christian worship

Although Christians are encouraged to worship individually as well as together, most forms of Christian worship centre on the gathering of the church congregation for praise, prayer the preaching of God's word, which usually takes verses from the Bible as its starting point. Different denominations place varying emphases on the main elements of worship, but in most church services today the congregation will take part in singing hymns (songs of praise), prayers will be led by the minister, priest or a member of the congregation, readings from the Bible will be given and a sermon preached. For many Christians the most important service is the act of Holy Communion (Protestant) or Mass (Catholic) which celebrates the death and resurrection of Jesus in sharing bread and wine, which are held to represent Christ's body and blood given to save people from their sin. Although Christian services may be held daily in some churches most Christian congregations in Sri Lanka meet for worship on Sun, and services are held in Sinhala and Tamil as well as in English. They are open to all.

Denominations

Between the 2nd and the 4th centuries AD there were numerous debates about the interpretation of Christian doctrine, sometimes resulting in the formation of specific groups focussing on particular interpretations of faith. One such group was that of the Nestorian Christians, who played a major part in the theology of the Syrian Church in Kerala. They regarded the Syrian patriarch of the E their spiritual head, and followed the Nestorian tradition that there were two distinct natures in Christ, the divine and human. However, although some believe that St Thomas and other early Christians came to Sri Lanka as well as S India the early church left no real mark on the island.

Today Roman Catholics account for 90% of the Island's Christians. The Roman Catholic church believes that Christ declared that his disciple Peter should be the first spiritual head of the Church, and that his successors should lead the Church on earth. Modern Catholic churches still recognize the spiritual authority of the Pope and cardinals.

The reformation which took place in Europe from the 16th century onwards resulted in the creation of the Protestant churches, which became dominant in several European countries. They reasserted the authority of the Bible over that of the church. A number of new denominations were created. This process of division left a profound mark on the nature of the Christian church as it spread into South Asia. The Dutch brought with them their Dutch Reformed faith and left a number of churches, and subsequently during British colonial period the Anglican Church (Church of England) also became established, and several Protestant missionary denominations including Baptist and Methodist, established small churches. The reunification of the Protestant Christian churches which has taken significant steps since 1947 has progressed faster in South Asia than in most other parts of the world.

CULTURE

Contents

Art and architecture	72
Language	79
Crafts	79

Art and architecture

Sri Lankan architecture has many elements in common with Buddhist and Hindu Indian traditions, but the long period of relative isolation, and the determined preservation of Buddhism long after its demise in India, have contributed to some very distinctive features.

In order to understand the distinctiveness of Sri Lanka's Buddhist architecture, however, it is helpful to trace its origins in early Indian architectural developments.

Over the 4,000 years since the Indus Valley civilization flourished art and architecture developed in India with a remarkable continuity through successive regional and religious influences and styles.

The Buddhist art and architecture of the 3rd century BC left few remains, but the stylistic influence on early Hindu architecture was profound. From the 6th century AD the first Hindu religious buildings to have survived into the modern period were constructed in S and E India, alongside a continuing development of the Buddhist tradition elsewhere. Although Hindu buildings across India had many features in common, regional styles began to develop.

Coming into India as vanquishing hordes, the early Muslims destroyed much that was in their path. Temples that had been encrusted with jewels were left bare. Mosques were built out of the stones of destroyed temples. To the E, the Muslims finally completed the decline of Buddhism in India by destroying the last remaining Buddhist monasteries, notably the great monastery at Nalanda.

Introducing concepts of religious building from a faith completely different from that of the Hinduism into which it was transplanted, the new Islamic rulers also brought alien cultural concepts – notably from Persia. Yet the greatest flowering of Islamic architecture India ever saw under the Mughals, was not simply a transplant from another country or region. It grew out of India's own traditions as a new and distinctive architecture, yet with recognizable links to the culture which surrounded it. That continuity reflected many forces, not least the use made by the great Mughal emperors of local skilled craftsmen and builders at every stage of their work. Constantly in contact not just with Hindu religious buildings, but with the secular buildings of the Rajputs to their S and W, the Mughal emperors took up themes present in the Hindu traditions of their time, and bent them to a new and developing purpose.

Painting, sculpture, inlay work, all blended skills from a variety of sources, and craftsmen – even occasionally from Europe. These were sometimes employed to embellish the great works. What emerged was another stepping stone in a tradition of Indian architecture, which, far from breaking the threads of Hindu tradition actually wove them into new forms.

These developments left Sri Lankan Buddhist architecture virtually untouched, thereby widening the gap between the two traditions. It is a distance which can be seen even in 19th and early 20th century architecture, for whereas the British encouraged an attempt to revive what they regarded as Islamic and Rajput ideals in some of their most ambitious building works, Sri Lanka's modern buildings make no attempt to recall such styles.

Sri Lankan Buddhist architecture

Buddhist and Hindu architecture probably began with wooden building, for the rock carving and cave excavated temples show clear evidence of copying styles which must have been developed first in wooden buildings. The 3rd-2nd century BC caves of the Buddhists were followed in the 7th and 8th centuries AD by free standing but rock-cut temples such as those at Mamallapuram.

Stupas were the most striking feature of Buddhist architecture in India. Originally they were funeral mounds, built to house the remains of the Buddha and his disciples. One of the first great stupas in India was built at Sanchi under the Emperor Asoka in the 3rd Century BC, and stupas were built as far afield as Taxila in what is today the NW of Pakistan and Amaravati in modern Andhra Pradesh. The tradition of building stupas was developed by Sri Lanka's Sinhalese kings, notably in golden age of the 4th and 5th centuries AD, and the revival during the 11th-12th centuries AD. Some of the stupas (*dagobas*) are huge structures, and even those such as the 4th century *Jetavana* at Anuradhapura, now simply a grassed-over brick mound, is impressively large.

Few of the older Buddhist monuments are in their original form, either having become ruins or been renovated. Hemispherical mounds built of brick and filled with brick and rubble, they stand on a square terrace, surmounted by three concentric platforms. In its original or its restored form, the brick mound is covered with plaster and painted white. Surrounding it on a low platform (*vahalakadas*) is the ambulatory, or circular path, reached from the cardinal directions by stone stairways. Around some of the dagobas there are fine sculptures on these circular paths at the head of each stairway.

The design is filled with symbolic meaning. The hemisphere is the dome of heaven, the axis of the cosmos being represented by the central finial on top, while the umbrella-like tiers are the rising heavens of the gods. Worshippers walk round the stupa on the raised platform in a clockwise direction (*pradakshina*), following the rotational movement of the celestial bodies.

Many smaller stupas were built within circular buildings. These were covered with a metal and timber roof resting on concentric rows of stone pillars. Today the roofs have disappeared, but examples such as the *Vatadage* at Polonnaruwa can still be seen. King Parakramabahu I also built another feature of Sri Lankan architecture at Polonnaruwa, a large rectangular hall in which was placed an image of the Buddha. Most of Sri Lanka's early secular architecture has disappeared. Made of wood, there are remnants of magnificent royal palaces at both Anuradhapura and Sigiriya.

Moonstones

Sri Lanka's moonstones (not the gem) are among the world's finest artistic achievements. Polished semi-circular granite, they are carved in concentric semi-circular rings ('half-moons', about 1m in radius) portraying various animals, flowers and birds, and normally placed at the foot of flights of steps or entrances to important buildings. There are particularly fine examples in Anuradhapura and Polonnaruwa.

The moonstones of pure Buddhist art at Anuradhapura comprise a series of rings and are often interpreted in the following way. You step over the flames of fire, through which one must pass to be purified. The next ring shows animals which represent the four stages of life: **1** Elephant, representing

SINHALESE STUPAS

The Sinhalese classify the domes into six different types, such as bell-shaped, or bubble-shaped. On top of the dome is a small square enclosure (*hataraes kotuwa*), which contained valuable offerings, surrounded by a railed pavilion. Above it is the ceremonial umbrella (*chatta*). The Sri Lankan parasols are furled into a staff-like shape (see page 72). Percy Brown suggests that they are more reminiscent of the totem poles of the Veddas, and may be derived from aboriginal symbols. Originally the cubical box housed the sacred relics themselves. However, the post left little room for the relics and offerings. A compartment was then hollowed out of the brickwork immediately below the staff. Into it was lowered the 'mystic stone', a granite block carved with nine recesses to contain the relics and offerings. The finial staff then sealed and surmounted the relic stone and the whole dagoba.

Many of these buildings are immense, and enormous effort went into ensuring that they would last. The Mahavansa records how King Dutthagamani prepared their foundations. The base was laid of round stones, crushed by pounding and then trampled by huge elephants with leather shoes to protect their feet. Clay was then spread over the hard core, followed by a layer of iron, another layer of stones and then a layer of ordinary stone.

birth; **2** Horse – old age; **3** Lion – illness; **4** Bull – death and decay. These continue in an endless cycle symbolizing the continuous rebirths to which one is subject. The third row represents the twisting serpent of lust and desire, while the fourth is that of geese carrying lotus buds, representing purity. The lotus in the centre is a symbol of nirvana.

Guardstones The steps have on either side beautifully carved guardstones with *makaras* designed to incorporate features from eight symbolically significant creatures: the foot of the lion, the crocodile's mouth and teeth, an elephant's tusk, the body of a fish, the peacock's feather,the serpent inside the mouth and the monkeys eyes.

Sri Lankan Hindu architecture

Hindu temple building

The principles of religious building were laid down in the *Sastras*, sets of rules compiled by priests. Every aspect of Hindu and Buddhist religious building is identified with conceptions of the structure of the universe. This applies as much to the process of building – the timing of which must be undertaken at astrologically propitious times – as to the formal layout of the buildings. The cardinal directions of N, S, E and W are the basic fix on which buildings are planned. The E-W axis is nearly always a fundamental building axis.

Hindu temples were nearly always built to a clear and universal design, which had built into it philosophical understandings of the universe. This cosmology, of an infinite number of universes, isolated from each other in space, proceeds by imagining various possibilities as to its nature. Its centre is seen as dominated by **Mt Meru** which keeps earth and heaven apart. The concept of *separation* is crucial to Hindu thought and social practise. Continents, rivers, and oceans occupy concentric rings around the mountain, while the stars encircle the mountain in another plane. Humans live on the continent of **Jambudvipa**, characterized by the rose apple tree (*jambu*).

The *Sastras* show plans of this continent, organized in concentric rings and entered at the cardinal points. This type of diagram was known as a **mandala**. Such a geometric scheme could then be subdivided into almost limitless small

Thuparama Dagoba, Anuradhapura
Illustrated by Rev W Urwick in 1885

compartments, each of which could be designated as having special properties or be devoted to a particular deity. The centre of the mandala would be the seat of the major god. Mandalas provided the ground rules for the building of stupas and temples across India, and provided the key to the symbolic meaning attached to every aspect of religious buildings.

Temple design
Hindu temples developed characteristic plans and elevations. The focal point of the temple lay in its sanctuary, the home of the presiding deity, known as the womb-chamber (*garbhagriha*). A series of doorways, in large temples leading through a succession of buildings, allowed the worshipper to move towards the final encounter with the deity himself and to obtain *darshan* – a sight of the god. Both Buddhist and Hindu worship encourages the worshipper to walk clockwise around the shrine, performing *pradakshina*.

The elevations are designed to be symbolic representations of the home of the gods the tallest towers rising above the *garbagriha* itself, symbolizing the meeting of earth and heaven in the person of the enshrined deity. In both, the basic structure is usually richly embellished with sculpture. When first built this would usually have been plastered and painted, and often covered in gems. In contrast to the extraordinary profusion of colour and life on the outside, the interior is dark and cramped. Here is the true centre of power.

Hindu architecture on the island bears close resemblances with the Dravida styles of neighbouring Tamil Nadu. Although all the important Hindu temples in Sri Lanka were destroyed by the Portuguese, the style in which they have been re-built continues to reflect those S Indian traditions.

Doorframe from Galapata Vihara in the Galle District
Source: Godakumbura, CE (1982) *Sinhalese Doorways*, Archaeological Department, Colombo

Tamil Nadu has been at the heart of S Indian religious development for 2,000 years. Temple building was a comparatively late development in Hindu worship. Long before the first temple was built shrines were dotted across the land, the focus of **pilgrimage**, each with its own mythology. Even the most majestic of S Indian temples have basic features in common with these original shrines, and many of them have simply grown by a process of accretion around a shrine which may have been in that spot for centuries.

Mythology The myths that grew around the shrines were expressed first by word of mouth. Most temples today still have versions of the stories which were held to justify their existence in the eyes of pilgrims. There are several basic features in common. David Shulman has written that the story will include "the (usually miraculous) discovery of the site and the adventures of those important exemplars (such as gods, demons, serpents, and men) who were freed from sorrow of one kind or another by worshipping there". The shrine which is the object of the story nearly always claims to be supreme, better than all others. Many stories illustrate these claims of superiority: for example, we are often told that the Goddess **Ganga** herself is forced to worship in a S Indian shrine in order to become free of the sins deposited by evil-doers who bathe in the river at Benares.

Early architecture Through all its great diversity Hindu temple architecture repeatedly expresses these beliefs, shared though not necessarily expressed, by the thousands of Sri Lankan Hindus who make visiting temples such a vital and living part of their life. In architecture as in religious philosophy, S India has derived much from its northern Hindu relations. The Buddhist *chaitya* hall with its apsidal plan had been the common form of most religious shrines up to the time of the Chalukyans in Karnataka, who in the 6th century started experimenting with what the Guptas in the N had already achieved by elaborating the simple square plan of earlier shrines. Developments at Aihole, Badami and Pattadakal led to the divergence of the two styles of Hindu temples and this became obvious in the shape of the spire. In the N, the *sikhara* was a smooth pyramidal structure, rising to a rounded top with a pointed end, while in the S the *vimana* was more like a stepped pyramid, usually square in plan and had at its top a rounded cupola.

The **Dravida** or Dravidian style underwent several changes during the reign of the different dynasties that held sway for about 1,000 years from the time of the Pallavas who laid its foundations. In Mamallapuram, just S of Madras, rock-cut cave temples, *mandapas* or small excavated columned halls and the *rathas* or monoliths in the shape of temple chariots, were carved out by the early Pallavas in the 7th century. These were followed by structural temples and bas relief sculptures on giant rocks, which added another dimension. The Shore Temple, built in the 8th century, was a structural expression of the Pallava style.

Various dynasties fought for the Tamil lands until the **Cholas** gained supremacy in the 9th century and established their kingdom in the Kaveri River valley later extending their realm to become rulers over a vast area from the Ganga to Sri Lanka. They did away with the rampant lion pilasters, introduced high relief, half-size sculptures of deities and the gryphon motifs. The Cholas are also remembered for the fine bronzes which adorned their temples.

Development of gopurams Today the most striking external features of Hindu temples in Sri Lanka as in S India are their elaborately carved towering gateways. These were first introduced by the **Pandiyas**, who succeeded the Cholas a century later. They built tall and prominent watch towers, the *gopurams* and concentric, often battlemented fortress walls which enclosed the courtyards with shrines.

The *gopuram* took its name from the 'cow gate' of the Vedic village, which later became the city gate and finally the monumental temple entrance. This type of tower is distinguished from the *vimana* by its oblong plan at the top which is an elongated vaulted roof with gable ends. It has pronounced sloping sides, usually 65°, so that the section at the top is about half the size of the base. Although the first two storeys are usually built solidly of stone masonry, the rest is of lighter material, usually brick and plaster.

By the 15th century the Vijayanagar kings established their empire across much of S India. Their temples were built on an unprecedented scale, with huge gopurams studding the outside walls. None of the Sri Lankan temples were built on a scale anywhere near that of the 16th and 17th century Vijayanagar temples of S India. Furthermore, all Hindu temples were destroyed by the Portuguese during the period in which Vijayanagar architecture was flourishing across the Palk Straits. Thus contemporary Hindu temples in Sri Lanka, while retaining some of the elements common to Hindu temples in Tamil Nadu, are always on a much smaller scale.

Sculpture

Early Sri Lankan sculpture shows close links with Indian Buddhist sculpture. The first images of the Buddha, some of which are still in Anuradhapura, are similar to 2nd-3rd century AC images from Amaravati in modern Andhra Pradesh. The middle period of the 5th to 11th centuries AC contains some magnificent sculptures on rocks, but there is a range of other sculpture, notably moonstones. There are decorated bands of flower motifs, geese and a variety of animals, both Anuradhapura and Polonnaruwa having outstanding examples. While the moonstones are brilliant works in miniature, Sri Lankan sculptors also produced outstanding colossal works, such as the 13m high Buddha at Aukana, now dated as from the 9th century, or the 13th century reclining Buddha at Polonnaruwa.

Painting

Sri Lanka's most famous art is its rock paintings from Sigiriya, dating from the 6th century AC. The heavenly nymphs (*apsaras*), scattering flowers from the

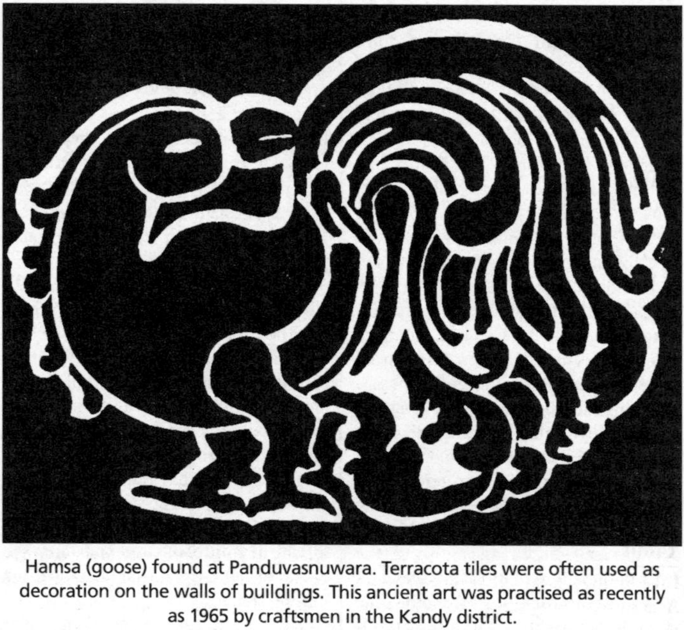

Hamsa (goose) found at Panduvasnuwara. Terracota tiles were often used as decoration on the walls of buildings. This ancient art was practised as recently as 1965 by craftsmen in the Kandy district.

Source: CE Godakumbura (1965) *Decorative tiles*, Archaeological Department, Colombo clouds, are shown with extraordinary grace and beauty. Polonnaruwa saw a later flowering of the painting tradition in the 12th and 13th centuries. The wall paintings of Dambulla are also noteworthy (although many of the original paintings were covered by later ones), but thereafter Sri Lankan art declined.

Language

Sinhala

Sinhala(or Sinhalese,) the language of the Sinhalese, is an Indo-European language with N Indian affinities, unlike the Dravidian language Tamil. The language brought by the N Indian migrants, possibly in the 5th century BC, can be traced from inscriptions dating from the 2nd century BC onwards which show how it had developed away from the original Sanskrit. The spoken language had changed several vowel sounds and absorbed words from the indigenous races and also from Tamil. The Sinhala language had acquired a distinct identity by the beginning of the 1st century.

The script Although at first glance the script might suggest a link with the S Indian scripts, it developed independently. The rounded form was dictated by the use of a sharp stylus to inscribe on palm-leaf which would later be filled in with 'ink' instead of the North Indian technique of writing on bark.

Literature

The early verse and later prose literature were religious (Buddhist) and apart from inscriptions, date from the 10th century although there is evidence of some existing 300 years earlier. Non-religious texts only gained prominence in this century.

Tamil

Like Sinhala Tamil is also one of South Asia's oldest languages, but belongs to the Dravidian language family. It originated on the Indian mainland, and although Sri Lankan Tamil has retained some expressions which have a 'pure', even slightly archaic touch to them, it remains essentially an identical language both in speech and writing to that found in Tamil Nadu.

Literature

The first Tamil literature dates approximately the 2nd century AC. At that time a poets' academy known as the Sangam was established in Madurai. The poetry was devoted to religious subjects. From the beginning of the Christian era a development began to take place in Tamil religious thought and writing. Krishna became transformed from a remote and heroic figure of the epics into the focus of a new and passionate devotional worship – *bhakti*. Jordens has written that this new worship was "emotional, ardent, ecstatic, often using erotic imagery". From the 7th to the 10th century there was a surge of writing new hymns of praise, sometimes referred to as 'the Tamil *Veda*'. Attention focused on the 'marvels of Krishna's birth and infancy and his heroic and amorous exploits as a youth among the cowherds and cowherdesses of Gokula'. In the 9th century Vaishnavite Brahmans produced the *Bhagavata Purana*, which, through frequent translation into all India's major languages, became the vehicle for the new worship of Krishna. Its tenth book has been called "one of the truly great books of Hinduism". There are over forty translations into Bengali alone. These influences were transmitted directly into Hindu Tamil culture in Sri Lanka, which retained intimate ties with southern Tamil region.

Crafts

Local craft skills are still practised widely in households across the country. Pottery, coir fibre, carpentry, handloom weaving and metalwork all receive government assistance. Some of the crafts are concentrated in just a few villages.

Brasswork, for example, is restricted to a small area around Kandy, where the 'city of arts', Kalapura, has over 70 families of craftsmen making superb brass, wood, silver and gold items. Fine **gold and silver chain work** is done both in the Pettah area of Colombo and in Jaffna. **Batiks**, from wall hangings to lungis (sarongs), and a wide range of handloom household linen are widely available. **Silver jewellery** (also from Kandy), trays, ornaments and inlay work is a further specialisation. **Masks** are a popular product in the SW of the island, based on traditional masks used in dance dramas while Galle and the S is famous for **lace-making**.

HISTORY

CONTENTS

Settlement and early history	81
The Kandyan Kingdom	84
Colonial power	86
The moves to independence	87

Settlement and early history

Stone tools from the Middle Palaeolithic Age have been found in several places, evidence of settlement in Sri Lanka perhaps as much as 500,000 years ago. Recent genetic research however suggests that Homo sapiens may not have evolved until very much later, and spread from Africa in the last 100,000 years.

The early record of settlement in Sri Lanka is scanty. Archaeologists believe today that the first Homo sapiens arrived perhaps 75,000 years ago, bringing with them a life of hunting and gathering centred on open-air camp sites. Evidence of their activity has been found in a variety of habitats. However, no Neolithic tools have been found, and and no tools from the Copper Age, which is so well represented in peninsular India from the 2nd millennium BC.

The picture changes with the arrival of the Iron Age, for the megalithic graves, associated with black and red pottery, suggest that Sri Lanka had direct contact with S India well before the Aryans immigrated from N India from around 500 BC. Sri Lanka's archaeological record remains comparatively sparse, with barely any evidence with which to date the development of Stone Age cultures or the later spread of domesticated animals and cultivation. At some point in the first millennium BC rice cultivation made its appearance, though whether as a result of migration from either N India or South East Asia remains controversial.

The earliest aboriginal settlers, of Australoid, Negrito and Mediterranean stock, have now been almost entirely absorbed in the settled populations. The earliest named culture is that of **Balangoda**, distributed across the whole island between 5000 and 500 BC. The **Veddas** are the only inhabitants today whose ancestors were in Sri Lanka before the Aryan migrations. Related to the Dravidian jungle peoples in S India, they dwelt in caves and rock shelters, and lived by hunting and gathering. They practised a cult of the dead, communicating with ancestors through reincarnated spirits. Today the Veddas have been largely absorbed into the Sinhalese community and have virtually ceased to have a separate existence. In the mid 1960s their numbers had shrunk to under 800, from over 5,000 at the beginning of the century.

Migration from India The overwhelming majority of the present population of Sri Lanka owes its origins to successive waves of migration from two different regions of India. Most people are of Indo-Aryan origin and came from N India. The earliest migrations from N India may have taken place as early as the 5th century BC. Although these migrants brought with them a N Indian language which had its roots in the Sanskrit tradition, they were not yet Buddhists, for Buddhism did not arrive in Sri Lanka until the 3rd century BC. It is most likely that the Sinhalese came from India's NW, possibly Punjab or Guyarat, and it seems probable that Guyaratic traders were already sailing down India's W Coast by this time. The origins of Tamil settlement are unclear, but are thought to go back at least to the 3rd century BC, when there is clear evidence of trade between Sri Lanka and S India.

Today the *Sinhalese* make up 74% of the total population. Sri Lanka's *Tamil* population comprises the long settled Tamils of the N and E (12.6%) and the migrant workers on the tea plantations in the Central Highlands (5.5%) who settled in Sri Lanka from the late 19th century onwards. By the middle 1990s over 340,000 adults from this Tamil community had been repatriated to India. The so-called '**Moors**', Tamil speaking Muslims of Indian-Arab descent, were traders on the E coast and now number over 1.1m (7.7%). A much smaller but highly distinct community is that of the **Burghers**, numbering about 50,000. The Dutch (mainly members of the Dutch Reformed Church), and the Portuguese intermarried with local people, and their descendants were urban and ultimately English speaking. There are similar numbers of Malays and smaller groups of Kaffirs. The Malays are Muslims who were brought by the Dutch from Java. The Kaffirs were brought by the Portuguese from Mozambique and other parts of E Africa as mercenaries.

Early history

With the development of agriculture came the origins of a literate and complex society. Tradition associates the founding of Sri Lanka's first kingdom with Devanampiya Tissa (250-21 BC) whom the great Chronicle the Mahavansa suggests was converted to Buddhism by Mahinda, son of the great Indian emperor Asoka. Myth and legend are bound up with many of the events of South Asian history, but the Sri Lankan historian KM de Silva has noted that the historical mythology of the Sinhalese "is the basis of their conception of themselves as the chosen guardians of Buddhism." The basic text through which this view of the island's history has been passed on by successive generations of Buddhist monks is the *Mahavansa* (the *Great Dynasty* or *Lineage*), which de Silva suggests possibly goes back to the 6th century AD, but is probably much more recent. It is the epic history from Vijaya, the legendary founder of Sri Lanka, to King Mahasena (d AC 303) and is a major source on early history and legend. It was continued in the 13th century text the *Culavansa*, which gives a very full account of the medieval history of the island. These works were compiled by **bhikkus** (Buddhist monks) and inevitably they have the marks of their sectarian origins.

Interpretation of Sri Lanka's early history does not depend entirely on the writings of the Buddhist monks who ultimately wrote the Mahavansa. The first known writings are inscriptions discovered near caves in several parts of the island. Written in the Brahmi script (which was also used in India on the great inscriptions of the Emperor Asoka to express his principles of government and to mark out the limits of his territorial power), in Sri Lanka the inscriptions are brief epigraphs, testifying to the donation of caves or rock shelters to Buddhist monks. Written in an early form of Sinhala, rather than in the Prakrit which was the language used by Asoka, they give vivid testimony to the existence of prosperous, literate agricultural societies. The alphabet and the language were common right across the country, and even from early times it is clear that wet rice cultivation using sophisticated irrigation technology was the basis of the economy. As the map shows, settlement spread steadily right through to the 13th century. A notable feature of this early settlement and culture was its restriction to the Dry Zone and to altitudes below 300m.

From the origins of this agricultural civilisation in the 3rd Century BC there was a progressive economic and social evolution. The economy and the culture developed around the creation of extraordinarily sophisticated irrigation systems, using the rivers flowing from the central highlands across the much drier N and E plains. Traditional agriculture had depended entirely on the rainfall brought by the retreating monsoon between Oct-Dec. The developing kingdoms of N Sri Lanka realized the need to control water to improve the reliability of agriculture, and a system of tank irrigation was already well advanced by the 1st century BC. This developed into possibly the most advanced contemporary system of hydraulic engineering in the world by the end of the 5th century AC. Many of these developments were quite small scale and today it is impossible to identify their creators. Others however were of a previously unparallelled size and are clearly identified with powerful kings. Thus King Mahasena, for example (274-302 AD) the 15m high dam which impounded the Kantalai Tank, covering 2,000 ha and served by a 40 km long canal. King Dhatusena (460-478 AC) constructed the Kalawewa Lake in Anuradhapura, then by far the largest tank in Sri Lanka, to be surpassed in the late 12th century by King Parakrama's Parakrama Samudra (Sea of Parakrama), retained by an embankment 14 km long.

Political developments in pre-Colonial Sri Lanka

Proximity to India has played a permanent part in Sri Lanka's developing history. Not only have the peoples of the island themselves originated from the mainland, but through more than 2,000 years, contact has been an essential element in all Sri Lanka's political equations.

According to the Mahavansa the Buddha commanded the king of the gods, Sakra, to protect Lanka as the home in which Buddhism would flourish. In recent years, much has been read into both the text and to more recent history to suggest that Sinhalese have always been at war with the Tamils. The truth is far more complicated. The earliest settlement of the island took place in the NE, the region now known as the Dry Zone. Until the 13th century AC this was the region of political and cultural development for Sinhalese and Tamil alike.

The political history of the island after the establishment of the first recorded kingdom was not as smooth as might be inferred from the steady expansion of settled agriculture and the spread of sophisticated irrigation technology. Before the 13th century AC three regions played a major role in the island's political life. **Rajarata** in the N central part of the island's plains grew into one of the major core regions of developing Sinhalese culture. To its N was **Uttaradesa** ('northern country'), while in the SE **Rohana** developed as the third political centre.

Periodically these centres of Sinhalese power came into conflict with each other, and with Tamil kings from India. The Mahavansa records how the Rohana Sinhalese King Dutthagamenu defeated the Chola Tamil King Elara, who had ruled N Sri Lanka from Anuradhapura, in 140 BC. Dutthagamenu's victory was claimed by the chroniclers as a historic assertion of Buddhism's inalienable hold on Sri Lanka. In fact it is clear that at the time this was not a Tamil-Sinhalese or Buddhist-Hindu conflict, for the armies and leadership of both sides contained Sinhalese and Tamils, Buddhists and Hindus. By that time Buddhism had already been a power in the island for 2 centuries, when the king *Devanampiya Tissa* (307-267 BC) converted to Buddhism.

Buddhism became the state religion, identified with the growth of Sinhalese culture and political power. The power of the central kingdom based at *Anuradhapura* was rarely unchallenged or complete. Power was decentralized, with a large measure of local autonomy. Furthermore, provincial centres periodically established their independence. Anuradhapura became one of Asia's pre-eminent cities, but from the 11th century AD *Polonnaruwa* took over as capital.

The Tamil involvement Although Buddhist power was predominant in Sri Lanka from the 1st century BC, Sri Lankan kings often deliberately sought Tamil support in their own disputes. As a result Sri Lanka was affected by political developments in S India. The rise of the expansionist Tamil kingdoms of the Pandiyas, Pallavas and Cholas from the 5th century AC increased the scope for interaction with the mainland. In de Silva's words, "South Indian auxiliaries became in time a vitally important, if not the most powerful element in the armies of the Sinhalese rulers, and an unpredictable, turbulent group who were often a threat to political stability. They were also the nucleus of a powerful Tamil influence in the court."

It was not a one way flow. Occasionally the Sinhalese were themselves drawn in to attack Tamil kings in India, as in the 9th century when to their enormous cost they joined with their beleaguered allies the Pandiyans and attacked the Cholas. The Chola Emperor Rajaraja I defeated them in India and then carried the war into Sri Lanka, adding Jaffna and the N plains, including Anuradhapura, to his empire.

The Cholas ruled from Polonnaruwa for 75 years, finally being driven out by the Rohana king **Vijayabahu I** in 1070 AC. He established peace and a return to some prosperity in the N before civil war broke out and disrupted the civil administration again. Only the 33 year rule of **Parakramabahu I** (1153-1186) interrupted the decline. Some of Sri Lanka's most remarkable monuments date from his reign, including the massive irrigation embankment 12m high and 15 km long which enclosed the *Parakrama Samudra* (*Sea of Parakrama*) at Polonnaruwa. However, it was the collapse of this kingdom and its ultimate annihilation by the Tamils in the 13th century that left not only its physical imprint on the N Sri Lankan landscape but also an indelible psychological mark on the Sri Lankan perception of neighbouring Tamil Hindus.

The Sinhalese move South

Other factors, such as the spread of malaria which occurred with the deterioration in maintenance of the irrigation system, may have led to the progressive desertion of the N and E plains and the movement S of the centre of gravity of the Island's population. Between the 12th and 17th centuries Sinhalese moved from the dry to the wet zone. This required a change in agriculture from irrigated to rainfed crops. Trade also increased, especially in cinnamon, an activity controlled by the rising population of Muslim seafarers. A Tamil Kingdom was set up in Jaffna for the first time, briefly coming back under Sinhalese power (under the Sinhalese king Parakramabahu VI, 1412-67, based in his capital at *Kotte*), but generally remaining independent, and a frequent threat to the power of the Sinhalese kingdoms to the S. Other threats came from overseas. As early as the 13th century, a Buddhist king from Malaya invaded Sri Lanka twice to try and capture the tooth relic and the Buddha's alms bowl. In the early 15th century the Island was even invaded by a fleet of Chinese junks sent by the Ming Emperors.

The Kandyan Kingdom

Between the S and N kingdoms, Kandy became the capital of a new kingdom around 1480. Establishing its base in the Central Highlands, it became a powerful independent kingdom by the end of the 15th century. By the early 16th century the Sinhalese kingdom of Kotte in the S was hopelessly fragmented, giving

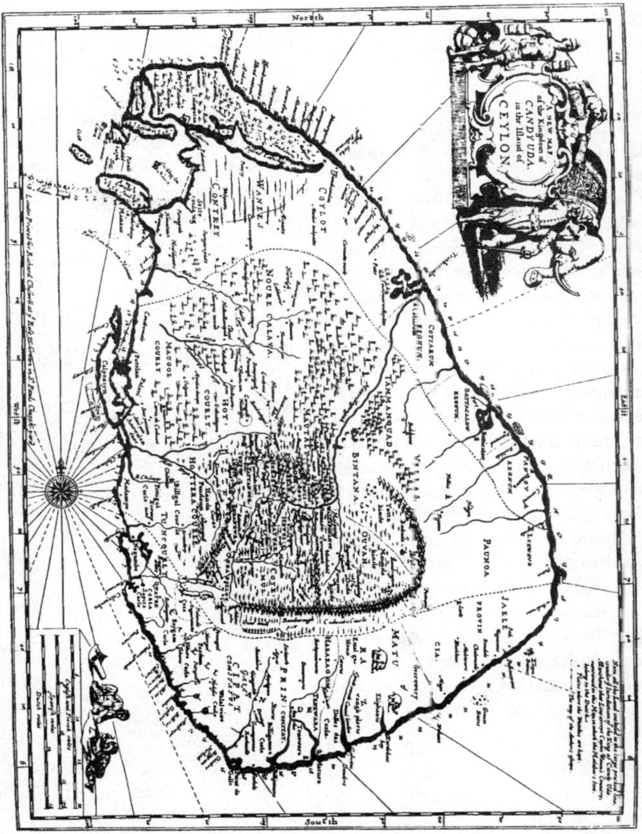

An early (1681) map of Sri Lanka. Known as Knox's Map it shows the Kingdom of Candy Uda in the Island of Ceylon.

impetus to Kandy's rise to independent power. Its remote and inaccessible position gave it added protection from the early colonial invasions. Using both force and diplomacy to capitalize on its geographical advantages, it survived as the last independent Sinhalese kingdom until 1815. It had played the game of seeking alliances with one colonial power against another with considerable success, first seeking the help of the Dutch against the Portuguese, then of the British against the Dutch. However, this policy ran out of potential allies when the British established their supremacy over all the territory surroundiong the Central Highlands in 1796, and by 1815 the last Kandyan King, a Tamil Hindu converted to Buddhism, was deposed by his Sinhalese chiefs, who sought an accord with the new British rulers in exchange for retaining a large measure of their own power.

Colonial power

The succession of three colonial powers, the Portuguese, Dutch and the British, finally ended the independent Sinhalese and Tamil rule. Expanding Islam, evidenced in the conversion of the inhabitants of islands on the Arab trading routes such as the Maldives and the Laccadives as well as significant numbers on the SW coast of India, had also been making its presence felt. The Portuguese arrived in Sri Lanka in 1605 and established control over some of the island's narrow coastal plains around Colombo. They were responsible for large-scale conversions to Roman Catholicism which today accounts for 90% of the island's Christians, leaving both a linguistic legacy and an imprint on the population, evidenced today in many names of Portuguese origin.

During this period the rest of the island was dominated by the rulers of Sitavaka, who overpowered the Kotte Kingdom in 1565 and controlled the whole of the SW apart from Colombo. For 10 years they occupied Kandy itself, nearly evicted the Portuguese and came close to reasserting Sinhalese power in the far N.

By 1619 the **Portuguese** had annexed Jaffna, which thereafter was treated by the Dutch, and more importantly the British, as simply part of the Island state. They were less successful in subjugating Kandy, and in 1650 the Portuguese were ousted by the Dutch. The Dutch extended their own colonial control from Negombo (40 km N of Colombo), S right round the coast to Trincomalee, as well as the entire N peninsula, leaving the Kandyan Kingdom surrounded in the Central Highlands. Because the Portuguese and Dutch were interested in little other than the spice trade, they bent most of their efforts to producing the goods necessary for their trade. The British replaced the Dutch in 1795-6 when British power was being consolidated in S India at the expense of the French and the Mysore Muslim Raja, Tipu Sultan. Their original purpose was to secure the important Indian Ocean port of Trincomalee. Initially the British imported administrators and officials from Madras, but as BH Farmer points out, by 1802 "it was apparent that Madras-trained officials were, apart from other disabilities, quite unable to understand the language and customs of the Sinhalese, and Ceylon became a Crown Colony."

When the **British** came to control the whole island after 1815 they established a quite distinctive imprint on the island's society and economy. This was most obvious in the introduction of plantation agriculture. During the British period coffee took over from cinnamon, but by the beginning of the 20th century, even though coffee had largely been wiped out by disease, plantation agriculture was the dominant pillar of the cash economy. Rice production stagnated and then declined, and Sri Lanka became dependent on the export of cash crops and the import of food. In 1948 it was only producing about 35% of its rice needs.

The colonial period also saw major social changes take place. Under the Portuguese and then the Dutch the development of commercial activity in the coastal lowlands encouraged many 'low-country' Sinhalese to become involved in the newly emerging economic activity. In a process which continued in the early British colonial period, the Low Country Sinhalese became increasingly westernized, with the widespread adoption of an English education and the rise of an urban middle class, while the Kandyan Sinhalese retained far stronger links with traditional and rural social customs. Despite British reforms in 1833 which introduced a uniform administrative system across the whole of Ceylon, wiping out the distinctive Kandyan political system, a contrast between Kandyan and Low-Country Sinhalese persisted into the modern period.

However, an even more significant change took place in the 19th century. British commercial interests saw the opportunities presented for the cultivation of cash crops. Cinnamon and coconuts had been planted by the Dutch and become particularly important, but the after 1815 coffee production was spread to the Kandyan hills. Despite ups and downs production increased dramatically until 1875, when a catatrophic attack of a fungus disease wiped out almost the entire crop. It was replaced, particularly in the higher regions by tea.

Labour had already begun to prove a problem on the coffee plantations, and as tea spread the shortage became acute. Farmer has shown how private labour contractors were recruited to persuade labourers to come to Ceylon from the Tamil country of S India. between 1843-1859 over 900,000 men women and children migrated to work as indentured labour. The cost of their transport was deducted from their wages after they had arrived, and they could not leave until they had repaid their debt. Immigration on that scale created a massive change in the ethnic mix of the Highlands, with a particularly significant effect on the Kandyan farmers, whose land was increasingly hemmed in by the spread of estates. The Indian Tamils however remained entirely separate from the Sinhalese, returning to S India whenever possible and sending cash remittances home.

The moves to Independence

Dominated by Buddhists and Sinhalese in its early stages, no one in the Independence movement at the turn of the century would have believed that British rule would end within 50 years – nor would many have wanted it to. The **Ceylon National Congress**, formed in 1919, was conservative and pragmatic, but the pressures of imminent democratic self-rule made themselves felt throughout the 1930s, as minority groups pressed to protect their position. Universal suffrage came in 1931, along with the promise of self-rule from the British Government. It had the positive benefit of encouraging the development of welfare policies such as health care, nutrition and public education. However, it also had the immediate impact of encouraging a resurgence of nationalism linked with Buddhist revivalism.

Independence came with scarcely a murmur on 4 February 1948, 6 months after that of India and Pakistan. Ceylon's first Prime Minister was Don Stephen Senanayake. His son **Dudley Senanayake**, who followed, was identified with a pragmatic nationalism. The heart of his programme was the recolonisation of the deserted Sinhalese heartlands of the Dry Zone. It was a programme deliberately calculated to recapture the glories of the past while laying the groundwork for post-Independence prosperity. In the event, its results have proved far more complex than even its critics fully recongized.

MODERN SRI LANKA

Contents

Government 88
Economy 90

Government

In its first 30 years of Independence Sri Lanka held eight general elections, sometimes accompanied by radical changes in political direction. Between 1956 and 1977 the governing party always lost. Power alternated between the socialist **Sri Lanka Freedom Party** (SLFP), and the free-market **United National Party** (UNP), which had formed the first government after Independence. Neither has succeeded in achieving the economic success which could keep pace with the growing demands of an increasingly young and literate population, struggling for jobs. Education has been one of the triumphs, with the country achieving high adult literacy figures. It has the sixth highest pupil-teacher ratio in the world, with 14 primary pupils per teacher (Asiaweek).

There has been a series of moves to turn away from British institutions and styles of government. Both parties have competed in the search for more and more potent symbols of national identity, largely Buddhist and Sinhalese. The last decade has seen the divisions worked out in ethnic conflict of these two fundamental aspects of political development.

Since Jul 1983, when an anti-Tamil pogrom devastated many Tamil areas of Colombo and led to the loss of hundreds of Tamil lives, Sri Lanka has been locked in a bitter conflict between the government forces and Tamil guerrillas. Over 150,000 Tamils fled as refugees to India. In the N and E, Tamil militancy rapidly gained ground, and between 1983 and 1987 the **Liberation Tigers of Tamil Eelam** (LTTE or just 'the Tigers') waged an increasingly successful battle for control of what they regarded as the Tamil homeland, both against rival Tamil groups and against the Sri Lankan armed forces. In response the Government mounted increasingly strong attacks into the N, and in summer 1987 launched what was hailed as a final offensive.

The conflict had been watched with growing concern by the Indian government, which opposed the creation of a separate Tamil State in Sri Lanka but feared the domestic political consequences of failing to support Sri Lankan Tamils in the face of increasingly genocidal attacks. In Jul 1987 the Indian Prime Minister Rajiv Gandhi forced President Jayawardene and the Sri Lankan Government to accept a peace accord, under which the Indian army would enter Sri Lanka to restore law and order and elections would be held to elect Provincial Councils.

In the event the Indian army became bogged down in a conflict with the Tigers themselves. At the same time the presence of the Indian forces roused fierce opposition from the Sinhalese, and the angry upsurge of support among young people for the fiercely anti-Tamil **JVP party** (Janatha Vimukhti Peramuna, People's Liberation Army) in the S of the island was accompanied by escalating violence and disruption. Many people 'disappeared' (presumed dead) at this time.

In Nov 1989 the two key leaders of the JVP were killed, and the new Sri Lankan Government of President Premadasa claimed its first major success. Soon it was able to claim another, for it appeared to have succeeded in reaching

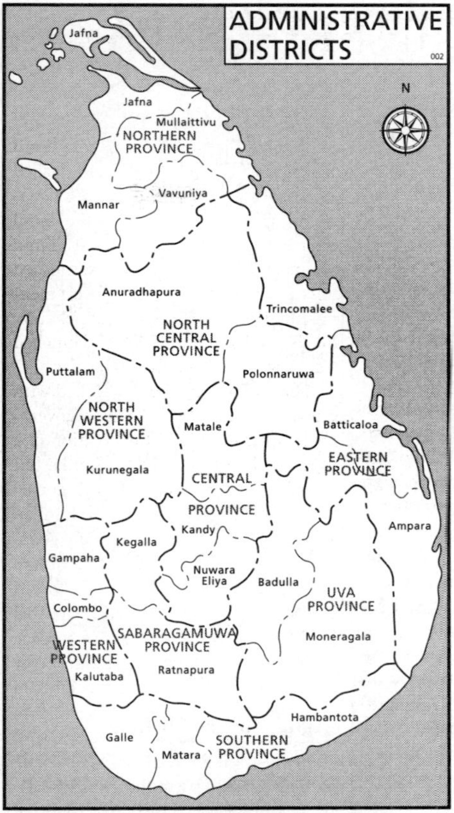

an agreement with the Tigers on a withdrawal of the Indian Peace Keeping Force, finally completed in Mar 1990. That accord soon broke down. Although the S was now quiet, in mid 1994 civil war continued in the far the N of the Island. The assassination of President Premadasa on 1 May 1993 at a Labour Day parade in Colombo marked a further destructive twist in the island's violent fabric. Following less than 2 weeks after the assasination of another high ranking former cabinet minister, Lalith Athulathmudali, President Premadasa's assassination by a suicide bomber was believed by the government to be at the hands of the Tamil Tigers (the LTTE). They disclaimed responsibility, though the method used was very similar to that of the woman LTTE member who was responsible for the death of Rajiv Gandhi in India in May 1991, and for which at the time the leadership had also disclaimed responsibilty. The Sri Lankan Prime Minister, Dingiri Banda Wijetunga, was elected President in Mr Premadasa's place on 7 May 1993.

District elections in 1994 suggested that there was a strong tide flowing against the UNP government. Mrs Bandaranaike's Sri Lanka Freedom Party, weakened for many years by internal factionalism and defeat at the hands of the UNP, was making a strong comeback. The SLFP itself underwent important changes in its leadership, Mrs Bandaranaike's son Anura deserting the party for the UNP, while her daughter Chandrika took up the mantle as her mother's chosen successor, leading the SLFP at the head of a rather loose grouping of parties in the anti-UNP People's Alliance.

On 24 Jun President Wijetunga dissolved Parliament and announced that parliamentary elections would be held on 16 August 1994, to be followed by a Presidential election on 9 Nov. In the Parliamentary elections the Alliance gained a narrow 49% to 44% majority over the UNP. The Presidential elections which followed were disrupted by the assassination of the UNP's candidate, Gamini Dissanayake, by a suicide bomber, and Chandrika Kumaratunge defeated Dissanayake's widow in the Presidential election which followed, gaining over 62% of the vote.

Those victories were followed by a set of political moves which triggered the most optimistic period in Sri Lanka's politics for over a decade. As President Mrs Kumaratunge put forward proposals for a truce with the LTTE, to be followed by new constitutional proposals which would create a devolved political structure for the Island's government, and give a large measure of autonomy to the Tamil N and E. The truce held into the early summer of 1995, when the LTTE once more launched a series of attacks on Sri Lankan Government positions. Through the latter half of 1995 the Government pursued a twin approach, arguing publicly for a peaceful resolution of the conflict on the basis of a new constitutional settlement while advancing steadily against Tamil Tiger positions in the far N. Despite continuing apparent military success in the northern campaign the Tamil Tigers demonstrated their ability to launch terrorist raids into the heart of the capital when they blew up one of the country's most important oil terminals in Colombo on 20 October 1995. The army pressed on and in Nov 1995 were in the suburbs of Jaffna. Virtually the entire population of the city was reported to have fled, while the LTTE continued to attack Sinhalese villagers elsewhere in the N and E of the island.

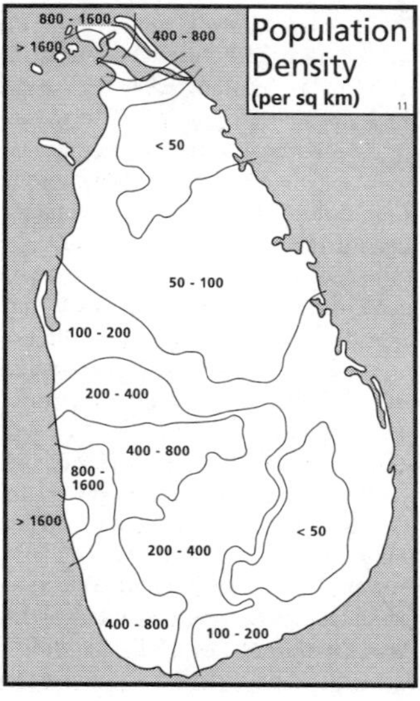

The constitutional proposals put forward on 3 August 1995 enviasaged a federal union of eight regions. Each would have an elected regional council with exclusive power to legislate over subjects ranging from health, industrial development, transport and education to land, the promotion of foreign investment and mineral rights. The Central Government would retain control among other things of national security, banking and customs duties and interregional irrigation schemes. It remains far from clear that the proposals will gain sufficient suport to be implemented.

Economy

Agriculture and fishing

About 25% of Sri Lanka's area is cultivated by sedentary farmers or under cultivated forests, a further 15% being under shifting cultivation. About half is under forest, grassland, swamp and waste land. In the wet zone virtually all the cultivable land is now taken up.

Sri Lanka has not produced enough food to meet the needs of its population since the 18th century, yet in many respects it has been the most obviously prosperous state in South Asia. In the 1970s more than half the money earned from the export of tea, rubber and coconuts was spent on importing foodgrains, leaving little for investment. Attempts to increase rice production have ranged from land reform to the introduction of high yielding varieties (hyv).

Rice Sri Lanka has two main rice growing seasons. The *Maha* crop is harvested between Jan and Mar, the *Yala* crop between Aug-Sep. By the early 1980s there was virtually a 100% takeup of new varieties. Yields have increased to over 4 tonnes per ha, and production has risen towards 80% of domestic needs despite the speed of population growth. In addition to the intensification programme the Government has also carried out major colonisation schemes, bringing new land under rice cultivation. This has been expensive and certainly not always cost effective, but in part has been a response to political pressures to reclaim land for Sinhalese cultivators.

The cash crops of tea, rubber and coconuts continue to contribute the lion's share of Sri Lanka's foreign exchange earnings. In 1950 this stood at 96%. In 1995 approximately 30% of foreign exchange earnings still came from these three products alone.

Tea has suffered from inadequate investment and fierce competition from expanding production in other countries of cheaper, lower quality tea. The area cropped under tea fell steadily, but production nearly doubled between 1948 and 1965. It declined to around 180 million kg in 1983. Tea alone still accounts for 15% of the total value of exports, followed by rubber (Rs 3bn) and coconuts (Rs 1.4bn).

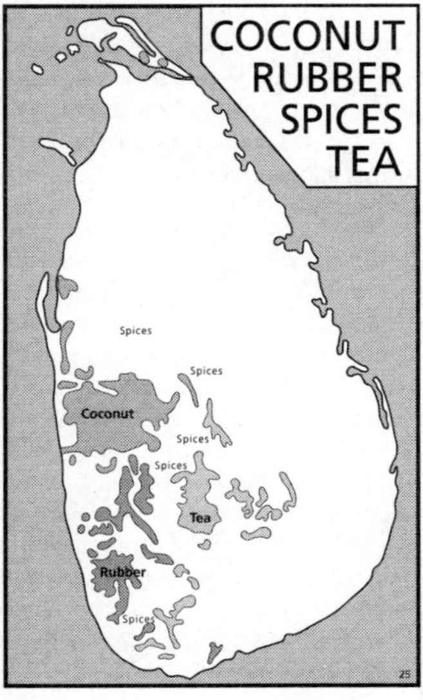

Fishing Potentially rich fishery resources have yet to be fully developed. Fresh water stocking programmes have increased the yield of rivers and lakes, and brackish water fishing is becoming increasingly commercialized. However, nearly 40% of households which depend on fishing have no boats or equipment, and despite the potential of the export market production does not meet domestic demand.

Resources and industry

Sri Lanka has few fossil fuels or metallic minerals. Gemstones, graphite (crystalline carbon) and heavy mineral sands are the most valuable resources, though clays, sands and limestones are abundant. Gemstones include sapphires, rubies, topaz, zircon, tourmaline and many others. Gem bearing gravels are common, especially in the SW around the appropriately named Ratnapura (*City of gems*). Other minerals are also concentrated in the SW. The greatest concentration of heavy mineral sands – ilmenite, rutile and monazite – is N of Trincomalee, where deposits are 95% pure. Monazite is found on the W coast. There are scattered deposits of iron ore in the SW and some veins of magnetite in the NW interior. High evaporation rates make shallow lagoons, as in the NE, suitable for salt manufacture. The most important salterns are at Puttalam and Elephant Pass in the N and Hambantota in the S.

Due to the lack of fossil fuel resources, 95% of the island's electricity is now generated by hydro power. The first HEP project was opened in the 1930s, but firewood still accounts for over half of all energy used. Supplies are under increasing pressure, and the Mahaweli Project undertaking has meant that most of the HEP is now developed.

Sri Lanka had very little industry at Independence, manufacturing accounting for less than 5% of the GDP. By 1996 a number of new industries had been developed – cement, mineral sands, ceramics, cloth. These were all planned originally in the state controlled sector. The socialist government under Mrs Bandaranaike envisaged public ownership of all major industries, but the United National Party government elected under President Jayawardene's leadership in 1977 reversed this policy, moving towards a free trade economy.

Among the leading sectors of the new policy was tourism, with particular efforts to exploit the superb beaches and equable climate. This programme was severely hit by the political troubles which dogged the island since 1983. In the 1990s, however, barring trouble spots in the N, tourists began to return. Sub-marine fauna and the opportunities for watersports have made some beaches particularly attractive along the SW, S and the SE of the island.

Since 1992 the overall economic performance has been remarkably strong in view of the continuing difficulty faced in resolving the underlying political crisis. A serious drought in 1992 hit agricultural production but was followed by a rapid recovery. Tea production, having declined by 26% during the drought year of 1992, recorded an increase of 35% the following year, and has continued to grow fast. Industrial output grew by 7%. Services, which account for about half of the Gross Domestic Product, also grew by just over 6%, and overall growth continued at over 5% per annum through 1995. However, inflation remained in double digits, and the new government showed little sign of getting it under control.

Export performance has continued to be strong, but the 1990s have seen a major change in the composition of Sri Lanka's exports. At the beginning of the decade tea (27% of the total) was still the nearly as important an export as manufactured goods, notably textiles and garments (32%), but by 1995 textiles accounted for over 55% compared with tea's 15%. The change partly reflected the rapid increase in foreign investment in the manufacturing sector which has continued into the mid-1990s. The government is now paying particular attention to the improvement of productivity through technology transfer and research and development.

COLOMBO

CONTENTS

Introduction	93
The Centre and North	95
The South	98
Excursions	98
Museums	99
Parks and zoos	100
Tours	101
Local information	101
Short excursions from Colombo	108

MAPS

Colombo	94
Fort and Pettah	97
Galle Face and Beira Lake Area	99
Kollupitiya	102
Bambalapitiya	103

INTRODUCTION

Sheltered from the SW Monsoon by a barely perceptible promontory jutting out into the sea, Colombo's bay was an important site for Muslim traders before the colonial period. However, it is essentially a colonial city, whose rise to pre-eminence did not start until the 19th century and the establishment of British power. Before that it was a much less important town than Galle, but when the British took control of Kandy and encouraged the development of commercial estates, the Island's economic centre of gravity moved N. The capital, Colombo offered two easy routes into the Kandyan highlands.

(*Pop* 2.1 million; *Alt* Sea level) Colombo's small promontory offered little protection for larger ships, and in the late 19th century the British started work on a series of breakwaters which were to provide an effective harbour round the year. The SW breakwater, over 1,000m long, was completed in 1885. It has the pilot station at its head. The NE breakwater, a rubble embankment 350m long, was completed in 1902, followed in 1907 by the NW breakwater. As this breakwater has no land connection it forms an artificial 'island' with a S entrance 250m wide and a N entrance 220m wide. Overall the breakwaters enclose an area of 3 sq km more than 8m deep.

The growth in shipping during the early 20th century reflected the advantages of Colombo's position on the Indian Ocean Sea route between Europe, the Far East and Australasia. However, the city also benefitted from its focal position on the rapidly expanding transport system within the Island. After 1832 the British had encouraged the rapid development of a road network

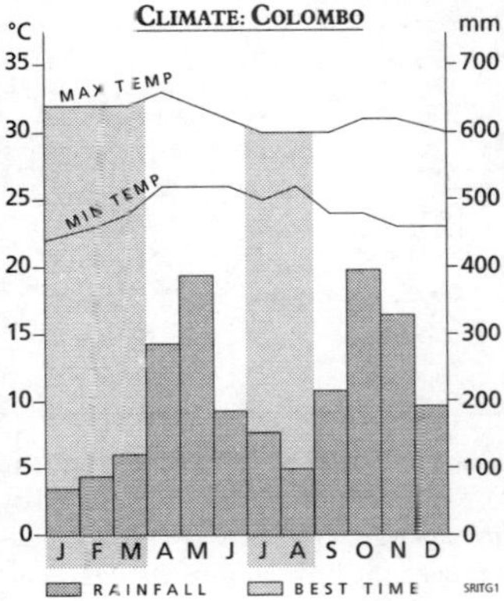

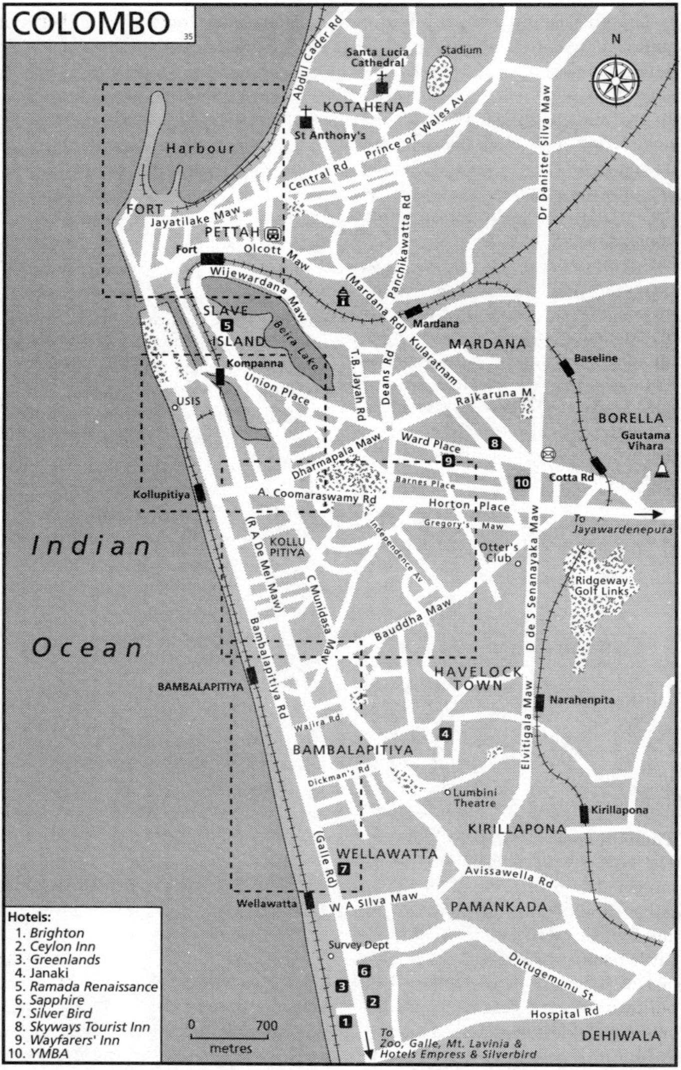

which radiated from Colombo. In the late 19th century this was augmented by an expanding rail network. Since Independence it has retained its dominant position. The harbour facilities are quite large and it remains the chief port. There are usually a large number of ships waiting to enter the harbour. There are, however, no beaches and the sea is quite dangerous.

The official limits of the city itself are quite confined, stretching just over 6 km S from the Kelaniya River and under 5 km E from the coast. However, the built up area now straggles indeterminately along all the major roads radiating from the centre, and it is difficult to tell where the city really begins and ends. Before the new harbour was built the centre of upper class Colombo was 3 km N of the Fort at Mutwal. Little remains from that period, and the city has grown S and E. Immediately next to the eastern flank of the city is the country's administrative capital Sri Jayawardenepura-Kotte. Just S of the commercial centre is the Beira Lake and to the SE again the high class residential area surrounding the attractive open spaces of the Viharamahadevi Park, with the museum and art gallery. Embassies are scattered on either side of Ananda Coomaraswamy Rd and Horton Place, running E from the sea towards Jayawardenepura-Kotte.

The Centre and North

Generally bustling with life, the roads can be very busy, making movement both within the city and attempts to get out of it frustratingly slow. Compared with much of the rest of the country, the air is quite polluted and consequently there is often a haze.

The Fort area

The **Fort**, no more than 500m sq, lies immediately S of the harbour. It is a rather disappointing commercial area, and not really worth wandering around. Little remains of either the Portuguese or Dutch periods. It is now largely rebuilt with tower blocks housing offices and some large department stores.

Marine Drive runs down the coast to the *Intercontinental Hotel* and across the wide open space of the Galle Face. Immediately inland of its N section is the narrow road now called Galle Buck, an English corruption of the old name Gal Bokka – rocky belly.

Galle Face Green The area between the mouth of the canal feeding Beira Lake and the *Galle Face Hotel* is currently dry and dusty; there are plans to re-lay the turf in the near future. It is a very popular area for Sri Lankans to walk and play – lots of food stalls and hawkers selling kites and other children's toys. You can walk along the wide path between the 'grass' and the sea. You need to be on guard for the inevitable pick-pockets especially at night when the whole area really comes alive.

From the N end of Marine Drive, Church St runs E, past **St Peter's Church** on the right. Part of the former residence of Dutch Governors, the Church **cemetery** contains the tombs of several British residents, including William Tolfrey (1778-1817), an army officer and the first translator of the Bible into Pali and Sinhalese. The nave of the church was originally a reception and banqueting hall, first converted into a church in 1804 and consecrated in 1821.

To the E is the *Hotel Taprobane* formerly the *Grand Oriental*, from which **York St**, one of the main shopping areas, runs due S. Halfway down it is **Sir Baron Jayatilleke Mawatha**, the main banking street. Nearly all the buildings are in red brick. Hospital St, running W at the S end of York St, is a lively centre of low cost restaurants, fruit sellers, and pavement merchants.

Running S from Church St to the W of St Peter's Church is **Janadhipathi Mawatha** (formerly Queen St). At the N end are Gordon Gardens, with a statue of Queen Victoria and a stone bearing the Portuguese Coat of Arms. Threats of terrorist violence have led to entrance to the Gordon Gardens being restricted, as it lies in Republic Square, alongside the offices of the Prime Minister and Cabinet. The N end of Janadhipathi Mawatha is normally closed to the public. Colombo is not graced with many fine buildings, but the GPO, on the E side of Janadhipathi Mawatha is a good example of Victorian colonial building. Opposite it is the President's House, *Janadhipathi Medura*. The Chartered Bank building is another imposing commercial structure, decorated with reliefs of domesticated elephants.

The statue in front of the **President's House** is of the 19th century British Governor Edward Barnes. An adjutant of the Duke of Wellington during the Battle of Waterloo, in Sri Lanka he is better known for building the Colombo-Kandy road. His statue is the point from which the distances of all towns in Sri Lanka from Colombo are measured. Just to the S again is the **Lighthouse Clock Tower** (1837), now replaced as a lighthouse by the new tower on Marine Drive. Sir Baron Jayatilleke Mawatha runs E, immediately N of the GPO, with a number of impressive commercial buildings, including a good example of inter-war architecture in the Bank of India.

East of the *Taprobane Hotel* is the Central YMCA, next to the Moors Islamic Cultural Home in Bristol St. Across Duke St is the Young Men's Buddhist Association. The shrine houses a noted modern image of the Buddha. The Fort Mosque, in a building of the Dutch period, is to the S on Chatham St.

The Pettah

While the Fort is the centre of Colombo's modern commercial activity, the Pettah (Tamil: *'pettai'* – suburb; Sinhalese: *'pitakotuwa'* – outer fort) is the hub of its traditional markets. The small shops and narrow streets are covered in advertising hoardings. Specialist streets house such craftsmen and traders as goldsmiths (Sea St), fruit and vegetable dealers (the end of Main St) and ayurvedic herbs and medicines (Gabo's Lane).

At the SE edge of the Pettah is the Fort Railway Station. In the market area to the N, Arabs, Portuguese, Dutch and British traded. Half way along Main St on the left-hand side after 2nd Cross St is the **Jami ud Alfar mosque** with its interesting white and red brick façade. It can be entered but there is little of architectural interest. It is clearly very much a working mosque and as such forms an important part of the bustle of life within the Pettah.

At the end of Main St, Central Road goes E from a large roundabout, just N of the Market. A left turn off Central Rd immediately after the roundabout, Brass Founder St, leads to a right fork, Ratnajothi Saravana Mawatha, formerly

SLAVE ISLAND

The high rise hotels and offices which have occupied the northward jutting peninsula in Beira Lake facing the Fort now leave no trace of the earlier uses of what was known as Slave Island. 'Island' was a misnomer, but slaves played a very real part in the colonial history of Colombo.

Brohier has recorded how in the Dutch period this tongue of open land was known as Kaffir Veldt. The Kaffirs – Africans from the East Coast around Mozambique – were brought to Sri Lanka for the first time by the Portuguese from Goa in 1630. When the Dutch ousted the Portuguese they made use of the slave labour force to build the fort in Colombo, when there may have been 4,000 of them. Their numbers grew, but after an unsuccessful insurrection in the 18th century the Dutch authorities decided to insist that all slave labour must be identifiably accommodated. The Kaffir Veldt was the nearest open space on which special shanty houses could be built, and a nightly roll call would be held to ensure that every slave was there.

In 1807 Cordiner reported that the number of slaves had fallen to 700, but the British did not abolish slavery in Sri Lanka until 1845. Nonetheless, the name Slave Island has persisted.

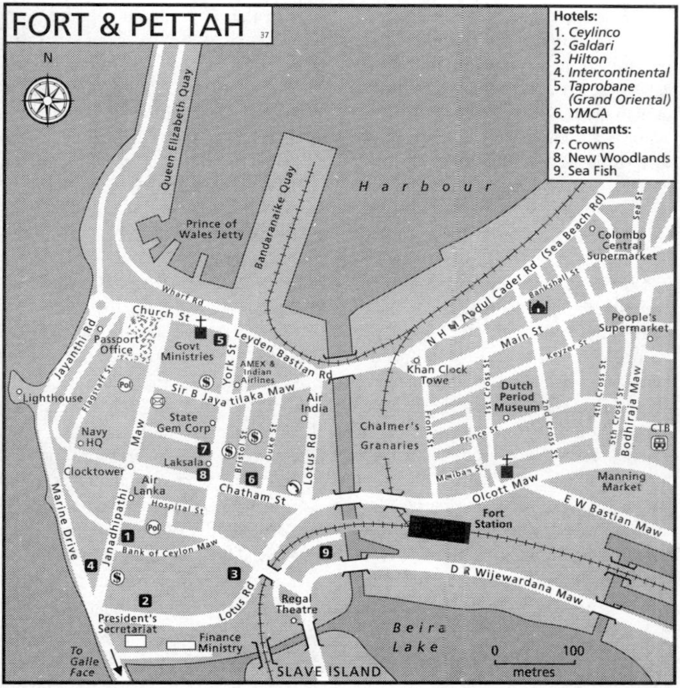

Wolfendahl St. At the end is the **Wolfendahl Church**. Built in 1749 on the site of an earlier Portuguese church, it is prominently placed on a hill, where its massive cruciform shape stands out, commanding a view over the harbour. Its Doric façade is solid and heavy, and inside it has many tombstones and memorial tablets to Dutch officials. It is the most interesting surviving Dutch monument in Sri Lanka.

To its NE is **Santa Lucia**, the Roman Catholic cathedral and in some people's eyes the most remarkable church building in Sri Lanka. It is a huge grey structure with a classical façade and a large forecourt. Begun in 1876 it was completed in 1910. Inside are the tombs of three French bishops but little else of interest. The Pope conducted a service here during his visit in 1994. **Christ Church**, the Anglican Cathedral, is just to the NW, the main church in a diocese which dates from 1845.

To the S in New Moor St is the **Grand Mosque**, a modern building in the style, as one critic puts it, of a modern international airport covered in metallic paint.

Also in the Pettah are three modest Hindu temples, of little architectural interest, but giving an insight into Hindu building style and worship. Perhaps the most striking is that of **Sri Ponnambula Vanesvara** at 38 Sri Ramanathan Rd. The gopuram (entrance gateway) has typical sculptures of gods from the Hindu pantheon. A Siva lingam is in the innermost shrine, with a Nandi in front and a dancing Siva (*Nataraja*) to one side, see page 65.

In **Borella**, 6 km E of the Fort, the modest building of the Gotami Vihara contains impressive modern murals depicting the life of the Buddha by the Sri Lankan artist George Keyt.

Further NE across the Kelaniya River is the **Raja Maha Vihara**, 13 km from the centre of the city and, after the temple of the tooth in Kandy, the most visited Buddhist temple in Sri Lanka. In the 13th century *Kelaniya* was an impressive city, but for Buddhists its chief attraction today is the legendary visit of the Buddha to the site. The Mahavansa recorded that the original stupa enshrined a gem-studded throne on which the Buddha sat when he supposedly visited Sri Lanka. Ultimately destroyed by the Portuguese, the present dagoba is in the shape of a heap of paddy. There is a famous image of the reclining Buddha, but there are also many images of Hindu deities. The temple is the meeting place for the **Duruthu Perahera** in Jan every year, which draws thousands of pilgrims from all over the Island.

The first city on the site was believed to have been built by King Yatala Tissa. According to legend this was destroyed by a flood from the sea, which was a punishment given to the king for mistreating the Buddhist *sangha*. He tried to placate the sea by setting his daughter afloat on a golden boat. Having drifted ashore in the S of the island she married King Kavan Tissa, and became the mother of one of Sri Lanka's great heroes, King Dutugemunu. The city is subsequently believed to have been destroyed by Tamil invasions, and was only re-built in the 13th century by King Vijayabahu. The present temple dates from about 1300.

The South

There are some attractive walks and drives to the S of the Fort area and Beira Lake. Galle Rd runs almost due S across the windswept open space of the Galle Face in the N, gradually moving away from the sea southwards, and separated from it by the railway. Inland and parallel with it runs RA de Mel Mawatha (formerly Duplication Rd, and still often referred to by the name which describes its origins as a duplicate of the Galle Rd), built up all the way S. Inland again lies the most prestigious residential area of Colombo, Cinnamon Gardens – widely referred to by its postal code, Colombo 7. Broad roads and shaded avenues make it a very attractive area.

There is a range of parks, the national museum, Town Hall and conference facilities. The **Viharamahadevi Park**, now named after an early Sri Lankan Queen, but originally named after Queen Victoria (see Parks and zoos below). A series of rectangular lakes to the E of the park leads to a golden statue of the seated Buddha. The impressive **Town Hall**, the Colombo 'White House', on Kannangara Maw, stands in the NE corner of the park. It was completed in 1927. At the De Soysa Circus roundabout is an equally interesting red-brick building, the **Victoria Memorial Rooms**, built around the turn of the century.

Excursions

Sri Jayawardenepura-Kotte

Despite being made the administrative capital in 1982, like some other 'artificially' planned capitals, it remains solely a centre of administration and has acquired no other significant functions. The decision to put the new 'Parliament' here was based partly on the fact that the site was formerly the almost sacred territory of Kotte, the ancient capital of Sri Lanka under Alakeswara who built a large fortress and defeated the Tamil leader Chakravarthi. Parakramabhu VI transformed the fortress into a prosperous modern city. However subsequent weak rulers left the city relatively defenceless and it fell easy prey to the Portuguese. They destroyed the city when

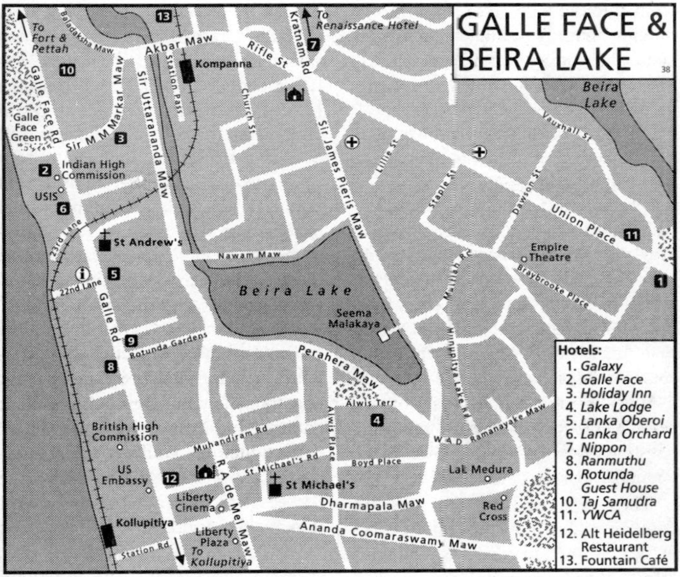

they attacked it from the N so that there are no traces of its former glory left. Built in the shadow of the modern city of Colombo, it is planned to relocate most government offices here, but Colombo will still retain its importance as the commercial capital.

Parliament building The impressive new parliament building, constructed with financial assistance from the Japanese government to a design by the well known Sri Lankan architect Geoffrey Bawa, stands in the middle of a lake. It is not open to the public and it is heavily fortified. The lake itself is surrounded by open park land. Approaching the new parliament building from Colombo you will pass **Independence Square** which contains a large open air construction. The 11 km drive from the Fort area, through the suburbs, takes about 30 mins.

The **Gramodaya Folk Arts Centre** has craftsmen working with brass, silver, leather, coir and producing jewellery, pottery, natural silk, lace and reed baskets. There is a shop, a herbal health drink counter, an aquarium and a restaurant serving Sri Lankan specialities.

Museums

National Museum, 8 Marcus Fernando Mawatha (Albert Crescent). 0900-1700, Sun-Thur. Closed on public holidays. Rs 100. (Bus 114, 138). The building is of typical English architecture with a statue of Sir William Gregory, governor 1872-77, in front of the imposing facade and a banyan tree in the large garden. Opened in 1877, it has a very interesting collection of paintings, sculptures, furniture and porcelain. Also masks and Kandyan regalia; and the library houses a unique collection of over 4,000 *Ola* (palm manuscripts) – an extremely rich archaeological and artistic collection. Very well labelled and organized, a visit is an excellent introduction to a tour of Sri Lanka. Exhibits include an outstanding collection of 10th-12th century bronzes from Polonnaruwa, and the lion throne of **King Nissankamalla**, which has become the symbol of Sri Lanka. There are interesting details and curiosities, eg the origin of Kolam dancing is traced back to the pregnancy craving of the Queen of the legendary King Maha Samnatha!

The ground floor displays Buddhist and Hindu sculptures, including a striking 1,500 year old stone statue of the Buddha from Toluvila. 'Demon-dance' masks line the stairs to the first floor. One visitor noted, "These are more 'satire in nature' than 'demon' with lots of characters of court officials, soldiers and 'outsiders' such as Muslims. Some were very elaborate and capable of moving their eyes etc. It is interesting to see how these evolved as different fashions swept the court."

The first floor has superbly executed scale reproductions of the wall paintings at Sigiriya and Polonnaruwa. Other exhibits include ancient jewellery and carvings in ivory and wood.

Natural History Museum, behind the National Museum has good natural history and geological galleries.

Dutch Period Museum, Prince St, Pettah. Open 0900-1700, Mon-Fri. Originally the residence of the Dutch governor, Thomas van Rhae (1692-97), it was sold to the VOC before becoming the Colombo seminary in 1696. This ceased in 1796 when it was handed over to the British. During this time it was a Military Hospital, Armoury Police Training Centre, Post and Telegraph Office and much altered. Now it has been restored and offers a fascinating insight to the Dutch period. It surrounds a garden courtyard and has various rooms dedicated to different aspects of Dutch life including some interesting old tomb stones. Upstairs are several rooms with Dutch period furniture on display. These are not always open and you may have to ask the curator to show you around.

Bandaranaike Museum, Bauddhaloka Maw. Open 0900-1600 except Mon and *Poya* holidays. Devoted to the life and times of the late prime minister.

National Art Gallery, 106 Ananda Coomaraswamy Maw. Open 0900-1800. Closed Poya Days. Permanent collection, mainly portraits.

Parks and zoos

Dehiwala Zoo, Dharmapala Maw (Allan Ave), 10 km SW from centre. 0830-1700. Entry Rs 30, plus charge for photography. One of the most attractive in Asia. 15 ha undulating ground, beautifully laid out with shrubs, flowering trees and plants, orchids, lakes and fountains. Over 2,000 animals include sloth bear, leopard, civets and other small cats, many kinds of lizard, crocodiles and snakes. Lions, tigers, jaguars,

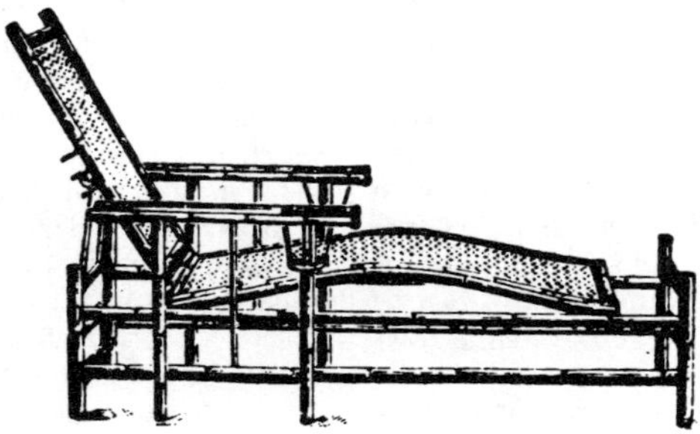

Planter's chair

black panthers, and many exotic species such as hippopotami, rhinos, giraffes and kangaroos. The zoo also has an aquarium with over 500 species of fish, and is particularly noted for its collection of birds. There is a troupe of trained elephants which are shown every afternoon. *Getting there*: bus No 132 or 176, also train to Dehiwala Station.

Vihara Mahadevi Park (formerly Victoria Park), on the site of the old Cinnamon Gardens, now re-named after the mother of the Sinhalese King Dutthugamenu. A botanical garden, including named species, it has a range of tropical trees, including a bo tree, ebony, mahogany, sal and lemon eucalyptus which attract a wide variety of birds. There is also an enormous profusion of climbing plants, parasites and rare orchids; it is particularly colourful in the spring. Early morning is an excellent time to visit (opens 0700).

Tours

City tours: by car with a chauffeur/Guide for three – Half day: 40 km, Buddhist Temple, Hindu Temple, Zoo and residential area. Full Day: also includes Kelaniya Temple. For nature safaris, hiking and bird watching contact Wildlife and Nature Protection Soc, Chaitiya Rd, Marine Drive, Fort, T 25248.

Local information

● Accommodation

Colombo now has several world class hotels, but is poorly provided with good cheap accommodation; budget travellers often find it can be difficult to get a suitable room. Mount Lavinia (listed separately), has the widest range of choice. Most hotels in the **B** category and above are comfortable with a/c, restaurant, exchange, shop and pool. Going S, along Galle Rd, which is busy and noisy, are several moderately priced hotels which vary: price is not always the best guide so you would do well to visit before booking.

Airport area: those arriving late or departing early may prefer to stay nr the airport; coach transfer is not always free. **A-B** ***Airport Garden***, 234 Negombo Rd, Seeduwa, 2 km towards Colombo (free airport shuttle), T 452950, F 452953, 120 rm (US$75), set back from main road, pool, watersports on lagoon, plush and convenient; **C** ***Goodwood Plaza*** and ***Orient Pearl***, Canada Friendship Rd, 1 km from airport (from terminal, across the road on right towards Colombo), T 452561, F 453847, 32 rm each, most a/c (Rs 1,150), twin hotels (former marginally better) with large rooms off long corridors, some refurbished to a good standard, reasonable restaurants, Colombo and Negombo buses pass the hotel, free airport transfer (driver may insist it is not free!); **D** ***Airlink***, 580 Negombo Rd, Seeduwa, 5 km from airport, towards Colombo, T 453607, F 453664, 11 simple rm with bath, 2 a/c, 24-hr meals brought in.

Fort and Pettah area (see page 97): **AL** ***Colombo Marriott***, 64 Lotus Rd, T 445860, F 575662, Europcar rentals; **AL** ***Galdari***, 64 Lotus Rd, corner of Janadhipathi Maw, T 544544, F 449875, 446 rm (US$85), overlooking Indian Ocean with golf nearby, French restaurant, *Café Fleuri* and *Colombo 2000* nightclub, good rooftop pool; **AL** ***Hilton***, 67 Lotus Rd, Echelon Sq, T 544644, F 544657, 387 rm (US$160), Japanese flr, special facilities for ladies; **AL** ***Intercontinental***, 48 Janadhipathi Maw, Fort, T 421221, F 547326, 250 rm (US$70), all with superb seaview, 9-storey seafront hotel, roof-top *Cats Eye* restaurant (good buffet lunches), *Pearl* for seafood and bar with panoramic views, snackbar serves Sinhalese specialities, open-air dining with live music, in season, well located, good bookshop; **B** ***Ceylinco***, 69 Janadhipathi Maw, Fort, T 20431, small with 15 rm in modern building, restaurant below has superb views; **B** ***Galaxy***, Union Place, Colombo 2, T 696372, F 699321, 52 a/c rm (US$35), restaurant, 24-hr coffee shop, bar, business centre, travel, pool; **B** ***Taprobane***, 2 York St, Fort, overlooking harbour, T 320391, F 447640, 62 comfortable rm (US$45), the old hotel for travellers arriving by sea, still full of sailors from port!, *Harbour Room* restaurant on top flr with excellent views, good bookshop; **C** ***Lanka Orchard***, 6 Galle Rd, Colombo 6, T 580809, modern, central; **C** ***Nippon***, 123, Kumaran Ratnam Rd, Colombo 2, T 431887, F 332603, 25 rm, some a/c (US$30); **D** ***YWCA International***, 393 Union Place, Colombo 2, 20 rm with bath (for women and couples), well located, in residential area, good restaurant and spice shop; ***YMCA***, 39 Bristol St, Fort, no longer has accommodation for visitors.

Galle Face Green area (see map page 99): **AL** ***Lanka Oberoi***, 77 Steuart Pl, Colombo 3, T 437437, F 449280, 600 rm with sea or lake-view (US$125), many recently refurbished, unimpressive exterior but atrium and very attractive public area roof-top nightclub, 9 restaurants incl excellent oriental cuisine in *Ran Malu* and western in *London Grill*, tennis, squash; **AL** ***Renaissance***, 115, C Gardiner Maw, Colombo 2, T 544200, F 449184, 358 rm (US$110), 5 speciality restaurants, casino and turkish bath, tennis, squash; **AL** ***Taj Samudra***, 25 Galle Face Rd, overlooking sea and Green, T 546622, F 446348, 400 rm (US$100, expensive suites), well designed, ideally situated in large well kept gardens; **A** ***Holiday Inn***, 30 Sir MM Markar Maw, T 422001, F 447977, 100 rm (US$60) in attractive Moghul style building, open-air pool and specialist *Alhambra Restaurant* for Muslim cuisine, *Golden Seer* for fish, rec; **A-B** ***Galle Face***, 2 Kollupitiya Rd, Colombo 3, T 541010, F 541072, 77 rm, much disliked by Edward Lear, who wrote in 1874 that it was "a very nasty, second-rate place, but now much improved!", old colonial room (US$65), modern room (US$45), quiet and best with sea-view (a splendid old-fashioned lift takes you up to your room but you have to walk down!), most bedrooms and reception rooms are enormous and lots of staff to cater for the guests' every need, restaurant food disappointing but is made up for by the atmosphere, indoor garden for breakfast and drinks, a nice pool overlooks the Indian Ocean, you can see Prince Philip's first car which he bought for £12 and imagine past glories in the ball room, travel desk arranges tours of island (eg 8-day car with driver visiting all main sites from Galle to Polonnaruwa, US$290 (Jo driver/guide specially rec); **C** ***Lake Lodge***, 20 Alvis Terrace, Colombo 3, T 326443, F 434997, 16 rm, 11 a/c (US$14 incl

breakfast), overlooking lake, quiet, very good value; **C** ***Ranmuthu***, 112 Galle Rd, Colombo 3, T 433968, 54 rm, pool; **D** ***Wayfarer's Inn***, 77 Rosmead Pl, Colombo 7, nr Town Hall, T 93936, some a/c rooms, restaurant, car hire, tours, pool, garden; **E** ***YWCA***, *Rotunda Guest House*, 7 Rotunda Gardens, Colombo 3, nr *Lanka Oberoi*, rooms with bath and dorms.

Kollupitiya, Bambalapitiya: **B** ***Havelock Tour Inn***, 20 Dickman's Rd, Bambalapitya, T 85251, charming, in quiet residential area, tropical garden and excellent restaurant, rec; **B** ***Renuka***, 328 Galle Rd, Colombo 3, T 573598, F 574137, 80 rm (US$40), basement *Palmyrah* restaurant serves good Sri Lankan curries; **C** ***Colombo House***, off Bagatelle Rd (nr Br Council), T 574900, large rooms (Rs 900) with bath, fan and terrace in a colonial house set in leafy suburb, reservation rec; **C** ***Duro***, 429 Kollupitiya Rd, T 85338, 27 rm; **C** ***Empress***, 383 RA de Mel Maw, Colombo 3, T 27205, 33 rm; **C** ***Sea View***, 15 Sea View Av, Colombo 3, T 573570, fairly large rooms but generally shabby and dirty – horrifc wiring, quiet, around large central courtyard, overpriced; **C** ***Skyways Tourist Inn***, 28 Cross Rd, off Ward Pl, Colombo 3, T 698313, some a/c rooms, restaurant, exchange, tours, pool; **D** ***Orchid Inn***, 571/6 Galle Rd, Colombo 6, T 83916; **E** ***Lanka Inns***, 239 Galle Rd, Colombo 4, T 84220; **F** ***Sri Lanka Youth Council***, 50 Haig Rd, Bambalipitiya, has basic dorm beds.

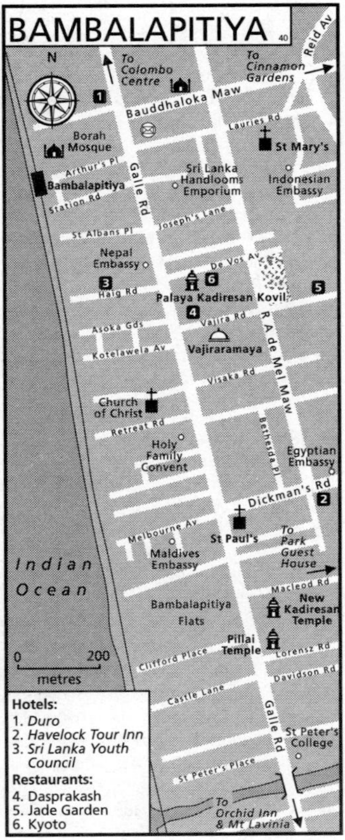

Welawatte and others: **C** ***Brighton***, 57 Ramakrishna Rd, Wellawatte, T 585211, 62 rm in a modern hotel on seafront close to railway line but away from busy road; **C** ***Ceylon Inns***, 501 Galle Rd, Wellawatte, T 580474, 74 rm some a/c, popular with tour groups, restaurant, bar, exchange, pool; **C** ***Sapphire***, 371 Galle Rd, Wellawatte, Colombo 6, T 583306, F 585455, 40 spacious rm mostly a/c (US$35), good beach nearby; **C** ***Silver Bird***, 382 Galle Rd, Wellawatte, T 83143, 50 rm.

Youth hostel: at 35/1 Horton Pl, Colombo 7, E of Viharamanadevi Park, affiliated to international YHA, some rooms and dorm, restaurant and cooking facilities.

● Places to eat

Some of the best restaurants are in hotels, but there is a wide range of restaurants outside. Chinese, Indian and continental specialties are all available. The list below contains some suggestions, but enquire locally for completely up-to-date advice.

Buffets: coffee shops in the city's top hotels offer a wide choice of dishes at lunch-time charging about Rs 300-350 plus tax (*Hilton* charges Rs 450); the *Inter-Continental* (rec) and the *Marriott* offer theirs' at a reduced rate if you choose not to have dessert. The venue gives you the added benefit of sitting in cool comfort during the hottest part of the day!

Chinese: ***Flower Drum***, Thurstan Rd, quiet atmosphere, excellent food, reasonable prices, rec; ***Jade Garden***, 126 Havelock Rd, Colombo 5; ***Kinjou***, 33 Amarsekera Maw, Colombo 5, opp BBC Grounds; ***Lotus Motel***, 265 Galle Rd, Colombo 3; ***Nanking***, 33 Chatham St, Colombo 1; ***Park View Lodge***, 70 Park St, Colombo 2; ***Peking Palace***, 3 Sellamuttu Ave, Colombo 3.

Continental: ***Alt Heidelberg***, 11 Galle Court 2, Colombo 3, German; ***Chasa***, Duplication

Rd, is Swiss, excellent dishes at a price (Rs 1,500); ***Da Guido***, 47/4 Dharmapala Maw, Colombo 7, Italian, excellent; ***Ginza Araliya***, 286 Galle Rd, Colombo 3, Italian; ***Max's San Remo Café***, 199 Union Pl, continental food with piano music at dinner, lounge cocktail bar, rec; ***The Fab***, Kolpiti, 474 Galle Rd, western food and excellent patisserie.

Fast foods: *Majestic City*, Galle Rd, has a new food park which brings together food from different continents; ***Max's San Remo Café***, 199 Union Pl, garden café with fast food, all day for cold drinks, ice creams, good value; ***Nectar***, Mudalige Maw, corner of York St, Fort for snacks, ice creams; ***Peera***, 217 Galle Rd, Colombo 3, for cakes, snacks, breads, mainly take-away; the Sri Lankan ***Vilasa Kitchen*** makes a feeble attempt to imitate a village home, is decorated with local clay pots and straw baskets.

Indian: *Kohinoor*, 49 Dharmapala Maw, Colombo 3; ***New Woodlands***, 108 York St, on the corner with Hospital St, is very good, rec; ***Palms***, 40 Galle Rd, Colombo 6, dosas and other Indian veg food, inexpensive; ***Saras Indian Restaurant***, 25 Charles Drive, Colombo 3.

Japanese: *Kyoto*, 19 De Vos Ave, Colombo 4; *Nippon*, 123, Kumaran Ratnam Rd, Colombo 2; ***Sakura***, 14 Rhineland Place, Kollupitya, Colombo 3.

Korean: *Ari Rang*, 16 Abdul Gafoor Maw, Colombo 3, with barbecues at tables, special eel dishes, also Chinese; ***Sam Gyup Sal*** and ***Sobul Gogi***, rec.

Philippino: the restaurant nr Fort railway station, behind the leather market, is rec.

Seafood: *Seafish*, 5 Sir C Gardiner Maw, Colombo 2, excellent fish, very reasonable prices, though lacks atmosphere, rec.

Sri Lankan: *Fountains*, Bridge St, Colombo 2, local and European food, excellent.

Vegetarian: for good vegetarian try ***Crowns***, next to *Laksala*, York St, S Indian style, simple, friendly, cheap.

● Bars

All the main hotels have bars.

● Airline offices

Aeroflot, 79/81 Hemas Bldg, York St, T 25580; **Air France**, 4 Leyden Bastion Rd, T 35333; **Airlanka**, 14 Sir Baron Jayatilleke Maw, T 21291; **British Airways**, *Ramada Renaissance Hotel*, 115 C Gardiner Maw, T 20231; **Cathay Pacific**, 94 York St, T 23048; **Emirates**, T 540709, *Meridien Hotel*, 64 Lotus Rd; **Ethiopian Airlines**, T 436724, and **TWA**, T 26611, 51 Janadhipathi Maw; **Gulf Air**, 11 York St, T 547627; **Indian Airlines and Maldives International**, 95 Sir Baron Jayatilleke Maw, T 26844; **Japan Airlines**, T 545480, and **KLM**, 61 Janadhipathi Maw, T 545531; **Lufthansa**, 8 Galle Face Rd, Colombo 3, T 35536; **Phillippine Airlines**, 41 Janadhipadhi Maw, T 44831; **PIA**, 432 Galle Rd, Colombo 3, T 573475; **Qantas**, 5 Upper Chatham St, T 20551; **Royal Nepal Airlines**, 434 Galle Rd, Colombo 3, T 24045; **SAS**, 16 Janadhipathi Maw, T 36201; **Singapore Airlines**, 15A Jayatilleke Maw, T 22711; **Thai International**, *Intercontinental Hotel*.

● Banks & money changers

Banks are usually open at 0900 and close 1300-1500, some branches open for Sat morning and have an evening service; most are closed on Sun, Poya days and national holidays. **Bank of Ceylon**, Bureau de Change, Gr Flr, York St, T 22730, 0900-1800, weekends and holidays 0900-1600. Also at New HQ Bldg, 1st Flr, Janadhipathi Maw, 0900-1300 Mon, 0900-1330 Tues-Fri. Airport counter, T 030 2424, open 24 hrs. Airlanka Office, GCEC Bldg, Sir Baron Jayatilleke Maw, issues TCs, daily 0900-1530. **People's Bank**, Foreign Branch, 27 MICH Bldg, Bristol St, T 20651, 0900-1330 Mon-Fri. Night Service at HQ Branch, Sir Chittampalam A Gardiner Maw, T 36948. **Card Centre**, 1st Flr, 20 CA Gardiner Maw, Colombo 2, T 434147.

● Cultural centres

Most have a library and reading room and have regular music and film programmes. ***Alliance Française***, 54 Ward Place, Colombo 7; ***British Council***, 49 Alfred House Gdns, Colombo 3, T 580301; ***Buddhist Cultural Centre***, 125 Anderson Rd, Nedimala, Deliwala, T 714256, F 723767, 8 km S of town centre, information, instruction and meditation by prior arrangement; ***Buddhist Information Centre***, 50 Ananda Coomaraswamy Maw; ***German (Geothe) Cultural Institute***, 39 Gregory's Rd, Colombo 7, T 694562, open 0900-1300, 1500-1700 weekdays; ***Soviet Cultural Centre***, 10 Independence Ave, Colombo 7, T 685429, open weekdays 0900-1700; ***USIS***, 44 Galle Rd, Colombo 3, T 332725, open Tues-Sat, 1000-1800.

● Embassies & consultate

Australia, 3 Cambridge Pl, T 59876; **Austria**, Colombo 2, T 91613; **Bangladesh**, Colombo 7, T 502397; **Canada**, 6 Gregory's Rd, T 595841; **France**, Colombo 5, T 583621; **Germany**, 40 Alfred House Av, T 580531; **India**, 18-3/1 Sir Baron Jayatilleke Maw, T 21604; **Indonesia**, 1 Police Park Terrace, T 580113; **Italy**, Colombo 5, T 588622; **Japan**, Colombo 7, T 93831; **Malaysia**, 63A Ward Pl, T 94837; **Maldives**, 25 Melbourne Av, T 586762; **Nepal**, Colombo 4, T 586762; **Netherlands**, 25 Torrington Av, T 589626; **Pakistan**, 211 De Saram Pl, T 596301; **Sweden,** 315 Vauxhall St, T 20201; **Thailand**, 26 Gregory's Rd, T 597406; **UK**, 190 Galle Rd, Colombo 3, T 27611; **USA**, Colombo 3, T 548007; **USSR**, Colombo 3, T 573555.

● Entertainment

Cinemas: the larger a/c cinemas along Galle Rd sometimes have English language films.

Cultural shows: performances of Sinhala dance and music can be seen at the YMBA Hall, Borella, Navarangahala, Cumaratunga Munidasa Maw, and at Lionel Wendt Hall, 19 Guildford Crescent both at Colombo 7. Lumbini Hall, Havelock Town specializes in Sinhalese theatre. Some top hotels put on regular folk dance shows and also have western flr shows and live music for dancing, open to non-residents.

● Hospitals & medical services

Chemists: a number on Galle Rd, Union Place, Pettah and Fort. ***State Pharmaceutical*** outlets at Hospital Junc, Colombo 7; Main St, Fort. Pharmacy attached to *Keells Supermarket*, Liberty Plaza, Dharmapala Maw, Kollupityia, quite reasonable prices (though expensive Sri Lankan standards).

Hospitals: *General Hospital*, Regent St, T 691111 (24-hr Accident and Emergency), Cardiology Unit, T 93059. Private hospitals incl *Nawaloka*, T 944444 (24-hr). *Ministry of Indigenous Medicine*, 385 Deans Rd, T 597345, has list of practitioners. Homeopathy and herbal medicine from *Govt Ayurvedic Hospital*, Cotta Rd, Borella, T 595855. *Siddhalepa Ayurveda Hospital*, Mt Lavinia (see below).

● Libraries

See Cultural Centres above. ***Colombo Public Library***, Ananda Coomaraswamy Maw, Colombo 7, T 695156, open daily except Wed and public holidays, 0800-1845, Rs 2 entry fee.

● Post & telecommunications

GPO: Janadhipathi Maw, Colombo 1; open 24 hrs for despatch, T 323140.

Poste Restante: will keep your mail (letters and packages) for 2 months.

Telegraph Office: Lower Chatham St, Colombo 1, T 331967.

Telephones: there are some International Direct Dialling centres outside hotels offering 24-hr service and far cheaper rates. One of the most accessible is in the Liberty Plaza, R.De Mel mawatha (Duplication Rd).

● Shopping

Most shops are open 1000-1900 on weekdays and 0845-1500 on Sat. Gemstones, batik, handlooms, silver jewellery, crafts (lac, reed, wood, brass, Demon dance masks, betel-nut boxes etc), spices and tea are best buys. You can shop with confidence at govt run shops although it may be interesting to wander in the bazaars and look for good bargains – ***Sunday Bazaar*** on Main St, Pettah and Duke St, Fort. The top hotels have good shopping arcades but prices are often higher than elsewhere.

Bookshops: good shops in the *Inter-Continental* and *Grand Oriental* Hotels. ***Cultural Bookshop***, 34 Malay St, Colombo 3, has a wide selection; ***Lakehouse***, 100 Sir C Gardiner Maw, particularly good for art books; ***KVJ de Silva***, 415 Galle Rd, Colombo 4; ***MD Gunasena***, Olcott Maw, Colombo 11; ***Vijitha Yapa Bookshop***, 376 Galle Rd, Colombo 3, is rec; others on Sir Baron Jayatilleke Maw, Fort. Second-hand books from ***Ashok Trading***, 183 Galle Rd, Colombo 4 and antiquarian from ***Serendib***, 100 Galle Rd. ***Children's Bookshop***, 20 Bogala Bldg, Janadhipathi Maw, nr Fort clocktower for Sri Lankan music cassettes. Books on Buddhism from ***Buddhist Information Centre***, 50 Ananda Coomaraswamy Maw, Colombo 7. ***Travel Information Centre***, 78 Steuart Pl, Colombo 3, has cassettes of words and music on pilgrim sites, booklets on the ancient cities, posters and picture post cards.

Gemstones, silver and gold: articles should only be bought at reputable shops – eg arcades in the top hotels (*Hotel Lanka Oberoi* rec). ***Premadasa***, 17 Sir Baron Jayatilleke Maw and 20 Duke St, Colombo 1; ***Zam Gems***, 81 Galle Rd, Colombo 4 with a few branches; ***Janab***, 9 Temple Lane, Colombo 3. Sea St in Pettah has a number of private jewellers; ***Hemchandra***, 229 Galle Rd, Colombo 3. ***State Gem Corpn*** sales section at the *Gem Exchange*, 310 Galle

SPORTS MAD SRI LANKA!

Sri Lankans are as sports mad as their neighbours in India. Cricket is the national sport and something that is given a high profile. Victories over New Zealand and Pakistan as well as de Silva playing for Kent for £50,000 in 1995 all did much for its image. During test matches, groups cluster around radios and TVs and people will try to take holidays so that they can watch them. Children are taught it from an early age. The season is from Jan to Apr. Most of the larger towns have pitches.

Cricket is not the only obsession. Football (soccer) is becoming increasingly popular, and there is much talk of national and international events, such as the BRISTOL SAARC Cup – a South Asian football festival held annually in March. India, Sri Lanka, Pakistan and Bhutan took place tin 1995.

Even rugby football is played in the highlands, which are quite a popular destination with overseas club and provincial sides. However, given their size, it is not surprising that the Sri Lankans have difficulty in putting out representative sides.

Rd which has several wholesalers and retailers; their laboratory on the 2nd flr, will test gems free (you have to pay about US$2 for a certificate), Mon-Fri, 0830-1630 (closed for lunch).

Handloom and handicrafts: Govt outlets incl ***Laksala***, Australia House, York St, Colombo 1 which carries a wide range. Other branches in Galle Face and Bambalapitiya. Open 0900-1700, except Sat and Sun, Apr-Oct. ***Viskam Niwasa*** (Department of Industries), Bauddhaloka Maw, Colombo 7 also has high quality craft goods. ***Handloom Shop***, 71 Galle Rd, Colombo 4. ***Ceylon Ceramics Corpn*** showroom in Bambalapitiya also has terracotta ware. ***Lakmedura***, 113 Dharmapala Maw, Colombo 7. For good batiks try ***Serendib***, 100 Galle Rd, Colombo 4, ***Fantasy Lanka***, 302 (1st Flr), Unity Plaza, 2 Galle Rd, Colombo 4, ***Barbara Sansoni***, Galle Rd, Bambalipitiya and ***Ena de Silva***, Duplication Rd, Kollupitiya.

Maps: *Survey Department*, *Map Sales Branch*, Kirula Rd, Narahenpita and *Map Sales Centre*, York St, Colombo 1.

Photography: numerous in town. ***Hayleys***, 303 Galle Rd, Colombo 3 offers special 1 hr service.

Shopping complexes: *Liberty Plaza* on Dharmapala Maw, Kollupitiya, ***World Market***, nr Fort Railway Station, ***Majestic City*** and ***Unity Plaza*** on Galle Rd. ***Duty Free Complex*** at Katunayake International Airport stocks the usual articles, to be paid for in foreign currency and noted in your passport. City shop on Galle Rd, Kollupitiya. Shops in the **Fort** tend to be good but more expensive than equally good quality items in Kollupitiya. Boutiquesin **Pettah** are worth a visit too. ***The Philatelic Bureau***, 4th Flr, Ceylinco House, Janadhipathi Maw, Fort has a good stock of stamps.

Supermarkets: ***Keells*** at Liberty Plaza, Dharmapala Maw, Kollupitiya – a very modern supermarket – (you can even pay by credit card); ***Cornell's*** nr the Duty Free Centre. Also ***Mlesna Tea Centre***, Liberty Plaza; ***Sri Lanka Tea Board***, 574 Galle Rd, Colombo 3; ***YWCA Spice Shop***, Union Pl.

● Sports

Visitors may take out temporary membership at various local clubs.

Golf: *Royal Colombo Golf Club*, Model Farm Rd, Colombo 8. Temporary membership.

Rowing: Colombo Rowing Club, C Gardiner Maw, Colombo 2 (entrance opp Lake House Bookshop), T 433758. Temp membership.

Squash: at the *Oberoi*, *Intercontinental*, *Taj Samudra* and *Ramada* Hotels. Also at ***Gymkhana Club***, 31 Maitland Crescent, Colombo 7, and Sri Lanka Ladies Squash Assoc, T 696256.

Swimming: *Colombo Swimming Club*, Storm Lodge, Galle Rd, Colombo 3, ***Kinross Swimming & Lifesaving Club***, 10 Station Ave, Wellawatte, and leading hotels allow temporary membership.

Tennis: at major hotels.

Watersports: ***Aqua Tours***, 108 Rosemead Place, Colombo 7, T 695170. ***Underwater Safaris*** 25 Barnes Place, Colombo 7, T 694255.

Yachting: *Royal Colombo Yacht Club*, welcomes experienced sailors.

● Tour companies & travel agents

Aitken Spence, 13 Sir Baron Jayatilleke Maw, Colombo 1; *Aset*, 315 Vauxhall St, Colombo 2, T 440480 for excellent car hire and tour service; *Ceylon Tours*, Colombo 2, T 21722; *Cox & Kings*, Colombo 2, T 34295; *Gemini Tours*, 40 Wijerama Maw, Colombo 7, T 598446; *Jetwing*, 503 Union Place, Colombo 2, T 689192, F 699226; *Paradise Holidays*, 5 Palmyra Ave, Colombo 3, T 380106; *Thomas Cook*, 15 Sir Baron Jayatilleke Maw, T 445971, F 436533 and 245C Galle Rd, Bambalapitiya, T 580141, F 580275; *Walkers Tours*, 130 Glennie St, Colombo 2, T 421101, F 439026.

● Tourist offices

TIC, Ceylon Tourist Board, 78 Steuart Pl Colombo 3, T 437059, F 437953, open 0830-1615, Mon-Fri, 0830-1230, Sat, free literature in English, German, French, Italian, Swedish and Japanese to personal callers, guide service arranged, tickets and permits for ancient archaeological sites; **The Railway Tourist Office** provides a very helpful service for journey details covering the island, T 435838.

● Useful addresses

Automobile Association of Ceylon: 40 Sir MM Markar Maw, Galle Face, Colombo 3, T 21528.

Central Cultural Fund (Cultural Triangle): 212 Bauddhaloka Maw, Colombo 7, T 500733, F 500731.

Department of Archaeology: Marcus Fernando Maw, Colombo 7.

Department of Immigration and Emigration: Marine Drive, Colombo 1, T 436353.

Department of Small Industries: 71 Galle Rd, Colombo 4, T 501209.

Forest Department: Rajamalwatta Rd, T 566631.

Investment Promotion Department: Greater Colombo Economic Commission, PO Box 1768, 14 Sir Baron Jayatileke Maw, Colombo 1, T 22447.

Ministry of Cultural Affairs (for visiting archaeological sites): Malay St, Colombo 2, T 587912. Open 0830-1615.

Police: T 433333. Police Station, S of Maradana Railway Station, Kollupitya, Bambalapitya and Wellawatte.

Tourist Police: Fort Police Station, Bank of Ceylon Maw, Fort, T 433744.

Wildlife Department: 493, TB Jaya Maw, Colombo 10, T 687347.

● Transport

Local Bus: good network of buses and mini-buses. Ceylon Transport Board (CTB), private and mini-buses compete on popular routes. Local CTB buses have white signs, yellow for long-distance. Central Bus Stand, Olcott Maw, SE corner of Pettah. **Car hire**: Avis, Hertz and Europcar are represented in town and also at the airport. **Europcar**, International airport, T 452388, F 575662. Self-drive cars for 25-65 year olds are available, though it is easier (and safer!) to have a chauffeur-driven car charged at a similar rate; Rs 14/kilometre or about US$40/day incl fuel and driver for out-of-town excursions. In 1995, petrol was about Rs 40/litre; diesel is much cheaper. Excellent car hire (usually Japanese cars) and tour service from *Aset*, 315 Vauxhall St, Colombo 2, T 440480, F 335520, efficient, providing 24-hr service; *Ceylon Tours*, Colombo 2, T 21722; *Mackinnons* (Avis), 4 Leyden Bastian Rd, Colombo 1, T 29881; *Aban Tours* (Europcar), 498 Galle Rd, Colombo 3, T 574160. *Inter Rent and Dollar*, Mercantile Tours, 51 Janadhipathi Maw, T 28708; *JJ & A Ltd*, 21 Modera St, Colombo 15, T 522282, F 575599; *Mercantile Tours*, 586 Galle Rd, Colombo 3, T 501946; *Quickshaw's* (Hertz), 3 Kalinga Place, Colombo 5, T 583133; *Sudans*, 18-1/2 Mudalige Maw, T 431 865 or at Airport; they will also arrange holidays in the Maldives. **Motorbike/bike hire**: *Gold Wing Motors*, 346 Deans Rd, Colombo 10. T 685750, F 698787, rental on daily, weekly or monthly terms. *Rent a Bike*, T 685750. **Taxis**: metered taxis have yellow tops and red-on-white number plates. Make certain that the driver has understood where you wish to go and fix a rate for long-distance travel. Radio cabs are more expensive having a higher min charge, but are fixed price and are reliable; they are available at the airport and in town. *Ace Radio Cabs*, T 501502; *Quick Cabs*, 911/1 Galle Rd, Colombo 4, T 502888, 24 hrs, no extra for 15 km of city, special rates for return trips of 60+ km. Min charge about Rs 30, extra km Rs 22. **Trains** (suburban): services to Bambalapitya, Kollupitiya, Dehiwala and Mt Lavinia all along the Galle Rd from the Fort Station, SW corner of Pettah. Airport Express, Enquiries T 687037. **3-wheelers** (no longer called trishaws, autos or autorickshaws): these are cheapest but have no meters so negotiate price before starting, normally to about 60/70% of asking price. Radio 3-wheelers are cheaper, charge a fixed

Colombo's Straggling Suburbs – A Traveller's Woe

Nearly 200 years ago the Rev James Cordiner, describing the road out of Colombo in 1807, wrote that "all the roads, in their commencement from the Pettah, are streets of a straggling village, having houses on each side extending to a considerable distance inland". A recent traveller's description suggests that little has changed, except that today modern traffic has been added to the congestion of narrow streets and straggling village houses: "Leaving Colombo was a hot and rather tedious business. Heavy traffic on the **A1** together with chaotic driving – minibuses, buses, cars, bicycles, cattle and people all conspiring to confuse and disorientate. At least the Indian-made small lorries are smoke-free, as there are strict Govt standards on emission, and they look far smarter than their Indian relatives, with often beautifully varnished wooden sides. Obtaining petrol or diesel can be a problem for those self-driving: there are comparatively few filling stations, all of which were overflowing with traffic. Great patience is needed. We were never quite sure when we actually left Colombo as the A1 seemed to be built up for many miles".

price and are reliable. **Warning** Beware of pickpockets on public transport.

Air International Airport, Katunayake, T 452861. TIC, 030 2411 (Flight times, day and night). Ratmalana Airport, T 716261. **Transport to town**: to Colombo: Airport Express Bus, T 687037, 24 hrs, one-way, a/c, Rs 500; minibus shuttles are cheaper. Commuter trains between Colombo and Negombo go via the airport. Radio cabs are available (see above). To Negombo: several hotels and guest houses willl arrange a pick-up; also see page 164. *Upali Travels* charter helicopter services to places of interest and resort hotels and charter aircraft for domestic airports. Air Taxi Ltd flies 5 passengers on Cessna aircraft and helicopters with landing facilities at Batticaloa, Hingurakgoda, Vavuniya, Anuradhapura, Kankesanthurai, Koggala, Sigiriya, Amparai, Puttalam, Katunayake and Trincomalee. Contact *Thomas Cook*, 15 Sir Baron Jayatilleke Maw, Colombo 1, T 545971. Helicopter hire enquiries, T 320465.

Train Trains to all important places of interest on 3 separate lines. Enquiries (express and commuter trains), T 434215. Airport Express, Enquiries T 687037. For foreign travellers, the Railway Tourist Office, T 435838, is particularly useful. **Anuradhapura**: *Yal Devi*, 77, daily, 0545, 4 hrs; *Rajarata Rajini*, 85, daily, 1405, 4¾ hrs. **Bandarawela**: *Podi Menike*, 5, daily, 0555, 7½ hrs; *123 Express*, daily, 0945, 8 hrs; *Colombo-Kandy Mail*, 45, daily, 2015, 8¼ hrs. **Galle**: (no 1st class on this service), 50, daily, 0730, 2¾ hrs; 52, daily, 0845, 2¾ hrs; *Galu Kumari*, 56, daily, 1335, 2¾ hrs; 775, daily, 1915, 3¼ hrs. **Kandy**: *Podi Menike*, 5, daily, 0555, 2¾ hrs; *Intercity Express*, 9, daily, 0655, 2½ hrs; *Intercity Express*, 29, daily, 1535, 2½ hrs. **Matara**: (no 1st class on this service), 50, daily, 0730, 4½ hrs; 52, daily, 0845, 4½ hrs; *Galu Kumari*, 56, daily, 1335, 4½ hrs. **Nanu-Oye (Nuwara Eliya)**: *Podi Menike*, 5, daily, 0555, 7½ hrs; *123 Express*, daily, 0945, 6 hrs; *Colombo-Kandy Mail*, 45, daily, 2015, 8 hrs. **Polonnaruwa**: *Udaya Devi*, 79, daily, 0605, 6½ hrs; *Mail*, 93, daily, 2000, 7½ hrs. Special a/c Hitachi trains for day tours to Kandy and Hikkaduwa. Inter-city Expresses to Kandy and Bandarawela. Occasional tours on vintage steam trains – details from the Railway Tourist Office, Fort Station, T 435838.

Road Bus: the Sri Lanka Transport Board has a good island-wide network and travel is cheap. Principal towns have an Express Service every 30 mins; Regular buses leave every 15 mins from Pettah and a fast Inter-city service operates to Kandy. Frequent services to Kandy, Galle, Ratnapura, Anuradhapura, Kurunegala, Matara. Eight buses daily to Kataragama, 2 to Medawachchiya. Minibuses also leave from the bus stop and from the railway station. Central Bus Stand, Olcott Maw, Pettah. Enquiries T 328081.

Short excursions from Colombo

It can make a pleasant change from the congestion of central Colombo to visit the beach at **Negombo** or **Mt Lavinia** (see below), either for the day or for a short break. Many travellers opt to stay outside the capital altogether. See below.

THE WESTERN AND SOUTHERN PROVINCES

Contents

Colombo to the Ruhunu-Yala National Park: the coastal route 112
Colombo to Ratnapura and Bandarawela 141
Colombo to Kandy 149
Colombo to Kurunegala and Anuradhapura: the western route 154
Colombo to Negombo, Puttalam and the Wilpattu National Park 157

Maps

Western and Southern provincces 110-111
Mt Lavinia 112
Hikkaduwa Area 117
Hikkaduwa Beach 118
Galle 121
Unawatuna 126
Weligama 127
Matara and Polhena 129
Tangalla 129
Hambantota 134
Hambantota to Tissamaharama and Kataragama 136-137
Ratnapura 143
Peradeniya Botanical Gardens 151
Kurunegala 154
Kurunegala Area 155
Negombo Town 158
Negombo Beach 160

Introduction

The heart of the western and southern provinces is the Wet Zone, but they stretch from the driest regions of the coast to the north of Colombo right round to Ruhunu-Yala National Park on the even drier south-easternmost coast. It is the region most strongly influenced by successive European colonial powers, the Portuguese leaving an imprint still visible on the region's religious complexion and the Dutch and the British on its economic and political life as well as some of its most important social features.

Today the western and southern provinces are also the most densely populated region in Sri Lanka. Inland of some of the world's most beautiful beaches for which the southwest coast is justly famous small rice holdings are interspersed with coconut and rubber plantations, while tea estates stretch from the highlands almost down to the coast just inland of Hikkaduwa. But it is the beaches themselves which are the most famous attraction, frequent long stretches of silver sand lined with coconut palms, sometimes narrow spits of land wedged between the sea on one side and quiet lagoons on the other. Some of the international class hotels which are the first destination of many visitors to Sri Lanka now occupy prime positions, but the region has much to explore beyond the beaches. Good roads also connect the main towns of the south and southwest coasts with the Central Highlands, making the provinces easily accessible to the Central Highlands themselves.

The Western and Southern provinces comprise North Western Province, Western Province, Sabaragamuwa, and Southern Province.

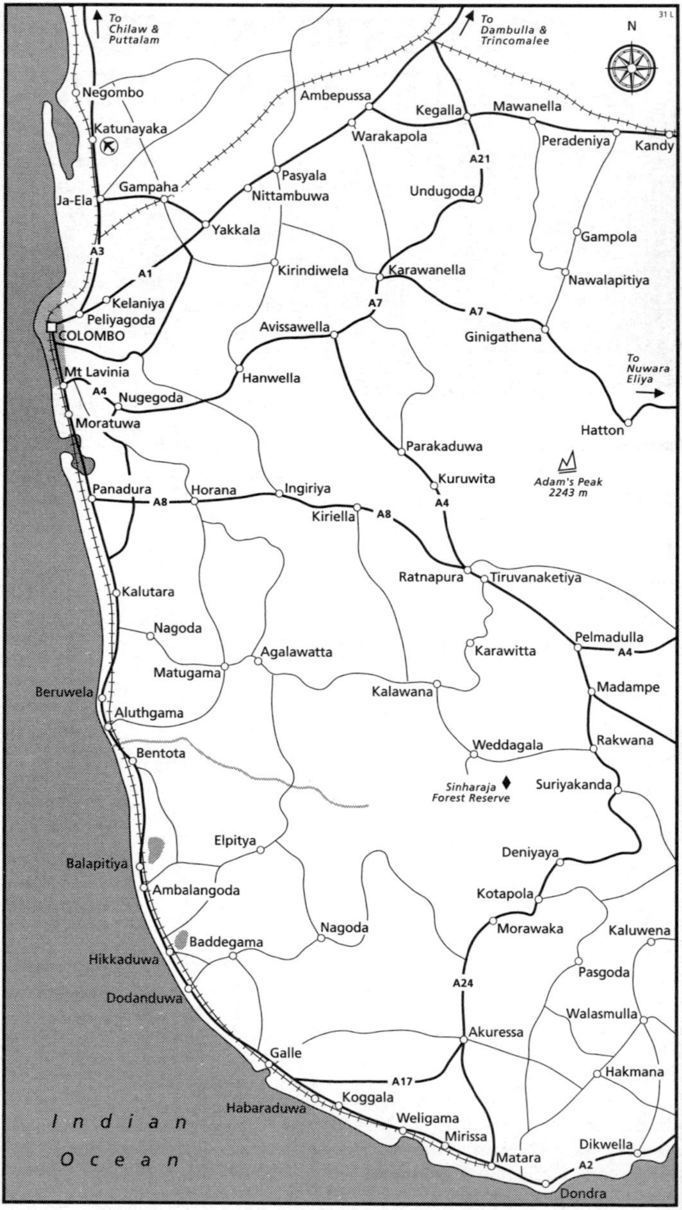
To Chilaw & Puttalam
To Dambulla & Trincomalee
N
Negombo
Katunayaka
Ja-Ela
Gampaha
A3
A1
Kelaniya
Peliyagoda
COLOMBO
Mt Lavinia
A4
Nugegoda
Moratuwa
Panadura
A8
Horana
Ingiriya
Kiriella
Kalutara
Nagoda
Matugama
Agalawatta
Beruwela
Aluthgama
Bentota
Elpitya
Balapitiya
Ambalangoda
Nagoda
Baddegama
Hikkaduwa
Dodanduwa
Galle
A17
Habaraduwa
Koggala
Weligama
Mirissa
Matara
Dondra
A2
Dikwella
Indian Ocean
Ambepussa
Warakapola
Kegalla
Mawanella
Peradeniya
Kandy
A21
Undugoda
Pasyala
Nittambuwa
Yakkala
Kirindiwela
Karawanella
A7
Gampola
Nawalapitiya
Avissawella
Ginigathena
Hanwella
To Nuwara Eliya
Hatton
Parakaduwa
Kuruwita
Adam's Peak 2243 m
Ratnapura
Tiruvanaketiya
Pelmadulla
Karawitta
Kalawana
Madampe
Weddagala
Rakwana
Sinharaja Forest Reserve
Suriyakanda
Deniyaya
Kotapola
Morawaka
Kaluwena
A24
Pasgoda
Walasmulla
Akuressa
Hakmana

Cottages near Galle
Illustratedby Rev W Urwick in 1885

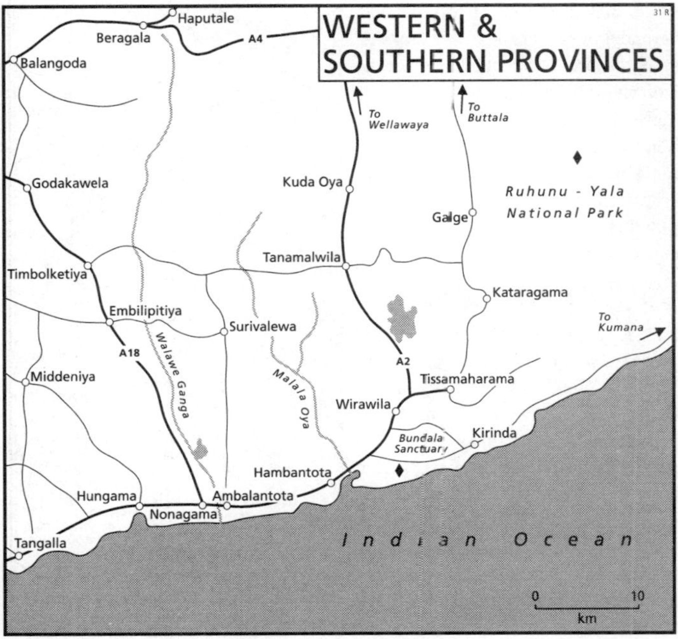

COLOMBO TO THE RUHUNU-YALA NATIONAL PARK: THE COASTAL ROUTE

The A2 S of Colombo follows close to the coast, with its magnificent bays and sandy beaches. It is a wholly distinctive drive, contrasting sharply with the routes into and through the hills or across the Dry Zone of the N and E. Some of the beaches are now developed, but even so they retain their largely rural settings. The railway line hugs the ocean as it goes S and is an exhilarating journey. The journey S is recommended.

The coastal area to the S is one of the most densely populated parts of the island. Many people depend on fishing, and every day fishermen bring in their catch at numerous points along the coast. The coconut palms that also line the shore all the way down to Galle and beyond provide fibre for local use as well as for export. The route also gives the most vivid impression in Sri Lanka of the transition from the Wet Zone to the Dry Zone, for the 20 km or so between Weligama and Dikwella the annual rainfall drops from over 3,500 mm a year to under 1,000 mm, with a corresponding contrast in vegetation.

Mt Lavinia

Galle Rd continues S to Mt Lavinia, one of the most popular excursions just 13 km from Colombo, and 3 km beyond the Dehiwala zoo. It takes its name from a corruption of the Sinhalese 'Lihinia Kanda' – *gull rock*. An attractive picnic spot, the original *Mt Lavinia Hotel* was Governor Edward Barnes' weekend retreat. He was forced to sell the house by the Government in England who approved neither the expenditure nor the luxurious style.

Local information

● Accommodation

A *Mount Lavinia*, T 715221, F 715228, 185 a/c rm (US$80), 40 non a/c rm cheaper, once British Governor's residence, now radically renovated and extended, massive white building – enormous public rooms, labryinthine corridors, excellent terrace with pool overlooking the ocean which gets blisteringly hot, guests avoid the indifferent, seedy beach,

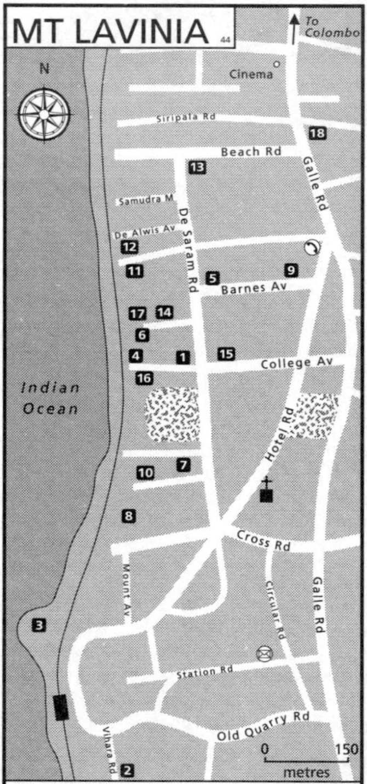

Hotels:
1. *Cottage Gardens*
2. *Lak-Mahal's Inn*
3. *Mount Lavinia*
4. *Mount Royal Beach*
5. *Mt Lavinia Inn*
6. *Oceanview*
7. *Palm Beach*
8. *Ranveli Holiday Village*
9. *Ratna Inn*
10. *Riviras & Saltaire*
11. *Sea Breeze Tour Inn*
12. *Shore Lanka Beach Inn*
13. *Sunray Beach Villas*
14. *Super Mount Rest*
15. *Tropic Inn*

Restaurants:
16. Connie's
17. Frankfurt Lavinia Beer Garden
18. Mount Grill

good evening buffet meals, good bar and shops; **A** *Mount Royal Beach*, 36 College Av, T 714001, F 713030, 90 a/c rm, private beach huts, pool, railway line behind can be a little noisy for some.

B *Lak Mahal's Inn*, 8 Vihara Rd, T/F 734848, German restaurant with rooms; **B** *Palm Beach*, 52 De Saram Rd, T 717484, F 712713, 50 rm, 10 a/c (US$35), restaurant, bar, exchange, pool, tennis; **B** *Ranwali Holiday Village*, T 031 2136, 84 rm.

C *Mt Lavinia Inn*, De Saram Av, mainly package tour groups; **C** *Ratna Inn*, Barnes Av, large, quiet family house, friendly; **C** *Riviras*, 50/2 De Saram Rd, T 717786, F 575294, 50 rm, some a/c (US$30) with bath (tub), villa style; **C** *Saltaire*, 50/5 De Saram Rd, T 717731, F 575294, wooden cabanas, in a large garden nr the sea, typical package hotel; **C** *Sea Breeze Tour Inn*, De Saram Rd, T 714017, 23 rm; **C** *Tropic Inn*, 6 College Inn Av, 16 small dark rm, overpriced.

D *Blue Whale Guest House*, De Seram Rd, expensive rooms (Rs 550) dirty sheet, no net, filthy, expensive and unpleasant; **D** *Cottage Gardens*, 42 College Av, T 713059, 3 bungalows (Rs 700) in small garden; **D** *Oceanview*, along railway line from Royal Beach; **D** *Shore Lanka Beach Inn*, De Alwis Av, slightly cheaper than others in the category; **D** *Sunray Beach Villas*, 3 De Saram Rd, T 716272, 3 rm (Rs 550) in a comfortable house with garden, meals available.

Budget hotels: on the seaward side of Galle Rd, S of St Mary's Church, there is some **E** category accommodation. **E** *Super Mount Rest*, De Seram Rd, T 811289, 7 rm with bath, net and fan (Rs 350), quiet, popular with travellers.

● Places to eat

Various restaurants advertise Bratwürst as a speciality. *Connie's Restaurant* is very popular for pizza, pasta and seafood; *Frankfurt Lavinia Beer Garden*, 34/8 De Saram Rd, Germam specialities, serves good European food, but expensive at around Rs 700/head.

● Hospitals & medical services

Ayurvedic treatment: *Siddhalepa Ayurveda Hospital*, 106 Templer's Rd, Mt Lavinia, T 722524, F 725465, herbal and ayurvedic health programmes incl herbal/steam baths and massage, large a/c rooms with TV, about Rs 2,500 for 3 days (2 nights) incl treatment.

ROUTES Continue on the **A2** S of Colombo, from Mount Lavinia to **Moratuwa** (28 km), noted for its furniture making and its college. Cross the 300m wide river Kalu Ganga ('Black River') to **Panadura**, see page 142, and Kalutara.

Kalutara

(24 km; 42 km from Colombo; *STD Code* 034) The Portuguese built a fort on the site of a Buddhist temple, the Dutch took it over and the British agent converted it to his residence. It now has a Buddhist shrine again. Wild hog deer, introduced by the Dutch from the Ganga Delta, are reputedly still found. The centre of the arrack industry, Kalutara is known for its basket making. Leaves of the wild date are dyed red, orange, green and black, and woven into hats and baskets. The area is also famous for its mangosteen fruit, and graphite is mined.

Kalutara has a huge stretch of fine sand.

● Accommodation AL *Tangerine Beach*, T 22640, F 22794, 166 a/c rm (US$80), beautifully laid out, enormous lawn stretches beneath the coconut palms to the sea; **A** *Hibiscus Beach*, Mahawaskaduwa, T 22704, F Colombo 433755, 48 a/c rm (US$37), more modest than some, but pleasantly laid out.

Beruwela

(16 km further S; *STD Code* 034) Derived from the Sinhalese word Baeruala (the place where the sail is lowered), is on the spot where the first Muslim settlers are believed to have landed. The Kitchimalai mosque, on a headland, is worth seeing; it is a major pilgrimage centre at the end of Ramadan. You can also go out to the lighthouse raised on a small island offshore. There is an excellent view of the coastline from the top. Most of the upmarket hotels are in Moragalla and cater for package tours, many from Germany.

● Accommodation AL *Bayroo*, T 76297, 101 a/c (US$90); **AL** *Eden*, is the newest in this category with 158 rm in 2 wings enclosing a large pool; **AL** *Neptune*, T 76031 or Colombo 326767, 104 a/c rm (US$75), beach

Returning home from a hog hunt from Kincaid, D (1938) *British social life in India*, Routledge, London.

and shady trees; **A** *Wornels Reef*, T/F 76041, 119 rm, most a/c (US$60), shaded garden fronting beach; **A** *Tropical Villas*, T/F 76156, 54 suites set in gardens around pool, not directly on beach; **B** *Barberyn Reef*, T 76036, F 76037, 66 rm, 5 a/c (US$40), cottage style without views, self catering possible, ayurvedic centre; **B-C** *Swanee*, 3 km from centre, 50 decent rm, mostly a/c with balcony on upper flrs, shady garden around pool; **C** *Ypsylon*, T 76132, 25 rm (Rs 1,000), restaurant, garden, diving school with German instructor. **Budget hotels**: **E** *Berlin Bear*, Maradana Rd opp the lighthouse, T 76525, 12 reasonable rm (Rs 450), pool; **E** *Rest House*, with view of the harbour and mosque on quiet village road away from tourist hotels, pleasant.

• **Useful addresses Tourist Police**: Galle Rd, Moragalla.

ROUTES The road and railway continue S to Aluthgama.

Aluthgama (5 km; *STD Code* 34) is the main bus and railway station for the beaches to both Beruwela to the N and Bentota to the S. The town is famous for its oysters, and as a weekend resort from Colombo. **Accommodation D** *Terrena Lodge*, Manju Sri Maw (River Ave), by the bridge, T 75001, 5 clean rm (Rs 800) opening on to terrace and riverside garden, good food, excellent service, Austrian management, location can be noisy, otherwise highly rec. There are some hotels and guest houses on Galle Rd at Kaluwamodara; several are more expensive than the Terrena.

Bentota

(3 km S; *STD Code* 034) The resort is built entirely for foreign tourists as a

specially designed National Holiday Resort, a beach complex with shops and cultural activities mainly catering for groups. The sand spit which separates the river from the sea where most of the hotels are built provides excellent waters for wind surfing and sailing. A full range of watersports is available plus tennis, mini golf, swimming pool etc. The sea is best between Oct and Apr; it is rough during the monsoons. River trips inland are best arranged through the hotel. The **Turtle Research Project** here welcomes visitors, entry Rs 50.

Excursions

From Aluthgama or Bentota, the road inland leads to Dharga (8 km) and a track further 2 km through rubber plantations takes you to the splendid **'Brief Garden'** laid out in 1929 by Bevis Bawa the landscape architect and sculptor. His private collection of paintings, sculptures, photographs and furniture (many colonial antiques) provides an added incentive to visiting the bird-filled landscaped garden with many mature specimen trees.

Local information

● Accommodation

Prices are considerably inflated in high season (mid-Dec to end-Mar) with top class hotels rising from about US$75 to $100.

AL *Bentota Beach*, nr the river bridge, T 75176, F Colombo 447087, 133 rm, extensive gardens, luxurious layout; **AL** *Ceysands*, between sea and Bentota River, approached by ferry, T 75073, F Colombo 447087, 84 a/c rm, beautifully built, floating disco and good food; **AL** *Robinson Club*, Paradise Island, T 75167, F 75172, 150 rm (US$125), in pagoda style buildings in tropical gardens, formerly private club now largely German package tour clientele.

A *Lihiniya Surf* (CHC), opp Bentota railway station, T 75126, F 75486, reservation T Colombo 323501, F 422732, 86 a/c rm (US$78) with the feel of a dated beach-side motel.

B *Club Villa*, 138/15 Galle Rd, off the main road, Mohotti Walauwa, T 75312, F 22530, 6 non-a/c rm (US$40), individually and tastefully decorated in large 19th century Dutch style villa, peaceful palm-shaded garden, small pool, direct access to beach, good service; further S, across Galle Rd, **B** *Warahena Walauwa*, Warahena, 2 km from Bentota, 3 mins from beach, 20 pleasant a/c rm around courtyards in old Dutch-style buildings furnished with antiques, reasonable restaurant.

● Places to eat

Outside hotels, *Sea View* behind *Bentota Beach Hotel*, National Holiday Resort Complex, no sea-view but a garden; good food all day especially sea-food and rice dishes, within walking distance of many hotels.

● Useful addresses

Tourist Police: Police Station, National Holiday Resort, T 75022.

ROUTES From Bentota to Galle the road is nearly always in sight of the sea.

Induruwa (5 km S; *STD Code* 034), has a pleasant stretch of beach and a **turtle** hatchery. **Accommodation** S from the railway station: **B-C** *Emerald Bay* on the beach, T 75363, 24 comfortable rm (US$30) with terrace, 4 a/c, restaurant, large garden, pool; **C** *Dream Cottage*, nearby, T 75186, 6 pleasant rm, Sri Lankan and continental meals to order; **D** *Long Beach Cottage*, N of the station, T 01 727602 (Mon-Fri), 5 clean sea-facing rm with fan, net and bath (Rs 500), local dishes and seafood to order, mangrove-shaded garden, Sri Lankan/German couple.

Kosgoda (*STD Code* 09), just S of Bentota has **AL** *Kosgoda Beach Resort*, T 54017 between sea and lagoon, rooms with open-air showers, lovely pool, excellent restaurant, the beach here attracts turtles.

Ahungalla (*STD Code* 09), a further 6 km S, has one of the region's most luxurious hotels at the **AL** *Triton*, in coconut groves, T 54041, 125 rm, superb in every detail on excellent beach; also, aimed at Austrian/German tourists, **AL** *Lotus Villa*, T 54082, F 54083, an exclusive, beachside villa with 14 rm, Austrian speciality restaurant, ayurvedic and herbal therapy, boating etc.

DANCE OF THE SORCERERS

The **Devil Dance** evolved from the rural people's need to appease malevolent forces in nature and seek blessing from good spirits when there was an evil spirit to be exorcised, ie a sickness to be cured. It takes the form of a ritual dance, full of high drama, with a sorcerer 'priest' and an altar. As evening approaches, the circular arena in the open air is lit by torches, and masked dancers appear to the beating of drums and chanting. During the exorcism ritual, which lasts all night, the 'priest' casts the evil spirit out of the sick. There are 18 demons associated with afflictions for which different fearsome *sanni* masks are worn and although there is an element of awe and grotesqueness about the whole performance, the audience is treated to occasional light relief. These dances have a serious purpose and are, therefore, not on offer as 'performances'.

The **Kolam Dance** has its origins in folk theatre. The story tells of a Queen, who, while expecting a child, had a deep craving to see a masked dance. This was satisfied by the Carpenter of the Gods, Visvakarma, who invented the dances.

The Kolam dances tell stories and again make full use of a wonderful variety of masks (often giant size) representing imaginary characters from folk tales, Buddhist *jatakas*, gods and devils, as well as well-known members of the royal court and more mundane figures from day-to-day life. Animals (lions, bears) too, feature as playful characters. This form of folk dance resembles the more serious Devil Dance in some ways – it is again performed during the night and in a similar circular, torch-lit, open air 'stage' (originally Kolam was performed for several nights during New Year festivities). Inspite of a serious or moral undertone, a sprinkling of cartoon characters are introduced to provide comic relief. The clever play on words can only be really appreciated by a Sinhalese.

Ambalangoda (*STD Code* 09) is the home of **Devil Dancing** and **masks** making which many families have carried out for generations. It may be possible to watch a performance of Kolam dance.

Traditional masks worn for dancing, using vegetable colours instead of the brighter chemical paints, are available on the N edge of the town. Masks sell from around Rs 400 to a few thousand rupees; traditional masks are more expensive. The colourful fish-market is worth visiting early in the morning.

Ariyapala Mask Museum, 426 Patabendimulla, 0730-1700. You can watch craftsmen at work carving traditional masks from the light *kaduru* (nux vomica) wood and buy them. The masks can be very elaborate, eg the *naga raksha* mask from the *Raksha Kolama* has a fearsome face with bulging eyes that roll around, a bloodthirsty tongue hanging from a mouth lined witzh fanglike teeth, all topped by a set of cobra hoods.

Further reading *The Ambalangoda Mask Museum*, ed by W Mey and others, Ambalongoda, Mask Museum Council, 1987.

• **Accommodation** **D** *Princess Guest House*, 418 Main St, Patabendimulla, nr Museum, 5 rm, Good home cooking, pleasant atmosphere, rec, good value; **E** *Rest House*, Beach Rd, 7 rm with bath, T 27299, next to the sea and good swimming, good food (excellent club-sandwich) but you might be plagued by flies, originally it was a Dutch warehouse for cinnamon and coconuts, the new, characterless wing has 8 rm, the old building houses restaurants and some rooms, the Old Dutch Chapel next door is used vehicles. About 2 km inland **D** ***Sena's Lake View House***, Maha Ambalangoda, very quiet, by attractive lake, rec.

Meetiyagoda, 6 km, has a moonstone quarry.

Seenigama 6 km has a Devil's Temple by roadside; Sri Lankan travellers pay their respects here bringing most traffic to a temporary halt.

Hikkaduwa

(13 km; *STD Code* 09) This has become the most popular and developed beach on the W Coast. It offers good swimming and a wide range of facilities for snorkelling and scuba diving with thtrr stations, including Poseiden on Main Road, T 3294. It is also known for its 'Coral Gardens' – you can hire a glass-bottomed boat from near the *Coral Gardens Hotel* to view the underwater collection. However, you may find, hiring a boat for Rs 600 (plus Rs 200 for turtles) is not worthwhile.

You can swim in front of the Coral Gardens but you have to be constantly aware of the glass bottom boats which come very close to the shore. In the spring, the sea can be quite choppy with a strong under current sweeping you along the beach which can make swimming quite uncomfortable.

The town is thriving again, and the guest houses and hotels are returning to normal, along with the shops and restaurants which line the road. Hikkaduwa is unique on this stretch of coast in having a full range of accommodation with over 50 hotels. Cheaper guest houses are along the S end of the beach, also the better end for surfing. Bikes and motor bikes can be hired in many places (shack opposite *Hikkaduwa Beach Resort*, ask for Neel) and there is a wide range of shops.

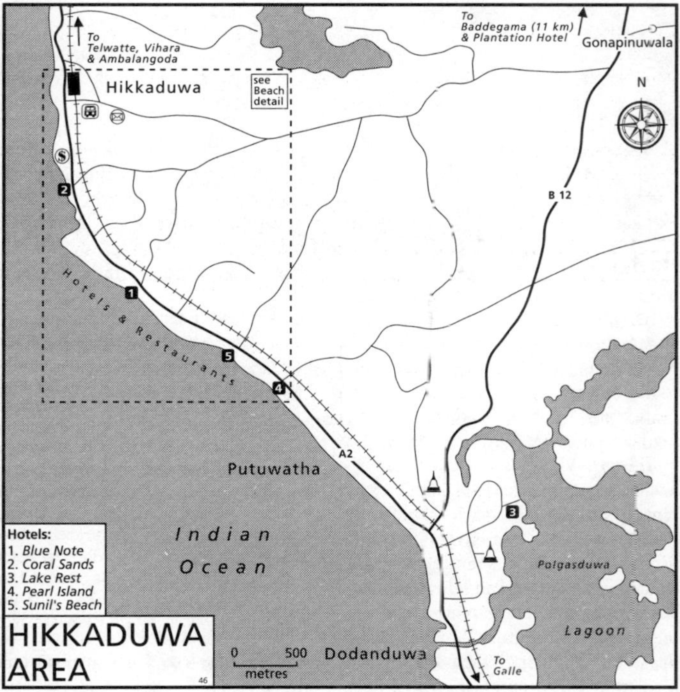

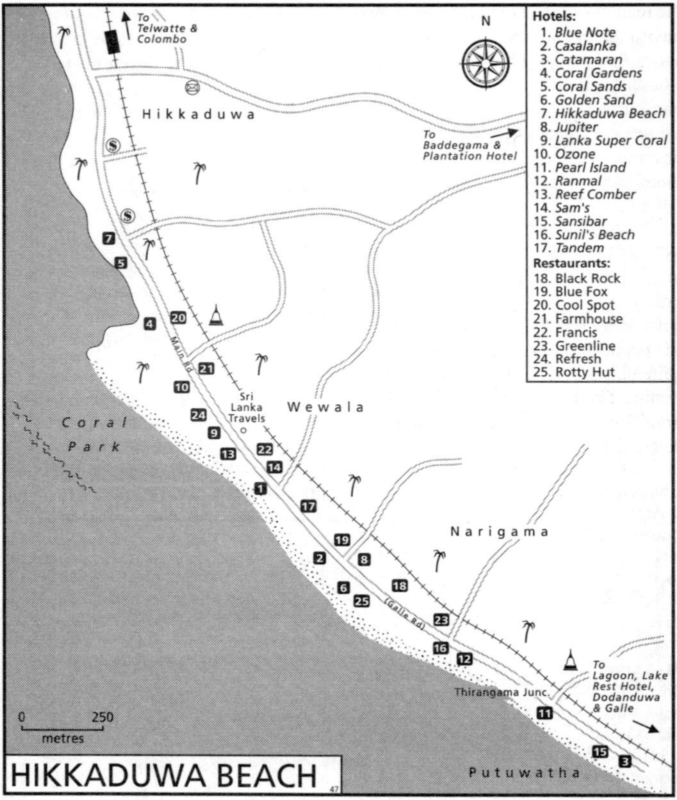

A major disadvantage here is the very busy main road which splits the town in two. the improved surface means the traffic moves very fast and makes it a death trap.The cheaper hotels and eating places are across from the beach.

Telwatte Vihara (Totagama Rajamahavihara) dating from the early 19th century is a short distance inland, about 2 km N of Hikkaduwa (a very pleasant bicycle ride away). It is the only temple to Anangaya on the island; lovers make offerings to him. The carvings between the fine *makara* ('dragon') arches leading to the sanctuary hide a cupid with his bow and flower-tipped arrows. The murals too are particularly impressive. It is hardly ever visited by travellers which adds to its charm.

Kumarakanda Rajamahavihara S of town also has fine murals and carvings but is on the tourist trail with a dancing monkey and 'school pen' collectors. Donations are expected.

Excursions

Baddegama (11 km inland) is within easy reach of Hikkaduwa by bicycle or motor bike. It is a very attractive road through coconut and banana groves, followed by several small plantations – rubber, tea and spices. About half way the road passes the **Nigro Dharama Mahavira** (stupa) in Gopinuwala. On a hill above the river in the grounds of Christ Church Girls College is the first **Anglican church** in Sri Lanka, built in 1818 and consecrated by Bishop Heber in 1825. It has noteworthy ironwood pillars. **Accommodation** **C** *Plantation Hotel*, Halpatota (10 mins drive from Hikkaduwa beach), T 587454, reservations T Colombo 587454, 4 rm (US$18), breakfast incl, set in small tea estate, this guest house is quite exceptional, surrounded by a beautiful quiet wooded garden, it has the feel of an old planter's house though the house is quite new, food excellent, hosts very welcoming. **Place to eat** *Banana House*, 4 km from Hikkaduwa does good fruit juices in delightful spice garden.

Local information

● Accommodation

Innumerable hotels line the beach with often very little to distinguish them. Negotiate discounts for longer stays; off-season upto 50% cheaper, some have bargained down to only 25% of peak-season rate. **Warning** Avoid hotel touts who offer cheap rooms, drugs etc.

AL-A *Coral Gardens*, T 57023, F 57189, 156 a/c rm (US$90+) top of its class, excellent restaurants (excellent lunch buffet, Rs 300, rec); **A** *Coral Sands*, 326 Galle Rd, T 57436, F 57189, reservations T 421101, 58 rm, 30 facing sea, 5 a/c, newest and best scuba diving equipment, German instructor; **A** *Reefcomber*, T 433268, F 57374, 54 a/c rm (US$65), all facing beach.

B *Hikkaduwa Beach Resort*, Galle Rd, modern block, slightly above average; **B** *Lanka Supercorals*, 390 Galle Rd, 1 km from Bus Stand, T 57897, F Colombo 957897, 100 rm, some a/c (US$45), large package tour hotel, beginning to fade; **B** *Ocean Beach Club*, Main Rd, 3 km from town centre, T 57366, F 32098, 16 clean, comfortable rm, excellent restaurant, rec; **B** *Sunil's Beach*, Narigama, just S of the marine gardens, T/F 57187, 56 seaview rm, 5 a/c (US$40), Sinhala architecture, bookshop, pool, tropical garden.

Most from **C** category have rooms with cold shower, western toilet, mosquito net and fan. **C** *Blue Note Cabanas*, 424 Galle Rd, T/F 57016, 9 very clean rm (Rs 1,000), restaurant; **C** *Sansibar*, Galle Rd, Thirangama, T/F 57081, 10 rm with terrace facing beach (Re 1,400), large well kept garden, ducks and rabbits, Swiss run, fairly smart but expensive; **C-D** *Pearl Island Beach*, new building in Thirangama, T/F 57251, 15 rm with cold showers (Rs 900 incl breakfast), restaurant overlooks beach, large garden.

Most in **D** category have rooms with cold shower, western toilet, mosquito net and fan. **D** *Catamaran Beach*, a newish building with 12 large rm, (Rs 750 incl breakfast), restaurant overlooking beach, rather pricey; **D** *Golden Sand Beach*, Narigama, T 57060, 12 clean (Rs 700), quite smart, good value, rec; **D** *Sea View*, 295 Galle Rd, nr *Coral Gardens*, T 22014, 6 large rm with bath, restaurant very good for Italian and fish dishes, sadly noisy main road; **D** *Tandem*, Main Rd, 100 km post, 6 rm with bath, modern, clean, comfortable, good though not on the beach.

Budget hotels: **E** *Casalanka*, Galle Rd, hippie haven, one long block of barracks-style rooms; **E** *Ozone Tourist Rest*, 374 Galle Rd, 5 rm, basic; **E** *Ranmal Rest & Tourist Home*, T 57114, rooms with terrace (Rs 400-600), beach facing restaurant, better value than similar hotels, rec; **E** *Red Lobster*, 6 clean rm with bath, good value, excellent restaurant; **E** *Wide Beach*, renovated after having been derelict, unpleasant atmosphere, not rec.

F *Hansa Surf*, on the beach, 20 rm (check whether fan is working first, Rs 200), adequate but very basic, 'main attraction is the hotel boy, the famous teeth-cleaner. His record – 30 mins!'; **F** *Jupiter*, 6 simple rm with net, shared shower and Indian toilet (Rs 250), beach restaurant (rice and curry and chutney especially rec, Rs 75, order chutney to take home!), jolly atmosphere, basic but good value; **F** *Sam's Surfers' Rest*, opp Blue Note, T 57184, 6 rm with fan, net and cold shower (Rs 200), garden setting, restaurant with pool table, videos, music, laid back surfing feel, very pleasant, meall about Rs 150, rec; **F** *Sunrise*, 4 basic rm with fan, net, shared bath (Rs 150), beach restaurant, pleasant atmosphere.

● Places to eat

Plenty of choice, especially for sea food *Black Rock*, S end of Galle Rd, delicious and inexpensive meals, friendly management; *Blue Fox*, large and popular, good food but service sometimes slow; *Cool Spot*, 327 Galle Rd, does good, cheap breakfasts, a backpackers' haunt with plenty of atmosphere; *Curry Bowl*, good food and service, 'delicious garlic toasts' and for those not keen on straight arrack try 'a very special mix of vanilla milkshake with arrack!'; ***Farmhouse***, 341 Galle Rd, offers a wide range of other services; ***Francis***, 389 Galle Rd, for wide choice of Chinese and Western, rec; ***Greenline***, opp *Sunil's Beach*, good food but grumpy staff; ***Red Lobster***, excellent food, good value, friendly owners; ***Refresh***, 384 Galle Rd, for sea food, pleasant ambiance; ***Rotty Hut***, S end, cheap, tasty meals of rice and curry (about Rs 30), excellent rotties, 'even the locals eat here'. Budget travellers sometimes choose the cool of a plush a/c restaurant in a top hotel at lunchtime (eg *Coral Garden*).

● Post & telecommunications

Reception desks usually sell stamps and accept letters for posting.

● Sports

Snorkelling equipment, surfboards, bikes and motorbikes are widely available for hire.

● Tour companies & travel agents

Sri Lanka Travels and Tours (opp *Reefcomber Hotel*), have taxis and minibuses.

● Useful addresses

Tourist Police: Police Station, Galle Rd, T 57222.

● Transport

Local Minibus: to Katunayake Airport from above, about Rs 1,400/bus. **Taxi**: good hire from MG Thomson, Lion Paradies, Wewala, T 571390 or Custom Rd, Dodanduwa.

Dodanduwa

6 km further S Dodanduwa has a beautiful lagoon which is popular for bird watching. Touts on the beach offer boat trips – Rs 100 per person includes a visit to Polgasduwa and bird watching. The beach has Sarath Nanda Hewawasam **Turtle Research Centre** at Kumarakanda is a small set up which works to protect this endangered species. Entry Rs 50. You can see eggs and different stages of a turtle's development. There is a rare albino too.

There is a fine Buddhist temple approached by a long steep and narrow flight of stone stairs. **Accommodation D** *Lake Rest*, Dodandugoda, inland towards lagoon (from Hikkaduwa take the next road after the turn-off to the vihara), 10 rm with fan, net and cold shower, in recently refurbished Sri Lankan house overlooking the lagoon, restaurant, quiet rural setting, facing forests, idyllic, bike hire to get to and from Hikkaduwa.

ROUTES After 15 km the road crosses the Dutch Canal to enter Galle.

Galle

(*STD Code* 09) Galle (pronounced 'Gaul') is the most important town in the S and has retained much of its colonial atmosphere. The Portuguese, Dutch and British used the natural harbour as their main port until 1875, when reconstruction of breakwaters and the enlarged harbour made Colombo the island's major port. Its origins as a port go back well before the Portuguese. Ibn Battuta, the great Moroccan traveller, visited it in 1344. The historian of Ceylon Sir Emerson Tennant claimed that Galle was the ancient city of Tarshish, which had traded not only with Persians and Egyptians, but with King Solomon.

The Portuguese Lorenzo de Almeida drifted into Galle by accident in 1505. It was a further 82 years before the Portuguese captured it from the Sinhala Kings, and they controlled the port until the Dutch laid siege in 1640. The old Portuguese Fort on a promontory was strengthened by the Dutch.

The crescent-shaped shoreline was dotted with islands, though some have now been joined up or altered by the harbour developments.

Places of interest

The Dutch left their mark on the town, building brick – lined sewers which the tides automatically flushed twice a day. The Fort's main streets run over the old sewers; you can still see the manhole covers every 20m or so.

The Fort The old Fort completely dominates the town.

The Ramparts, surrounded on three sides by the sea are marked by a series of bastions covering the promontory.

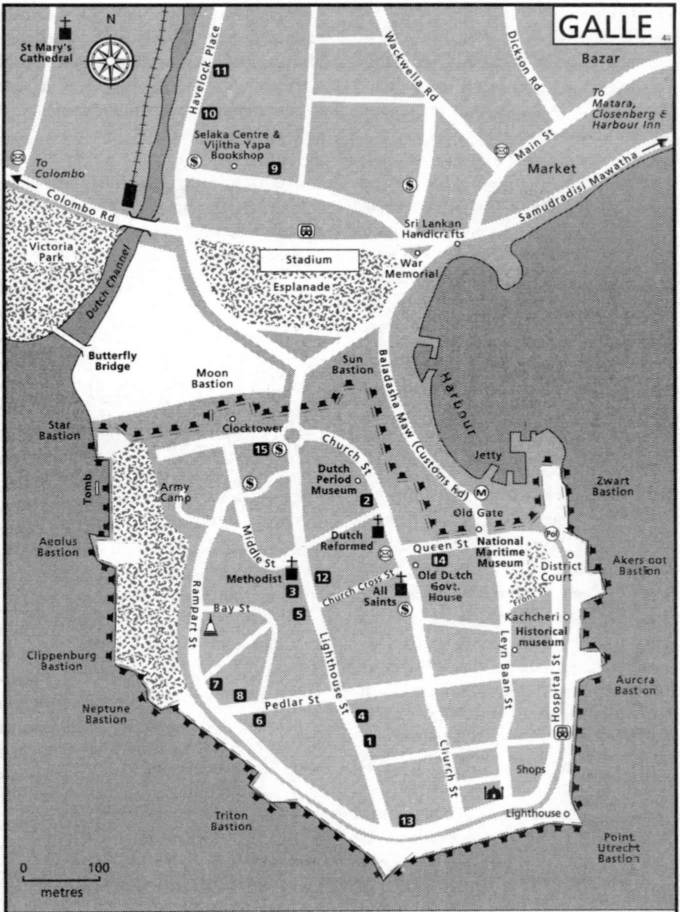

Hotels:
1. *Beach Haven Guest House*
2. *New Oriental*
3. *Old Dutch Guest House*
4. *Orchard Holiday Home*
5. *YMBA*
6. YMCA
7. *RK Kodikare Guest House*
8. *Weltreveden & Mrs Khalid's Guest House*
9. *Sydney*

Restaurants:
10. Chinese Globe
11. The Snack Bar
12. Kaln Snacks
13. Vegetarian Café
14. Queens Court
15. Vegetarian

The two nearest to the harbour are *Sun* and *Zwart*, followed by *Aurora* and *Point Utrecht* bastions before the lighthouse, then *Triton*, *Neptune*, *Clippenburg*, *Aeolus*, *Star* and *Moon*.

There are two entry points; the more impressive gate is under the clock tower. The ramparts just here are massive, partly because they are the oldest and have been reinforced over the years on many occasions. There are three quite distinct bastions (*Star* in the W, *Moon* and *Sun* in the E). The clocktower (1883) itself, is quite modern, and usually has a huge national flag flying from it. The ramparts on the W side are more accessible and stand much as they were built, although there is evidence of a signals post built in WW2 on top of *Neptune*. The Sri Lankan army still has a base in the Fort and so have a use for the *Aeolus* bastion. Under the ramparts between *Aelous* and *Star* bastions is the tomb of a Muslim saint neatly painted in green and white, said to cover an old fresh water spring. The open space between Rampart St and the ramparts is used as a recreational area and there is often an unoffical game of cricket in progess in the evenings and at weekends. Also on the green is a small shrine – the main one, Sri Sudharmalaya temple, being across the street.

The walk around the ramparts is a must. Try to do it on a clear evening and aim to reach the clock tower at sunset. A walk around the ramparts is a must. Try to start at about 1630 and wander slowly from the New Oriental clockwise. The views over the roofs of the houses and the sunset out over the sea is unforgettable.

Part of the charm of the fort is being able to wander around the streets. Nothing is very far away and, by and large, there are only a few curio shops. You will not get pestered very much either although on the ramparts you may be offered coral (near the Neptune bastion) and there are usually vendors near the New Oriental.

A tour An interesting route is to walk S along Church St, E to the 20m high lighthouse which was built by the British in 1934, nearly on top of the old magazine (with its inscription AJ Galle den 1st Zeber 1782). You can get good views from the top. You then return back down Hospital St past the Police Barracks (erected in 1927 but failing to blend in with the older parts of the fort); the Government offices on Hospital St were once the Dutch 'Factory' (warehouse). The walk ends at the square with the district court near the *Zwart* Bastion. Note the sign: "All vehicles should proceed slowly and noiselessly. Horns or other warning signals should not be given beyond this point. By order". Turn W along Queen St and end back at the post office.

The quiet Fort streets are lined with substantial buildings, most with large rooms on the ground floor and an arched verandah to provide shade. The arched windows of the upper floors are are covered by huge old louvered wooden shutters – the lower ones have glass nowadays. Unfortunately, quite a few of these fine houses are in need of restoration.

The **Dutch Reformed Church** (1754), next to the New Oriental, is certainly worth visiting. It was built as a result of a vow taken by the Dutch Governor of Galle, Casparaous de Jong, and contains a number of interesting memorials. Inside, the floor is covered by about 20 gravestones, some are heavily embossed, others are engraved, which originated in older graveyards which were closed in 1710 and 1804. The British moved them into this church in 1853. There is a splendid wooden memorial to EAH Abraham, commander in Galle who died 3 May 1766. Note the hour glass and skull on top of it. The barrel roof is painted blue. The organ loft has a lovely semicircular balustrade surrounding the organ. The pulpit with an enormous canopy was being repaired in Apr 1995. Opposite the church, is the old bell tower erected in 1701. The bell, open to the elements, is hung in a belfry with a large dome on top of it.

The old **Post Office** was restored by the Galle Heritage Trust in 1992. It is a long low building with a shallow red tiled roof supported by 13 stout columns. It still operates as the post office although it is very run down inside.

All Saints Church Further down Church St is All Saints Church. It is not always open. This was built in 1868 (consecrated in 1871) after much pressure from the English population who had previously worshipped at the Dutch Reform Church. Its bell has an interesting history as it came from the Liberty ship 'Ocean Liberty'. When the vicar asked the Clan Shipping Company whether they could help with a bell, the chief officer who had acquired the bell when the Liberty ship was scrapped (and named his daughter Liberty!), willingly presented it to the church in its centenary year, 1968. There is a particularly good view of the church with its red tin roof surmounted by a cockerel and four strange little turrets, from Cross Church St. The old Dutch Government House opposite the church, is now Walker & Sons.

At the end of Church St, lies the old Arab quarter. Here you will find the mosque in a tall white building with the crescent clearly visible; it was rebuilt at the turn of the century where the original stood from c1750s. The Muslim Cultural Association and Arabic College which was established in 1892, are here. It is still very active and you will see many Muslims in the distinctive skull caps hurrying to prayer at the appointed hours.

In Queen St is the second and much older gate: the British arms are on the outside of the gate. On the inside, monogrammed arms of the Dutch East India Company, VOC (*Vereenigde Oost Indische Campagnie* –) arms can clearly be seen with the date MDCLXIX (1669), above it. On the ground floor of this imposing building is the National Maritime Museum (see below).

Modern Galle has not much to offer. It is quite good to wander around though and its bustle contrasts with the more measured pace of the fort. It is an easy walk either out of the old gate and along by the sea with its rows of fishing boats neatly drawn up on the beach or through the main gate and around by the cricket ground. Near the main post office on Main St, there is a splendid equestrian statue. You can walk along side of the old Dutch canal – very dirty at low tide. Monitor lizards can often be seen.

On the Colombo Road to the W of Victoria Park, are several gem shops. If you take the road opposite them you can walk up to **St Mary's Cathedral** which was built in 1874 and has a very good view over town. There is little of interest inside, though. SCIA handicraft centre factories are nearby (see Shopping below)

Museums

National Maritime Museum, the Old Dutch Gate, Queen St. Entrance Rs 50, normal opening times. The exhibition is housed in the basement of what was originally storehouses (*Pakhus*) and you can really appreciate the strength of the building with 1m thick walls and huge stone pillars to keep the building from collapsing. There is much of interest inside the museum but regrettably it is not well exhibited. There is a small collection illustrating the island's maritime history including trade, spices, sea products (a pickled cuttlefish), fibreglass whales, models of different styles of catamarans. At the far end there is an interesting exhibit about fishermen – they make annual pilgrimages to Kataragama to offer alms and carry with them a sea horse which they believe brings Good

luck. They perform the *Gara Yakuma* dance on the sea shore as *shanthl karma* in an attempt to increase yields.

Historical Museum, 31-39 Leyn Bann St (well signed). Open 0830-1800, free admission. It describes itself as an "art gallery, museum and arcade". The old house was restored in 1992 by Mr Gaffar, the owner, in some ways similar to the Dutch Museum in Colombo. There are a number of rooms including the kitchen and bedroom containing a collection of colonial artefacts – glasses, VOC china (rather repetitious), pens, record player. The exhibits are quite interesting although unfortunately, not labelled. There are workshops for gold work and gem cutting and a large 'exhibit' of a 20th century gem shop. The real aim of the 'museum' becomes apparent when the obligatory guide leads visitors to the gems for sale in the shop (all guaranteed by the Ceylon Gem Corporation)!

Local information

● Accommodation

New Oriental (NOH), 10 Church St, Fort, T/F 934591, 36 large rm, the oldest registered hotel on the island run by the Brohier family since 1899, in an historic building dating from 1684 which originally was the Army barracks, Mrs Nesta Brohier is still very much in evidence and likes to meet 'suitable' guests, refuses to have tour parties, she is 92 (having survived her children) and fascinating to talk to, furnished with Dutch period furniture, not all in very good repair but charming (rumours that millions of Far East money will be spent on it), best room on 1st flr (US$40), No 7 has excellent view of the Fort, public rooms also full of old prints and furniture and a grand piano which guests can play, food mediocre and quite expensive, lovely little garden with pool surrounded by frangipani trees (chameleons drop out of them!), good atmosphere, good value, highly rec.

A *Closenberg*, 11 Closenberg Rd, Magalle, Unawantana Road (3-wheeler from Fort, Rs 80), T 32241, F 32441, 21 non a/c comfortable rm (US$35+) in colonial house built in 1858, old rooms are noisy though, modern wing has great sea views set apart from the terrace and restaurant which is pleasant and quiet in the evenings, good restaurent but busy at lunchtime, on the promontory overlooking the bay 3 km E of Galle with boating, sea fishing, with character and pleasant ambiance, lacks the atmosphere of the fort at night, still rec, **NB** Beach nearby polluted, bus to Matara (for good bathing) stops close to hotel; **A** ***Lighthouse Hotel***, with 60 luxury rm (open late 1995), details from Jetwing, T/F 698818.

D *Beach Haven Guest House*, 65 Lighthouse St in Fort, T 22663, 4 rm, 1 a/c (Rs 600), excellent restaurant, immaculate and highly rec; **D** *Old Dutch House*, 46 Lighthouse St, inside Fort, T 34370, F 34445, 8 rm (Rs 450), good restaurant (possibly cheapest beer in town), spotless, excellent service, Old Dutch furniture and architectural features (original walls left exposed to show some interesting historical notes), rec.

Budget hotels: most have fans and nets. **D-E** *Mrs Shakira Khalid's Guest House*, 106 Pedlar St, T 22725, 4 rm with toilet (Rs 300-600), family atmosphere, delicious Sri Lankan food, small shady garden; **E** *Dr Ladduwahetty*, Rampart House, 3 Rampart St, T 34448, 4 rm (Rs 300); **E** *Weltrevreden*, 104 Pedlar St, 8 rm with toilet (Rs 400 with bath Rs 300 shared toilet), simple meals, noodles and rice, Rs 150-250, courtyard with lush garden, clean and quite good value; ***Orchard Holiday Home***, rooms Rs 400; **F** ***RK Kodikara's Beatrice House***, 29 Rampart St (S end, 50m from Buddhist temple), T 2351, rooms with toilet (Rs 200-300) in colonial house with seafacing garden, meals, good for budget travellers; **F** ***Railway Retiring Rooms***. In the Bus Station to the N you can see the *Sydney Hotel*, once Galle's premier hotel for tourists but now one of the seediest.

● Places to eat

Consider taking a 3-wheeler to *Closenberg Hotel* across the bay (see above) which has a good restaurant, heavily used by tour groups so service can be slow, try sitting under the pergola – you get a lovely view over the harbour and are far from the crowd. Outside hotels:

In the Fort: *Kaln's*, 21 Lighthouse St, worth trying for snacks; ***New Shan Lanka***, Rampart St, for Chinese, is more expensive than it looks; ***Queens Court Tea Centre***, Queen St, at the back of the old Dutch Government building, serves Chinese and Western food and has cool drinks and a pleasant enough garden; ***Vegetarian Café*** nr Neptune Bastion, at the end of Lighthouse St, is a good place to sample short eats, clean and fresh; ***Vegetarian Restaurant***, does traditional veg Sinhalese curries, hot and tasty (Rs 20), not frequented by tourists. Good breakfasts in the Fort, on Pedlar St nr crossing with Church St.

Station area: *Ceylon Restaurant*, next to Bus Station for a good range of dishes (try pineapple curry or cashew nut curry), clean, reasonable prices, Western-style decor; ***Chinese Globe Restaurant***, 38 Havelock Pl, opp railway station; ***Mayura*** nr the bus stand, corner of Hospital and Pedlar sts, serves teas and snacks but has very loud music; ***Selaka Shopping Centre***, 1st flr, by the Bus Stand, has a good, clean and reasonably priced restaurant.

● Banks & money changers

Bank of Ceylon, Lighthouse St; **People's Bank**, Middle St. Money changing at Historical Museum, 31-39 Leyn Baan St.

● Post & telecommunications

Post Office: behind the Bus Station has Poste Restante. Church St GPO is on the site of the old Dutch burial ground.

Telecommunications: faxes and ISD calls from a shop in the Selaka Bldg by the Bus Station.

● Shopping

Galle is famous for its lace-making, gem polishing and ebony carving, all of which make good souvenirs. There are a few curio shops around. ***Laksana***, 30 Hospital St, carries a selection; ***Lihinya Trades***, just by the lighthouse, good selection, knowledgeable, helpful owners.

Bookshops: *Vijitha Yapa Laitiru Bookshop*, 2nd Flr, Selaka Bldg, 34 Gamini Maw, next to the Bus Station, carries a good selection of English books.

Gems and jewellery: in Modern Galle, on Colombo Rd, W of Victoria Park are several gem shops incl ***Star Jewellers*** at 41 Colombo Rd. Nearby is ***Sapphire Gem Centre***, 5 Mosque Lane, Kandewatte; also ***Universal Gems***, 42 A Jiffriya St (Cripps Rd).

Handicrafts: *SCIA Handicraft Centre* on Kandewatte Rd (T 94-9-34304, F 94-9-34505), accepts credit cards and approved for foreign exchange. There are 5 factories producing polished gems, tortoise shell goods, carvings (ebony), batik and lace, and leather bags etc emploing about 50 people (approved by the State Gem Corp and Tourist Board). Visit the factories before buying. **NB** Unofficial guides posing as 'friends' have been a problem recently – girls in particular are advised to be very careful.

● Tour companies & travel agents

Southlink Travels, 2nd Flr, Selaka Bldg, 34 Gamini Maw, next to the Bus Station.

● Useful addresses

Police Station: is in the Zwart Basion.

● Transport

Train Colombo: *Samudra Devi*, 327, daily, 0500, 3¼ hrs; *Ruhunu Kumari Express*, 57, daily, 0825, 2½ hrs; 51, daily, 1456, 2¾ hrs; 53, daily, 1700, 2½ hrs. 2nd class, Rs 55, seat reservation Rs 15. **Matara**: 50, daily, 1022, 1¼ hrs; 52, daily, 1123, 52; *Ruhunu Kumari*, daily, 1815, 1 hr. The journey to Colombo by rail is preferable to road; quite pleasant, provided you travel outside the rush hour.

Road Bus: buses from Central Bus Stand, Pettah, Colombo. Less comfortable and picturesque than by train. Rs 25. **Taxi**: Rs 3,000+ from Colombo.

ROUTES The **A2** continues SE along the coast. Just S of the '74 mile' marker a narrow coastal road, Bona Vista offers excellent views across Galle Harbour towards the Fort. It is worth doing a detour for the views. Walk up along the tarred road (to Home for the Aged) and when you reach the highest point. On a clear day look inland to catch sight of Adam's Peak.

Unawatuna

(*STD Code* 09 or 072) 5 km E of Galle, Unawatuna has a picturesque beach along a sheltered bay, good for swimming and diving. More relaxed than Hikkaduwa and with fewer package tourists. The area is, however, developing rapidly.

A traveller in 1995 found "this was not the idyllic, quiet beach we imagined. Many places to stay and even more to eat at. Very narrow beach. For those arriving from elsewhere in Asia (eg Thailand) it may well be a disappointment. Getting ever more popular with city dwellers and tourists alike. Cloudy water, dead coral."

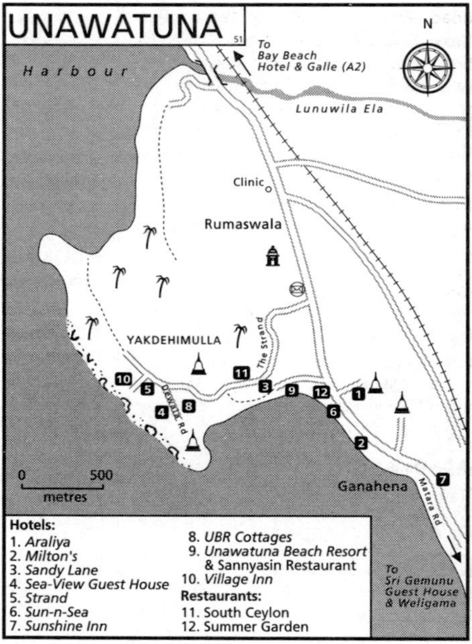

Local information

● Accommodation

Reserve ahead.

A *Milton's*, Ganahena, E end of beach, T 57088, F 949 53312, 23 rm, 15 a/c (US$65), good restaurant with views, sheltered pool in sea, relaxed, diving possible; **A** *Secret Garden*, nr the beach, T Colombo 685564, an old bungalow, full of character, in large grounds, 4 rm sharing a bath, catering, peaceful, bookings for a week (min).

B *Bay Beach*, T 0415 201, en route from Galle, 56 rm, restaurant, pool; **B** *Unawatuna Beach Resort* (*UBR*), 500m from Galle Rd, Parangiyawatta, T/F 32247, 56 comfortable rm (US$26-43), 20 a/c (US$8 extra) with hot water (rates for half-board), good seafacing restaurants, bar, disco, watersports; **B-C** *Sea-View Guest House*, Dewala Rd, opp *UBR cottages*, T 30013, F 34445 (Attn 'Sea-View'), 14 clean rm with fan, net and bath, most with verandah (various prices), good restaurant, family guest house in pleasant garden nr the beach; also cheaper rooms in *Cottages* on Dewala Rd further W; **B-C** *Strand*, W end of beach, T 30010 (book very early in peak season, ie Nov to end-Mar), friendly family guest house described as 'colonial style homestay', highly rec; **B-C** *Sun-n-Sea*, E end of beach, nr *Milton's*, 8 rm by the sea, excellent restaurant, rec.

D *Sandy Lane*, beyond *UBR*, simple rooms on 3 flrs with sea view, good Sri Lankan food; **D** *Sunshine Inn*, Dalawella, S of *Milton*, 15 rm with bath, net and fan, 2 a/c dearer, restaurant, bar; **D** *Village Inn*, beyond *Strand*, F 53387 (Attn Village Guest House), cleaner than average rooms and decent breakfasts (good hoppers), 15 simple rm in 5 bungalows, 3 with balconies overlooking a small coconut grove, rec.

Many cheaper **D/E** rooms can be found in private houses by the beach and along the main road; ask locally and inspect. Even cheaper a little inland from the main road: **D-E** *Araliya*, clean rooms with bath, restaurant; S along the main road *Sri Gemunu*, Dalawella, past Police Station, 10 clean rm in friendly guest house, nr peaceful beach, good Sri Lankan food.

● Places to eat

Apart from the hotel restaurants there is ample choice along the beach. *Lucky Tuna*, on the beach, beyond *UBR*, is rec for good, inexpensive rice and noodle dishes; however, *Paradise*, you may wait 20 mins for a pot of tea, better ask for the bill when you order, 'food smells and tastes funny ... and amazing that it is always empty, considering everyone must spend 2 hrs there!'. A few rec behind the *UBR* incl 2 offering good western veg dishes: *Sannyasin* and *South Ceylon* across the road. *Summer Garden* on the beach, off Matara Rd is rec for seafood.

● Shopping

Good for picking up bangles.

● Transport

Train From **Colombo**, get any Galle or Matara train (many); change at Galle if your train does not stop at Unawatuna (next stop). From **Kandy** see Matara trains below.

Road Bus: from Colombo, best to get Colombo-Matara bus; alternative go to Galle first, and then frequent connection. **3-wheeler**: to/from Galle, Rs 60-70.

Koggala, 3 km, has a free trade zone and there is some light industry, with plans to expand. **Accommodation A** *Koggala Beach*, reputedly the longest hotel in Asia, T 53260, 200 rm, 30 a/c, a package tour hotel, with large restaurant, 2 pools; *Horizon*, T 2528 or through *Ruhunu Hotel*, Colombo T 580493. At **Talpe**: **C** *Beach Haven*, T 53362, 25 rm, good restaurant, beautiful situation.

Weligama

(23 km; *STD Code* 0415) 1 km before the town there is a 4m high statue of Kushta Raja, sometimes known as the 'Leper King'. Various legends surround the statue believed by some to be of Bodhisattva Samantabhadra. Look out for the *mal lali* fretwork decorated houses along the road from the centre towards the statue. There is a tiny island in the lovely bay known as **Taprobane** once owned by the French Count de Maunay who built a house on it.

The bay is best known for its remarkable fishermen who perch silently for hours on stilts out in the bay, and also for locally made lace (see Shopping). **Devil Dances** are held in neighbouring villages.

Local information

● Accommodation

B *Bay Beach*, Kapparatota, reservations T 201, F 423741, 58 a/c rm (US$45), watersports, good pool on the beach, attractive garden, scenic location with views.

D *Bay Inn Rest House* (CHC), on the bay, 5 mins drive from railway station, reservations

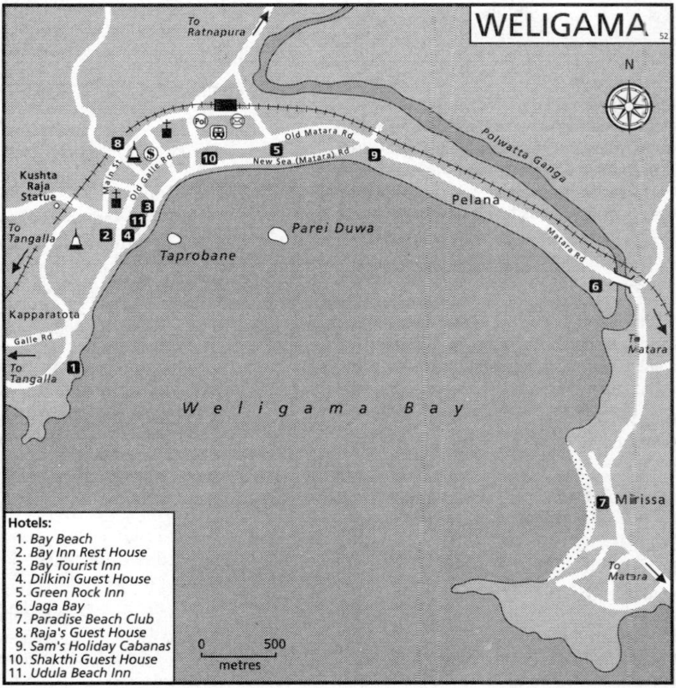

T Colombo 323501, F 422732, 12 rm (US$11) with bath, fan, net and balcony, some with seaview, pleasant restaurant serves good sea food, bar, exchange; an old house in a beautiful large garden, rec; **D** *Jaga Bay*, Pelena (3.5 km E of railway), 6 rm (Rs 550) in new house, beach restaurant, quiet garden.

Budget hotels: **E** *Bay Tourist Inn*, 10 New Matara Rd, 8 rm with bath (about Rs 300) in a traditional house, dated fittings but all in good condition, beautiful large garden, boat trips, bike and motor bike hire, very good value, our researcher's favourite in Weligama; **E** *Green Rock Inn*, 427 Pelana, 4 rm with bath, no windows, not good value; **E** *Raja's Guest House*, 245 Main St, Kanthi Nivasa, Paranakade (W of railway station, 500m from bus stop) in old building, 3 rm with shared bath, fan and net, in friendly family home, warm welcome, very good seafood (especially lobster), rec; **E** *Sam's Holiday Cabanas*, 484 New Matara Rd, on the beach nr main junction with Old Matara Rd, 7 clean, good value rm with bath, fan and net (Rs 400), seafood restaurant, pleasant garden, surf boards and bikes for hire, free taxi from railway station; **E-F** *Udula Beach Inn*, Beach Rd, 7 rm with bath (Rs 250-500 incl breakfast), expensive for what it is, next to main road hence noisy.

F *Dilkini Guest House*, T 281, 6 rm in converted modern house, good value at Rs 200; **F** *Shakthi Guest House*, New Sea Rd nr Bus Stand (5 mins from railway), 2 rm with bath, good home-cooking, friendly, popular with budget travellers, owner Prince Charles look-alike!

● **Places to eat**
Bay Inn Rest House, *Raja's*, *Sam's* and *Shakthi* are rec.

● **Shopping**
Lace workshops along road opp Taprobane Island. Snorkelling equipment in shops in Station Rd.

● **Sports**
Watersports: *Bay Beach Aqua Sports*, Kapparatota, T 32295, F 437376.

● **Transport**
Local Bike and motorbike hire: from *Bay Inn*, 10 New Matara Rd.

Road Colombo, 4½ hrs.

ROUTES From Weligama to Tangalle is an outstandingly beautiful stretch of road. There is an endless succession of bays, the road often running right by the startling blue sea and palm fringed rocky headlands. The district is famous for the manufacture and export of citronella perfume.

Mirissa

For a pleasant excursion travel 6 km along the coast across Weligama Bay to Mirissa which has a staggeringly beautiful small rocky beach which is almost private. You can try deep sea fishing, river trips, snorkelling or visit rubber and tea factories or a snake farm (enquire at the *Paradise Beach Club*).

● **Accommodation** **D** *se Beach Club*, 140 Gunasiri Mahima Maw, T 071 24665, 16 cabanas (Rs 660) or 12 rm with bath right on the beach (Rs 1,000 with a/c), good range of food at the reasonably priced large rustic restaurant in tropical garden serving seafood dishes (around Rs 150) and huge jumbo prawns (Rs 450), not forced to eat seafood though, plenty of other choice, organizes tours, clean and comfortable, 'luxurious atmosphere for less than a tenner'; **D** *Giragala Village*, Bandaramulla, nearby, 6 small rm with bath in a converted house on the same beach, much less luxurious at Rs 400.

● **Transport Road Bus**: from Weligama or 3-wheelers.

Matara

(15 km; *STD Code* 041) The Ruhuna University 3 km out of town has brought students into this old town of narrow streets and an old market place where you might see the local wooden carts ('hackeries') used for races!

It is a town divided by the Nilwala Ganga; two Dutch forts stand on either side. The larger **Main Fort** is to the S which holds most of the old town with a *Rest House* and the Church dating from 1769. It was badly damaged by attackers from Kandy who occupied it for a time. Following this, the Coral Star Fort was built in 1763 which has a moated double-wall and five bastions. The gateway (1770) is particularly picturesque; it houses the library now. The fort itself is private property.

The Buddhist hermitage, *Chula Lanka*, on a tiny island joined by causeway

to the mainland, was founded by a Thai Prince priest.

Polhena 2 km E (towards Galle) has become dominated by the most exploitative kind of tourism. Hotels vie with each other to gain business and unabashadly claim that others have closed or insist you place your order for dinner in the morning to obviate the opportunity to sample food anywhere else. It however has a good coral **beach** with good value guest houses and a reef within easy reach.

Reef visit

Ask for Titus at the *TK Guest House* (below) – he is a good snorkelling guide who is knowledgeable about the reef and arranges night-trips to see Moray eels for Rs 250; recommended.

Museums

The Archaeological Department Museum, closed Thur, entry free. The exhibition traces history through reproductions of Sri Lanka's prehistoric cave paintings from major archaeological sites, right up to the 20th century.

Street names

The Broadway is also known as Dharmapala Mawatha, Colombo Rd or New Galle Rd.

Local information

● Accommodation

At Matara: **C-D** *Mayura Beach Resort*, 33 Beach Rd, desolate beach-front setting, T 3274, rooms with bath much the same as elsewhere but ridiculously overpriced at Rs 750, Chinese and Sri Lankan restaurant; **C-D** *Rest House* in the main Fort by the sea, nr Bus Stop, T 2299, 18 rm, better in new part with bath, very attractive, good food, good value.

Budget hotels: **E** *River Inn*, 96/1 W Gunasekhara Maw, Fort, next to Matara Prison, T 2215, 11 rm with bath (Rs 275), rather shabby but they do overlook the river; **F** *Blue Ripples*, 38 W Gunasekhara Maw, Fort, T 2058, best rooms with bath, balcony and river view (Rs 225).

At Polhena the comfortable **D** *Reef Garden*, 30 Beach Rd, T 2478, off the main road, 20 rm with seaview (Rs 450), good restaurant, bar, good for snorkelling ('underwater safari'); **D** *TK Guest House*, 116/1 Beach Rd, T 2603 has 11 rm at the same price, restaurant (insists on taking orders for dinner at breakfast!), good diving beach, peaceful, see above for reef visit.

Budget hotels: **E** *Saranga Travellers Nest*, Madiha (10 mins walk from Walgama Bus stop, Bo Tree Junc), T 25917, 4 rm with bath (RS 300), slightly worn, seafood restaurant, big garden; **E** *Sunny Lanka Guest House*, Polhena Rd, 9 rm with bath (Rs 350) in modern building, Sri Lankan and western meals, skin diving equipment; **F** *Holiday Resort*, relocated at Madiha, 50m from beach, 4 simple rm with shared bath (Rs 150), good seafood at *Sepalika* restaurant, friendly atmosphere, free use of snorkelling equipment.

Paying guest: you can rent simple rooms in family homes in beautiful rural setting for only Rs 50; contact HK Shantha, Paluwata, Walgama S, 5 mins walk from Polhena.

● Places to eat

In Matara: *Chinese Dragon*, 62 New Tangalle Rd, good meals for around Rs 150; *Galle Oriental Bakery*, Dharmapala Maw, next to the crisp Broadway Cinema, does good Sri Lankan meals for Rs 40 as well as snacks. A local delicacy is curd served with honey or jaggery. There are numerous outlets; the *Fine Curd Food Cabin* is rec.

● Shopping

Bookshops: *HB Eramanis Appuhamy*, 87 Dharmapala Maw, has some English books.

Handicrafts: you will also find good batik (58/6 Udyana Rd) and citronella oil in town. You can buy, or simply watch craftsmen producing musical instruments (particularly drums) at 21 Dharmapala Maw.

● Transport

Train Trains to **Colombo (Maradana)**: daily, *Ruhunu Kumari*, 0540, 3½ hrs; *Mail* (2nd and 3rd class), 1530, 4½ hrs; *Galu Kumari*, weekdays, 0730, 4½ hrs. To **Kandy**: 1325, 7½ hrs. From **Kandy**: *direct train*, 0500, 5½ hrs; Rs 118, 2nd class. The train is very busy (2nd and 3rd only which do not guarantee a seat) still, rec if you can get on the train by 0440.

Road Bus: frequent service to coastal towns nearby; to **Nuwara Eliya**: depart am, 8 hrs; to **Hambantota**: every 30 mins.

ROUTES The road crosses the Nilwala Ganga. After 5 km a road to the left goes to what has been described as a new Buddhist sanctuary at **Werahena**, in 'stupefyingly bad taste'. There is a statue of the Buddha 40m high; *Perahera* at Nov/Dec full moon. The road goes on to Dondra.

Dondra

7 km Dondra or Devinuwara (City of Gods), a fishing village which marks the southernmost point of Sri Lanka. **Galge** has an ancient shrine possibly dating from the 7th century AD which may be the oldest stonebuilt structure on the island. The 50m high **lighthouse** on the S promontory at Dondra Head was built in 1899; entry Rs 50.

Local festivals

End-Jul/Aug: there are spectacular *Perahera* with processions and a fair for 12 days at the site of the old Vishnu temple which was destroyed by the Portuguese. Even now the Buddhist pilgrims, continuing the ancient tradition here, venerate Vishnu of the Hindu trinity. There is a modern stupa now.

● **Accommodation** There is no accommodation in Dondra.

Dikwella The road passes through Dikwella (12 km) where there are superb statues and tableaux, and a Buddhist temple. **Accommodation B** *Dikwella Relais Club Village Resort*, Bahteegama, 1 km W, T 2961, 53 rm in bungalows (up to US$55), good restaurant, cultural shows, tennis, watersports, very attractive location on the promontory, beautifully laid out, Italian owned and managed; **D** *Country Comfort*, Kemagoda, has 20 rm.

ROUTES The **A2** continues E along the coast. Take the turn off S at the Naakulagamuwa School for 2 km. The rocky coast here near Mawella, is Hummanaya, a very impressive 'blow hole' where the water spray can rise as high as 25m when the waves here are big. Its name originated from the sound that emerges. Take care not to get too close.

Tangalla

(16 km; *STD Code* 047) Tangalla (or Tangalle) is famous for its turtles and its beach of pink sand. It is an attractive fishing port with a palm fringed bay with extensive irrigation to N.

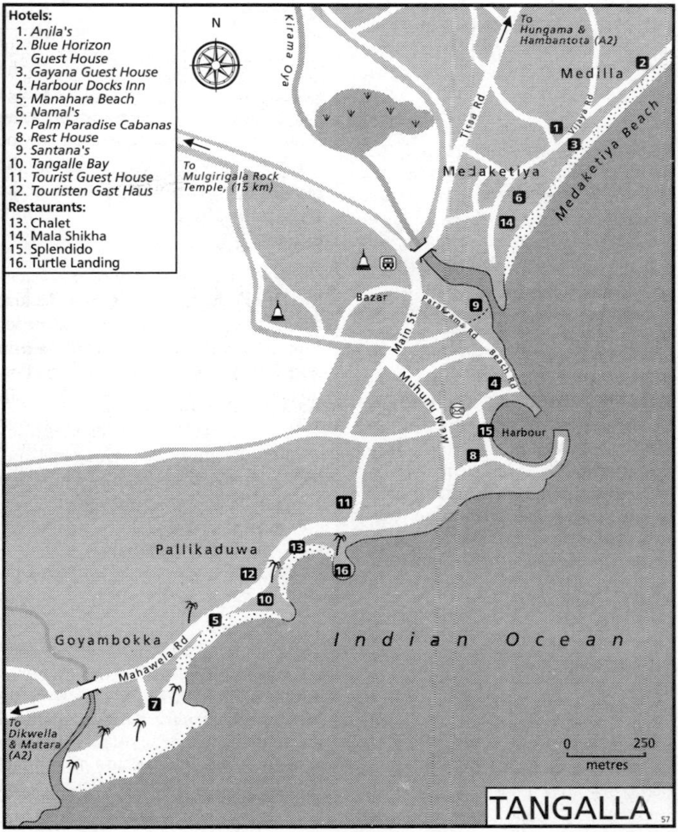

Excursions

Mulgirigala 20 km N, just off the road towards Wiraketiya (B52), stands the isolated 210m high rock. The monastic site was occupied from the 2nd century BC, and was again used as a place of Buddhist learning in the 18th century. In 1826, the discovery at this site by George Turnour, of the commentaries on the *Mahavansa* and *Culavansa* (the *Tika*) allowed the ancient texts, which chronicle the island's history from the 3rd century BC, to be translated from the original Pali to English and Sinhala.

Although not a citadel it is in some ways similar to Sigiriya. At the base of the rock there are monks' living quarters. The fairly steep paved path goes up in stages to the main temple and image house at the top. Along the way there are three platforms with temples, monasteries, *stupas*, a water pool and a Bodhi tree. The site has been renovated; several Buddha statues and good wall paintings were found in the monasteries. Although it is a fairly strenuous climb it is well worthwhile; there are good views across the surrounding countryside from the top.

Local information

● Accommodation

Full-board can double the price of a room. Most **D/E** hotels give discounts out of season.

B ***Tangalle Bay***, Pallikudawa, T 40346, F Colombo 449548, 40 rm, 15 a/c (US$27), restaurant, exchange, pool, watersports, helpful knowledgeable manager will help you plan your tour of the area, pleasant 70s feel, unusual 'ship' design (no straight lines except for bedrooms), attractive setting on rocky promontory, rec.

C ***Manahara Beach***, Moraketiyara, Mahawela Rd, 2 km W, 6 cabanas and 3 rm (Rs 1,000), good food, clean, by the sea in large grounds; **C** ***Palm Paradise Cabanas***, Goyambokka, 2 km W, T 40338, F 40401, 20 simple cabanas with showers on stilts built in the 1980s under shady palms nr beach, airy restaurant serves mild Sri Lankan meals and seafood, eco-conscious attractive setting, popular with German groups (ask bus to drop you on main road and walk 500m), rec; **C-D** ***Rest House***, Dutch building (1774) on promontory overlooking harbour in town centre, T 40229, 26 rm (better in new building), overpriced at Rs 850.

D ***Gayana Guest House***, 75 Vijaya Rd, 8 rm, better on beachside, restaurant, basic but friendly; **D** ***Namal's***, Medaketiya Rd (on the beach), T 40352, 18 rm with bath and balcony with seaview (up to Rs 525), seafood restaurant, bar; **D** ***Tourist Guest House***, opp *Tangalle Bay Hotel*, T 40389, 4 clean rm with bath (up to Rs 600), breakfast incl, quiet, good value; **D** ***Touristen Gast Haus***, 13 Pallikudawa Rd, T 40370, 2 bungalows and 7 rm with bath, spotless, good service, rec.

Budget hotels: **E** ***Anila's***, 23 Vijaya Rd, Medaketiya Beach, T 40446, 7 rm with bath, garden restaurant, bike hire, peaceful; **E** ***Blue Horizon Guest House***, 'Lakmal', Medilla, 1.5 km from harbour, T/F 40401, 2 rm with 4-posters, rattan rocking chair, bath, good, inexpensive Sri Lankan food, peaceful spot, very good value; **E** ***Harbour Docks Inn***, 145 Beach Rd, T 40567, F 40401, clean rooms with bath (up to Rs 450), lobster restaurant (good food but quite expensive), tours near and far; **F** ***Santana's***, 55 Parakrama Rd, T 40419, 4 rm with bath (Rs 200), most basic of the lot but still clean, nonchalant service.

● Places to eat

Many hotels serve good seafood in particular *Blue Horizon*. Others incl ***Chalet***, Mahawela Rd, for seafood (try shear fish with garlic sauce), also sells postcards; ***Mala Shikha***, good, inexpensive food on the beach; ***Splendido***; ***Turtle Landing Beach Restaurant***, basic seafood inspite of evocative name.

● Transport

Train Up to Matara.

Road Colombo (5 hrs).

Going W, you pass from the Wet Zone to the Dry Zone, through **Ranna** (12 km) where there is a Buddhist temple on summit of hill, **Hungama**, where a road leads to Kalametiya Bird sanctuary.

Kalametiya Bird Sanctuary

Take the signposted right hand turning a short distance after Hungama and walk 2 km to the lagoon if on a bus (best to organize your own transport). There are no facilities, nor entry fees. It is a beautiful beach and lagoon, excellent for birdwatching undisturbed save for a few fishermen who might pester you for money.

ROUTES The **A2** continues along the coast and beyond the left turn (A18) towards Embilipitiya and after crossing the Walawe River you reach **Ambalantota** (16 km from Ranna). The attractive coastal area just before the A18 turn-off and S of the Ambalantota is good for exploring and camping.

Madungala, Karambagala Caves and Mahapalessa hot springs

15 km inland from Ambalantota, the road along the Walawe River runs through the Dry-Zone where the forest deteriorates to a dirt track for the last 7 km. The **Madungala** hermitage reputedly has remarkable paintings. In fact, all that remains of the old monument is a square white base and some writing engraved in the rock. There is a new concrete dagoba with murals on a hilltop. There are fine views of Ridiyagama Tank and Adam's Peak from there. A walk through the forest takes you to another dagoba under construction in 1995.

The hot springs at **Mahapalessa** are N of the tank and N of **Ridiyagama** village which is well known for its fine curd and honey. If you approach the hot springs from the A18, take the road to the right (E) at **Siyambalagoda**, cross the Welawa River and follow the track along the stream for about 5 km. Also close to the A18 on the other side, are the 100 or so ancient rocky **Karambagala Caves** which were discovered in the scrubland, once occupied by Buddhist hermits.

Getting there: as this is not on a regular bus route, you need to arrange your own transport (1½ hrs by car). It is possible to cycle but watch out for elephants!

ROUTES On the **A2** towards Hambantota is **Godaraya** Junction. A turn right (1 km S) has a cave with King Gajabahu's inscription but these are difficult to find amidst the cacti.

Hambantota

(14 km; *STD Code* 047) This is a small fishing port with a large Muslim population and is the centre for producing salt from evaporated sea water. The *lewayas*, or shallow salt pans, are by the road, the white salt stunningly bright in the hot sun. You can see the salt flats of Lanka Salt Ltd stretching away inland.

The town square has its usual clock tower together with a curious statue of a coolie. The small bay offers excellent swimming, but the beaches, where you will see outriggers, are not so good. There are sand dunes immediately around the town.

Local information

● **Accommodation**

On the beach at Galwala: **A** *Peacock Beach Hotel*, T 20377, F Colombo 449325, 105 a/c rm, secluded but indifferent gardens, pool amidst frangipanis open to non-residents, often full with tour groups, self-contained resort with security guards; **C-D** *Seaspray*, 1 km from Bus station, T 20212, 15 rm (cheaper for Sri Lankans), rather rundown, threadbare carpets, peeling paint, overpriced at Rs 800; **D** *Aparna Tourist Rest*, off Tissa Rd, opp *Seaspray*, 5 rm with bath, basic, expensive at Rs 450.

In town: **C-D** *Rest House*, T 20299, 15 rm overlooking the coast, situated in a superb position on a promontory, with a restaurant with seafood (unexciting), described as 'the bright spot of Hambantota'; **E** *Lake View*, W of Bus Station, T 20246, has 5 similar rm at the same price but is not very clean; **E** *Sunshine Tourist Rest*, 47 Main Rd (150m N of Bus Station), T 20129, 5 simple rm with bath (Rs 300), mosquito net and fan in friendly family guest house, restaurant (excellent curries); **E-F** *Hashim Pushena's*, 33 Terrace St, up stairs from Bus Station, 6 rm with bath (squat wc), fan and net (Rs 200), good food, simple clean family guest house popular with travellers; **F** *Joy*, off Matara Rd, T 20328, 6 similar rm with bath in well-run guest house with restaurant.

● **Places to eat**

In addition to hotel restaurants, ***Jade Garden*** in Galawala, opp *Peacock Beach Hotel*, is smart, modern and western style with prices to match; ***Fire Curd***, Tissa Rd, opp Bus Station (beach side) does delicious curd and treacle and inexpensive meals.

● **Transport**

Road Bus: buses to Colombo takes about 5½ hrs and to Ratnapura about 3½ hrs.

ROUTES You can enjoy some birdwatching by taking a diversion off the A2 towards Tissamaharama.

Malala Lagoon

Follow the Malala River from the second bridge after '246 km' towards the lagoon and you will reach this a birdwatcher's paradise. You will probably see several crocodiles sunbathing undisturbed and numerous species of Dry Zone and water birds here including flamingo near the mouth of the channel. The bonus is you are free to wander around at leisure since there are no guides as when visiting a 'Park' (eg Bundala) and no hassle.

Bundala Bird Sanctuary

Approach From the A2, a right turn at Weligatta (SE at 250 km) leads to coastal lagoons with a wealth of birdlife (there are lots of stalls on the main road here selling

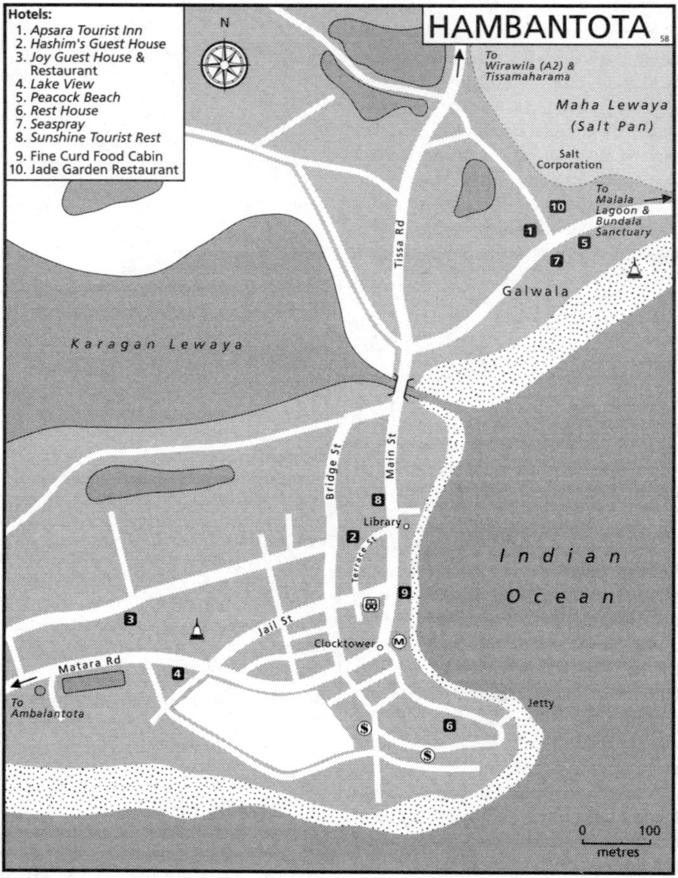

curd in attractive clay pots). The entrance to the park is about 1 km down this road. Jeep hire Rs 1,200. Entry Rs 470, children Rs 235 (students may get a discount on showing ID). Allow about 3 hrs and do take drinks as it can be very hot. Early morning/late afternoon are best times.

Background The reserve consists of a series of shallow lagoons. These are surrounded by low shrubs which make really quite dense bush. Tracks go through the bush and connect each lagoon. The sanctuary skirts the sea and it is possible to see the lighthouse on the Great Basses some 40 km away to the E.

Wildlife You are likely to see elephants (though often difficult to see), jackals, monkeys, rabbits (apparently very rare and carry a Rs 1,000 fine for killing) crocodiles and snakes. Apart from peacocks and other bush birds, there is a good variety of water birds including spoonbills, ibis, pelicans,

Shooting water fowl

Source: Kincaid, D (1938) ***British social life in India***, Routledge, London

painted storks, flamingos and different egrets, mostly concentrated around the lagoons.

Viewing You travel around the park in hired jeeps with guides (who cannot be too knowledgeable if they insist that flamingos are summer visitors from Australia and that peacocks are female!). Unfortunately, the jeep drivers do not seem to be very willing to stop and let you just observe. Tracking an elephant appears to be the high point of the day. When one is sighted, all jeeps home in on it and follow it so closely that ultimately the animal is angered enough to turn and charge one of the jeeps which sends all the vehicles to burn off down the track. Some visitors find this quite distasteful.

ROUTES The **A2** continues northwards, away from the sea, past Wirawila where a right fork goes to Tissamaharama. The main road crosses a large tank on a causeway to Pannegamuwa towards Wellawaya. The **Wirawila Wewa** is a Bird Sanctuary which attracts large numbers of waterfowl.

ROUTES The **alternative route** from the N, on the A2 road from **Wellawaya** to Tissamaharama is not very interesting. Shortly after Wellawaya, the road finishes descending the 150m or so to the flat plain. There are only two or three small towns (the biggest of which is at Tanamalwila) and not much can be seen of the Lunuganwehera reservoir although there is the occasional glimpse of the Kataragama peak. For Tissam turn E off the A2, just before the Sri Lankan air force base at Wirawila.

Tissamaharama

(*STD Code* 047) 32 km NE of Hambantota, 'Tissa' is one of oldest of the abandoned royal cities where King Dutthagamenu had his capital here

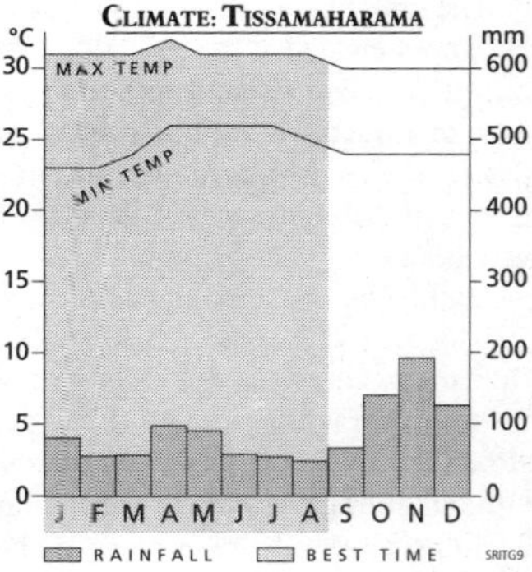

before recapturing Anuradhapura. The ruins had been hidden in jungle for centuries and today there is little of interest visible. It does not, in any way, compare with the better preserved Polonnaruwa or Anuradhapura.

The tank at **Tissawewa**, thought to have been created at the end of the 3rd century BC, was restored with two others and attracts a lot of water birds. At dawn, the view of birds roosting on large trees and then moving over the tank is very beautiful.

Numerous dagobas, including one 50m high, which too had been lost under the sand having been destroyed by the invading Dravidians, have been restored entirely by local Buddhists. Other buildings resemble a palace and a multi-storeyed monastery. The Yatala Wehera (originally the tooth relic shrine) houses a new **museum** with a collection of low-impact, but charming, Buddha and *Bodhisattva* statues.

There are a lot of unofficial 'safari' companies on the main street in Tissa. You will probably be able to negotiate a much lower rate to visit the Ruhunu-Yala National Park, than those on offer from the hotels. Beware though, as the transport is not always serviceable and if you have not already booked accommodation, you may well be taken to a different hotel from the one you want to go to.

Excursion

Kirinda, on the coast, is 7 km S of Tissamaharama, and has a good beach and some Buddhist ruins on the rocks. It is historically linked to the King Duttha-gamenu. His mother, having been banished by her father, landed at the village

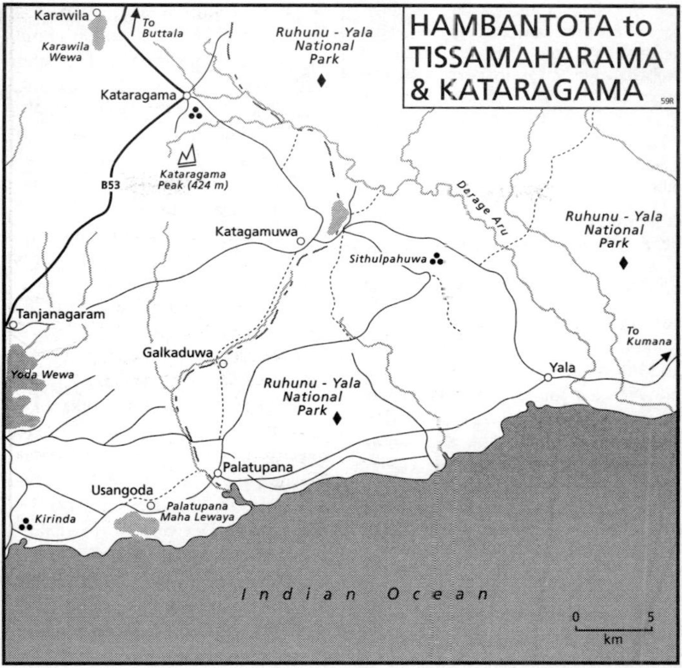

and married the local king. Although popular with scuba divers who are attracted by the reefs at Great and Little Basses off the coast, the currents can be treacherous. If you walk E along the coast towards Yala there is an area of Dry Zone scrub land along the coast, contiguous to Yala itself. Good for birdwatching but keep a look out for elephants! **Accommodation E** *Kirinda Beach Resort* has rooms with bath, fan and net, Rs 350, good restaurant. *Getting there*: buses run between Tissa and Kirinda.

Local information

● Accommodation

B-C *Tissamaharama Rest House* on lakeside, T 37299 (reserve T Colombo 323501, F 422732), 62 rm, 5 a/c (US$25), all with a balcony with a nice view of the tank, a large concrete building and consequently the rooms are very box-like, rooms vary in comfort (some with a/c can be freezing, others may be stuffy), restaurant (limited menu but tasty curries), open-air bar, exchange, nice pool overlooking the tank, gardens, lacks personal touch but still rec, one of the larger CHC rest houses but very popular with groups so book ahead. Others nearby are simpler guest houses.

C *Lakeside Tourist Inn*, facing the lake, T 37216 comfortable rooms, some a/c (Rs 1,100), great restaurant, warm and friendly, good base for touring Yala, jeep hire arranged (Rs 1,600 for 2); **C** *Priyankara Tourist Inn*, Kataragama Rd, T 37206, F 37326, 26 rm, 8 a/c (US$20) with balcony overlooking paddy fields, pleasant restaurant, good atmosphere, very clean.

D *Chandrika*, Kataragama Rd, 8 rm, good restaurant; **D** *Queen's Rest House*, 169 Kachcheriyagama, T 37264, 10 clean, modern rm with fan, net and bath (Rs 450), restaurant (bland food, popular with those avoiding curries!); **D** *Singha Tourist Inn*, Tissawewa Maw, nr *Rest House*, T 37099, F 37080 (T Colombo 587737, F 421381), 15 rather dark rm (Rs 600), 3 a/c (Rs 800), restaurant, bar, residential block in family home's garden, friendly, often full, rec; **D** *Tissa Inn*, Wellawaya Rd, 2 km from Tissa town, between Debara Wewa and Wirawila Wewa, T 37233, F 37080 (Attn Tissa Inn), 8 rm (Rs 700), restaurant, bar.

E *Hatari*, Kataragama Rd, 7 modest rm, Chinese restaurant.

● Transport

Road 6 hrs drive from Colombo.

Kataragama

16 km N from Tissamaharama, is Kataragama, well off the beaten track and not often visited by tourists. It is, however, a popular pilgrimage centre throughout the year, even outside of the great festivals. A small town with clean, tree lined roads with rows of stalls selling garlands and platters of fruit (coconut, mango, watermelon) it attracts people of all faiths from across the island.

The largest draw is the *Esala* (Jul/Aug full-moon) festival. Thousands of pilgrims flock to the Hindu temple for the *Perahera* which ends with fire-walking and 'water cutting' ceremonies. They come to perform penance for sins they have committed and some of the scenes of self-mutilation, performed in a trance, are horrific.

The Hindu and Buddhist sanctuaries are quite separate. Buddhists visit the ancient Kirivehera dagoba, 1 km W of the plain white Hindu temple but also consider the 'Kataragama Deviyo' here sacred. Muslims associate the town with two saints and come to pray at the Khizr Takya at the mosque nearby.

There is quite a large car park on the S side of the river which is busy with garland and fruit stalls. A short walk takes you to the Menik Ganga. Steps lead down to the water which is quite shallow in places allowing pilgrims to take their ritual bath almost in the middle of the river. It is a very attractive area with large trees on the banks providing plenty of shade. Cross the bridge to enter the main temple complex.

The wide street lined with tulip trees leads to the Hindu temple (300m). You may see groups of pilgrims performing the *Kavadi* dance when men, women and children hold semicircular blue arches above their heads as they slowly progress towards the temple.

The **Hindu Temple (Maha Devale)** dedicated to Skanda (see page 138) (Kataragama Deviyo) is not particularly impressive: a small gate with a large wrought iron peacock on the reverse, leads onto the rectangle. Immediately, there is a small area where the pilgrims throw coconuts onto a stone slab to split them before making the offering. Trees in the rectangle are surrounded by brass railings and there are a number of places where pilgrims can light leaf-shaped candles. Here, you can see men in 'ritualistic trances': some are professionals, though, since you might see the same man, a little later, making his way to the Buddhist dagoba, carrying a briefcase and umbrella!

There is often a long queue to enter the shrine where platters are offered to

Barefoot Over Hot Coals

Fire-walking, a part of the Kataragama festival, may hark back to the story of Sita in the epic **Ramayana**. Ravana, the King of Lanka, abducted Rama's wife Sita, an Indian princess, from the forest and carried her away to his island. After she is finally rescued by her husband, Sita proves her purity (chastity) by walking barefoot over fire and emerging unhurt. In southern Sri Lanka, devotees of Kataragama and Pattini follow her example and seek their blessing as they undergo the purification ritual.

the priests. The idea seemed to be to 'hide' a note in the platter. Some say, anything less than Rs 200 may be unacceptable and the gift might be refused. There is certainly evidence that the platters are 'recycled': men on bicycles can be seen returning them to the market, covered in garlands – nobody seems to mind though! There is no image of the god Skanda in the shrine; simply his *vel* or lance. There are separate small shrines to others in the Hindu pantheon, including Vishnu, Ganesh and Pattini, the last also linked to the fire-walking ceremony. Nearby are the two Bodhi trees.

Kirivehera Beyond the Hindu shrine and a meeting hall on the N side of the square, starting from the E gate, there is another tulip tree avenue which leads to the milk-white Budhhist dagoba, about 500m away. Stalls selling lotus buds line the route but here there is competition with girls shouting out the bargains and pressing people buy. Clearly those on the shady side of the road won! You can often see the temple elephant shackled to the trees here, being fed a copious diet of palm leaves. The dagoba itself is a very peaceful place and, as usual, beautifully maintained. It is not especially large and its spire is quite squat compared with those farther N.

Archaeological Museum There is a small museum near the Hindu temple, with Buddha statues, moonstones and ancient inscriptions; closed on Tues.

Local information

● Accommodation

There are a number of hotels and guest houses.

C ***New Rest House***, off Sithulpahuwa Rd, T 35299, 18 rm.

Nearby, **D** ***Kataragama Rest House***, nr the river, has 23 simple rm and dormitory, simple Sri Lankan food.

Enquire in Colombo about rooms at the attractive ***Bank of Ceylon Guest House***, Sri Lankan meals; also ***Robinson's Resthouse***, attractive building, in a pleasant garden and the ***Safari Park***, signed from the road has about 60 rm and a pool.

● Transport

Road Bus: services in all directions incl direct bus to Nuwara Eliya, Galle and Colombo.

Ruhunu-Yala National Park

Approach The entrance to the reserve in the Dry Zone (*STD Code* 047) is 20 km from Tissamaharama, bounded by the river and the sea. Kumana (see page 237) to the E is a Bird Sanctuary, reached from Pottuvil and Arugam Bay. Open 0600-1800 daily mid-Oct to end-Jul. Entry permits from the Park Office at Palatupana to the S which has a small museum. Visitors must be accompanied by a Park Tracker or Guide who will charge a fee in addition to the entry.

Background The Park comprises five blocks and Yala Strict Natural Reserve; the central area was originally a Sportsmens' Shooting Reserve which was established as a protected area in 1938. The 1260 sq km Park varies from open parkland to dense jungle on the plains, scrubland with rocky outcrops and several streams, small lakes and lagoons. The picturesque ocean frontage to the E has wide beaches and high sand dunes.

The archaeological remains of ancient sites suggest that many centuries ago the area was a part of the Ruhunu Kingdom; Akasa Chetiya and Magul Mahavihara date from the 2nd and 1st centuries BC, while thousands of Buddhist monks resided at the monastery at **Situlpahuwa** where the white Akasa Chitiya dagoba which has now been restored.

Wildlife Elephants are the main attraction and are easily seen especially near water sources from Jan-May. Others seen throughout the Park include macaque and langur monkeys, sambhur, spotted deer, wild boar, buffaloes and crocodiles. Bears are occasionally spotted, particularly in Jun, when they feed on local fruit while the magnificent leopard may sometimes be seen in the dry sandy and rocky areas; Vepandeniya is considered a favourite spot.

There are about 130 species of birds including barbets, hoopoes, Malabar pied hornbills, orioles, Ceylon shamas, paradise flycatchers, and peacocks. The expanses of water attract Eastern grey heron, Painted stork, Serpent-eagle and White-bellied Sea-eagle. In addition a large number of migrant water-fowl arrive each winter to augment the resident population. You may be lucky enough to spot the rare Black-necked stork near Buttawa on the coast.

Viewing Best time to visit is Oct-Dec, early morning and late afternoon (it is possible to spend the middle of the day at one of the coastal hotels at Amaduwa). Walking is not permitted within the park. Buses or jeep tours within the Park, 0630, 1500. Safari tours, about Rs 200 per person in a jeep carrying six passengers, last 2½-3 hrs. Some are disappointed by the difficulty of seeing wildlife.

• **Accommodation** **E** *Park Bungalows*, 7 simple bungalows in scenic locations: Old and New Buttuwa, Mahaseelawa, Patanangala along the coast, Heenwewa facing a tank, Yala and Thalgasmankada on the Manik Ganga River (tourists may only stay in Patangala and Heenwewa). Each has a cook who can prepare Sri Lankan meals but take the ingredients; no electricity. Reservations up to 3 months in advance: Department of Wildlife Conservation, 82 Rajamalwatta Rd, Battaramulla nr Sri Jayawardenepura (Kotte) or T 433012. Also 2 ***Camp Sites***, on the bank of the Manik Ganga. At Amaduwa on the coast, S of the Main Gate: **A** *Yala Safari Beach Hotel*, T 20471, Colombo 688421, F 699226, 56 rm, 6 a/c (US$60), restaurant, bar, diving, safari jeep; **C** ***Brown's Safari Beach***, T 20326, Colombo 326767, F 433755, 8 rm (US$16), restaurant, pool open to non-residents.

COLOMBO TO RATNAPURA AND BANDARAWELA

The most attractive route to Ratnapura goes via Avissawella through the Wet Zone, before reaching the centre of Sri Lanka's gem producing region. It is a gentle drive to the foot of the hills, with superb views of Adam's Peak and the hills when they are not shrouded in heavy cloud. This is the heart of the Wet Zone and one of the wettest regions of Sri Lanka. From Ratnapura the A4 circles to the S of Adam's Peak, climbing into the hills through Balangoda to Bandarawela. The A8, which also runs through attractive countryside, offers an alternative route to Ratnapura.

ROUTES The **A4** runs SE past Nugegoda. The slower but more attractive route, the **B1**, follows the left (S) bank of the Kelaniya River. *Kelaniya River Villa*, on the river bank, 20 mins drive from Colombo on Biyagama Main Rd, Enquiries, T 536820.

Kaduwela (16 km), also on the **B1**, has a *Rest House* in a beautiful position overlooking the river with a constant succession of varied river traffic. There is a fairly large Buddhist temple and the irrigation tank of Mulleriyawa. Continuing along the Kelaniya River the road passes through Hanwella.

Hanwella (33 km) On the site of a Portuguese fort, Hanwella is noted as the place where the last king of Kandy, **Sri Vikrama Raja Sinha**, was defeated. There is an excellent **E** *Rest House*, (CHC) on the Kelaniya River, rooms with bath (US$7) with a beautiful view along the river. Reservations T Colombo 323501, F 422732. The Prince of Wales' visit is commemorated by the planting of a jackfruit tree. At Hanwella the road joins the **A4** and turns left towards Avissawella.

Avissawella (18 km), the ancient capital of the Sitawaka kings and now the centre of rubber industry, is in beautiful wooded surroundings. The ruins of the royal palace of Rajasinha, a Buddhist king who converted to Hinduism can still be seen. He was responsible for starting work on the unfinished Berendi Kovil temple, which still has some fine stonework despite the destructive efforts of the Portuguese. It is just off the Ginigathena road on the opposite bank of the river.

ROUTES Avissawella to Watawala, Hatton and Nuwara Eliya. In some senses Avissawella is one of the gateways to the Central Highlands. The **A7** goes E out of the town and then NE into the hills towards Kandy. Just before **Ruwanwella**, where the old rest house occupies the site of a former Dutch Fort, the **A7** turns E directly into the hills, following the valley of the Maskeliya Oya for 20 km before climbing steeply to Ginigathena. It continues to the **Ginigathena Pass**, offering magnificent views at the top including Adam's Peak on a clear day. The road decends to **Kitulgala**. **Accommodation C-D** *Kitulgala Rest House* (CHC), on the river Kelaniya, T 7528, reservations, T 323501, F 422732, 18 rm (US$15), restaurant, bar, exchange, picturesque location for David Lean's "Bridge on the River Kwai".

From here on the road runs through tea country. Ginigathena is a small bazaar for the tea estates and their workers. The road winds up through a beautiful valley, surrounded by green, evenly picked tea bushes to Watawela.

Watawala (10 km). The air becomes noticeably cooler, and occasionally there are views right across the plains to Colombo and the Kelaniya Valley. At Watawala the **Carolina Falls** are spectacular in the wet season. Follow the lower road to Hatton (12 km), then through Talawakele and Nanu Oya to Nuwara Eliya (see page 184).

ROUTES Avissawella to Ratnapura and Bandarawela The **A4** takes a more circuitous route into the Highlands. It turns sharply S in Avissawella, passing first through low gaps between the Central

Highlands to the E and the outermost ranges of the hills to the W, and periodically crossing rivers that come tumbling down from the SW Highlands. It passes through Pusella and crosses the river Kuruwita, running through a landscaspe that was the site of some of Sri Lanka's earliest settlements. At the Batadomba-lena Cave near **Kuruwita**, Deraniyagala reported the find of fragmentary skeletal remains, as well as those of several large mammal skeletons, including elephants and cattle, dating back at least as far as 28,000 years ago, and possibly very much earlier. *Palm Garden Travellers Paradise Restaurant* on the right of the road is hard to miss. Pleasant gardens, open-sided seating, good for a stop for drinks and simple snacks. The road goes on to Ratnapura.

ROUTES The southern route from Colombo to Ratnapura The **A8** goes S from Colombo to **Panadura** (27 km) and then turns left towards **Horana** (16 km).

Kiriberiya A left turn at Eluwila Sub-Post Office, 4 km beyond Panadura, takes you to the **Kiriberiya** Estate (15 mins drive) which has the attractive **B** *Paradies* 'Country House', T 034 32356, F Colombo 652045, with 4 large comfortable rm (US$25) with period furniture, meals to order, spacious grounds amidst rubber plantations in a peaceful, rural setting, fresh water pool, boats, bird-watching and possibility of pony/elephant rides. Kiriberiya Bus Station is 3 mins walk; pick up from the airport can be arranged. At **Horana** the **D** *Rest House* (good value) is built in the remains of an ancient Buddhist monastery. On the opposite side of road is a large Buddhist temple with a particularly noteworthy bronze candlestick, over 2m tall.

ROUTES From Nambapane (29 km) the road keeps quite close to the Kalu Ganga River, staying in its valley to Ratnapura.

Ratnapura

(21 km; *STD Code* 045) The climate of Ratnapura has been likened to a Turkish bath. One of Sri Lanka's wettest towns, even Feb, the driest month, normally has nearly 100 mm of rain, while May, the wettest, has nearly 500 mm. The vegetation is correspondingly luxuriant, but the city is best known for its gem stones, washed down the river bed so it is aptly named the 'City of Gems'. However, the gravel beds which contain the gemstones are also the source of evidence of some of Sri Lanka's earliest cultures and of the fauna which are now extinct. Discoveries of animal bones as well as of a variety of stone tools have made it clear that the area is probably one of the first sites to have been occupied by humans in Sri Lanka.

The quality of Ratnapura's gems is legendary. In the 7th century Hiuen Tsang claimed that there was a ruby on the spire of the temple at Anuradhapura whose magnificence illuminated the sky. Today sapphires are much more important. A number of precious stones are found nearby including sapphire, ruby, topaz, amethyst, cat's eye, alexandrite, aquamarine, tourmaline, garnet and zircon. Several are mined from pits dug into a special form of gravel. Genuine stones are common; valuable stones by definition are rarer. Advice given to travellers at the beginning of the century still holds:

CLIMATE: RATNAPURA

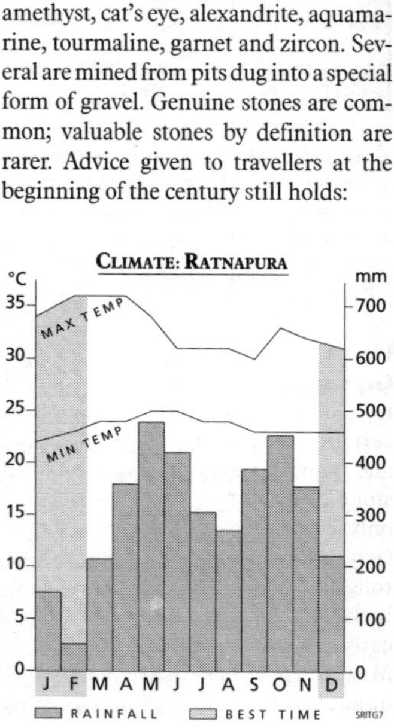

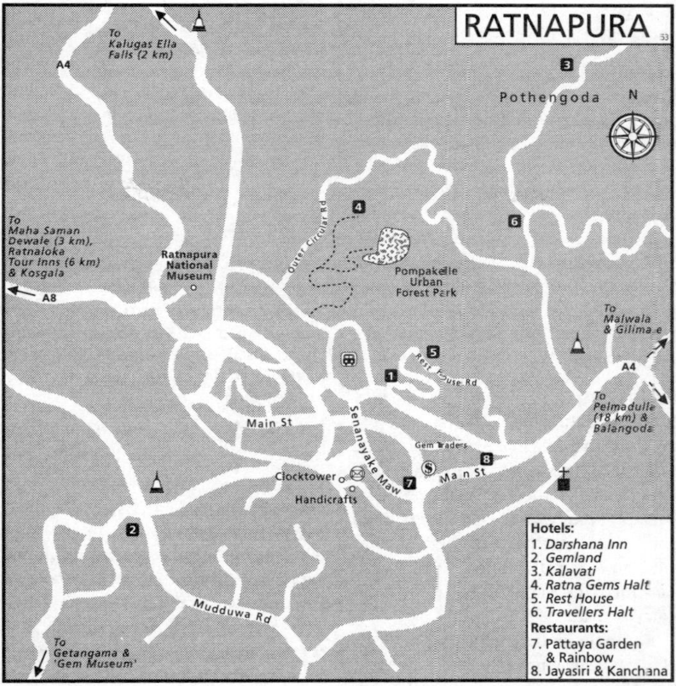

"As regards buying stones, it is a risky business unless the passenger has expert knowledge or advice. It is absolute folly to buy stones from itinerant vendors. It is far better to go to one of the large Colombo jewellers and take the chance of paying more and obtaining a genuine stone."

Places of interest

Gem market Although people seem to trade gems all over town, there are certain areas that specialize in uncut and unpolished stones, polished stones, cut stones, other streets will only deal in star sapphires or cat's eyes. Gem traders usually wear a white sarong and white shirt to bring them luck. Most of the trading takes place early in the morning. On Saviya Mawatha (off Main St) you can watch hundreds of people buying and selling gems every morning.

Ratnapura is surrounded by rubber and tea estates in a lush and beautiful setting, and gives better views of Adam's Peak than almost anywhere else on the island. It is well worth going to the top of the fort for the views. Driving up to Gilimale from the bridge gives you a chance to see the massive curtain wall of the central highlands to the N. Pilgrims walk the 25 km from Ratnapura to Adam's peak during the winter months. The surrounding forests are rich in flowers, one of the most notable being the *Vesak Orchid*, which takes its name from the month of Vesak in which it flowers.

Maha Saman Dewale 4 km W of town is the richest Buddhist temple in Sri Lanka. Built by Parakrama Bahu in the 2nd-3rd century it is dedicated to the guardian god of Adam's Peak. There is a major *Perahera* procession at the time of the Jul-Aug full-moon.

Museums

Ratnapura National Museum, on A4 going W, near the Bus Depot. Open 0900-1700, closed Fri. Small exhibition of pre-historic fossil skeletons from the region of elephants, hippos and rhinoceros found in gem pits. Also jewellery, gems, textiles and flags. **Gem Museum**, Pothgul Vihara Rd, Getangama (2 km S). 0900-1700. Gems from different parts of Sri Lanka and an exhibition of gem polishing. **NB** Travel agents can organize visits to gem mines.

Excursions

Adam's Peak This is the base for the much steeper and more strenuous route which leads to Adam's Peak. Route: Malwala (8 km) on the Kalu Ganga to Palabadalla (11 km; 375m), then a very steep path to Heramitipana (13 km; 1,100m) and the summit (5 km; 2,260m). The imprint of the Buddha's foot gives it the name Sripada.

Pompakelle Urban Forest Park (NE of town, near swimming pool, Reservoir Rd) Signposted trails lead you through the surprisingly large forest – a welcome change of pace from Main St.

Kalugas Ella Falls (2 km N from centre) Attractive waterfall with opportunity to swim in the river. Snack bars. Avoid Sun which can get busy.

A **Buddha Statue** overlooks the town. You can climb up to it through low woods.

Caves There are impressive caves at Kosgalla (8 km from Ratnapura) and at Eratna/Batatota (19 km).

Local information

● Accommodation

Most hotels from **D** category down have rooms with cold shower, western toilet, fan and mosquito net.

B-C *Ratnaloka Tour Inns*, Kosgala, Kahangama (6 km from town), T 2455, 53 rm, central a/c, good restaurant, exchange, pool, gem museum.

C-D *Kalavati*, Polhengoda Village, Outer Circular Rd, 1.6 km from Bus Stand, T 2465, 23 rm, some a/c (Rs 800), restaurant, house decorated with collector's pieces (antiques cabinets, palm leaf manuscripts, statues, betel cutters etc), beautiful tropical garden, tours (Dec to May), natural theraphy 'Healing arts' practised here incl oil baths and massage (about Rs 650), herbal treatments (Rs 450-800), floral baths, 3-wheeler from Bus Stand, R 50.

D *Nilani Lodge*, 21 Dharmapala Maw, T 2170, 10 rm with balcony (Rs 650), some a/c, in large modern white apartment-style building, restaurant and Gem Museum and shop on site, tours to mines and cutters – a gem shop with beds!; **D** *Rest House*, Rest House Rd, on a hill, 1 km from centre, T 2299, 11 rm, food also excellent value, outstanding views and delightful site, peaceful.

Budget hotels: **E** *Darshana Inn*, 68/5 Rest House Rd, T 2674, 4 clean rm (Rs 350), restaurant, bar; **E** *Gemland*, 12 Mudduwa Rd, T 2153, 10 rather dingy rm (some a/c) in a large hotel but with not much going on; **E** *Ratna Gems Halt*, 153/5 Outer Circular Rd, has 4 pleasant rm (Rs 300) in family house overlooking paddy fields, meals available; **E** *Travellers Halt*, T 3092, acceptable rooms (Rs 330) in family house but no one speaks English.

● Places to eat

Jayasiri Hotel & Bakery, 198 Main St, Sri Lankan rice and curry dowstairs, Chinese on 1st flr, meals about Rs 75, bustling with activity, friendly staff, full of local colour; *Kanchana*, 189 Main St, Indian veg meals (Rs 25), 1st flr overlooking busy Main St. *Pattaya Garden Palace*, 14 Senanayake Maw, modern a/c upmarket restaurant with a wide choice of Chinese and Thai dishes, average meal Rs 500; *Rainbow*, opp at 163 Main St, good for Rice and Curry 'meals' (Rs 50), large airy room looking onto part of gem traders street market.

● Transport

Road Bus: regular buses to Colombo, every 15 mins, takes 3 hrs, Rs 50. Buses to other destinations do not originate here so have no fixed timetable. However, they are regular and frequent. To Balangoda, 2 hrs, Rs 11.

Longer excursions

Sinharaja Biosphere Reserve

The Sinharaja forest reserve lies approximately 30 km S of Ratnapura, and can easily be reached by road from Ratnapura. The shortest route leaves the A4 E of Ratnapura at Tiruwanaketiya and runs to Kalawana, where a road turns left to Weddagala. The reserves can also be reached from the A17 at Rakwana (see below).

Approach From Colombo the usual entry route is via the Kalawana-Weddagala road from the NW. There are three other options: from the NE via Rakwana-Morningside Estate; Deniyaya-Pallegama Rd from the SE; Hinduma-Neluwa road from the SW. Lying in the SW lowland Wet Zone, the Reserve's rolling hills with ridges and valleys between 200-1,300m stretch 21 km from E to W. However, it is less than 4 km wide, bounded by the Kalu Ganga in the N and the Gin Ganga in the S. The area receives over 2,500 mm of rain annually, most falling between May-Jul and Oct-Dec. Afternoons can be wet so be prepared! The average temperature is 23.6°C. *Best time to visit*: Dec-early Apr and Aug-Sep. Suggested min stay, 2 nights; 3 nights give you an opportunity to see a good cross-section of the forest.

Background Sinharaja is a unique stretch of rain forest on the island which apart from very limited use by tribal peoples has been left largely undisturbed. Designated a Man and Biosphere Reserve in 1978, it is now Sri Lanka's first Natural Heritage site. In 1989 it was recognized by UNESCO as one of the international Biosphere Reserves and is a World Heritage Site. The forest with the name meaning 'Lion King' is believed to have been the final refuge of the now extinct lion.

It rains in Sinharaja most afternoons; it does not have the modern accommodation and prestige animal spotting facilities of some of the other Reserves or National Parks, eg Yala, yet just being in the thick of the rain forest is a unique experience. Besides, you are not confined to a jeep.

22 villages surround the reserve and the villagers make free use of the resources within, eg collecting *kitul* sap for jaggery (see box) and leaves and wood for construction and fuel, making the task of conservation and forest management more difficult.

Wildlife The animals include sambhur, barking deer, mongoose and the Golden palm civet; the Purple-faced leaf monkey is common. Although leopard tracks have been seen frequently, it is much more difficult to sight than many of the other animals. Birds include some rare endemics such as Red-faced malkoha, Sri Lanka Blue magpie, and the White-headed starling and plenty of others including orange minivets, orioles and babblers. Reptiles include the endemic Green pit viper and the Hump-nosed viper.

Viewing You need an Entry Permit; apply in advance (see Accommodation below) and take your identity card or passport. Foreigners are charged Rs 50 per day for entry. You have to be accompanied by a guide to enter the forest, Rs 100 min. Guides are very knowledgeable but do not always speak English. There are three main nature trails with good guide leaflets available. Binoculars are worth taking.

NB Leeches are everywhere and can be a nuisance as bites may become septic, so carry a repellent. They sway on the ground waiting for a passer by and get in boots when you are walking. When they are gorged with blood they drop off. To remove do not pull away but use a spray (eg *Waspeeze*), some salt, a lighted cigarette or match or, as a last resort, a sharp knife to encourage it to drop off. It is a good idea to spray socks and boot laces well with an insect repellant before setting off each day.

Waturawa Trail, 4.7 km: the path starts 250m from the Camp and leads through the forest up to the visitors centre. There are 14 Observation Posts which are marked on the relevant guide.

To Drink Or Not To Drink

Villagers make free use of the sap from the fishtail or *kitul* palm (*Caryota urens*) and can sometimes be seen carrying pots of this home. The sap which drains from a cut at the end of the main stalk of the inflorescence is collected in clay pots. This liquid produces not only the fermented toddy (distilled to yield arrack), but also the unfermented treacle produced by heating it (*peni*) which in turn is used to make the dry brown sugar, jaggery (*hakuru*). Both forms of sugar are excellent served with curd or when used in preparing sweets. The Sinharaja jaggery is particularly fine.

It is about 3 hrs of gentle walking with two good places for spotting birds and watching monkeys; a good introduction to the rain forest.

Moulawella Trail, 7.5 km, taking about 7 hrs. A fairly strenuous trek which takes you through primary forest up to Moulawella peak (700m). From there you can see Adam's Peak and look over the forest canopy. The walk gives you a chance to see fascinating leaf-shaped frogs, lizards, tropical fish, snakes, crabs and a 300-year-old vine (which features on Rs 10 notes).

Sinhagala Trail, 14 km, takes a full day. The trek leads through the heart of the rain forest to 'Lion Rock' from where you can look out over the unbroken tree canopy of an undisturbed forest and see the various hill ranges – 'twice as good as Moulawella'.

• **Accommodation** *Forest Department Camp*, Kudawa, NW entrance, simple dormitory style with some partitions, shared western toilets, showers (sometimes 'out-of-order'), forest river for washing and bathing, not really aimed at tourists as majority using the accommodation are on research or educational programmes. Rs 150/night, hire of sheet and pillowcases, Rs 25. Reservations are essential; contact Conservator of Forests, Forestry Department, Rajamalwatta Rd, Battaramulla, Colombo outskirts, T 566626.

• **Places to eat** You can arrange rice and curry meals (Rs 35) by speaking to the cook. Day visitors should carry food and drink.

• **Transport Road Bus**: from Colombo, public buses to Weddagala, 117 km via Mathugama, 154m via Ratnapura. Turn off the main road to Kudawa (6 km) with the *Forest Department Camp*.

ROUTES Ratnapura to the East and South East coast The **A4** between Ratnapura and Pelmadulla (18 km) continues across the fertile and undulating low country, while the hills on either side come closer and closer to the road. Pelmadulla is at the junction of three major routes. The **A4** runs E and then NE, curving round the southern flank of the Central Highland massif. The A18 goes SE to **Madampe** (13 km), and continues Almost due SE to the S coast at Nonagama near Hambantota. From Madampe the **A17** goes S to the coast at Matara.

ROUTES Pelmadulla to Balangoda and the caves beyond From Pelmadulla the **A4** continues to Balangoda through superb lush scenery all the way. This is the heart of the rubber producing area, and there a many rubber estates. Adam's Peak and the Maskeliya Range rise magnificently to the N, although during the SW monsoon they are almost permanently covered in cloud.

Balangoda

(24 km; *STD Code* 045) There is little to do in Balangoda but it is a base for excursions into Peak Wilderness Sanctuary and to visit prehistoric cave sites.

Excursions You can visit the **Kuragala Cave** with the Jailani Muslim shrine nearby, and the **Budugala Cave Temple** (25 km). The road to **Uggal kaltota** follows the downward sloping ridge (buses go most of the way).

For Kuragala, which is at an altitude of 350m, you have to follow a path uphill from Taniantenna on the Kaltota road.

For Budugala, the 3 km track from Uggal Kaltota is safe for 4WD in dry weather.

From Balangoda, after passing Rajawaka on the Kaltota road, a track leads 4 km down to the S to **Diyainna Cave**, near the village of the same name, which was also inhabited between 8000 and 2500 BC. If you continue along the track SE towards Uda Walawe Reservoir, you will reach **Handagiriya** on the river bank. It is claimed that the old Buddhist stupa once held the Tooth Relic. This is close to **Bellan Bendi Pelessa**, the plain where large finds of prehistoric skeletons has confirmed it as an open-air site once used by *Homo Sapiens Beangodensis*.

• **Accommodation** Most hotel rooms here have cold shower, western toilet, fan and mosquito net. **E** *Charika Rest*, Pettigala Rd, T 7530, 6 rm (breakfast incl, Rs 350), meals available, quiet rural setting, 1 km along Pettigala Rd; **E** *Rainbow Guest House*, rooms (Rs 400) with nets with holes and too small for the bed, damp, dingy, filthy rooms, friendly eager staff let down by inadequate infrastructure, not rec; **E-F** *Balangoda Rest Inn*, 110 Old Rd, T 7207, 5 quiet rm (Rs 250), if you are looking for a decent hotel, not too close to the centre, then this is a good choice; **E-F** *Samanala*, in town centre, clean and light rooms (Rs 250) in large rundown, modern building in the centre of town, Rice and Curry restaurant.

• **Transport Road Bus**: for visiting the S coast, there are buses to Tangalle via Pelmadula and Embilitipiya (2 hrs), Rs 40.

ROUTES The densely forested land to the E has now largely been cleared, and the road goes on through Belihuloya.

Belihuloya (19 km; *STD Code* 045) with tea estates and a 'honeymooners' hotel. **Accommodation C-D** *Rest House* (CHC), nr the bridge in an over 100-year-old building by an attractive – though very noisy – stream, T 7200, Reservations T Colombo 323501, F 422732, 11 rm (US$15) some in a newer extension, restaurant on a pleasant side-terrace, bar, exchange, restaurant may be slow as it is a popular lunch stop for coaches and busy at weekends; **D** *West Haputale Estate Bungalow*, T 0578104, 4 beds and water only, best in Apr, can pick up from Ohiya station. Also *River View Inn* on the Colombo side of the bridge.

ROUTES The road then rises to **Haldummulla** (15 km; *Alt* 1,020m). which has excellent views across to the sea. The **A16** goes NE shortly after Haldummulla, a short but steep climb through Haputale to Ella in the Uva Province, see page 197.

ROUTES Pelmadulla to the South Coast From Pelmadulla the A18 runs SE through Kahawatta Ford. After 10 km the A17, the main road to Galle and Matara, branches off to the right. **Rakwana** is the chief village of a tea-growing district. Good **D** *Rest House*, with views that are some of the most beautiful in Sri Lanka. There are many beautiful flowering trees in season and wild orchids, notably the large flowered *Dendrobium maccarthaie*. It is possible to reach the Sinharaja Forest Reserve from Rakwana by taking the road W to Weddagala. This road climbs to over 1,200m before descending into the valley of the Delgoda Ganga along the northern flank of the Reserve.

The **A17** crosses the Bulutota Pass and passes just to the E of Gongala Peak (1,358m) running down the easternmost edge of the Wet Zone. Just S of Akuressa the road forks, the A24 turning left to Matara down the valley of the Nilwala Ganga, and passing from one of the wettest areas of Sri Lanka to one of the driest in under 20 km. The right fork continues as the A17 to Galle, remaining in typically Wet Zone vegetation and cultivation throughout.

ROUTES Pelmadulla to Hambantota From Pelmadulla the **A18** goes SE from Madampe to **Maduwanwela** (35 km), one of best known *walauwas* of the Kandyan chiefs where small inward-looking courtyards were built on the 'Pompeiian plan'.

The A18 continues SE into the Dry Zone and through areas with over 90% of the land under shifting cultivation. At the small village of **Embilipitiya**, on the edge of a great rice growing area, is a paper mill set up to use rice straw. Intended to be an environmentally friendly development, it is causing some water pollution problems with its

Rubber

Third in importance after tea and coconuts as a plantation crop, the first rubber trees were introduced to Sri Lanka from their native Brazil via Kew gardens in London in the last quarter of the 19th Century. In the decade after 1904 Sri Lanka experienced a rubber boom, the Wet Zone land between the sea and the Central Highlands being found particularly well-suited. The apparently sparsely populated land, combined with an ideal climate, encouraged widespread planting. In fact the shifting cultivation which had dominated much of the region around Kalutara, now one of the most important centres of the rubber industry, was severely curtailed by the planting of rubber trees, which spread up the valley sides, leaving paddy the dominant crops in the valley bottoms.

The pale cream sap (latex) of the rubber plant is gathered (or 'tapped') from a fine cut in the bark, renewed between two and three times a week. The latex is collected in a tin cup or coconut shell hung beneath the cut. You can easily ask to be shown round a rubber estate and the processing plant, where you can see the latex being mixed with water, strained and hung out to dry after having been rolled into sheets.

waste. Embilipitiya is a convenient base for trips to Uda Walawe National Park. **Accommodation** *Centurian Guest House*.

Uda Walawe National Park

Approach From Pelmadulla (A18) and Timbolketiya to the S of the reservoir, by 4WD only (Rs 1,000) which are allowed to use the dry-weather roads and jeep tracks.

Background In 1972, the 308 sq km park originated from the necessity to protect the catchment of the Uda Walawe Reservoir which is at the S end of the Walawe Oya. Along the river there is thick woodland but the rest of the area is mainly open parkland traversed by streams, which makes elephant viewing easy.

Wildlife It has similar wildlife to Ruhunu-Yala with particularly large herds of elephants. Birdwatching is more rewarding than searching for any other wildlife.

Viewing Elephants can be seen along the river and near the numerous streams and tanks.The water birds are seen in large numbers around the tanks, (best around Magam, Habarlu and Kiri Ibban). The best season is Nov-Apr when the resident population is joined by migrants from the N.

- **Accommodation** *Campsites* are nr the river at Pransadhara and Wehrankade. Reservations: Wildlife Conservation Department, 82 Rajamalwatta Rd, Battaramulla, T 433012.

You may also be able to stop at the following: on the Palugaswewa tank approached from the A18, about 8 km along a dry weather track from Galpaya to the W of the reservoir

To the N of the reservoir: **Timbirimankada** 3 km from **Sinnukgala**, at the N end of the reservoir, particularly good for birdwatching. These are not far from Handagiriya village which has a prehistoric site nearby (see page 147). **Ranagala** reached in dry weather, about 7 km from Sinnukgala. Good for birdwatching; elephants too may come to the river here.

The road joins the **A2** on the coast at Nonagama which continues to Hambantota, see page 133.

COLOMBO TO KANDY

The route runs NE from Colombo across the coastal plain. Lush and beautiful scenery continues 65 km, through paddy fields interspersed with coconut and areca nut palms, endless bananas and above all pineapples. Taking 11 years to complete, the trunk road from Colombo to Kandy was the first modern road to be opened in Sri Lanka (in 1832), when the first mail service ran between the two cities. Although the road route is quicker, the train often gives better views, the last hour being through stunning scenery.

ROUTES Colombo is strung out in a long suburban sprawl up the A1 to the 'Clocktower junction' just beyond Warakapola, where it separates from the A6 which goes to Kurunegala and Trincomalee. The really attractive scenery on the Kandy road does not start until after this point.

Sapugaskanda Leaving Colombo on the A1 a minor road at 12 km leads off to the right to the minor temple of Sapugaskanda, on a low hill 3 km away. There are beautiful views from the terrace of the small stupa, but the temple is famous for its murals which show the arrival of the Burmese saint Jagara Hamuduruvo in Sri Lanka.

ROUTES The A1 goes through **Mahara** (15 km; excellent *Rest House*). The small town was once a Dutch cantonment. 5 km off the main road to the left, just before Yekwala, is Heneratgoda.

Heneratgoda Botanical Gardens
The beautiful garden town near Gampaha is well signed. It is particularly famous as the nursery of Asia's first rubber trees introduced from the Amazon basin over a century ago. Several of the early imports are now magnificent specimens; No 6, the first tree planted, is over 100 years old, but the most famous is No 2 because of its remarkable yield. The trees include *Hevea brasiliensis*, *Uncaria gambier*, rubber producing lianas (*Landolphia*), and the drug *ipecacuanha*. A female of the Coco de Mer was imported from the Seychelles and bore fruit in 1915.

The road passes by the former estate of Sir Solomon Dias Bandaranaike, aide de camp to the British Governor at the time of WW1. His son, **Solomon Western Ridgway Dias Bandaranaike**, became Prime Minister of independent Ceylon in 1956, but was assassinated in 1959. His widow succeeded him as Prime Minister and his

FIRST IMPRESSIONS ... FROM A TRAVELLER'S DIARY

"We actually left the suburbs quite quickly though the ribbon development along the road gave a rather misleading impression. Most of the way, houses were interspersed with small stores selling cold drinks 'Cool spots', tyres and bicycle repair shops, green groceries and small clothing stores. I was quite surprised by their construction: red roofs on solid concrete walls. On reflection, I think that may have something to do with the climate: this type of construction was much less visible in the Dry Zone where mud walls and tin roofs were the order of the day.

Slowly we became more aware of paddy fields. Despite the land slowly getting higher and consequently more 'crumpled', there was no evidence of terracing. We were also quite surprised by the lack of colour in the countryside. There were few flowering trees or shrubs in evidence although it was fabulously green. This was usually made up for in the villages and towns with lots of people queuing for buses in brightly coloured saris and holding colourful umbrellas."

Alcohol Is A Wonderful Stain Remover

"Alcohol is a wonderful stain remover.
It removes stains from day and night materials.
It also removes your home, furniture, cars, carpets, wife and children.
It removes your judgement,
your ability to think,
your clothes and even your self-respect.
It removes your good name
and even your job
and if used too much it will remove even you.
Try it, why not?
After all, it is an excellent remover."

(Warakapola innkeeper's words of caution, painted on his garden wall)

daughter, Mrs Chandrika Kumaratunge, was elected President in 1994. The family home, where visitors such as King George V and Jawaharlal Nehru stayed, can be seen nearby. The Bandaranaike memorial is by the side of the road at **Nittambuwa**, 38 km from Colombo. A broad walkway, about 10m wide and 100m long, leads to a raised plinth with six stone pillars behind it, the whole, surrounded by a coconut grove.

After a further 7 km **Pasyala** is on the W edge of the central highland massif. The area is noted for its graphite (*plumbago*)' mines, betel nuts and cashew. Passing through **Cadjugama** ('village of cashew nuts'), you will see women in brightly coloured saris selling cashew nut from stalls lining the road. The nuts are relatively expensive, but freshly roasted, they are well worth it.

ROUTES The road passes through a series of small villages and towns including Warakapola and, where the **A1** turns E towards Kandy, via Kegalla.

Warakapola

(*STD Code* 072) Warakapola provides an outlet for locally made cane baskets and mats in its bazar. It is also a popular halt for those with a sweet tooth searching for seasame seed *thalagulis* (see page 27) which are freshly made at *Jinadasa's* shop, among others.

• **Accommodation E** *Navimana Inn*, Kandy Rd, Warakapola, just S of clocktower junc at Weweldeniya, T 51339, 10 rm, (Rs 350), good quality, restaurant and take away. Good tea and snacks inside or on verandah, pleasant atmosphere, small garden with a new tiger-cage to house a young cub (which proprieters think will be an attraction), popular stop en route to Kandy or Kurunegala and beyond.

Ambepussa, is just off the road to the W, with a train station (60 km from Colombo; *STD Code* 035) **Accommodation D** *Rest House* (CHC), pleasantly located, T 7299, Reservations T Colombo 323501, F 422732, 8 rm, restaurant, bar, exchange.

ROUTES The **A1** begins to climb into the hills at **Rambukkana**.

Pinnawela, 3 km S of Rambukkana (a 15 mins bus ride from Kegalla) has the government's **Elephant Orphanage** where several dozen young animals, some only a few weeks' old and a metre high, are kept in parkland where they are nursed by five adult elephants. Set up by the Government in 1975 to rescue orphaned baby elephants; the babies are introduced to the herd once they have been thoroughly checked.

They are 'herded' just before feeding time which is very photogenic, until they start charging the tourists! You can actually get injured, so stand well back. The feeding is done in a couple of large sheds. Each elephant is tied to a post and then bottle fed with copious amounts of milk. Adults are fed with palm leaves. You can usually watch them browsing, bathing in the river at 1030 and 1430, and sometimes being trained to work. Best time to visit is in the morning, around 0900. **Accommodation and places to eat** There is quite a good cafe here where you can wait for feeding time and also a few *Guest Houses* nearby.

Down the road is the **Concept Elephant Bath**. You can ride elephants, either on land or through water.

Kegalla (19 km) is a long straggling town in a picturesque setting. Some beautiful hill scenery lies between Kegalle and Mawanella. On either side the vegetation is stunningly rich. At the top of the **Balana Pass** is a precipice called **Sensation Point**. The railway goes through two tunnels to **Peradeniya** (10 km), where the road crosses the Mahaweli Ganga, Sri Lanka's longest river.

Peradeniya

(*Alt* 500m) Famous for its magnificent Botanical Gardens, Peradeniya is also the home of the Sri Lanka University and almost a suburb of Kandy which is 6 km away (see page 170).

Places of interest

The Botanic Gardens Entry Rs 100, children Rs 50. You may take a car in and drive around (minivans are not admitted). However, it is very pleasant to walk around; even at mid-day there are walks under shady trees. Best to visit in early morning or late afternoon.

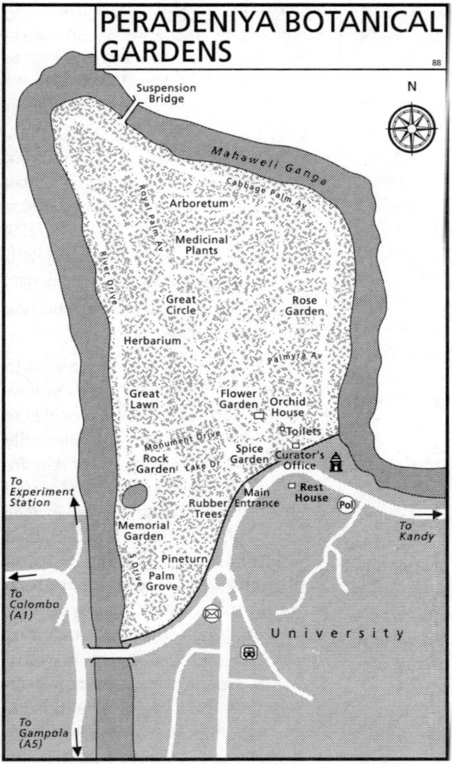

Conceived originally in 1371 as the Queen's pleasure garden, Peradeniya became the residence of a Kandyan Prince between 1741-1782 where royal visitors were entertained. The park was converted into a 60 ha Botanical Garden in 1821, 6 years after the fall of the last Kandyan King. It is still beautifully maintained with about 4,000 labelled species.

There are extensive well-kept lawns, pavilions, an Orchid House with an outstanding collection, an Octagon Conservatory, Fernery, banks of bamboo and numerous flower borders with cannas, hibiscus, chrysanthemums, croton and colourful bougainvilleas. The central tank has water plants including

Forest Hermitages With Pretty Carved Latrines!

The *Pansukulika* or *Tapovana* sect of ascetic Buddhist hermits who lived a simple life of deep meditation in forests and caves are associated with Arankale, Mihintale and Ritigala, around the 7th to the 11th centuries. The monks were expected to wear ragged clothing and to immerse themselves in seeking the Truth, devoid of ritualistic forms of worship associated with Buddha images, relics and relic chambers. Such communities often won the admiration and support of Kings, Sena I (831-851).

The sites had certain features in common. There was a porched entrance, ambulatories, a water pool for cleansing and the *padhanaghara*. One was an open terrace, possibly intended as a 'chapter house' connected to a smaller section which was usually roofed. These 'double platforms' were aligned E-W, the two raised stone-faced platforms were connected by a narrow walkway or bridge. An interesting contradiction of the austere life was the beautifully carved latrines or urinal stones the monks used, examples of which can be seen in the Anuradhapura Archaelogical Museum, see page 207.

the giant water lily and papyrus reeds. You will see unusual exotic species, especially palms (palmyra, talipot, royal, cabbage), and *Ficus elastica* (latex-bearing fig or 'Indian rubber tree' with buttress roots) and some magnificent old specimen trees. Try not to miss one of the rarest plants in the gardens – the *Coco de Mer*. You will find it on the path leading to George Gardner's monument. This is on your left (W) as you enter the park. This plant has the largest and heaviest in the plant kingdom, weighing on average some 10-20 kg. They take between 5-8 years to mature and are surprisingly productive; it is not unusual to have over 20 nuts on a tree. They are all carefully numbered. Native *Coco de Mer* are only found on the island of Praslin in the Seychelles. Carry on along this path to get to the Memorial, a dome shaped structure. George Gardner was superindent of the gardens from 1844 to 1849. From here you overlook the lily tank which is surrounded by giant bamboo, some 40m in height; it grows at 2-3 cm a day!

A suggested walk Riverside Drive follows the course of the Mahaweli Ganga. Follow the road to the right (E) to take in the Orchid House, then walk along the Royal Palm Ave (planted 1885) to meet the drive. You will notice the fruit bats in quite large colonies hanging in many of the trees. Follow the drive to the suspension bridge. Here there is a useful notice board and map to enable you get your bearings. An enterprising industry has sprung up in the river – men dive to fill shallow bowls with sand which are then emptied onto a barge before being offloaded on the opposite bank.

This is about half way around the River Drive and you can if you wish go back via the Central Drive. This goes through the central area – a large grassy area around which visiting dignatories have planted further species. King George V and Queen Mary planted a Cannon Ball Tree on 14 April 1901. Their great grand daughter Princess Anne planted a *saraca asoca* on 11 March 1995.

A bridge across the river, takes you to the **School of Tropical Agriculture** at Gannoruwa, where research is undertaken into various important spices and medicinal herbs as well as into tea, coffee, cocoa, rubber, coconuts and varieties of rice and other cash crops. The **Economic Museum** has botanical and agricultural exhibits.

Excursions

The **University** (1942) is nearby, built in the old Kandyan style in an impressive setting of a large park with the river Mahaweli Ganga and the surrounding hillocks.

Local information

● Accommodation

Peradeniya Rest House 5 km SW from the railway station.

● Places to eat

There is the ***Royal Park Cafeteria*** in the garden and a '*Cool Spot*' nr the ticket office.

COLOMBO TO KURUNEGALA AND ANURADHAPURA: THE WESTERN ROUTE

The first part of this route follows the A1 out of Colombo to just beyond Warakapola, where the A6 takes a left turn at the Clocktower. It climbs gently over attractive rolling low hills, the site of *chena* (shifting) cultivation for generations. Leaving the Wet Zone just N of Colombo, rainfall declines steadily NW.

ROUTES From the junction of the A1 (Kandy road) with the Anuradhapura road just N of Warakapola (see page 150) the **A6** continues straight (N), through **Polgahawela** ('the field of the coconut') to Kurunegala.

The road follows the main line railway from Colombo and Anuradhapura and Kandy (*Inter-City Exp*). The road is relatively quiet and follows the forested banks of the Maha Oya for several miles before crossing it at Alawwa. The area often suffers from drought at the end of the dry season. The Maha Oya flows slowly between sand-banks – more grit than sand. The grit is used as building material and you can see women digging the river bed by hand before carrying it up the 3m high banks to stock pile it for small lorries to transport.

Kurunegala

(37 km) Kurunegala is an important cross-roads town, astride the route from Kandy to Puttalam and Colombo to Anuradhapura. It is a very pleasant town overlooked by huge monoliths some of which have been the given names of the animals they resemble: – elephant rock, tortoise rock etc. It is at the foot of the 325m black rock **Etagala**; there are excellent views across the lake from the top.

The town has all services and is within easy reach of quite a few sites which are not very often visited, eg Arankele.

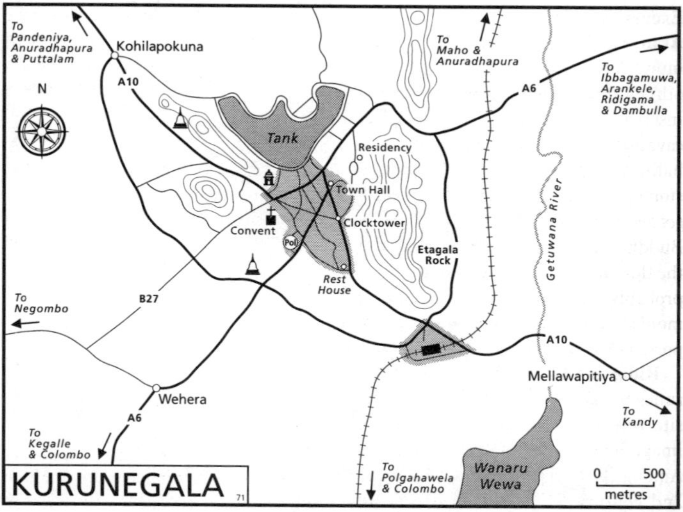

Excursions

Arankele, 24 km N (W of the Ibbagamuwa-Moragollagama Rd) which has a 6th century cave hermitage with Brahmi inscriptions, up a forested hillside. Excavations have revealed meditation halls, double-platform strucures and stone-paved ambulatories for the *tapovana* (forest-dwelling) sect of austere Buddhist hermits here. The smaller of the double-platform structure here was probably divided into nine 'cells' or monks' dwellings – the roof being supported on columns.

Ridigama Vihara, 18 km NE of Kurunegala is an ancient Buddhist temple site with rock cave hermitages and an image house with Kandyan paintings. Among the finds which date from the 2nd century BC to the 18th century AD, are Buddha statues, a door frame beautifully carved and inlaid with ivory and an altar with Dutch (Delft) tiles with Biblical figures! There is an attractive artificial lake at the foot of the hills.

Local information

● Accommodation

C-D *Bunaweka*, clean and attractive; **D** *New Rest House*, W bank of lake, 1 km N of town centre, 10 clean and pleasant rm, restaurant, beautiful position; **D** *Old Rest House*, in town centre, 10 simple rm, restaurant, noisy.

● Places to eat

Diva Dahara Hotel, 7 North Lake Rd, pleasant terrace overlooking lake for drinks where you may find elephants bathing.

ROUTES From Kurunegala two routes go N to Anuradhapura. The E route takes the A6 to Dambulla and then A9 to Anuradhapura, see page 201. The W route (106 km) on the **A10** goes N from Pandeniya to **Maho** (19 km), the base from which to see the 13th century capital of Yapahuwa.

Yapahuwa

From Maho take the road to the left, which leads to the foot of the rock (5 km) at Yapahuwa, on which the **fortress** stands. The **tooth relic**, now enshrined at Kandy, was carried from the temple here to India, then recovered in 1288 by Parakramabahu III. It was built as the fortress capital of the Sinhalese kings in 1301, and when abandoned, was inhabited by Buddhist monks and religious ascetics. The remains of a temple to the NE, outside the fortification has some sculptures visible and may well have temporarily housed the tooth relic.

A vast granite rock rising 100m from the surrounding plain, is encircled by a 1 km long path rising to the top. The fort is surrounded by two moats and ramparts, and there are signs of other ancient means of defence. The impressive ornamental staircase is still well preserved, and the ruins at the head of the remarkable flight of granite steps are unique. One of the two window frames is now exhibited in the Colombo Museum.

ROUTES Return to the main road and turn N to **Mahagalkadawala** (24 km; turn left in town to see Rajagane (1 km) and Anuradhapura (37 km).

COLOMBO TO NEGOMBO, PUTTALAM AND THE WILPATTU NATIONAL PARK

The coastal road runs through the region most affected by Portuguese colonialism. Their imprint is clearly visible in the high proportion of Roman Catholics and the number of Catholic churches in the numerous villages through which the road passes. Dutch influence is also in evidence in the now unused canal which was built between Colombo and Negombo. Once it was busy with the flat-bottomed boats which travelled the 120 km between Colombo and Puttalam, As the Rev James Cordimer wrote in 1807 "the top of the canal (near Colombo) is constantly crowded with large flat-bottomed boats, which come down from Negombo with dried fish and roes, shrimps, firewood, and other articles. These boats are covered with thatched roofs in the form of huts." The Dutch built canals extensively not just around Colombo but also around Galle in the S, but they were relatively minor works compared to the 1,000 km of irrigation canals already dug by the Sinhalese by the 12th century. The boats on the Dutch-built canals were often pulled by two men in harness, but now the canal banks are largely the preserve of people strolling along the waterway. You can hire bikes at several points, including Negombo, and ride along a section of the banks.

ROUTES The coastal route to Puttalam (A3) runs due N through apparently endless groves of coconut palms. It passes the International Airport about 6 km S of Negombo, then runs close to the coast and coastal lagoons all the way to Puttalam. The road from Puttalam to Anuradhapura crosses much more open terrain, the dryness leading to much less dense forest and sparser cultivation. The A1 runs N, 3 or 4 km inland of the coast.

At **Dalugama** the A3 leaves the A1 to the run N to **Wattala** (11 km from the city centre). It passes the *Pegasus Reef Hotel*, through some built up areas and an industrial estate. **Accommodation A** *Pegasus Reef*, Santa Maria Maw, Hendala, Wattala, by old Dutch canal, 11 km from city centre, 18 km airport, T 530205, F 549790, 150 rm, 500m of coconut-fringed beach, good restaurants, pool.

ROUTES Half way to Negombo the road passes through Kadana and **Ja-ela**, at the heart of what used to be one of Sri Lanka's main cinnamon producing areas. Now the road runs through coconut groves, following the line of the Dutch canal up to the Negombo lagoon and beyond to Chilaw.

Negombo

(*Pop* 60,000; *Alt* Sea level; *STD Code* 031) Negombo is 6 km N of the international airport. The Dutch had captured it from the Portuguese in 1644, and made it an important centre. It has a high reputation for its brasswork, and today the Negombo Lagoon has become the country's main fishing port and a centre for prawn and shrimp fishing and research.

The principle resort on the W coast, Negombo is a rather characterless town. The main tourist area lies some 3 km N of the town itself which is rather scruffy and contains little of genuine interest. You can walk most of the way along the beach towards the town (which gets progressively less inviting) or take a 3-wheeler (Rs 50) or the Kochchikade bus (No 905) from the bus station. Some travellers have found it "a rather grotty tourist ghetto, but still a pleasant way to begin (or end) a trip".

There are a few shops and a Bank of Ceylon on Main St leading from the square in front of St Mary's Church towards the train and bus stations. If you follow Main St W, there are some fine

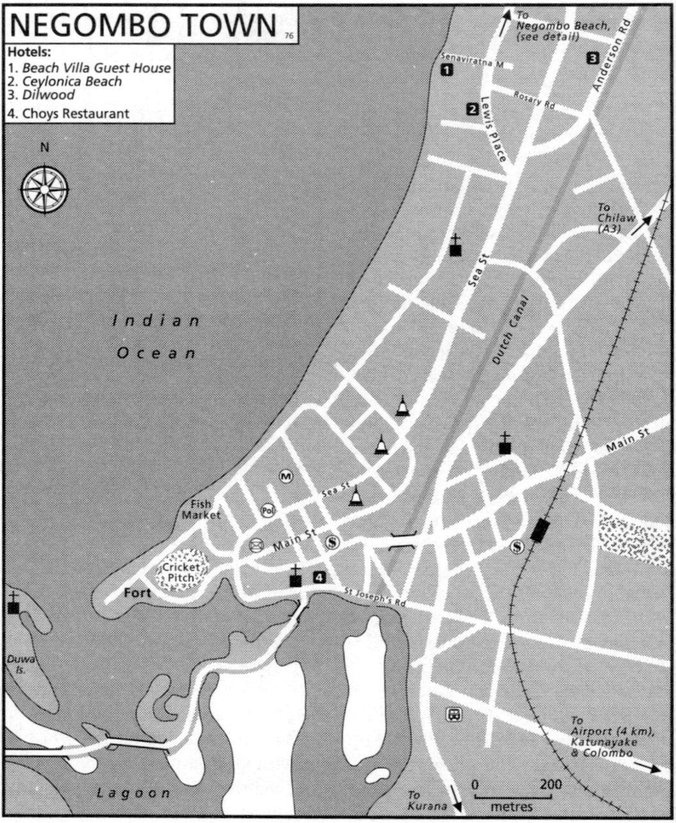

buildings with attractive balconies. At the end of the street is a curious roundabout guarded by a fish, the cricket ground, and opposite it the remains of the fort.

The Portuguese originally built a **fort** on the headland guarding the lagoon in about 1600. Since the area was rich in spices and particularly the much prized cinnamon, it changed hands several times before the Portuguses were finally ousted by the Dutch in 1644. It was the Dutch who built a much stronger structure. However this was largely destroyed by the British who pulled much of it down to build a jail. Today only the gatehouse (dated 1678) with its rather crooked clock tower survives. The place is still used as a prison and the District Court is tucked away in a corner of the grounds.

A more enduring monument to the Dutch is the canal system (see page 157). You can see this if you follow St Joseph St around the headland. It skirts the lagoon where mainly fishing boats are moored (witness to its thriving fishing industry). The junction of the canal is just past the bridge crossing the lagoon. Unfortunately at its mouth it is rather dirty and not very appealing.

THE LURE OF THE UNDERWATER WORLD

Sri Lanka with its warm coastal waters, its reefs with a wealth of corals and colourful tropical fish and the comfortable resort hotels, has invited divers to return to search for new excitement, once they have been hooked to the pleasures of underwater life. The delights on offer among the varied corals and rocks include invertebrates and a dazzling number of fish – blue surgeon, comical parrot, butterfly, lion, several large and small angels which are not camera shy – to the larger snappers, groupers, barracudas, jackfish. See also wildlife section in the centre.

Snorkelling for the not-too-adventurous, skin diving, as well as SCUBA to take the serious seeker further down, are possible from a number of the coastal resorts. The best time for the SW of this island is the winter, from Nov to Mar when the sea is relatively calm and clear. The far S and the E coast are better from Apr to Sep (but avoid Jul).

Snorkels, masks and flippers can be bought in Colombo (if you cannot carry your own), and specialist diving gear is available for hire. Air tanks can be rented from Colombo, Hikkaduwa and Koggala (and possibly from Trincomalee and Nilaveli when the area is free from political troubles); it is best to only go to a reputable, established company (eg Underwater Safaris, 25 Barnes Place, Colombo; Poseidon Station and Coral Garden Hotels, Hikkaduwa; Browns Beach, Negombo, Bay Beach Aqua Sports, Weligama). The only decompression chamber is at the Naval Base at Trincomalee's Fort Ostenburg. It is best to carry your own underwater photographic equipment and films.

The better diving to the NW and W are out of bounds and the E coast is often inaccessible. If you wish to dive along the SW coast, a specialist company will advise you on good reefs. To avoid disappointment seek out clearer waters by taking a boat further out to sea and avoid outlets of rivers. Negombo's reef is 3 km out and really only worthwhile with SCUBA to descend from 15-20m; Ambalangoda, Belapitiya and particularly Hikkaduwa are popular for corals and exploring around wrecks and Galle and Gintota offer opportunities on off-shore rocky islands and wrecks. From Apr to Jun, in the far S, Dondra to Tangalle are fine in calm seas while 4 km off Hambantota rewards you with a reef and a shipwreck. For the more adventurous, enquire about the delights off the Great and Little Basses before setting sail.

NB Carry antihistamine for stings.

The area is very rich in marine life and although there is much evidence of a motorized fleet in the harbour, you can still see fishermen using catamarans and ancient outrigger canoes to bring up their catch onto the beach every day. The outrigger conoes known as *oruva* here are not made from hollowed-out tree trunks but rather the planks are sewn together and caulked to produce a fairly wide canoe with an exceptionally flat bottom. Look out for them as some are often beached in front of the hotels. You can often see the fleet early in the morning returning to harbour, each canoe under a three-piece sail. Their catch includes seer, skipjack, herring, mullet, pomfret, amber-jack, and sometimes sharks. Prawns and lobster are caught in the lagoon. There are a number of fish markets – one is located near the bridge on Duwa Island across the lagoon and there is another beyond the fort.

The reef is 3 km W of the beach hotel area with corals within 10-20m and the marine life includes barracuda, blue-ringed angels and unusual star fish. Tourists are attracted here for the exciting

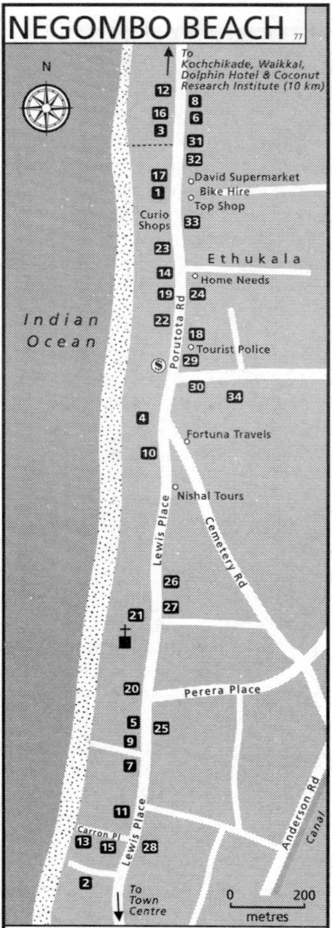

Hotels:
1. *Beach View Tourist Guest House*
2. *Beach Villa Guest House*
3. *Blue Oceanic*
4. *Browns Beach*
5. *Catamaran Beach*
6. *Club Oasis Beach*
7. *De-phani*
8. *Dippeguker*
9. *Don's Beach*
10. *Golden Beach*
11. *Golden Star Beach*
12. *Goldi Sands*
13. *Interline Beach*
14. *Oasis Beach Resort*
15. *Rainbow Guest House*
16. *Royal Oceanic*
17. *Sea Garden*
18. *Silva's Beach*
19. *Sea Sands*
20. *Silver Sands*
21. *Sunflower Beach*
22. *Topaz Beach*

Restaurants:

23. Alt Saarbrucken
24. Bijou
25. Blonghe's & Blue Moon
26. Curry Bowl
27. Delhi
28. Join Us
29. Pri-Kin
30. Seafood
31. Seawirt & Jetwing Tours
32. Sherryland
33. Spice
34. Vasana

diving Negombo offered as well as other watersports. However, in mid-1995 there were very limited diving facilities in evidence.

Warning It is often dangerous to swim, particularly during the SW monsoon, May-Oct. Warning notices are now posted on the beach.

Places of interest

The town still has a few remains from its period as a Dutch settlement, notably the residence of the District Judge, the Dutch church, and the impressive gateway to the Fort.

St Mary's Church which dominates the town, is one of many that bears witness to the extent of Portuguese conversions to Roman Catholicism, especially among the fishermen in Negombo District. Started in 1874, the church was only completed in 1922. There are a number of alabaster statues of saints and of the Easter story as well as a colourfully painted ceiling. Easter holds a special place in this strongly Catholic area. There are numerous passion plays usually held on Easter Saturday, the most famous of which is on Duwa Island. If you are short of time, it is worth stationing yourself between the two churches on Sea St (about 1 km S of Lewis Place). Young girls in spotless white dresses are carried shoulder high by four men between the churches. This takes place in the afternoon but preparations take most of the day.

There are three **Hindu temples** on Sea St – the largest, Sri Muthu Mari Amman has a colourful gopuram in the inner courtyard.

Excursions

Colombo It is perfectly feasible to go into Colombo for a day's visit by hiring a car (hotels will often arrange for a driver to take you to the main sights). It is worth returning via **Hendola** by leaving the main road at Wattala. This route follows the course of the old Dutch Canal for much of the way. Keep an eye out

SRI LANKA
WILDLIFE GUIDE

A SHORT GUIDE TO THE FAUNA AND FLORA OF SRI LANKA

MARGARET CARSWELL

ILLUSTRATIONS BY JOAN ROCHE

For one island Sri Lanka packs an enormous variety of wildlife into a relatively small space. This is largely because in that small space there is a wide range in altitude, probably the single most important factor for giving rise to a large number of species in any one area. The Central Highlands rise to over 2,500m with damp evergreen forests, cool uplands and high rainfall. Within 100 km there are the dry coastal plain and sandy beaches. The climatic division of the island into the larger, dry, mainly northern and eastern region, and the smaller, wet, southwestern section is of importance to observers of wildlife. In the Dry Zone remnants of evergreen and deciduous forests are interspersed with cultivation, and in the east of this region the savanna grasslands are dominated by the metre high grass, *Imperata cylindrica*, widely regarded as a scourge. The whole vegetation complex differs sharply from both the Central Highlands and the Wet Zone of the SW. These different areas support very different species. Many species occur only in one particular zone, but there are some, often the ones associated with man, which are found throughout.

The Maldives support a much less varied habitat. Most of the vegetation is rather scrubby and coconut palms dominate. The wildlife here is richest around the hundreds of underwater coral reefs.

ANIMALS

Animals seen mainly in the wildlife sanctuaries

Sri Lanka has a number of wildlife sanctuaries and in many of these the **Asiatic Elephant** *(Elephas maximus)* is common. The animals come down to the water in the evening, either in family groups or herds of 20 or so individuals. Occasionally larger herds occur. The 'Marsh Elephants', an interesting sub-species significantly larger than the others, are found in the marshy basin of the Mahaweli River. Elephants are also frequently domesticated and are important beasts of burden. Another animal which is present both in the wild and in association with man is the **Asiatic Wild Buffalo** *(Bubalus bubalis)*, which when domesticated is known as the **Water Buffalo**. It is a solid looking beast, standing about 170 cm at the shoulder. The *black coat* and *wide-spreading curved horns*, which are carried by both sexes, are distinctive. The **Leopard** or **Panther** *(Panthera pardus)*, the only big cat in Sri Lanka, is found both in the dry lowland areas and in the forested hills. Although it is widespread it is not easy to observe, being shy and elusive. The **Sloth Bear** *(Melursus ursinus)*, about 75 cm at the shoulder, can be seen in areas of scrub and rock. It is unkempt looking with a *shaggy black coat* and a *yellowish V-shaped mark on the chest*. The *hairless eyelids* and *long dull grey snout* give it a mangy look. It has a distinctively *long and pendulous lower lip*.

The deer of Sri Lanka are widespread, particularly in the wildlife sanctuaries. The commonest, the **Chital** or **Spotted Deer** *(Axis axis)* is quite small being only some 90 cm at the shoulder. The *bright rufous coat, spotted with white* is unmistakable. The stags carry *antlers with three 'spikes' or tines* on each. Chital occur in herds of 20 or so in grassy areas and are very tolerant of man, so are often seen near the lodges in wildlife sanctuaries. Much larger, 150 cm at the shoulder, is the magnificent **Sambhur** *(Cervus unicolor)*. It has a noticeably *shaggy coat*, which varies in colour from *brown with a yellowish or grey tinge*, through to *dark, almost black* in older stags. The females tend to be somewhat lighter in colour. The coat of the stag is thickened around the neck to form a *mane*. The mature stags carry *large three-tined antlers*. Immature males carry 1 to 3 tines depending on age. The Sambhur is a forest dwelling deer often found on wooded hillsides. They do not form large herds, but live in groups of up to 10, or sometimes as solitary individuals. The **Barking Deer**, or **Muntjac** *(Muntiacus muntjak)*, 60 cms at the shoulder, is a small shy deer, which is usually glimpsed as it darts for cover. In general colour, it is *brown* with *darker legs*. It has *white underparts* and a *white chest* and *white under the tail*. The stag carries a *small pair of antlers* which arise from bony, hair covered protuberances and has *one short tine just above the brow*. The main part of the antler is only about 10-12 cm long and curves inwards slightly. Barking deer are usually seen in pairs and their staccato bark is heard more often than they are seen.

The **Wild Boar** *(Sus scrofa)* is easily identified with its *sparse hair* on a mainly *black body* and a *pig-like head*. The hair thickens down the spine to form a sort of *mane* or crest. A well-grown male stands 90 cm at the shoulder and bears tusks, which are absent in the female. The young are striped. Commonly seen in grass and light bush, near water it often causes great destruction among crops.

The interesting **Purple-faced Langur** *(Presbytis senex)* is one of the species that occurs only in Sri Lanka. A long-tailed, long-legged monkey about 125 cm in length, 70 cm of which is tail, it has a *dark coat* contrasting with the *pale, almost*

Elephant

Leopard (Panther)

Wild Boar

Wild Buffalo

Sloth Bear

Sambhur

Chital
(Spotted Deer)

Barking Deer
(Muntjak)

Purple-faced
Langur

Common Langur

Tocque Macaque

Five-striped Palm Squirrel

Flying Fox

Common Mongoose

white head. Hair on the head grows long to form swept back *whiskers*, but the *face itself is very dark*, almost black. The *tip of the tail is pale*. It lives mainly in the dense, damp mountain forests, but is also found in open woodland, both in the trees and on the ground, and can often be seen in groups of a dozen or so walking over broken ground.

Animals seen also outside the sanctuaries

There are a number of animals in Sri Lanka which have taken to village and urban habitats, including various monkeys, squirrels, bats and mongooses, all often seen near temples. In the countryside they are found in a variety of wooded habitats. The most widespread of the monkeys is the **Common** or **Hanuman Langur** (*Presbytis entellus*), another long-tailed monkey with a *black face, hands and feet*. Its body is up to 75 cm long with a 95 cm tail. The **Tocque Macaque** (*Macaca sinica*) 60 cm, is a much more solid looking animal with shorter limbs, though its black tinged tail is long. It has rather variable colouring being *grey with a yellowish tinge, brown* or even *reddish brown above*, with much *paler limbs and underparts*. The face is pale, sometimes reddish, with *whorls of hair* on the cheeks. On top of the head the hair grows *flat and cap-like*, from a parting.

In the gardens and parks in many of the towns you cannot fail to notice the small palm squirrels which abound. These **Five-striped Palm Squirrels** *(Funambulus pennanti)*, are about 30 cm in length, about half of which is tail. Be sure to look out for the so-called **Flying Fox** *(Pteropus giganteus)* which has a wing span of 120 cm. These are actually fruit-eating bats and are found throughout, except in the driest areas. They roost in *large, sometimes huge, noisy colonies* in tree tops, often in the middle of towns or villages, where they look like folded umbrellas hanging from the trees. In the evening they can be seen leaving the roost with *slow measured wing beats*. The **Common Mongoose** *(Herpestes edwardsi)* in the wild is an inhabitant of scrub and open jungle, but it can also be seen in gardens and fields. It is well known as a killer of snakes, but will also take rats, mice, chickens and birds' eggs. The mongoose is *tawny with a grey grizzled tinge*. It is about 90 cm in length, of which half is tail. This *long tail always has a pale tip*.

BIRDS

Birds of towns and villages

There are very many bird species which have adapted to man's ways and now live in the towns and villages. Some of these perform a useful function by scavenging and clearing refuse. One of the most widespread of these is the **Pariah Kite** *(Milvus migrans)* 65 cm. This is a *brown* bird with a *longish tail* which looks either *forked* when the tail is closed or *slightly concave* at the end when spread. It has buoyant flight and bold way of swooping down to pick up scraps of food. The much more handsome **Brahminy Kite** *(Haliastur indus)* 48 cm, is also a familiar scavenger, but is largely confined to waterside places such as docks and the coastal strip. Its *chestnut and white* plumage is unmistakable. Two members of the pigeon family are often seen in built-up areas. The **Feral Pigeon,** or **Blue Rock Dove** *(Columba livia)* 32 cm, is found in towns and villages everywhere, while the **Spotted Dove** *(Streptopelia chinensis)* 30 cm, frequents gardens and parks, where it is often seen feeding on the ground. It can be identified by the *speckled appearance of its back* and by the *wide half-collar of white spots on a black background*. The head and underparts are a pale pink. Also common in gardens and cultivated fields is the **White-breasted Kingfisher** *(Halcyon smyrnensis)* 27 cm. This kingfisher is frequently found away from water and is readily seen as it perches on wires and posts. The *rich chestnut of its body plumage* contrasts with the *brilliant blue of its wing feathers*, particularly noticeable when it swoops down to capture its prey. The *red bill* and *white front* make it unmistakable.

Some birds are seen in almost every town and village. Of these ubiquitous birds the **House Sparrow** *(Passer domesticus)* 15 cm, is almost world-wide in its distribution. The **House Crow** *(Corvus splendens)* 45 cm, is a very smart looking bird with a *grey body* and *black tail, wings, face and throat*. Both frequent the centre of towns. The **Red-vented Bulbul** *(Pycnonotus cafer)* 20 cm, is well known and widespread in parks and gardens throughout the area. A mainly brown bird, it can be identified by the slight *crest* and a *bright red patch under the tail*. The **Common Myna** *(Acridotheres tristis)* 22 cm, is often seen feeding on lawns, especially after rain or watering, rather in the manner of the European starling. Look for the *white under the tail* and the *bare yellow skin around the eye*, *yellow bill and legs*, and in flight, the *large white wing patch*. Another inhabitant of parks and gardens is the **Magpie-robin** *(Copsychus saularis)*, 20 cm. In the male the *wings, head and upperparts are mainly black*, but with a noticeable *white wing bar*. Below it is *white*. The *long black and white tail is often held cocked up*. The female's colour pattern is similar, but the black is greyish. It is a delightful songster, and has a trim and lively appearance. The **White-headed Babbler** *(Turdoides affinis)* 23 cm, an inhabitant of gardens and bushy country, is basically *brown, with a scaly throat and breast*. The *top of the head is creamy white*, which contrasts with the *darker brown at the sides of the head*. Weaver birds are a family of mainly yellow birds which are all remarkable for the intricate nests they build. The commonest and most widespread is probably the **Baya Weaver** *(Ploceus philippinus)* 15 cm. They nest in large colonies often in palm trees and near villages. The male in the breeding season can be distinguished by the combination of *black face and throat* and contrasting *yellow top of the head and yellow breast band*. In the non-breeding season the male and female are both brownish sparrow-like birds.

Birds of the lowland Dry Zone

Bird watching is rewarding in this zone as the birds are plentiful and easily seen

Birds of towns and villages

in the open countryside. One of the most conspicuous of these is the **Malabar Pied Hornbill** *(Anthracoceros coronatus)* 90 cm, which is a large, heavy looking bird, seen in small noisy flocks, often in fruiting trees. The plumage is *black and white,* and the long tail has white edges. The *massive bill* is mainly yellow and carries a *black and yellow protuberance* known as a casque, along the top. Another bird seen in noisy flocks, often in hundreds, in similar countryside is the **Rose-ringed Parakeet** *(Psittacula krameri)* 40 cm, which is found in the dry NE and in the coastal strip, where they often roost in the coconut groves. The *long tail is noticeable* both in flight and when the bird is perched. Females lack the collar. They can be very destructive to crops, but are attractive birds which are frequently kept as pets. The *all black* **Drongo** *(Dicrurus adsimilis)* 30 cm, is almost invariably seen perched on telegraph wires or bare branches. Its *distinctively forked tail* makes it easy to identify. The related **Racquet-tailed Drongo** *(Dicrurus paradiseus)* 35 cm, can be distinguished by its distinctive tail, which ends in *long streamers with broadened tips*. The head bears a *tufted crest*. It is more commonly seen in the Dry Zone, but another sub-species occurs in the wooded highlands. It is the habit of sitting on conspicuous perches in the open country that makes certain species so easy to observe. The **Paradise Flycatcher** *(Terpsiphone paradisi)* frequents woods and gardens in the Dry Zone and lower hills. It is seen flitting from its perch in pursuit of insects in woodland, and gardens. The *head is a shiny metallic black* with a *noticeable crest*, which contrasts with the white of the underparts. The wings and tail can be either white or chestnut. The male has particularly *long tail feathers*. The **Little Green Bee-eater** *(Merops orientalis)* is common in open countryside, gardens and fields and is usually seen in pairs, perching on posts and dead branches. The *green* of its plumage contrasts with the *bluish throat* and *chestnut top of the head*. Common in the extreme SE of the Dry Zone is the well-known **Peafowl** *(Pavo cristata)* male with tail 210 cm, female 100 cm, which is more commonly known as the peacock.

Birds seen at the tanks in the Dry Zone

A feature of the Dry Zone is the presence of shallow, man-made reservoirs (tanks). They vary considerably in size, and form an important habitat for a variety of wildlife, particularly birds. One of the largest and most easily identified is the **Spot-billed Pelican** *(Pelecanus philippensis)* 150 cm. This has the typical pelican-shaped *bill with the fleshy pouch below*. It is often seen soaring overhead, and can be identified by its all *grey, or off-white plumage*. It breeds colonially in trees. Another big bird is the **Painted Stork** *(Ibis leucocephalus)* 100 cm, which is also mainly *white*, but has a *pinkish tinge* on the back and *greenish black marks on the wings and a broken black band on the lower chest*. The *bare yellow face and yellow down-curved bill* are conspicuous. Two egrets are particularly common: the **Little Egret** *(Egretta garzetta)* 62 cm, and the **Cattle Egret** *(Bubulcus ibis)* 50 cm. In the non-breeding season both birds are pure *white*, but can readily be distinguished by their different coloured *bills*: *yellowish* in the cattle egret, but all *black* in the little egret. In addition the legs of the little egret are black with yellow toes, but this is not always easy to see. The little egret is a taller more elegant looking bird than the cattle egret, which often has a hunched appearance. In the breeding season the cattle egret develops *golden or buffish plumes* on its head and back. A bird usually seen in pairs in open countryside near tanks is the **Red-wattled Lapwing** *(Vanellus indicus)* 33 cm. In the field it gives the impression of being a *black and white bird* with *long yellow legs* and a *red bill*. In flight the black and white plumage and rounded wings can be seen. It is a

Birds of the lowland Dry Zone

Birds seen at the tanks in the Dry Zone

Painted Stork

Spot-billed Pelican

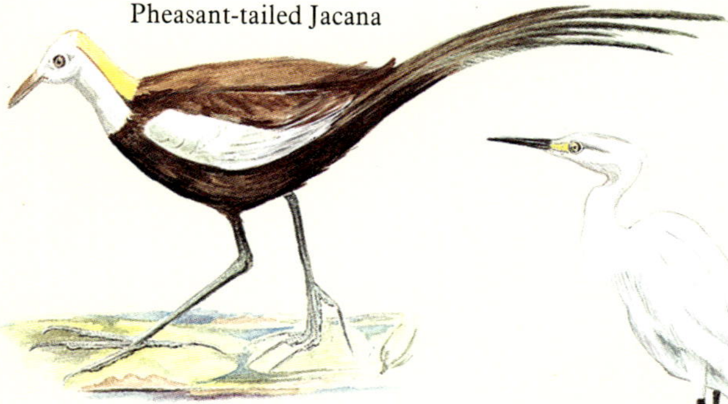

Pheasant-tailed Jacana

Little Egret

Red-wattled Lapwing

Birds of the Wet and Highland Zone

Ceylon Lorikeet

Layard's Parakeet

Grackle or Hill Myna

Ceylon Grackle

Yellow-eared Bulbul

Dusky Blue Flycatcher

Black-headed Babbler

noisy, neurotic bird given to calling out loudly at real or imagined danger. Among the floating vegetation in the tanks you will see the lovely and very distinctive **Pheasant-tailed Jacana** *(Hydrophasianus chirurgus)* 58 cm including tail, which cannot be mistaken for anything else.

Birds of the Wet and Highland Zone

The bird life of the Central Highlands and the SW of the country includes many of the common species associated with man throughout the island, but in addition has a rich variety of species found only in this area. Many of the 21 birds endemic to Sri Lanka are found here, including two members of the parrot family. The **Ceylon Lorikeet** *(Loriculus beryllinus)* 14 cm, is a *bright green short tailed* parrot-like bird, seen in small flocks in wooded areas in fruiting and flowering trees. The *bill, top of the head and the rump are bright red*, and there is a patch of *orange on the back* which shades into the red on the head. The male has a blue throat. **Layard's Parakeet** *(Psittacula calthorpae)* 32 cm, is a *long tailed* bird with a *soft grey head and back*, the *wings and underparts are green* and there is a mainly *black collar* round the neck. The male has a red bill, and the female a black one. It is seen in noisy flocks, especially in hilly forests. The **Grackle** or **Hill Myna** *(Gracula religiosa)* 28 cm, is generally well-known as it is often kept as a pet being such an excellent talker. In the wild, noisy flocks are found in highland forests, in fruiting trees. The **Ceylon Grackle** *(Gracula ptilogenys)* 25 cm, found only in Sri Lanka, also lives on the wooded hillsides in noisy flocks. Both Grackles are *black* with *white wing patches* and can be distinguished from each other by the wattles on the head. The Ceylon Grackle has only *two small yellow wattles* on the back of the head, whereas the wattles in the Grackle are more extensive. The species described above tend to be found high in the tree canopies, the next four species are usually found in the lower branches of trees or in bushes. The **Yellow-eared Bulbul** *(Pycnonotus penicillatus)* 20 cm, (another species found only in Sri Lanka) is common in the highland forests, usually in pairs, but sometimes in small flocks. It is *olive green above*, with the *underparts* being more *yellow*. The *head is dark brown* with a *white throat*, and white eyebrow. It gets its name from the prominent tuft of *yellow feathers* on the side of the head. The **Dusky Blue Flycatcher** *(Muscicapa sordida)* 14 cm, is an attractive and noticeable *blue-grey* bird with a *brighter blue forehead* and a *black patch* in front of the eye. It occurs in scrub, bush and gardens and in forest undergrowth in the hills. It behaves in typical flycatcher fashion, capturing its prey by flying out from a look-out post or branch. The **Grey Tit** *(Parus major)* 13 cm, also widespread in Europe, is common in hills and lowland areas in gardens, cultivation and light woodland. Above, it is *grey* and the *head is black with large white cheek patches*. Below, the *white underparts have a broad black stripe* running down the middle. On the forest floor, or low down in thick undergrowth is the common **Black-headed Babbler** *(Rhopocichla atriceps)* 13 cm. It is often in small flocks and is a restless bird, constantly on the move. The *upperparts are rich brown*, and the *black on the head contrasts with the clear white of the throat and chest*. The *pale yellow eye* is noticeable.

REPTILES

Two species of crocodile are found in Sri Lanka. The most widespread is the **Mugger** or **Marsh Crocodile** *(Crocodilus palustrus)* 3-4m in length, which lives in freshwater rivers and tanks in many parts of the island. In the brackish waters of the larger rivers lives the enormous **Estuarine** or **Saltwater Crocodile** *(Crocodilus porosus)*. It is as much as 7m in length, and is a much sleeker looking species than the mugger. Unlike the rather docile mugger, the estuarine crocodile has an aggressive temperament. The rather spectacular **Monitor** *(Varanus)* is a very large lizard which can be over 2m in length. A common type is basically greyish brown with black and yellow markings, but individuals vary somewhat in appearance. They live in a great variety of habitats from cultivation and scrub to waterside places and even the outskirts of towns. Because they are not persecuted, they have become quite tame and can be seen scavenging in the rubbish dumps and market places.

Monitor

Estuarine (Saltwater) Crocodile

Marsh Crocodile or Mugger

TREES AND PLANTS

Flowering trees

Visitors to Sri Lanka cannot fail to notice the many flowering plants growing in both town and countryside. The following flowering trees are often planted along roadsides and in towns. The **Gul Mohur** *(Delonix regia)*, is a native of Madagascar which is now grown throughout the island. It is particularly suitable for a shade tree in towns as it grows only to about 8 or 9m in height and has branches which spread out like an umbrella. Its flowers appear after it has shed its leaves, and the fiery coloured flowers make a magnificent display. The leaves themselves when they do appear are an attractive feathery shape, and a bright light green in colour. The **Jacaranda** *(Jacaranda mimosaefolia)*, originally from Brazil, is sometimes a rather straggly tree, though the feathery foliage is attractive. The flowers are purple-blue and thimble-shaped up to 40 mm long. When not in flower it bears a superficial resemblance to the gul mohur, but, though the leaves are similar, the shape of the two trees is quite different. The **Tamarind** *(Tamarindus indica)* is an evergreen with feathery leaves and small yellow and red flowers which grow in clusters. It has a short straight trunk and a spreading crown. The bark is often thickened with scar tissue, which gives it an irregular appearance. The noticeable fruit pods are long, curved and swollen at intervals down their length. The large and dramatic **Silk Cotton Tree** *(Bombax ceiba)* can be up to 25m in height. The bark is light coloured, often grey and usually bears conical spines. In big trees there are noticeable buttresses at the bottom of the trunk. It has wide spreading branches, and though deciduous, keeps its leaves for most of the year. The flowers appear when the tree is leafless and have rather fleshy red, curling petals up to 12 cm long forming a cup shape, from the middle of which the stamens all appear in a bunch. The fruit pod produces the fine silky cotton which gives it its name. The **Ceylon Ironwood** *(Mesua ferrea)* is a medium-sized tree often planted near Buddhist temples. It has long slender leaves which are reddish when young, and white four-petalled flowers with yellow centres.

Fruit trees

Widespread throughout is the well known **Mango** *(Mangifera indica)*. It is a fairly large tree being 6-15m high or more, with spreading branches forming a rounded canopy. It is often planted on roadsides and the dense shade it casts makes it a very attractive village meeting place. The distinctively shaped fruit is quite delicious and unlike any other in taste. Another widely grown fruit tree is the **Jakfruit** *(Artocarpus heterophyllus)*. A large evergreen with dark green leathery leaves, it may lose some of its leaves in the cold weather. The bark is warty and dark brown in appearance. The huge fruit, which can be as much as 90 cm long and 40 cm thick, grows from a short stem directly off the trunk and branches. The skin is thick and rough, almost prickly. The fruit is itself an acquired taste and some find the strong smell of the ripe fruit unpleasant. The **Banana** plant *(Musa)* is actually a gigantic herb arising from an underground stem. The very large leaves grow directly off the trunk which is about 5m in height. These leaves are often tattered and the single fruiting stem bears a large purple flower, which yields up to 100 fruit bunched up the stem. The **Papaya** *(Carica papaya)* has a slender palm-like trunk up to 8m tall, though it is usually much shorter. The large hand-shaped leaves come off near the top of the tree. Only the female tree bears fruit, which hang down close to the trunk just below the leaves. The **Cashew**

Flowering trees

Silk Cotton

Silk Cotton flower

Jacaranda

Gul Mohur

Ceylon Ironwood

Tamarind with flower and fruit

Fruit trees

Mango

Mango fruit

Cashew Nut

Jakfruit

Papaya fruit

Papaya

Banana fruit and flower

Banana plant

Flowering plants

Rhododendron

Bougainvillea

Pitcher plant

Hibiscus

Water Lily

Canna Lily

Frangipani flower

Frangipani

Nut *(Anacardium)* tree, a native of tropical America, was introduced into Sri Lanka, but now grows wild as well as being cultivated. Usually less than 7m in height, it has bright green, shiny, rounded leaves. The rather thick foliage casts a dense shadow. The nut is suspended from a fleshy fruit called a cashew apple. Originally from tropical America, the **Avocado Pear** *(Persea)* has been widely introduced and grows well in the Wet Zone. It is a fairly large broad-leaved tree up to 10m in height. The oval, pointed leaves are as much as 20 cm in length, and the familiar fruit grows towards the end of the branches.

Flowering plants

Common in the highland regions is the beautiful flowering **Rhododendron**. It grows as either a sprawling shrub or a tree which can be as tall as 12m. In the wild the commonest colour of the flowers is crimson, but other colours, such as pale purple occur too. Many other flowering plants are cultivated in parks, gardens and roadside verges. A particularly attractive small tree or bush is the **Frangipani** *(Plumeria acutifolia)*. It has a crooked trunk and rather stubby branches, which if broken give out a white milky juice, which can be irritating to the skin. The leaves, with noticeable parallel veins running at right angles to the main vein, are big and taper to a point at each end. The flowers which have a sweet scent, are rather waxy in appearance and usually white in colour, but sometimes pale yellow or pink. Perhaps even more common is the **Bougainvillea**. This is a dense bush, or sometimes a climber, with oval leaves and rather long spines. The flowers often cover the whole bush and can be a variety of striking colours, including pinkish-purple, orange, yellow and white. If you look carefully at one of the flowers you will see that the brightly coloured part is not formed by the petals, which are quite small and undistinguished, but by large bracts. The unusual shape of the **Hibiscus** flower makes it easy to identify. It is a fairly large bush and is cultivated in many forms. The trumpet-shaped flower, as much as 7 or 8 cm across, has a very long 'tongue' growing out from the centre. In colour it varies from scarlet and pink to yellow or white. The leaves are heart-shaped with jagged edges. In municipal flowerbeds the commonest planted flower is probably the **Canna Lily**. It has large leaves which are either green or bronze, and lots of large bright red or yellow flowers. The plant can be more than 1m high. Common in many of the tanks is the beautiful **Water Lily** *(Nymphaea)* which is generally white. The unusual **Pitcher Plant** *(Nepenthes)* looks very strange indeed. It is basically a climber, the leaves of which have become modified to form the brightly coloured pitchers. These pitchers, which can be up to 20 cm in length, are traps for unwary insects. Attracted by the sweet substance secreted within the pitcher, insects tumble down into it and are digested by the enzymes in the juice. **Orchids** abound but, sadly, most go unnoticed because of their tiny flowers. The large flowered, deep mauve *Dendrobium macarthiae* can be seen around Ratnapura in May. From spring to summer you may find the varicoloured, sweet-scented *Vanda tessellata* in bloom everywhere.

Other trees and plants

The **Rain Tree** *(Enterlobium saman)* is a large tree from South America, with a spreading canopy, and is often planted as a roadside shade tree. The dark green feathery leaves are peculiar in that they become horizontal in the daytime, thus maximizing the amount of shade thrown by the tree. At night time and in the rain they fold downwards. The flowers are pale pink, silky looking tufts. The **Eucalyptus** or **Gum Tree** *(Eucalyptus grandis)*, introduced from Australia in the 19th

Other trees and plants

Rain Tree

Rain Tree Flower

Sago Palm

Coconuts

Coconut

Coconut Palm

century, is now widespread and is planted near villages to provide both shade and firewood. There are various forms of eucalyptus, but they can all be readily recognized by their height, their characteristic long, thin leaves and the colourful peeling bark. The leaves and fruit of the tree often have a pleasant fresh smell. **Bamboo** *(Bambusa)* strictly speaking is a grass which is found almost everywhere. It can vary in size from small ornamental clumps to the enormous wild plant whose stems are so strong and thick that they are used for construction and as pipes in irrigation schemes in small holdings. The **Banyan** *(Ficus benghalensis)*, featured widely in eastern literature, is planted by temples, in villages and along roads. Curiously its seeds germinate in cracks in walls and in crevices in the bark of other trees. In a wall, the growing roots will split the wall apart, and this can be seen in many old temples and forts. If it grows in the bark of another tree, it sends down roots towards the ground. As it grows, more roots appear from the branches, until the original host tree is surrounded by a cage-like structure which eventually strangles it. So a single banyan appears to have multiple 'trunks' which are in fact roots. Related to the banyan, and growing in similar situations, is the **Peepal** *(Ficus religiosa)*, which also cracks open walls and strangles other trees with its roots. It has a smooth grey bark, and is commonly found near temples and shrines. It can easily be distinguished from the banyan by the absence of aerial roots, and by the leaves which are large, rather leathery and heart shaped, the point of the leaf tapering into a pronounced 'tail'. In a slight breeze the leaves quiver and make a gentle rustling sound. It bears abundant figs of a purplish tinge which are about 1 cm across.

The **Coconut Palm** *(Cocos nucifera)* is extremely common all round the coasts, with its tall (15-25m), slender, unbranched trunk, feathery leaves and large green fruit, so different from the brown fibre-covered inner nut which makes its way to Europe. A slightly different, golden coloured variety of coconut called the **King Coconut** yields a particularly sweet 'milk'. Another common palm is the **Sago** or **Fish-tail Palm** *(Caryota urens)*, locally called 'kitul'. Not as tall as the coconut palm, only some 6 to 8m in height, it has a smooth grey trunk. The leaves are very large and consist of many small leaflets, each of which is shaped like a fish tail. The flowers and associated parts hang down like horses' tails. The sago palm is commercially useful. The fibres are used to make bristles in brushes, as well as rope. Sago is obtained from the pith, and toddy from the sap. Sri Lanka, in most people's minds is second only to India as the home of **tea**. This is a vital commercial crop grown in tea gardens in highland areas and almost down to sea level near the wet SW coast. Left to itself, tea grows into a tree 10m tall. In the tea gardens it is pruned to waist height for the convenience of the tea pluckers and forms flat topped bushes, with shiny bright green oval leaves. The other commercially important plant is **rubber** *(Hevea brasiliensis)*. This large tree (24m) is cultivated in plantations in areas of high rainfall. The raw rubber (latex) oozes out through cuts made in the bark and runs into collecting cups suspended on the trunk. **Pineapples** are often grown under trees, especially under coconut palms on the coast. The pineapple fruit grows out of the middle of a rosette of long, spiky leaves. Probably the single most widespread crop is **rice**, the most important staple food. The grass-like rice plant grows in flooded paddies. The tending of rice paddies is very labour intensive, planting and harvesting often being done by hand.

Other trees and plants

Banyan

Banyan leaves

Eucalyptus leaves

Rubber Plant

Eucalyptus

Rice

Peepal

Tea

SEASHORE AND MARINE LIFE

The sandy beaches of Sri Lanka and the Maldives are a paradise for wildlife with a fantastic variety of fish, shells and corals which abound in the shallow warm waters, the sand banks and the reefs. Only the more common ones have universally recognized English names.

Corals are living organisms and consist of two basic types: the typical hard coral and the less familiar soft coral. There are several different species. Two common hard corals are the **Staghorn Coral** and the **Orange Tube Coral**. Look out also for the **Soft Corals** and **Sea Fans** which anchor themselves to the hard coral. One form of soft coral looks a bit like the familiar sea anemone, and is a pretty greyish pink in colour. One of the commonest sea fans is a reddish orange.

Among the living coral swim a bewildering variety of colourful fish. Shoals of silvery **Sardinella** dart about in great numbers, whereas the various sorts of surgeon fish and angelfish are somewhat more stately. **Angelfish** (*Pomacanthus*) are colourful with flattened bodies and some species have long streamers growing out of their dorsal and ventral fins. They have noticeable mouths which, being of a different colour from the body, look painted. One common type, the **Imperial (Emperor) Angelfish** (12 cm), is shown. Butterfly fish (*Chaetodontidae*) are similar to angelfish in general appearance, but smaller, about 9 cm. Their fins are rounded at the end and they lack the long streamers of the angelfish. They appear to flutter among the coral, hence their name. The **Red-fin Butterfly Fish** is one common species. The **Long-nosed Butterfly Fish** is unmistakable with its long snout, bright mustard yellow body and black mask. The various species of surgeon fish (*Acanthuridae*) abound and are generally unafraid of man. They get their name from the sharp blades at the base of their tails. They are rounded in outline, with compressed bodies and pouting lips. They are often very brightly coloured and the **Blue Surgeon** (17 cm) is often seen in shoals among coral and seaweed. Also common and colourful is the **Scorpion Fish** (*Pteriois*) (25 cm) seen among live coral, and sometimes getting trapped in the deeper pools of the dead reef by the retreating tide. It is easily recognized by the peculiar fins and its zebra-like stripes. Although it has poisonous dorsal spines it will not attack if you leave it alone.

The commonest shells are the **cowries**. Live cowries occur on the reef, but many dead ones can be found on the beach. The two commonest, the **Ringed Cowrie** (*Cypraea annulus*) and the **Money Cowrie** (*Cypraea moneta*) are shown. They are both about 2.5 cm long. The Ringed is a pretty grey and pinkish white shell with a golden ring. The Money Cowrie, so-called because it was once used as money in Africa, varies in colour from greenish grey to pink, according to its age. The big and beautiful **Tiger Cowrie** (*Cypraea tigris*) which can be up to 8 cm in length, is also seen occasionally. The colouring varies, but it is basically a very shiny shell with many dark round spots on, much more like a leopard than a tiger. Even bigger (15 cm) and more spectacular is the **Spider Conch** (*Lambis*). There is more than one species and a typical one is shown. They can be found on sandy beaches. Another large (20 cm) and common shell which occurs in a variety of forms is the **Murex** (*Chicoreus*). These shells all look basically similar and are found on the reefs. **Sea Urchins** (*Echinoidea*) are fairly common on sandy beaches and dead coral. The spines are extremely painful to tread on, so be sure to wear shoes when beach combing. Sea turtles are found on the sandy shores where they come to lay their eggs. Though often present in thousands when breeding, they are much preyed on and disturbed by man as well as animals, and are thus all on the endangered list. The giant **Leather-back Turtle** (*Dermochelys coriacea*) which grows to 2m in length, does not have a typical shell, but instead the back is covered with a ridged leathery skin. **Loggerhead Turtles** (*Caretta caretta*) can also grow to a considerable size. Both they and the smaller **Olive Ridley Turtle** (*Lepidochelys olivacea*) have the typical rows of shields along the shell.

Long-nosed Butterfly Fish

Imperial (Emperor) Angel Fish

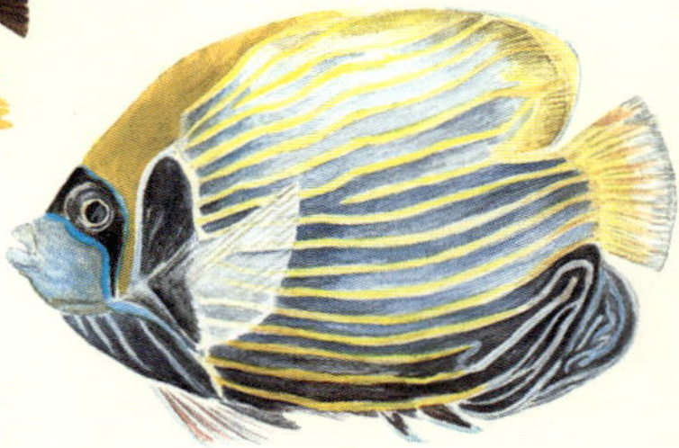

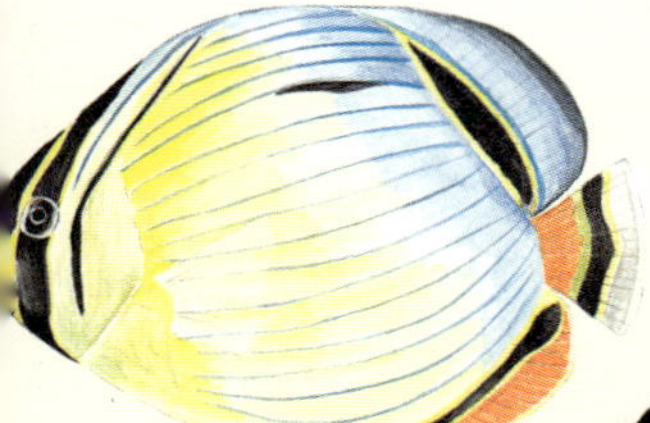

Red-fin Butterfly Fish

Blue Surgeon

Scorpion Fish

Loggerhead Turtle

Seashore and marine life

Money Cowrie

Ringed Cowrie

Sea Fan

Tiger Cowrie

Short-needled
Sea Urchin

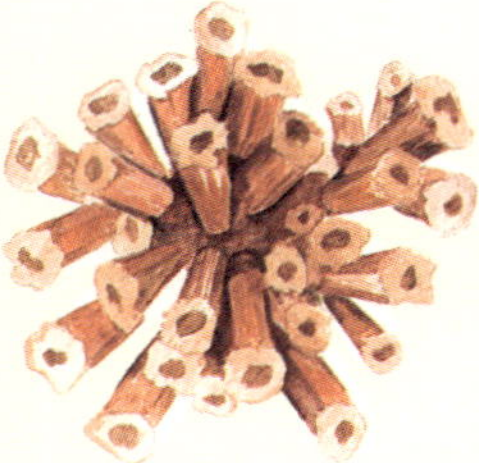

Orange Tube Coral

Staghorn Coral

Murex

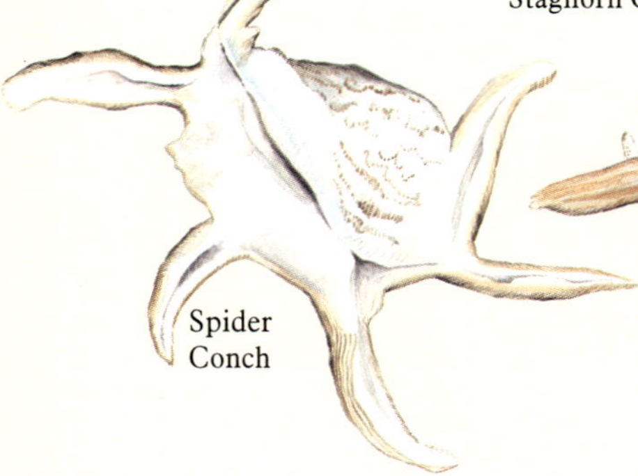

Spider
Conch

for the birds. If you follow the road to Pamunugama which skirts the lagoon along a narrow spit of land it will take you to the heart of Catholic Sri Lanka and you will pass numerous churches and shrines. You cross Pitipani and Duwa Islands which guard the mouth of the lagoon before entering Negombo Town. The road is virtually free from traffic and makes a very pleasant alternative to the bustle of the main road.

Kandy Many hotels will organize a day-trip to Kandy and although this is possible it is not really recommended as it takes about 3-4 hrs and means you have little time to sample its delights. A shorter trip is to the Elephant Orphanage near Kegalle, see page 151. **Warning** In the past, unauthorized 'travel agents' organizing excursions to Kandy and other towns have sometimes abandoned travellers with no money or obvious means of returning to the hotel.

Local festivals

Mar-Apr: *Easter* is celebtrated with passion plays, particularly on Easter Saturday on Duwa island.

Jul: *Fishermen's festival*, St Mary's Church; a major regional festival.

Local information

● Accommodation

This is spread out along almost 2 km, mostly along Lewis Place, the beach road due N of the lagoon, and further N in Ethukala and beyond. There are 2 small *Rest Houses* in Negombo itself. The beach gets progressively better the further away from Negombo you get and consequently the accommodation falls into 2 sections: *Browns Beach Hotel* forming the mid-point at the junction with Lewis Place, Poru Tota and Cemetery Roads. To its S are most of the cheaper guesthouses whilst to the N are the more expensive package hotels. Resort hotels usually offer watersports. Meals are normally incl in the price, especially in the peak season (mid-Dec to end-Jan) when a large supplement may be added. **NB** Some hotels do not allow Sri Lankans accompanying tourists, to stay.

A *Blue Oceanic* (Jetwing), Poru Tota Rd, Ethukala, T 4307, F 4277, 30m from beach, 105 large pleasant a/c rm (US$60) (ground flr ones not very private) are fairly spread out along the beach, 2 restaurants (1 seafood) can be disappointing – small portions and slow service,diving courses in swimming pool, the 'garden hotel'; **A** *Browns Beach* (Aitken Spence), 175 Lewis Place, T 2638, F 4303, 140 a/c rm (US$60), 10 bungalows, largest in Negombo, rooms are rather small and despite the impressive facilities it is slightly characterless, full facilities incl 3 restaurants, nightclub (opens 2130) and Barracuda diving centre, large pool, mainly catering for English package tours; **A** *Royal Oceanic* (Jetwing), Poru Tota Rd, Ethukala, T 4306, F 4277, 91 comfortable a/c rm with balconies (US$60), overlooking beach or 'tropical garden', pleasant bar overlooks nice pool, diving can be arranged, caters mainly for packages, 'grand experience' but reports of poor service from some independent travellers.

B *Golden Beach* (Adams), Lewis Place, T 2318, F 4285, 100 a/c rm, refurbished in 1995, restaurants, nightclub, pool, pleasant; **B** *Golden Star Beach*,163 Lewis Place, T 3564, F 8266, 61 rm, 25 a/c (US$35), full facilities incl pool and Arrack Bar in garden, pleasant enough. Sri Lankan/Dutch management; **B** *Goldi Sands*, Poru Tota Rd, Ethukala, T 2021, F 4227, 75 rm rather utilitarian, spartan, most overlook the beach, with uninteresting public area, most northernly of the 'package' hotels (mostly German guests); **B** *Sunflower Beach*, Lewis Place, T 2841, F 4227, 66 slightly shabby rm (10 a/c) arranged in L-shape around pool, balcony gives sea view (in theory).

C *Catamaran Beach*, 209 Lewis Place, T 2206, F 8026, 50 rm, 15 a/c with balcony (US$20), spartan rooms overlook central courtyard with pleasant garden, 5-bedroom bugalow good value, tastefully decorated reataurant, nice open air pool bar and good-sized pool are slightly above the fishing beach, billiards, watersports, island tours through travel counter; **C** *Dippeguker*, Poru Tota Rd, Ethukala, T (071) 23559, 6 rm with fans and nets, clean tidy rooms with spacious bath, bit dark but good value, small bar and restaurant overlook garden; **C** *Icebear*, 103 Lewis Place 5 quite large and comfortable rm in a nice garden fronting the beach, extras are available but essentially just a room, Swiss-owned; **C** *Oasis Beach Resort*, Poru Tota Rd, Ethukala, T/F 8002, F 4238, 30 rm, 10 a/c rm built around pool are good value, 2 restaurants, brick contruction makes a pleasant change from the ubiquitous concrete, tours US$15 Kandy (min number required); **C** ***Sea Garden*** (Jetwing), Poru Tota Rd, Ethukala, 72 rm (all non a/c) have nice balconies with planters chairs, restaurant, guests can use the facilities at *Blue* or *Royal Oceanic* hotels, the snack bar on the road side is good value for drinks; **C** ***Silva's Beach Guest House***, 5 Poru Tota Rd, Ethukala, across the road from the beach, T 3408, 7 large a/c rm on road, smaller rooms above owner's home are well back from the road and have nice sitting area, 4 bungalows (beware electric showers) at Rs 1,200, good beach restaurant well used by locals, bar, pool planned for end-1995, very helpful owners, rec; **C** ***Silver Sands***, Lewis Place, 17 rm (2 with hot water), fan, nets and bathroom, nice balconies overlook pleasant central courtyard garden, bicycle hire Rs 75; **C** ***Topaz Beach***, Poru Tota Rd, Ethukala, 30 rm (5 a/c), comfortable rooms but only the end rooms get much of a view, helpful owner, no pool, money changing (rate better than most), trips to Kandy for about US$50 organized by Ceylon Resorts, rec; **C-D** ***Don's Beach***, 75 Lewis Place, T 2342, 60 rm, watersports, disco underneath.

D ***Aquarius Beach***, off Lewis Place, 6 rm, dirty, not rec; **D** ***Beach View Tourist Guest House***, Poru Tota Rd, Ethukala, 15 rm, shower and fan, no nets, rather gloomy rooms overlooking central corridor, palm thatched restaurant on beach, *Beachview Restaurant* on roadside reasonable value, motorbikes for hire (Rs 400/day), bicycles (Rs 75); **D** ***Beach Villa Guesthouse***, 3/2 Senaviratna Maw, off Lewis Place, T 2833, F 3383, 14 rm with fan, slightly more expensive rooms upstairs, restaurant overlooks the beach, Mr Nissanka, the owner, acts as a guide and can organize island tours, car hire Rs 1,200/day, bicycles, boat trips Rs 1,000, transport to Colombo Rs 1,000, rec; **D** ***Club Oasis Beach***, Poru Tota Rd, over the road from beach, Ethukala, 25 rm comfortable with fan, nets and bathroom built around interior courtyard with small seating area on each flr, *Octupus* 'Bar in the Sky' attached but not always open, tours.

Budget hotels: **D-E** ***Interline Beach***, 5 Carron Pl (off Lewis Place), T 2350, 26 small rm with fan but no nets, scruffy reception, large restaurant with grassed sitting area overlooks beach; **D-E** ***Rainbow Guest House***, 3 Carron Place opp *Aquarius Beach*, T 2082, good food, rec.

Guest houses: there are several along Lewis Place. Among them **D-E** ***De-phani*** at 189/15, T 8225, 8 small, rather dingy rooms with shower (cold water only), pleasant restaurant overlooking beach open until 2100, good food; **D-E** ***Star Beach***, next to *De-phani*, T 2606, 15 clean and tidy rm, bigger dining room with good choice of food, barbecue on Fri, bar 'happy hour' 1700-1800, marvellously antequated switch board, rec; **E** ***Ceylonica Beach***, 29 Lewis Place, T 2976, 20 rm (1 a/c), run down rooms, questionable management, no bulb in lightholder, not rec. The cheapest guest houses tend to be away from the beach: **E** ***Red Sun Guesthouse***, 129 Lewis Place, dark and dingy rooms on the main road but cheap; **E** ***Sea Sands***, Poru Tota Rd, Ethukala, 12 rm, fan, net and balcony, small beach front, no restaurant (breakfast in room), one of the cheapest places N of Lewis Place but not very good value; **E** ***Srilal Fernando's***, 67 Parakrama Rd, Kurana towards airport (nr Kurana Railway Station, RAC Motors Bus Stop), T 2481, 5 rm with bath in family home in large garden, meals on request, phone from airport for free pick-up; **E-F** ***Dilwood***, 71 Anderson Rd, T 2810, 4 clean rm with bath, breakfast; Mrs Ranasinghe's **F** ***Vishwa Guest Rooms***, 91 Pallansena Rd, Kochchikade (1 km from railway station, 4 km N of Negombo on Bus route 905), T 7215, 3 rm in house with large garden, Sri Lankan veg meals, peaceful, walking distance of beach N of Ethukala, the Institute of Oriental Medicine is here.

Talahena: **B** ***Blue Lagoon*** (Serendib), across the lagoon to the 6 km S of Negombo Town, T 3004, 28 rm (US$25), full facilities incl restaurant, pool, attractive garden and watersports but unfortunately rather remote.

Waikkal: Waikkal is quite remote and separate from Negombo (40 mins from the airport). Once you are in your hotel you have to have transport of some kind to go anywhere. **A** ***Dolphin*** (Serendib), Kammala S, sandwiched between the sea and the old Dutch canal, T 3129, F Colombo 438933, 73 a/c rm, (US$65), traditional decor, good seafood restaurant, surrounded by a garden and palm trees, superb swimming pool (claims to be the largest on the island) which zig-zags most attractively between the rooms, whilst the hotel has full facilities, its remoteness is a decided drawback; attached are the cheaper non-a/c ***Dolphin Cottages*** which share the facilities of the main hotel, 50 fairly large and well furnished rm

(US$40); **B** *Ranweli Holiday Village*, T 2136, 84 chalets (35 a/c), restaurant, nightclub, pool and various watersports; **C** *Palm Village*, Uswetakeiyawa, 20 km from the airport, T 433755, F 446838, 50 a/c rm, attractive location by seaside.

● Places to eat

Seafood is the speciality of many hotels and restaurants; lobsters, crabs and prawns are all excellent. Even though in 1995 tourist hotels carried notices advising guests not to venture out (possibly because of the difficult political situation in the past), it is possible to eat out at restaurants which is much the cheaper option.The majority are clustered around *Browns Beach Hotel*.

North of Browns Beach Hotel:

Chinese: *Pri-Kin*, just up from the *Browns Beach* on the roadside is good for Chinese although ***Vasana***, past *Pri-kin* down a side street, (also Chinese) is much cheaper. Across the street from the *Pri-kin* is ***Seafood***, moderately priced but very plain surroundings.

Continental: *Alt Saarbrucken*, 35 Poru Tota Rd, is on the beach side just N of *Oasis Beach Resort*, where the Alpine influence is obvious with heavy wooden furniture and fondues at Rs 1,000 for 2; ***Rudis Bar***, next door, slightly less expensive than *Alt Saarbrucken*, cheap wine and reasonable food make this a popular place with travellers as witnessed by the grafitti on the walls; ***Bijou***, on the road side, opp *Rudies*, Swiss owned and moderately expensive (although much cheaper than the tourist hotels), excellent for seafood and noodles; further N is ***Sherryland***, opp *Sea Garden Hotel*, set back from the road in a garden, moderately priced with attentative service, lively bar, good value; ***Seawirt***, opp *Blue Oceanic Hotel*, good for chicken and amongst the cheapest beer in town (bicycles and motor bikes can be hired next door, altough rates are not very competitive); ***Silva's Beach Restaurant*** and bar, 5 Poru Tota Rd, is rec, great seafood, friendly owner will advise on the catch of the day.

Snacks: *Curry Bowl* and *Spice Restaurant* serve cheap snacks.

South of Browns Beach Hotel: ***Restaurant Delhi***, opp *Sunflower Beach Hotel*, good Indian food but rather the wrong end of town. There is also a little cluster of restaurants opp *Catamaran Hotel*, ***Join Us***, ***Blue Moon*** and ***Blonghe's*** all offer reasonable fare and are quite good value.

In Negombo Town: *Choys* is about the only choice, quite pleasant on St Joseph's Rd overlooking the harbour.

● Banks & money changers

Bank of Ceylon on Main St nearly opp St Mary's. A new branch of **Seylan Bank** has opened on Poru Tota Rd just N of *Browns Beach Hotel*, open 1000-1800, it is very efficient and has much better rates than those on offer in the hotels.

● Entertainment

Disco: Outside of the main hotels (see above) ***Club Tropicana*** on Poru Tota Rd (also supposed to have a skittles alley).

Herbal massage: ***Kräuter Shop***, 32 Poru Tota Rd, offers massages from Rs 750/30 mins as well as various other herbal treatments, open daily 0930-1730. The owner is confident that his herbal treaments offer relief from various allergies (incl mosquitoe bites!), sunburn and rheumatism. Food and drinks are available.

● Hospitals & medical services

Most large hotels (as well as the smaller guesthouses) have doctors on call. There is a hospital just off main street on the main Colombo road in Negombo Town.

● Post & telecommunications

The post office is on Main St towards the fort. Hotels also sell stamps and will arrange for the collection of post; most have IDD dialing as well as access to fax machines.

● Shopping

Handicrafts: the curio stalls nr the large hotels are handy for getting last-minute presents. Quality varies considerably and they are not nearly so good as buying direct up country. Visit them all before deciding and then bargain hard.

Supermarket: ***Davids***, opp *Sea Garden*, carries a range of basic goods as well as a selection of teas and spices, good medical supplies and bottled water. ***Home foods***, opp *Oasis Beach Resort*, has frozen food.

Tailors: ***Chandi Schneiderei***, 166 Lewis Place and ***Schneiderei Gaffal***, 266 Lewis Place, will make suits etc (silk and cotton) in about 2 days.

● Sports

Watersports: deep-sea fishing from *Halcyon Beach Hotel*, US$40/hour for 4 hrs (4pp), US$200 for 6 hrs; 'Leisure' fishing US$40/hour for 6pp, rods US$10-20. Ask for Gerhard, *Serendib Watersport Paradise*, Paragliding Rs 185, Banana boat Rs 440 pp, Ski boat Rs 2,900/hour, Waterskiing Rs 750, Windsurfing US$250 for 4-day course. Scuba diving can be arranged here or through *Blue Oceanic Hotel*, contact Franz or Marie on (078) 60798.

Tennis & squash: can be arranged through most hotels.

● Tour companies & travel agents
In addition to hotel travel desks, independent travel agents incl ***Jetwing Tous***, Ethukala, opp *Blue Oceanic Hotel*; ***Top Shop***, small travel counter, and ***Fortuna Travels and Tours***, opp *Browns Beach Hotel* on Cemetery Rd, T 2774, F 8239. For a trip around the lagoon or canal you should not pay more than Rs 350 and Rs 4 50 respectively; you may be able to negotiate a substantially lower rate.

● Tourist offices
Ceylon Tourist Board, 12/6 Ethukala, Lewis Place, 0900-1715, Mon-Sat.

● Useful addresses
Tourist Police: at Ethukala.

● Transport
Local Bicycle hire: from many hotels, usually Rs 75/day. **Bus**: frequent buses run along the main beach road from the bus and railway stations. Also **3-wheelers**. The flat roads make a short trip out of Negombo attractive. Transport is well regulated and hotel receptions should display a list of the agreed taxi rates. You may well be able to negotiate better rates with 3-wheelers, who will usually wait (or return at a specified hour) if you want to go visiting the surrounding countryside. **NB** Negotiate the return trip before setting foot in the vehicle, only pay for a single journey at the outset, never the return trip, otherwise you could be in for a very long wait! **Car hire**: mostly through hotels; inspect vehicles carefully and expect to pay Rs 1,000 plus Rs 250/day for car and driver. *Beach Villa Guest House*, 3/2 Senaviratna Maw; ***Charisma Tours*** just S of *Golden Beach Hotel* can arrange vehicles (also motor bikes); ***Nishal Travel***, 274 Lewis Pl, T 2725 and from the jeweller's shop opp. **Motorbike hire**: expect to pay Rs 400/day. Some hotels (eg *Beach View Tourist Guest House*, Ethukala) and ***Gold Wing Motors***, 546 Colombo Rd, T 2895, rent on daily/weekly terms.

Air Transport to airport, 10 km from Katunayake, takes about 20 mins in the quiet of the night, longer in the day due to very heavy traffic. **Bus**: every 30 mins at least, from early morning until late evening. **Taxi**: Rs 350-400 (after bargaining) to/from Ethukala hotels. **3-wheelers**: charge Rs 250. **Train**: the commuter train to Colombo goes via the airport.

Train For **Colombo**: train services are not frequent.

Road Bus: for **Colombo**: frequent Bus service, takes about 1 hr.

ROUTES Negombo to Puttalam The **A3** goes on to **Marawila** (20 km), one of many villages with large Roman Catholic churches. Strongly influenced by the Portuguese, the coastal strip has a high proportion of Catholics. In the mid-1990s 23% of the population immediately inland from Negombo was Christian, increasing N to 38%. Crossing the estuary the road passes between the coastal lagoon and the railway through **Madampe** (13 km; known for its Coconut Research Institute) to Chilaw.

Chilaw (12 km) is a small village, but an important Roman Catholic centre, with another very large church. There is also an interesting Saivite Temple at **Munneswaram** (or Munnessarama, 5 km E of Chilaw) with Tamil inscriptions. It is an important pilgrimage centre.

ROUTES The **A3** runs due N. A left turn at Battulu Oya leads to Udappawa.

Udappawa, 12 km N of Chilaw. A tiny Tamil Hindu village, it is noted for its **fire-walking** ceremonies which take place in Jul-Aug every year. Experiments conducted in 1935-36 showed that the coals were heated to about 500°C during the ceremony.

ROUTES Marshes and lagoons lie between the road and the sea for much of the route N to **Puttalam**, which crosses a series of minor rivers and a few major ones such as the **Battulu Oya**. At **Palavi**, 3 km S of Puttalam, a left turn goes up the W side of the Puttalam lagoon to Kalpitiya. You can cross the Puttalam Lagoon by ferry to Karaitivu, travelling S to complete a round trip to Puttalam.

Kalpitiya (25 km) The town has an old Dutch Fort, and an attractive 18th century Dutch church (1 km W of the fort) which was renovated by the British in the 1840s. Continuing up the main road to Puttalam is the *Lake View Restaurant*, 139 Colombo Road, which is clean and serves good food. The political troubles have resulted in the town now accommodating large numbers of regugees in camps. **NB** In 1995 the Tourist Board did not recommend a visit.

ROUTES From Puttalam the **A12** goes NE to Anuradhapura, fringing the Wilpattu National Park. 30 km before Anuradhapura, turn off the A12 to reach the entrance to the park (7 km).

Wilpattu National Park

Approach The Park covers 1,900 sq km and The park entrance is 7 km from Timbriwewa, 29 km from Anuradhapura. **NB** Due to the unstable political situation the park has remained closed from the mid-80s and was not accessible in 1995; enquire from the Department of Wildlife Conservation, State Timber Corp Bldg, 82 Rajamalwatte Rd, Battaramulla near Sri Jayawardenepura (Kotte) or Wildlife Department, 493, TB Jaya Maw, Colombo 10, T 687347.

Background The largest reserve in Sri Lanka, this is best seen by staying at **Kala Oya** (30 km) and taking advantage of the government organized tours. Private cars are not allowed into the reserve, which, unlike some of the island's other parks, has some dense jungle, interspersed with savannah and sand dunes. A number of *villus* – the small lakes which attract animals to drink, have crocodiles; Wil-pattu means 'the land of lakes'. Some of these were used by earlier kingdoms as reservoirs. Some Sinhalese ruins have been discovered in the forested areas to the E.

Wildlife The park is particularly famous for its leopards and sloth bears. True to its name, the sloth bear is slow to move and survives on honey, soft fruit and white ants (termites). Other wildlife includes a variety of deer, mongoose, wild buffaloes and wild boar; Kumbukwila and Nelunwila have watch-huts.

There is a wide variety of water birds, especially winter migrants from Nov-Jan, as well as those of the Dry Zone jungle.

Viewing About 300 km of jeep track cover the area. If you have not come on a tour from Kala Oya, you will have to choose between hiring a jeep with driver/guide (min charge is high) or taking a seat in a mini-bus. Although a jeep is more expensive, unless you can share with others, it is by far the best way to get a glimpse of a leopard and see the sloth bear.

The best months are Feb-Aug and Oct. Early morning or late afternoon are the best times for a visit, to avoid the heat of the day and also to see the animals. First light is best for viewing birds and deer. From 0800-1100, if you drive around the park you may spot leopard by the lakes and a variety of deer. At mid-day, sloth bears sometimes bask in the sun on sandy patches. After 1600, you will again see activity in the park; leopards possibly and certainly bear near the *villus*. In the dry season (Aug-Sep), elephants can be spotted as they come out to the water-holes.

• **Accommodation** Several very basic *Park Bungalows* are located by *villus* within the perimeter. There is no electricity; the cook will prepare a simple meal but visitors must bring the main ingredients. Two bungalows are available to foreign tourists: from Maradanmaduwa, 25 km away **Manawila** on the edge of a *villu*, and 20 km away **Panikkarvillu** along a trail, Reservations: Wildlife Conservation Department, 82 Rajamalwatta Rd, Battaramulla, T 433012. At **Maradanmaduwa**, 15 km from main gate, by the *villu*. *Bungalow* sleeps 10, *Log Cabin*, 4. Very good for bird-watching and spotting elephants in the dry months. 18 km away at **Manikapolauttu**, nr the centre of the park with several *villus* around, the *Bungalow* is nr a small lake with crocodiles. Good viewing from verandah. 8 km away, 3 km E of the old

Great North Rd, is **Kalivillu** which has the *Bungalow* on the water's edge. Good for spotting leopards, and in the dry season, elephants which frequent the large *villu*. On the N boundary, by the Moeragam Aru, a river attracting anglers, is the **Kokomattai** *Bungalow*. **Talawila** was once hunting territory; the *Bungalow* overlooks a lake. The plain Nature and Wildlife Conservation Soc ***Bungalow*** can sleep up to 10. Reservations: Soc Offices, Chaitiya Rd, Marine Drive, Fort, Colombo, T 25248. At **Kala Oya**: **C** ***Wilpattu Hotel***, T 29 752, 41 rm with fan, shower and mosquito nets, dining room overlooks Kala Oya River, excellent bungalows, rec; ***Pershamel Safari Hotel***, Pahamaragahawewa has 12 rm.

• **Transport Road Bus**: from Anuradhapura, twice daily; also jeep or taxis.

Nochchiyagama From Kala Oya the road passes NE through this small Tamil village of potters, famous for producing black clay cooking pots known as *chutties*.

ROUTES It is about 20 km to Anuradhapura along the rather poor quality **A12**.

KANDY, THE CENTRAL, NORTH CENTRAL AND UVA PROVINCES

Contents

Kandy	170
Kandy to Nuwara Eliya and Horton Plains	183
Kandy to Nuwara Eliya via Hatton and Talawakele	192
Kandy to the cultural triangle	198
Anuradhapura and Mihintale	202
Sigiriya	214
Polonnaruwa	219

Maps

Central, N Central and Uva Provinces	169
Kandy	172-173
Southern Highlands	190
Nuwara Eliya	185
Dambulla	129
Anuradhapura	203
Mihintale	210
Mihintale Sacred Centre	211
Sigiriya	215
Polonnaruwa	220
Polonnaruwa – quadrangle	222
Mahiyangana	226

Introduction

The stunning view over Kandy's 18th century lake towards the Temple of the Tooth hints at some of the reasons for Kandy's unique character. In the heart of the island's interior, protected for centuries from direct external control by its mountains and forests as well as by a fierce desire by a succession of leaders to protect its independence, Kandy and its region offers rich insights into Sri Lanka's cultural traditions.

On the northwestern edge of the Central Highlands, Kandy is a gateway not just to the Highlands themselves but to the whole of the Central and North Central Provinces. Thus it has become the natural centre for most visitors to the island who want to explore some of its outstanding scenery and cultural history, as it is easily accessible from most of the coastal resorts, but also provides an excellent base from which to explore Sri Lanka's cultural triangle of Anuradhapura, Polonnaruwa and Sigiriya, all located in the North Central Province.

Uva Province, occupying a basin on the SE edge of the Central Highlands, has sometimes been held to be the original home of the Kandyan civilization. Farmer has suggested that the river valleys draining into the Mahaweli Ganga would have provided a natural route from the N and E Dry Zone for Sinhalese migrating up into the hills. The relatively bare landscape, with trees restricted to the rivers' edges, suggest the difficulty of cultivation, and Uva has witnessed ancient irrigation systems, including, as Brohier has pointed out, tunnels through hills. Uva today is also one of the few remaining homes for the Veddas, living in isolated pockets, normally out of sight, though some of these aboriginal peoples can still be seen.

Uva Province is associated by popular legend with the Buddha who is believed to have made two visits to the area. In the E it has some high water falls, spectacular 'gaps' in its precipitous ridges, some interesting wildlife and is also famous for spices and Ayurvedic herbs which grow in the SW of the province.

Ayurvedic Healing

Ayurveda (science of life/health) is the ancient Hindu system of medicine – a naturalistic system depending on diagnosis of the body's 'humours' (wind, mucus, gall and sometimes, blood) to achieve a balance. In the early form, gods and demons were associated with cures and ailments; treatment was carried out by using herbs, minerals, formic acid (from ant hills) and water, and hence was limited in scope. Ayurveda classified substances and chemicals compounds in the theory of *panchabhutas* (5 'elements'). It also noted the action of food and drugs on the human body. Ayurvedic massage using aromatic and medicinal oils to tone up the nervous system, has been practised for centuries.

This ancient system which developed in India over centuries before the Buddha's birth was written down as a *samhita* by Charaka. It probably flourished in Sri Lanka up to the 19th century when it was overshadowed by the western system of allopathic medicine. However, with the renewed interest in alternative forms of therapy in the West, Sri Lanka too considers it a serious subject for scientific research and has begun exploring its wealth of wild plants. The island has seen a regerneration of special Ayurvedic herbal cure centres which are increasingly attracting foreign visitors.

In addition to the use of herbs as cures, many are used daily in the Sri Lankan kitchen (eg chilli, coriander, cumin, fennel, garlic, ginger, onions, turmeric), some of which will be familiar in the West, and have for centuries been used as beauty preparations.

CENTRAL, N CENTRAL
& UVA PROVINCES
85
Bay of Bengal
To Mannar
Vavuniya
To Jaffna
Kuchchaveli
Nilaveli
A29
A14
Kebitigollewa
A12
A9
Trincomalee
Ratmalgahawewa
Horowupotana
Medawachchiya
Malwatu Oya
Kinniyai
Rambewa
Kahatagasdigiliya
Kantale
Anuradhapura
Mihintale
A15
A12
Galkulama
Galenbindunuwewa
To Batticaloa
To Puttalam
Migaswewa
A 9
Gal Oya
Maradankadawala
Eppawala
Mahaweli Ganga
Kalawewa
Habarana
A 11
To Batticaloa
Polonnaruwa
Sigiriya
A28
Dambulla
Manampitiya
Maduru Oya
To Puttalam
Maho
A 9
Galewela
Elahera
A10
Naula
Dehiattakandiya
Pandeniya
A 6
Wariyapola
Nalanda
To Batticaloa
Ibbagamuwa
Pallegama
Maha Oya
Kurunegala
To Madampe
Matale
Girandurukotte
To Ampara
A6
Padiyatalawa
Victoria Reservoir
Polgahawella
Kandy
Mahiyangana
Peradeniya
A 26
Ambepussa
Mawanella
A5
Randenigala Reservoir
A1
Kegalla
Galaha
Rikillagaskada
Bibile
To Colombo
Gampola
A5
Ramboda
Pidurutalagala 2524 m
To Pottuvil & Arugam Bay
Ginigathena
Dimbula
Badulla
Nuwara Eliya
Talawakele
Hali Ela
A7
Nanu Oya
Ella
A 22
Hatton
Welimada
Monaragala
Adam's Peak 2243 m
A4
Beragala
Haputale
Buttala
0
25
km
Wellawaya
To Balangoda & Ratnapura
A4

KANDY

(*Pop* 55,000; *Alt* 488m) Kandy is a modest sized town, but it stands as one of the most important symbols of Sinhalese national identity. The last bastion of Buddhist political power against colonial forces, the home of the Temple of the Buddha's tooth relic, and the site of one of the world's most impressive annual festivals, the city is the gateway to the higher hills and the tea plantations. Its architectural monuments date mainly from a final surge of grandiose building by King **Vikrama Raja Sinha** in the early 19th century, so extravagant, and achieved only with such enormous costs for the people of Kandy, that his nobles betrayed him to the British rather than continue enduring his excesses. The result is some extraordinary buildings, none of great architectural merit, but sustaining a genuinely Kandyan style going back to the 16th century, and rich in symbolic significance of the nature of the king's view of his world.

History

Although the city of Kandy (originally *Senkadagala*) is commonly held to have been founded by a general named Vikramabahu in 1472, there was a settlement on the site for at least 150 years before that. On asserting his independence from the reigning monarch, Vikramabahu made Kandy his capital. He built a palace for his mother and a shrine on pillars. In 1542 the **Tooth Relic** was brought to the city, stimulating a flurry of new religious building – a 2-storey house for the relic itself, and 86 houses for the monks. As in Anuradhapura and Polonnaruwa, the Tooth temple was built next to the Palace.

Defensive fortifications probably only came with the attacks of the Portuguese. Forced to withdraw from the town in 1594, King Vimala Dharma Suriya set half the city on fire, a tactic that was repeated by several successors in the face of expulsion by foreign armies. However, he won it back, and promptly set about building a massive wall, interspersed with huge towers. Inside, a new palace replaced the one destroyed by fire, and the city rapidly gained a reputation as a cosmopolitan centre of splendour and wealth. As early as 1597 some Portuguese showed scepticism about the claims that the enshrined tooth was the Buddha's. In 1597 De Quezroy described the seven golden caskets in which the tooth was kept, but added that it was the tooth of a buffalo. The Portuguese were already claiming that they had captured the original, exported it to Goa and incinerated it.

By 1602 the city had probably taken the form (though not the actual buildings) which would survive to the beginning of the 19th century. The major temples were also already in place. Kandy was repeatedly attacked by the Portuguese. In 1611 the city was captured and largely destroyed, and again in 1629 and 1638, and the Tooth Relic

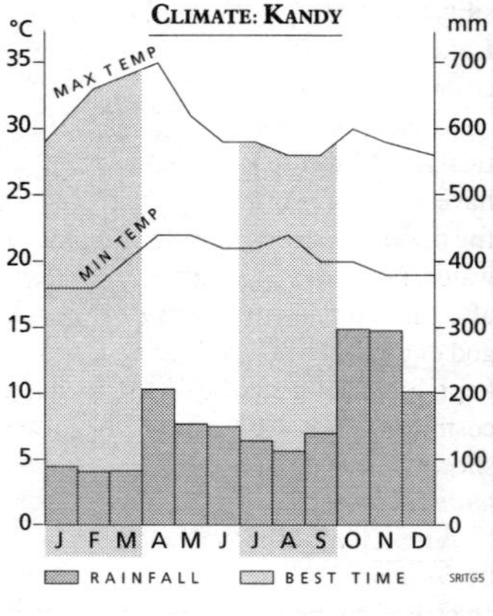

Worship Of the 'Tooth Relic'

The eyewitness account of **Bella Sidney Woolf** in 1914 captures something of the atmosphere when the Tooth Relic could be viewed by pilgrims: "The relic is only shown to royal visitors, or on certain occasions to Burmese and other pilgrims. If the passenger happens to be in Kandy at such a time he should try to see the Tooth, even though it may mean many hours of waiting. It is an amazing sight. The courtyard is crammed with worshippers of all ages, bearing offerings in their hands, leaves of young coconut, scent, flowers, fruit. As the door opens, they surge up the dark and narrow stairway to the silver and ivory doors behind which lies the Tooth.

The doors are opened and a flood of hot heavy scented air pours out. The golden'Karandua' or outer casket of the tooth stands revealed dimly behind gilded bars. In the weird uncertain light of candles in golden candelabra the yellow-robed priests move to and fro. The Tooth is enclosed in five Karanduas and slowly and solemnly each is removed in turn; some of them are encrusted with rubies, emeralds and diamonds.

At last the great moment approaches. The last Karandua is removed – in folds of red silk lies the wondrous relic – the centre point of the faith of millions. It is a shock to see a tooth of discoloured ivory at least 3 inches long – unlike any human tooth ever known. The priest sets it in a golden lotus – the Temple Korala gives a sharp cry – the tom-toms and conches and pipes blare out – the kneeling worshippers, some with tears streaming down their faces, stretch out their hands in adoration."

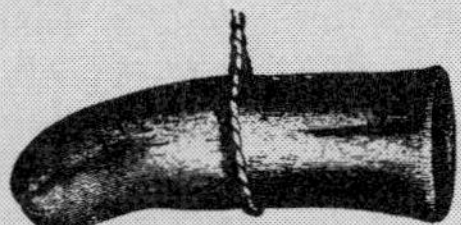

Buddha's tooth
Illustrated by Rev W Urwick in 1885

was removed for a time by the retreating King Senarat. A new earth rampart was built between the hills in the S of the city. In 1681 there is evidence of a moat being built using forced labour, and possibly the first creation of the **Bogambara Lake** to the SW, as a symbol of the cosmic ocean.

Vimala Dharma Suriya I had a practical use for the lake, for he is reputed to have kept some of his treasure sunk in the middle, guarded by crocodiles in the water. Duncan suggests that there was also the symbolic link with Kubera, the god of wealth, who was believed to have kept his wealth at the bottom of the cosmic ocean. Crocodiles are often shown on the dragon gateways (*makara torana*) of temples.

A new **Temple of the Tooth** was built by Vimala Dharma Suriya II between 1687-1707, on the old site. Three storeys high, it contained a reliquary of gold encrusted with jewels. Between 1707-1739 Narendra Sinha undertook new building in the city, renovating the Temple of the Tooth and enclosing the **Natha Devala** and the sacred **Bodhi tree**. He established the validity of his royal line by importing princesses from Madurai, and set aside a separate street for them in the town.

Major new building awaited King Kirti Sri (1747-1782). He added a temple to Vishnu NW of the palace, but at the same time asserted his support for Buddhism, twice bringing monks from Thailand to re-validate the Sinhalese order of monks. The Dutch, who captured the city in 1765, plundered the temples and palaces. The Palace and the Temple of the Tooth were destroyed and many other buildings were seriously damaged.

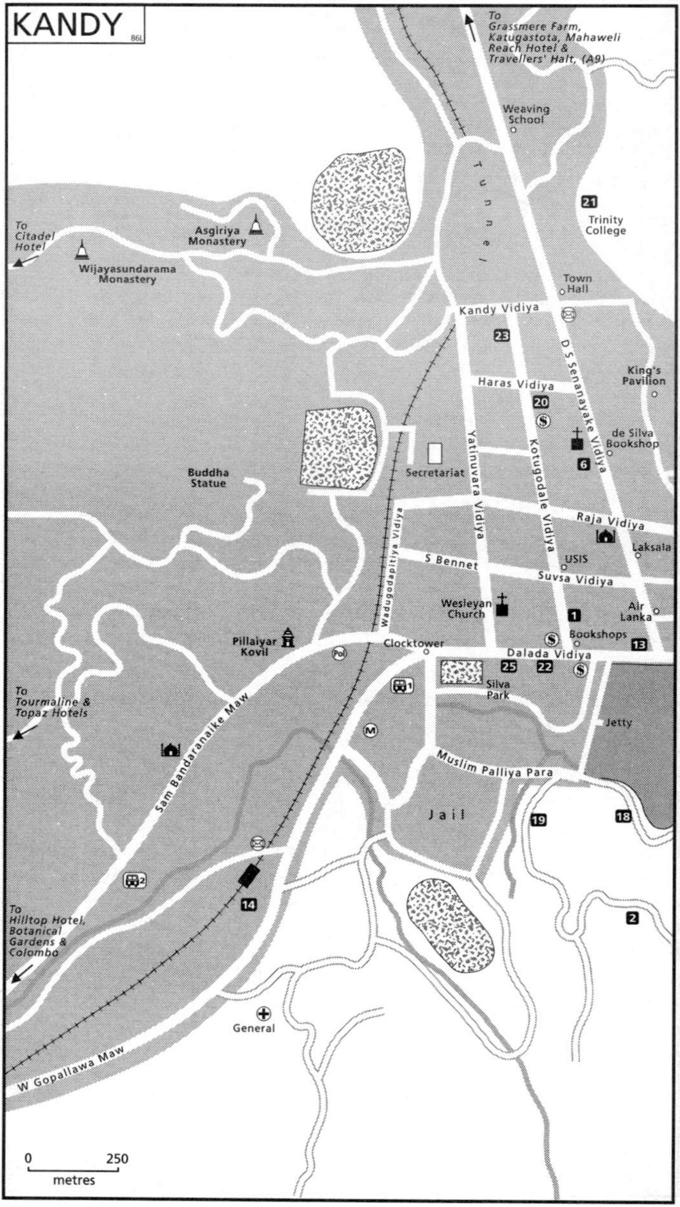
KANDY
86L
To Grassmere Farm, Katugastota, Mahaweli Reach Hotel & Travellers' Halt, (A9)
Weaving School
Tunnel
21
Trinity College
To Citadel Hotel
Asgiriya Monastery
Wijayasundarama Monastery
Town Hall
Kandy Vidiya
23
D S Senanayake Vidiya
King's Pavilion
Haras Vidiya
20
de Silva Bookshop
6
Yatinuvara Vidiya
Kotugodale Vidiya
Secretariat
Buddha Statue
Raja Vidiya
Laksala
Wadugodapitiya Vidiya
S Bennet
USIS
Suvsa Vidiya
Wesleyan Church
1
Air Lanka
Pillaiyar Kovil
Clocktower
Bookshops
13
Dalada Vidiya
25
22
Silva Park
To Tourmaline & Topaz Hotels
Jetty
Sam Bandaranaike Maw
Muslim Palliya Para
Jail
19
18
14
2
To Hilltop Hotel, Botanical Gardens & Colombo
General
W Gopallawa Maw
0
250
metres

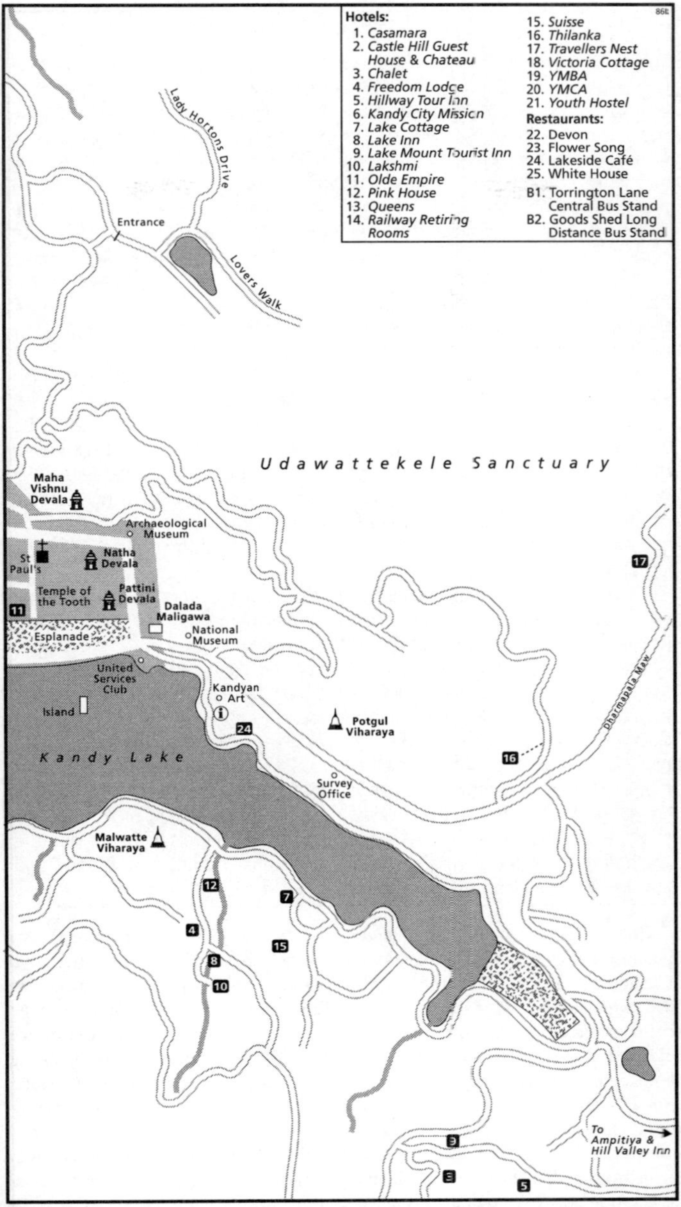
Hotels:
1. Casamara
2. Castle Hill Guest House & Chateau
3. Chalet
4. Freedom Lodge
5. Hillway Tour Inn
6. Kandy City Mission
7. Lake Cottage
8. Lake Inn
9. Lake Mount Tourist Inn
10. Lakshmi
11. Olde Empire
12. Pink House
13. Queens
14. Railway Retiring Rooms
15. Suisse
16. Thilanka
17. Travellers Nest
18. Victoria Cottage
19. YMBA
20. YMCA
21. Youth Hostel
Restaurants:
22. Devon
23. Flower Song
24. Lakeside Café
25. White House
B1. Torrington Lane Central Bus Stand
B2. Goods Shed Long Distance Bus Stand
Lady Hortons Drive
Entrance
Lovers Walk
Udawattekele Sanctuary
Maha Vishnu Devala
Archaeological Museum
St Paul's
Natha Devala
Temple of the Tooth
Pattini Devala
Dalada Maligawa
Esplanade
National Museum
United Services Club
Island
Kandyan Art
Potgul Viharaya
Dharmapala Maw
Kandy Lake
Survey Office
Malwatte Viharaya
To Ampitiya & Hill Valley Inn

KANDY'S ESALA PERAHERA

The entire organisation of the Perahera was designed to symbolise the flow of cosmic power through the god-chosen king to the people – and to enable it to be renewed for the following year. It was rich with potent symbolism. Seneviratne shows how the ritual pole used in the processions represents the cosmic axis. Cut specially each year from a male tree with milk-like sap, symbolising fertility, milk and semen, the chosen tree was encircled with a magic symbol to transform it into the axis of the world. An E facing branch (the auspicious direction) would be cut and divided into four sections, one for each of the four temples: each piece (*kapa*) would then be taken to its respective temple, linking the temple with the cosmic axis and thereby renewing its access to the source of all power. Further rituals at each of the temples, in which the kapa were taken round the temple three times, linked the temple directly with the three worlds. The planting of the kapa then inaugurated the Perahera.

In the 2nd stage – ***Kumbal Perahera,*** the symbols of the 4 gods were joined with the Tooth Relic and processed for the first time with elephants. Duncan suggests that at this stage there were five processions joined in one; that of the *Tooth Relic*, which was started by King Kirti Sri in 1747; of *Natha*, the next Buddha; of *Vishnu*, due to be Buddha after Natha; of *Katagarama*, the general; and of the goddess *Pattini*. This procession marched round the sacred Bo tree in the centre of the square for several nights in succession, drawing on the strength which flowed through the Bo tree as another representation of the central axis of the city and of the world.

The 3rd and last stage – ***Randoli Perahera***, saw the procession move out to encompass the whole city, at which point the king made his first entry. He would be seen first at the windows of the *Pattirippuwa*, and then went to the Temple of the Tooth, raised the relic and placed it on the elephant. Duncan points out that the 8-sided building symbolically controlled the eight directions, and that it was built specifically for this ritual purpose. The procession then moved off clockwise round the city. The king led the representatives of the 21 Kandyan provinces in a parade that was itself intended to secure fertility. The 21 days of the festival may themselves have been symbolic of the 21 provinces. Seneviratne has suggested that the Perahera was believed to be capable of producing light rains, symbolised by the flowers strewed in front of the elephant carrying the Tooth Relic. Elephants themselves were seen as able to bring rain, for grey and massive, like rain clouds themselves, they could attract the clouds of heaven.

Kirti Sri started re-building, more opulently than ever, but it was the last king of Kandy, Sri Vikrama Raja Sinha (1798-1815) who gave Kandy many of its present buildings. More interested in palaces and parks than temples, he set about demonstrating his kingly power with an exhibition of massive building works. Once again he had started almost from scratch, for in 1803 the city was taken by the British, but to avoid its desecration was once again burned to the ground. The British were thrown out, and between 1809-1812 there was massive re-building. The palace was fully renovated by 1810 and a new octagonal structure added to the palace, the **Patthiruppuwa**. 2 years later the royal complex was surrounded by a moat and a single massive stone gateway replaced the earlier entrances.

In the W Sri Vikrama Raja Sinha built new shops and houses, at the same time building more houses in the E for his Tamil relatives. But by far the greatest work was the construction of the lake. Previously the low lying marshy land in front of the palace had been drained for paddy fields. Duncan records that between 1810-1812 up to 3,000 men were forced to work on building the dam at the W end of the low ground, creating an artificial lake given the cosmically symbolic name of the Ocean of Milk. A pleasure house was built in the middle of the lake, connected by drawbridge to the palace. At last the city had taken virtually its present form.

Car parking Those visiting Kandy by car may find it difficult to park. You can park opposite the church; dozens of signs painted in white on black mark the legal quarter where the streets are quite wide and fairly clean. Alternatively, try the backstreets to the W of the sanctuary. The area is dominated by a large white Buddha on a prominent hill.

Places of interest

Today, Kandy has the reputation of being something of a tourist trap, as it is on the itineraries of most travel groups. Despite this, the clarity of the air and its position on hills around the lake (with its lovely pink blossom in the spring) make it a nice place just to wander around.

The chief focus of interest is the **Palace area**, with the Temple of the Tooth and associated buildings.

Entry The entrance is in Palace Square opposite the Natha Devala. **Note** Long skirt or trousers essential; otherwise *lungis* (sarongs) must be worn over shorts. No entry charge; the only charge is for photography, Rs 250 for videos, Rs 50 for cameras. According to one traveller "the charge appears to be arbitrary, sometimes depending on the number of foreign visitors, not the number of cameras! You may not find a great deal to photograph inside anyway". The Cultural Triangle Permit to photograph does not cover the temple here. You are virtually forced to take a guide (Rs 100 for about 15 mins).

Temple of the Tooth (Dalada Maligawa) is a genuine place of worship. The original dated from the 16th century, though most of the present building and the *Pathiruppuwa*, or Octagon, were built in the early 19th century. The gilded roof over the relic chamber is a recent addition. The oldest part is the inner shrine, built by Kirti Sri after 1765. The drawbridge, moat and gateway were the work of Sri Wickrama Raja Sinha. There is a moonstone step at the entrance to the archway, and a stone depicting Lakshmi against the wall facing the entrance. The main door to the temple is in the wall of the upper veranda, covered in restored frescoes depicting Buddhist conceptions of hell. The doorway is a typical *makara torana* showing mythical beasts. A second Kandyan style door leads into the courtyard, across which is the building housing the Tooth Relic. The door has ivory, inlay work, with copper and gold handles. The **Udmale** – upper storey – houses the Relic.

Caged behind gilded iron bars is the large outer casket (*karandua*), made of silver. Inside it are seven smaller caskets, each made of gold studded with jewels. Today the temple is controlled by a layman (the *Diyawadne*) elected by the high priests of the monasteries in Kandy and Asgiriya. The administrator holds the key to the iron cage, but there are three different keys to the caskets themselves, one held by the administrator and one each by the high priests of Malwatte and Asgiriya, so that the caskets can only be opened when all four are present.

The sanctuary is opened at dawn. Ceremonies start at 0530, 0930 and 1830. These are moments when the temple comes to life with pilgrims making offerings of flowers amidst clouds of incense and the beating of drums. The casket is displayed for only

Buddhist temple, Lake of Kandy
Illustrated by Rev W Urick, 1885

a part of the day. You are very unlikely to be allowed to see the relic itself, which for many years has only been displayed to the most important of visitors. You can join pilgrims to see the casket but may well have to overcome pushing and jostling by those desperate to see the holy object. There is a separate enclosure in front of the relic which wealthy Sri Lankans pay to go into.

The library (in its octagonal room) contains 800-year-old palm leaf manuscripts. It has a balcony for important people. The hall behind the tooth relic sanctuary is also interesting for its collection of old documents and pictures describing the history of the tooth.

The **Tusker Raja museum** is next door; entry free. The much venerated elephant Raja, who carried the Tooth Relic casket in the *Esala Perahera*, was 85 when he died in 1985. Raja, who was gift from the Prime Minister of India, is stuffed and preserved after 50 years of service. There is much memorabilia and the caretaker will attempt to explain it all in expectation of a tip.

The **Audience Hall** was rebuilt in the Kandyan style with a wooden pillared hall (1784). The historic document ending the Kandyan Kingdom was signed here, and the territory was handed over to the British. There is excellent carving on the pillars.

Across from the complex is a working monastery and beyond its walls is **St Paul's** church which was constructed in 1843 although the earliest minister, George Bisset, was here in 1816. Regimental colours were removed to the National Army Museum, England in 1916. There are various memorials to the British Army including one to those lost at the battle of Alma in the Crimea (1854).

On the lakeside is the 18th century **Malwatte Vihara** (Flower Garden) decorated with ornate wood and metal work where important ordinations take place. This and the **Asigiriya** are particularly important monasteries because of the senior position of their incumbents. There is a large recumbent Buddha statue at the latter, and the mound of the old Royal Burial Ground nearby.

The lake walk An attractive 4 km walk round the lake, named by its creator 'King Vikrama' the 'ocean of milk' after its cosmic parallel. There are some beautiful views, especially of the island pavilion in the lake. The Royal Palace Park (*Wace Park*), overlooks the lake and also has superb views.

Udawattekele Sanctuary, the 'forbidden forest of the kings of Kandy'. Kandy Vidiya, past the Post Office takes you to the entrance gate to the Sanctuary. Lady Horton's Drive takes you into the tropical rain forest and further E offers good views of the Mahaweli River.

Museums

Archaeological Museum, Palace Sq. Open 0900-1700, closed Tues. Superb sculptures, wood and stone housed in what remains of the old Palace. Some architectural pieces, notably columns and capitals from the Kandyan Kingdom. **Kandy National Museum** in the Queen's Palace, behind Temple of the Tooth. Open 0900-1700, closed Fri. A vivid history of the development and culture of the Kandyan Kingdom. Jewels, armaments, ritual objects, sculptures, clothes, games, medical instruments – an enormous range of everyday and exceptional objects.

Excursions around Kandy

Elephant Bath is close to the Mahaweli Ganga near *Mahaweli Reach Hotel* at **Katugastota**. Elephants are brought to the river for their bath twice a day and their mahouts brush, sponge and splash them with water (essential for the animals' health). **NB** Since most visitors choose to travel to the Pinnawela elephant orphanage (see page 150), the bathing at Katugastota has been virtually abandoned.

Elephants are sometimes bathed at the riverside on Rajasinghe Mawatha opposite Military Cemetery, 4 km. Open 0900-1800. Entry free.

Western Shrines

On the Kadugannawa-Peradeniya Rd, 16 km away, is a group of 14th century temples.

The **Gadaladeniya Temple** is in a beautiful setting, built on a rock, about 1 km from the main road. The stone temple, influenced by Indian temple architecture, has lacquered doors, carvings and frescoes and a moonstone at the entrance of the shrine. The inscriptions on rock by Dharmakirti, date it to 1344. The principal image of the Buddha (18th century, which replaced the original destroyed by the Portuguese) is framed by elaborate *makara* decoration. Unusually, there is also a shrine to Vishnu here. Outside, there is a covered stupa and a Bodhi tree.

The **Lankatilaka Viharaya**, the second monument of the group, is 3 km along the road, on top of the rock Panhagala. The white painted brick structure with a tiled roof was originally four storeys high but was renovated in 1845 after the two top storeys had fallen. You climb up a rock cut stairway to the moonstone at the entrance and the finely carved wooden doorways. The inner image house containing fine gold plated images of the Buddha is completely surrounded by a devale with carved figures of other gods (Saman, Skanda, Ganapathy, Vibhisena among others). The walls and ceiling have well preserved frescoes. This is one of oldest and best examples of the Kandyan temple style.

The **Embekke Devalaya** (dedicated to God *Kataragama* or *Skanda*) along a path 1.5 km away. The temple with its sanctuary, Dancing Hall and the Drummers' Hall, is famous for its carved wooden pillars (which may have once adorned the Audience Hall in Kandy) with vibrant figures of soldiers, wrestlers, dancers, musicians, mythical animals and birds. You can see similar carved pillars at the remains of the old

Pilgrim's Rest nearby. The village has craftsmen working in silver, brass and copper.

Getting there: there are buses from Kandy to the temples and to the Botanical Gardens. The turn off from the main Colombo-Kandy road is at the 65th mile towards Davulagala from which the temples can be reached.

Eastern Temples

Medawela Temple, 10 km NE of Kandy, though built in the 18th century is on an ancient site. The interesting features include the shrine room built in wood and wattle and daub, similar to the old Kandyan grain stores, and the wall paintings. Medawela, at the junction of B36 and B37, is a metalworkers village. The Kandyan Dance academy near **Amungama** is 3 km S (see Entertainment below). *Getting there*: bus No 603 from Market Bus Stop.

Galmaduwa Temple

The unusual incomplete 14th century Galmaduwa Temple on the Kundasala road, was an attempt to combine the features of Sinhalese, Indian, Islamic and Christian architectural styles. Nearby, **Kalapuraya Nattarampota** Craft Village in the beautiful Dumbara Valley (7 km E of Kandy along A26), is worth a visit. The **Degaldoruwa Temple**, 3 km away has interesting wall paintings. *Getting there*: bus No 655 from the Market Bus Stop drops you at the bridge across the river from the temple.

Dumbara Hills (Knuckles Range) The hills acquired the English name because of the distinctive clenched-hand profile seen from a distance. The altitude (with peaks above 1,500m) and the variation in the climate (annual rainfall range is 2,500-5,000 mm) allows a variety of forest types from Lowland Dry *patana* to Montane Wet Evergreen, with their associated trees, shrubs, plants and epiphytes to flourish.

These forests, in turn, harbour a number of wildlife species, eg leopard, sambhur, barking deer, mouse deer, wild boar, giant squirrel, Purple-faced langur, toque macaque and loris, as well as the otherwise rarely seen otter. Over 120 bird species recorded here include many endemic ones including the Yellow-fronted barbet, Dusky-blue flycatcher, Ceylon lorikeet, Ceylon grackle, Yellow-eared bulbul and Layard's parakeet. In addition, endemic amphibians and reptiles include the *Nannophrys* frog and Pigmy tree-lizard, which are only found here.

The importance of the range as a watershed for the Mahaweli River and the Victoria reservoir has led the Govt to designate the area over 1,500m as a Conservation area. Soil and water conservation have become critical issues because of the way the area has been exploited so far. Cardamom cultivation, the removal of timber and fuelwood, the use of cane in basket making and the production of treacle and jaggery from *kitul* (*Caryota urens*) have all been sources of concern.

Local festivals

End Jul/Aug: *Esala Perahera* Sri Lanka's greatest festival is of special significance. It is held in the lunar month in which the Buddha was conceived and in which he left his father's home. It has also long been associated with rituals to ensure renewed fertility for the year ahead. The last Kandy kings turned the Perahera into a mechanism for reinforcing their own power, trying to identify themselves with the gods who needed to be appeased. By focusing on the Tooth Relic, the Tamil kings hoped to establish their own authority and their divine legitimacy within the Buddhist community. The Sri Lankan historian Seneviratne has suggested that fear both of the king and of divine retribution encouraged nobles and peasants alike to come to the Perahera, and witnessing the scale of the spectacle reinforced their loyalty.

Today the festival is a magnificent 15-day spectacle of elephants, musicians, dancers and tens of thousands of pilgrims in procession, Buddhists are drawn to the temple by the power of the Tooth Relic rather than by that of the King's authority. The power of the Relic certainly long preceded that of the Kandyan Dynasty. **Fa Hien** described the annual festival in Anuradhapura in 399 AD, which even then was a lavish procession in which roads were vividly decorated, elephants covered in jewels and flowers, and models of figures such as *Bodhisattvas* were paraded. When the tooth was moved to Kandy, the Perahera moved with it. However, today the Tooth Relic itself is no longer taken out.

The first 5 days of the festival are celebrated only within the grounds of the four Hindu *devalas* (temples). On the sixth night the torchlight processions set off from the temples for the Temple of the Tooth. Every night the procession grows, moving from the *Dalada Maligawa* along **Dalada Vidiya** and **DS Senanayake Mawatha** (Trincomalee St) to the *Adahanamaluwa*, where the relic casket is left in the keeping of the temple trustees. The separate temple processions go back to their temples, coming out in the early morning for the water cutting ceremony. Originally, the temple guardians went to the lake with golden water pots to empty water collected the previous year. They would then be refilled and taken back to the temple for the following year, symbolising the fertility protected by the gods. On the last day of the festival a daylight procession accompanies the return of the Relic to the Temple of the Tooth.

You do not necessarily need to buy tickets to watch the processions since you can good views by standing along the street.

Note Change in street names: **Gregory Rd** to *Rajapihilla Maw*; **Lady Blacke's Drive** to *Devani Rajasinghe Maw*; **Lady Horton's Drive** to *Vihara Mahadevi Maw*; **Lady McCallum Drive** to *Srimath Kuda Ratwatte Maw*; **Trincomalee St** to *DS Senanaycke Vidiya* etc.

Local information

● Accommodation

Owing to its elevation, a/c is not normally necessary. **NB** Prices during *Perahera* are highly inflated and accommodation is difficult to find; out-of-town hotels can be expensive to reach by taxi (or 3-wheeler) and are sometimes off the main road and can involve a climb up-hill. **Warning** Hotel touts are extremely persistent (sometimes boarding trains before they arrive at Kandy) and should be avoided at all costs. Insist on choosing your own hotel as otherwise prices for you will be raised by small hotels and guest houses to pay off the tout. You can telephone a hotel and reserve a room and may then be sent transport or have the taxi fare paid. Several visitors have been disappointed by the size and cleanliness of swimming pools in some of the Kandy hotels. If this will influence your choice of hotel it is best to check the pool before you check in.

A *Topaz*, Anniewatte, T 24150, F 32073, 75 rm, half a/c (US$67), pool, tennis, well kept, quiet, good mountain views; **A** *Tourmaline*, Anniewatte, 1.6 km from town, T 32326, F 32073, 25 a/c rm with balconies (US$70), mountain views, pool; **A-B** *Queens*, Dalada Vidiya, T/F 32079, 100 rm (US$50), 5 a/c, quieter rm on garden side best, others noisy, good restaurant, bar, beer garden, pool, nr lake and palace, one of the oldest in the country (c1838 when the Pavilion Hotel was built on Trincomalee St; in 1815, a Kandyan Chieftain's house was converted into an Officers' mess by the British, later amalgamated into the hotel), its position opp the Temple of the Tooth allows most guests excellent vantage point for seeing the procession from their balcony; **A-B** *Suisse*, 30 Sangaraja Maw, T 33025, F 32083, 100 rm, 15 a/c (US$50), rooms vary, best with balcony on lakeside, good restaurant (excellent buffet lunch), friendly and helpful staff, good pool in attractive garden, tennis, colonial style hotel (c1920s) in quiet lakeside location, 15 mins walk from Temple, reserve in advance, rec. The Suisse was Lord Mountbatten's war time HQ.

B *Casamara*, 12 Kotugodalle Vidiya, T 34327, F 32050, 35 clean a/c rm, restaurant, bar, fairly modern town-centre hotel but unimaginative;

B *The Chalet*, 32 Rajapihilla Maw, T/F 34571, 36 rm, 5 a/c (US$35-60) upper flrs more expensive, restaurant (variable, poor breakfast), bar, tennis, small pool, boating. 1.5 km centre, located among wooded hills, good views being quite high above the lake, building with character with attractively decorated lounge, pleasant garden but pool not well maintained, somewhat overpriced; **B** *Hill Top*, 200 Bahirawakanda, Peradeniya Rd, 2 km from centre, T 34317 or Colombo T/F 433755, 80 rm, 36 a/c, modern, attractive and comfortable hotel with pool; **B** *Thilanka*, 3 Sangamitta Maw, beyond the Temple of the Tooth, T 32429, F 25497, 45 well-furnished rm, 1st flr better(US$40), good restaurant and pool, very clean, beautiful views from terrace, rec.

C *Castle Hill Guest House*, 22 Rajapihilla Maw, T 24376, 4 large beautifully decorated rm, 2 on garden-side with views (Rs 1,000), meals in dining room, good view over town, rec; **C-D** *Olde Empire Hotel*, 21 Temple St, T 24284, 10 clean rm with bath, large 1st flr verandah for Nos 1, 2 and 3, shared bath, good restaurant (try curry), well placed for temple and lake, popular with younger travellers seeking atmosphere.

D *Hill Valley Inn*, Ampitya, 3 km from town centre (buses available), comfortable large rooms with bath in Sri Lankan home, good food, peaceful, rec; **D** *Lake View Rest*, 71 Rajapihilla Maw, T 32034, 30 clean rm (Rs 600) with good views.

Guest Houses: many good-value rooms in private homes are available; the Tourist Office has a list of small guest houses. There are several by the lake with meals available. Most will offer transport from station on request. Some are within easy reach of the *Hotel Suisse* swimming pool which non-residents pay to use. **C** *Chateau*, 20 Rajapihilla Maw, T 32272, 3 rm with bath (US$15), good views, peaceful, rec; **D** *Gem Inn*, 39 Anagarika Dharmapala Maw, E of town, T 24239, pleasantly located on a ridge with good views, good rooms with bath; **D** *Lake Inn*, 43 Saranankara Rd (behind *Suisse*), T 22208, 10 rm (Rs 500), meals; **D** *Lake Mount Tourist Inn*, 195A Rajapihilla Maw, below *The Chalet*, T 33204, 8 spotless rm with modern showers in new building (Rs 600+), meals, part Japanese management, free pick-up from anywhere in Kandy, peaceful, highly rec; **D** *Lakshmi*, 57 Saranankara Rd, uphill nr the *Suisse*, T 22154, has clean rooms with bath; **D** *Travellers Nest*, 117/4 Anagarika Dharmapala Maw, T 22633, 26 rm, popular with backpackers; **D** *Victoria Cottage*, 6 Victoria Drive, next to YMCA on the lake room with bath.

Budget hotels: inexpensive **D-E** category incl **D-E** *Hillway Tour Inn*, 90A/1 Rajapihilla Maw (15 mins walk from centre), T 25430, 4 rm with toilets (Rs 400), meals, good value; **D-E** *Kandy City Mission*, 125 DS Senanayake Vidiya, 150m from Dalada Maligawa, 12 good rm, the limited menu restaurant rec, good value for snacks, clean, comfortable, home made bread and cheese; **E** *Freedom Lodge*, 30 Saranankara Rd (15 mins walk to centre), T 23506, a small guest house with spotless rooms with bath and hot water (Rs 300 incl breakfast), excellent curry and rice with family, very friendly 'excellent stop for tired travellers', highly rec; **E** *Lake Cottage*, 28 Sangaraja Maw, T 23234, adjoins *Hotel Suisse*, rooms with bath (Rs 350), meals; **E-F** *Pink House*, 15 Saranankara Maw, simple rooms, meals, pleasant garden nr lake.

Youth Hostels: offer **F** dormitories with shared facilities which may not be too clean; some have double rooms. *YMCA*, 90 Kotugodalle Vidiya, T 23529, 32 beds. The cheaper *YMCA* is at 4 Sangaraja Maw, on the lakeside, 10 basic rm. *YMCA Sports Hall* will allow visitors to sleep there for Rs 30 during the *Perahera*, together with hundreds of mosquitoes. *YMBA* (Young Men's Buddhist Assoc), 5 Rajapihilla Maw, nr Wace Park, overlooks lake. *Railway Retiring Rooms* at Kandy station. *Youth Hostel*, Trinity College, DS Senanayake Vidiya. See also **Travellers Halt** below

Out of town:

At Katugastota: by river Mahaweli, 5 km N, **AL** *Mahaweli Reach*, 35 PBS Weerakoon Maw, by Katugastota Bridge, T 32062, F 32068, 115 rm mostly a/c (US$100), striking, modern hotel in commanding position overlooking river, family run, excellent pool, relaxed atmosphere; **E** *Travellers Halt*, 53/4 Siyambalagastenna, 25 beds, 4 km from centre, bus from opp Police Station (Railway Crossing Bus Stop) to Katugastota, where you cross the bridge to reach the youth hostel.

At Ukuwala: 17 km N, on Wattegama, Matale Rd, **D** *Grassmere Farm*, Alupothuwala, Ukuwala (between 5th and 6th km posts), T 072 41110, in beautiful grounds, 3 large rm with bath (US$14), meals, friendly family, pick-up from Kandy station. Bus 636 stops at Farm.

On Mahaweli River: 5 km W, **A** *Citadel*, 124 Srimanth Kuda, Ratwatte Maw, T 34366, F Colombo 447087, 121 rm, mostly a/c (US$70+) on 3 flower-filled terraces, good restaurant, modern but in local architectural style, tour groups make it noisy (ineffective soundproofing).

At Elkaduwa (27 km, 45 mins drive from Kandy): higher in the hills, is the modern Jetwing hotel, **B** *Hunas Falls*, T 08 76402, F Colombo 699226, 30 a/c rm (US$70), restaurant, bar, exchange, pool, boating, fishing, tennis, beautifully located in a tea garden by a waterfall with excellent walks, visits to tea estate, factory and spice gardens.

At Rajawella: 14 km E, on Teldeniya Rd via Kundasale, **D** *Digana Village Resort*, T 08 74255, 12 rm in 3 villas (Rs 600), restaurant, pool.

● Places to eat

The top hotels in the town are good but can be expensive. ***Avanhala Royal Garden***, 72 Sangaraja Maw, is nr the Tourist Office; ***Devon***, 4E Sangaraja Maw, (1st flr), serves excellent food at a reasonable price, rec; ***Flower Song***, 137 Kotugodalle Vidiya (1st Flr, a/c) serves excellent Chinese, good portions (Rs 135/dish); ***Nawa Surasa***, 30 George de Silva Maw, SW of town, does good continental and Chinese; ***White House*** open during the day, slow service, but very good coffee and good food. For breakfast and snacks try the good value ***Lakeside Café*** nr *Olde Empire Hotel*; ***Lyon's***, 27 Peradeniya Rd, nr the main roundabout serves cheap snacks and some Chinese dishes. ***Bake House***, 36 Dalada Vidiya, has had poor reports.

● Bars

There are English style pubs at *Queens* and *The Olde Empire*.

● Banks & money changers

Bank of Ceylon on Dalada Vidiya.

● Entertainment

Daily performances of highland Kandyan dancing in different parts of the town (enquire at Tourist Office). Usually worth going to even if you have had dancing laid on in your hotel. **Kandyan Arts Assoc**, 72 Sangaraja Maw, around 1930. **Kandy Lake Club Dance Ensemble** performs Dances of Sri Lanka, at 7 Sangamitta Maw (off Malabar St), T 23505, daily at 1930, Rs 150, rec. **YMBA Hall**, Kandyan and Low country dancing, at about 1900, 1 hr, good value. Most performances offer a helpful programme sheet with explanations. Keppetipola Hall and the Lake Club performances are rec. At Amungama, 10 km from Kandy, is the **Kandyan Dance Academy** where the art and skill is handed down from father to son. The show usually lasts about 90 mins, ending with the fire dance.

● Hospitals & medical services

Chemist: *New Kandy Dispensary*, Brownrigg St.

● Libraries

Alliance Française, 412 Peradeniya Rd. **British Council** is opp the Clock Tower, the **USIS** on Kotugodalle Vidiya and **United Services Library** by the Lake, opp the Temple of the Tooth.

● Post & telecommunications

Post Offices: are opp the Railway Station and on Senanayake Vidiya (crossing with Kandy Vidiya).

Telecommunications: outside hotels are cheaper. Some, incl ***Matsui Communications***, 3A Temple St, T 32647, F 32343, will receive fax messages.

● Shopping

Batik: good batiks from ***Fresco***, 901 Peradeniya Rd. Also in curio shops on S Bandaranaike Maw, towards Botanical Gardens, just past railway station.

Bookshops: ***KVJ de Silva***, 86 DS Senanayake Vidiya has a good selection of local history. ***Lake House Bookshop*** and ***Vijitha Yapa Bookshop***, 9 Kotugodalle Vidiya, are rec; ***The Wheel*** by the Lake sells Buddhist literature.

Handicrafts, jewellery etc: ***Laksala***, Dalada Vidiya and ***Kandyan Arts Association*** (Tourist Office), 72 Sangaraja Maw, are govt sales outlets where you can watch weavers and craftsmen working on wood, silver, copper and brass, and buy lacquerware and batik. There are several shops on Dalada Vidiya nr the Temple of the Tooth. ***Kandyan Handicrafts Centre***, 10/4 Kotugodalle Vidiya has good metalwork. Also several antique shops, many along the lake and on Peradeniya Rd. The **Crafts village** set up with govt help is at ***Kalapuraya Nattarampota***, 7 km away (see Excursions above) where craft skills have been handed down from father to son.

Markets: a visit to the ***Municipal Market***, W of the lake is worthwhile even if you are not planning to bargain for superb Sri Lankan fruit and spices.

Photography: *Midland Studio*, 46 King St.

Textiles: shops along Colombo St sell material.

● Sports

Swimming: *Hotel Suisse* has a large pool but during the peak season (Dec-Feb) it can be fairly crowded. The cleanest pool is at *Queens* (no chlorine) which is usually very quiet. The *Tourmaline/Topaz* shared uncrowded pool is worth visiting for an afternoon for the spectacular hill-top views. Non-residents pay about Rs 50 (incl use of towel) at these hotels.

● Tourist Offices

Kandyan Arts Association Bldg, 72 Sangaraja Maw between the Temple of the Tooth and Queens Hotel. Not very useful, literature give out generally poor, only 2 books for sale. **Ceylon Tourist Board**, Headman's Lodge Raja Vidiya, 0830-1645, Mon-Fri, 0830-1230, Sat, T 22661.

● Useful addresses

Tourist Police: Pushpadana Rd, T 22222.

● Transport

Local Bus: local buses use the Central/Torrington Bus Stand nr the market. **Car hire**: if time is very limited for sightseeing, it is possible to hire a car for the day to visit Dambulla, Sigiriya and Polonnaruwa in 1 day. While this is a very full day it can be very rewarding.

Train Note The train journey between Kandy and Colombo is far more comfortable, quieter and more scenic than going by road. From Colombo the journey is best if you sit on the left, facing the rear in a 1st class 'observation carriage'. The last hour of the journey is memorable, climbing slowly into the mountains (thankfully away from road-fumes) through terraced paddy fields, lush home gardens and managed forests. Watch out for monitor lizards and flying squirrels; best at dusk (take the 1530 train from Colombo, Rs 90). **Badulla**: *Podi Menike*, 5, daily, 0906, 7¾ hrs; *Mail*, 45, daily, 2355, 7¾ hrs. **Colombo**: *Intercity Express*, 30, daily, 0630, 2½ hrs; *24 Exp*, daily, 1000, 3 hrs; *Intercity Exp* 10, daily, 1500, 2½ hrs. **Nanu Oya** (for Nuwara Eliya): *Podi Menike*, 5, daily, 0906, 4¼ hrs. Taxis and 3-wheelers are available for transport to hotel (see Warning under Accommodation).

Road Bus: long distance buses leave from the Goods Shed Bus Stand nr the station. CTB buses leave from the Central Bus Stand, in front of the market. Frequent buses to Colombo regular Rs 20, a/c Rs 60, (mini bus from behind the Temple); a/c buses (Intercity Expresses) take 2½ hrs, Rs 75, but are often congested, nerve wracking and far less pleasant than the train. Your life is in their hands – but so are the lives of many others on the road. Also direct bus services to Nuwara Eliya, Polonnaruwa and Anuradhapura.

KANDY TO NUWARA ELIYA AND HORTON PLAINS

There are two main routes from Kandy to Nuwara Eliya. Both start by passing through Peradeniya to the former capital, Gampola. The shorter 80 km route then takes the A5, crossing the Mahaweli Ganga and climbing SE through some of the highest tea gardens in the island. The longer alternative, which runs close to the railway line for much of the way, is a full day's journey, and goes from Gampola to Nawalapitya and Ginigathena, before climbing through Hatton and Talawakele.

From the humid heat of Kandy itself the freshness of the highlands comes as a welcome relief, whether travelling by road or taking the slow winding railway route via Ginigathena and Talawakele. The Horton Plains, Sri Lanka's highest plateau, offers the chance to trek through an area rich in bird and animal life.

ROUTES The shorter route takes the **A5** to Nuwara Eliya. Initially it continues along the Mahaweli valley. Shortly after **Gampola** (a pleasant town with most services), the road crosses the river and starts the long climb of almost 1,000m up to Nuwara Eliya passing through Pussellawa.

Pussellawa is a busy shopping centre and has a *Rest House* where you can stop for a meal or a drink. **Accommodation D** *Rest House* (CHC), in an attractive location, 4 rm with bath in a colonial bungalow (US$9), rather dated but with pleasant though steep terrace garden at back with good views across the valley, seating under large permanant sun umbrellas permanantly covered with the exotic 'ladies' slipper' vine.

ROUTES Tea gardens begin just below Pussellawa. The craggy hill, Moneragala appears to the S; legends tell that this is where King Dutthagamenu hid in a rock while escaping from his father, who had imprisoned him. The road passes the Helbodda Oya (5 km) as the **A5** continues to **Ramboda** (*Alt* 1,000m) with a fine 100m waterfall with a twin stream, just off the road. After 54 km from Kandy the road climbs through a series of hairpins to the Weddamulla Estate with great views to the W over Kothmale Reservoir. The whole area is covered with pine trees and ferns. These slowly give way to a large tea estate.

The **Labookellie Tea Estate** (*Alt* 1,570m) follows the twisty road for miles along the hillside. You will be able to see squads of women plucking the tea on fairly steep slopes. Picking goes on in all weathers – the women using plastic sacks as raincoats. The women labourers are all Tamils, descendants of the labourers who migrated from Tamil Nadu before independence.

The tea factory, an enormous corrugated iron building, welcomes visitors to drop in to the teashop and sample a free cup of tea, and perhaps to buy a

April In Nuwara

Around the April full moon, the town is invaded by the Colombo set. A banner across the road proudly announces *"Nuwara at 6,128 ft: Welcome to the salubrious climate of Nuwara Eliya: cultured drivers are welcomed with affection!"*.

For about a week, prices become inflated (tripled) and it is virtually impossible to find accommodation. Stallholders, mostly selling food and drink, pay vast amounts of money to rent a pitch alongside the main road by Victoria Park. Most hotels run all night discos (the best is said to be at the *Grand Hotel*) and the crowds roam the streets for much of the night. During the day, horse races, hill climbs and other sporting events are held.

packet or two (there is no pressure). Pieces of coffee (!) cake are also for sale, but beware of the flies.

Groups of visitors are taken on free guided tours of the factory, between 0900 and 1700 (you may need to wait in a queue on a busy day). The tour is quite informative. – all stages of the process from picking, drying, oxidation and grading are shown if you go in the morning. **Accommodation** Estate *bungalows* are available for hire at Rs 1,500 incl cook.

ROUTES From the Labookellie Estate it is a short climb through more tea gardens to the narrow pass above Nuwara Eliya, and the road then drops down into the sheltered hollow in the hills now occupied by the town.

Nuwara Eliya

Nuwara Eliya (pronounced Noo-ray-lee-ya; *Alt* 1,990m; *STD Code* 052) which sits in a little valley, is the highest town in Sri Lanka and a major hill resort. In 1846, when Samuel Baker first visited the semi-enclosed valley, surrounded by hills on the W and overlooked by Pidurutalagala, the island's highest peak (2,524m), he singled it out as an ideal spot for a hill country retreat. Today, with its television aerials, the highest on the island, and modern hotels, golf course and country walks, his rural idyll is being brought increasingly into the modern world.

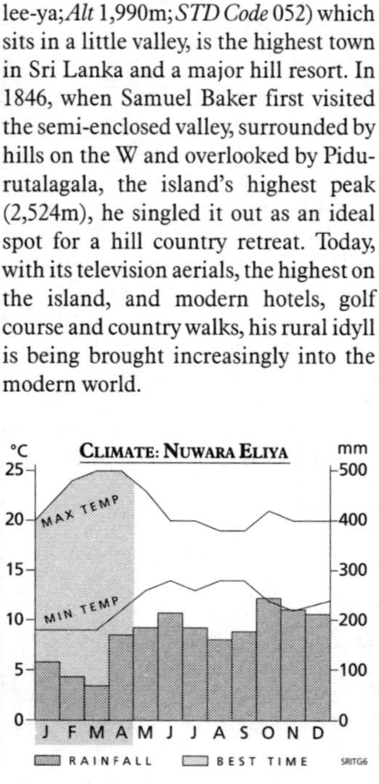

'The City of Light' was a favourite hill station of the British. Some feel its charm has faded, but it retains some distinctive features. The main street is the usual concrete jungle of small shops with the pink post office being an obvious exception. One of the distinctive features of Baker's plans was the introduction of European vegetables and fruit. The evidence of such innovations is readily evident. Flowers are extensively cultivated for export to Colombo and abroad. The road out of Nuwara Eliya towards Hakgala passes through intensively cultivated fields of vegetables, again produced for the urban market, and a short walk up any of the surrounding hillsides shows how far intensive cultivation methods have transformed Nuwara Eliya into one of Sri Lanka's most productive agricultural areas.

The key to Nuwara Eliya's prosperity lay in the railway connection from Colombo to the hills. The line was extended from Talawakele to Nanu Oya in 1885, and in those days, with a coach transfer up to Nuwara Eliya itself, the journey could be completed in under 9 hrs. A very steep narrow gauge line right into Nuwara Eliya was opened in 1910, but subsequently closed to passenger traffic in 1940 as buses began to provide effective competition.

Without the pretensions or political significance of the Raj hillstations in India, Nuwara Eliya nonetheless was an active centre of an English-style social life, with county style sports including a hunt, polo, cricket and tennis.

Nuwara Eliya offers a cool escape from the plains (nights can be very cold) and it has retained all the paraphernalia of a British hill station, with its colonial houses, parks, an 18-hole golf course which runs through much of the centre of town, and trout streams; there are brown trout in the lake for anglers. The real clue to its past perhaps lies in its gardens: dahlias, snap-dragons, petunias and roses, all amongst immaculately kept lawns.

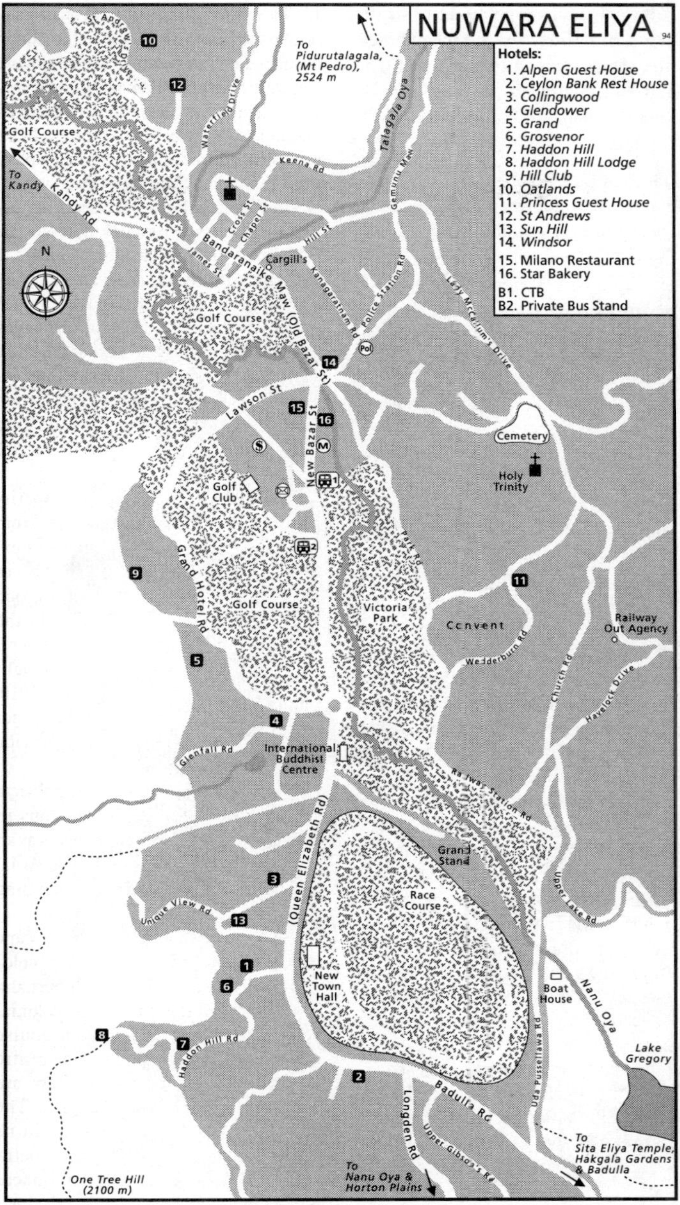
NUWARA ELIYA
Hotels:
1. Alpen Guest House
2. Ceylon Bank Rest House
3. Collingwood
4. Glendower
5. Grand
6. Grosvenor
7. Haddon Hill
8. Haddon Hill Lodge
9. Hill Club
10. Oatlands
11. Princess Guest House
12. St Andrews
13. Sun Hill
14. Windsor
15. Milano Restaurant
16. Star Bakery
B1. CTB
B2. Private Bus Stand
To Pidurutalagala, (Mt Pedro), 2524 m
Golf Course
To Kandy
Kandy Rd
Waterfield Drive
Talagala Oya
Keena Rd
Cross St
Chapel St
Gemunu Maw
Hill St
Bandaranaike Maw (Old Bazar St)
James St
Cargill's
Kanagaratnam Rd
Police Station Rd
Lady McCallum's Drive
Golf Course
Lawson St
New Bazar St
Cemetery
Holy Trinity
Golf Club
Park Rd
Grand Hotel Rd
Golf Course
Victoria Park
Convent
Railway Out Agency
Wedderburn Rd
Church Rd
Havelock Drive
Glenfall Rd
International Buddhist Centre
Railway Station Rd
Queen Elizabeth Rd
Grand Stand
Race Course
Upper Lake Rd
Unique View Rd
New Town Hall
Boat House
Nanu Oya
Haddon Hill Rd
Lake Gregory
Uda Pussellawa Rd
Longden Rd
Badulla Rd
Upper Gibson's Rd
To Sita Eliya Temple, Hakgala Gardens & Badulla
One Tree Hill (2100 m)
To Nanu Oya & Horton Plains

It is particularly popular during the New Year holidays in Apr when hotels raise their prices and are still full. The Golf is thought to be exceptionally good but there are added attractions (see box).

Places of interest
Some of the buildings are of Georgian and Queen Anne periods, and there are attractive walks round the small town, which has lawns, parks, an Anglican church and the *Hill Club*. To the S of town is the race course with the Council Building in the middle of the oval (politicians on the inside track?). The lake (about 1 km from the town centre) has boats which can be hired from Chalet du Lac.

The **Hakgala Botanical Garden** and Strict Natural Reserve (10 km) was once

A Morning Climb To Pidurutalagala

In 1911 Hermann Hesse wrote an evocative description of his climb to the top of Pidurutalagala at the end of a journey round India and Ceylon. He wrote "To bid India a proper and dignified farewell in peace and quiet, on one of the last days before I left I climbed alone in the coolness of a rainy morning to the highest summit in Ceylon, Pidurutalagala.

The cool green mountain valley of Nuwara Eliya was silvery in the light morning rain, typically Anglo-Indian with its corrugated roofs and its extravagantly extensive tennis courts and golf links. The Singhalese were delousing themselves in front of their huts or sitting shivering, wrapped in woollen shawls, the landscape, resembling the Black Forest, lay lifeless and shrouded.

The path began to climb upward through a little ravine, the straggling roofs disappeared, a swift brook roared below me. Narrow and steep, the way led steadily upward for a good hour. The rain gradually stopped, the cool wind subsided, and now and again the sun came out for minutes at a time.

I had climbed the shoulder of the mountain, the path now led across flat country, springy moor, and several pretty mountain rills. Here the rhododendrons grow more luxuriantly than at home, three time a man's height, and there is a furry silvery plant with white blossoms, very reminiscent of the edelweiss; I found many of our familiar forest flowers but all were strangely enlarged and heightened and alpine in character.

I was approaching the last ascent of the mountain, the path suddenly began to climb again, soon I found myself surrounded once more by forest, a strange, dead, enchanted forest where trunks and branches, intertwined like serpents, stared blindly at me through long thick, whitish beards of moss; a damp, bitter smell of foliage and fog hung between.

Then the forest came to an end; I stepped, warm and somewhat breathless, out onto a gray heath, like some landscape in Ossian, and saw the bare summit capped by a small pyramid close before me. A high, cold wind was blowing against me, I pulled my coat tight and slowly climbed the last hundred paces.

What I saw there was the grandest and purest impression I took away from all Ceylon. The wind had just swept clean the whole long valley of Nuwara Eliya, I saw, deep and immense, the entire high mountain system of Ceylon piled up in mighty walls, and in its midst the beautiful, ancient and holy pyramid of Adam's Peak. Beside it at an infinite depth and distance lay the flat blue sea, in between a thousand mountains, broad valleys, narrow ravines, rivers and waterfalls, in countless folds, the whole mountainous island on which ancient legend places paradise."

a Cinchona Plantation. The Botanical Garden now is famous for its roses. The name *Hakgala* or 'Jaw Rock' comes from the story in the epic *Ramayana* where the Monkey god, takes back a part of the mountainside in his jaw, when asked by Rama to seek out a special herb! There are monkeys here which are quite used to visitors. The different sections covering the hillside include a plant house, Japanese garden, wild orchid collection, old tea trails, arboretum, fruit garden, rock garden and oaks. **Place to eat** *Humbugs Restaurant* and bar, 100m beyond the entrance is beautifully located opposite the gardens, with extensive views across the Uva basin, particularly attractive in the early morning mist. It serves good snacks (strawberries and cream in season).

You will pass the **Sita Eliya Temple** to Rama's wife a short distance before you reach the gardens which is thought to mark the spot where she was kept a prisoner by King Ravana. There are buses from Nuwara Eliya. There are magnificent views.

Excursions

Pidurutalagala (Mt Pedro) is the island's highest peak (2,524m) and is a 2 hrs climb up the track from near the RC Church, N of the town, in places still through dense forest. It is a steep but quite manageable climb.

The **Horton Plains** can be visited on a day trip if you have a car, but involves an early start (breakfast at 0600) as the Plains have a reputation for bad weather after noon (see below).

Local information

● Accommodation

NB Beware of hotel touts – see note under Kandy. The 2 best hotels are by the golf course and are in the Raj style, well kept, with good restaurants and plenty of atmosphere. Some mid-price hotels offer excellent value.

A ***The Grand***, Grand Hotel Rd, T 2881, F 2265, 114 rm (US$50), more being added, ball-room sized restaurant (buffets catering for package tourists, Rs 420 dinner), adjoins golf course, tennis, billiards, cultural shows, considerable colonial character in century old hotel, efficient but can lack personal touch; **A** ***Hill Club***, up path from Grand Hotel Rd, 22 rm, somewhat modernized in century old Coffee Planters' Club (building 1930s), formal restaurant (tie essential for dinner), 5 mins walk from Golf course, billiards, rather run-down and over priced; **A** ***St Andrews***, 10 St Andrews Drive, overlooking golf course, T/F 2445, F Colombo 699226, 52 rm in over a century old building, good restaurant, rec. A new 4-storey **A** ***Holiday Inn*** is scheduled to open in winter 1996 with 98 rm and a fully equipped health club in addition to all usual facilities, enquiries, T Colombo 591947, F 586014.

B ***Ceylon Bank Rest House*** (Govt), Badulla Rd, T/F 3053, 20 rm (some family rooms) in newly tastefully refurbished building opp Park, pleasant and efficient service; **B** ***Glendower***, 5 Grand Hotel Rd, overlooking the 2nd Tee of the golf course, T/F 2749, 7 large comfortable rm, stylishly decorated (Rs 1,100, triple Rs 1,400), some slightly dark with rather old fashioned bathrooms, fire in evening, attractive modern half-timbered bungalow-style hotel, pleasant lounge, superb billiard table, good King prawn restaurant, beautiful garden, efficient service and personal attention, convenient for town, rec; **B** ***The Windsor***, 1 Kandy Rd, T 2554, F 2889, 48 rm on 3 flrs, many recently tastefully refurbished (US$35), good restaurant though lacking ambiance, modern hotel with attractive plant-filled inner garden, quiet interior in spite of busy town location, efficient, popular, rec.

C ***Haddon Hill Hotel***, 24/3 Haddon Hill Rd, T 2087, modernized bungalow with 11 clean, well-furnished rooms with good views (log fires/heaters), meals in pleasant dining room, a little overpriced.

D ***Collingwood***, Badulla Rd, T 3009, 6 fairly comfortable rm, best with modern bath, in old planter's house retaining its old-world British character with dark wood panelling, restaurant alongside; **D** ***The Grosvenor***, 6 Haddon Hill Rd, T 2307, 19 rm in old colonial house requiring modernizing; **D** ***Haddon Hill Lodge*** 29 Haddon Hill Rd, at the top end, in enviable position with attractive garden, T 2345, 8 clean, comfortable rm with modern hot showers (1 bath tub), some with good views, breakfast incl, dining room serves reasonably-priced, good meals to order (Rs 140), homely atmosphere, personal service, rec; **D** ***Oatlands***, 124

St Andrews Drive, T 2572, 7 comfortable rm most with bath, family-run guest house serving good food; **D** ***Princess Guest House***, 12 Wedderburn Rd, T 2462, 7 rm in 19th century home; **D** ***Sun Hill***, 18 Unique View Rd, T 2878, F 3237, 15 rm (various prices), some with modern bath, hot water, restaurant (Indian, Chinese), travel, friendly; **D-E** *Alpen Guest House*, 4 Haddon Hill Rd (6 mins walk from bus stand) T 3009, 13 rm generally clean (prices vary), some with modernized bath, hot water, some in run-down annexe at rear cheapest, good food (home grown vegetables), attractive prize-winning garden, travel section, hires tent (Rs 450/night), motorbike (Rs 450/day), jeeps (Rs 1,500), arranges treks, friendly management, very popular with travellers.

● Places to eat

Milano, Central market, 'first Halal restaurant' here, upstairs a/c, tasty Chinese and Sri Lankan (about Rs 130), tempting *wattapalam* dessert, sales counter; ***Star Bakery***, opp.

● Bars

Ceylon Brewery's English-style Pub serves draught stout as well as in bottles, closes 2030!

● Banks & money changers

Bank of Ceylon, nr Post Office.

● Hospitals & medical services

Chemists: *Cargills*, Kandy Rd.

● Sports

Golf: beautiful and superbly maintained golf course. Temp membership Rs 100, Rs 600/day.

The Refreshing Cup

An ancient Chinese legend suggests that 'tay', tea, originated in India, although tea was known to have been grown in China around 2700 BC. It is a species of Camellia, *Camellia thea*. After 1833, when its monopoly on importing tea from China was abolished, The East India Company made attempts to grow tea in Assam using wild 'chai' plants found growing there and later introduced it in the Darjiling area and in the Nilgiri hills in the S. Some believe that plants were smuggled in from China. Certainly, Chinese experts had to be asked to advise on improving the method of processing the leaves in the early days while horticulturists at the Botanical Gardens in Calcutta worked on improving the varieties.

In Sri Lanka, the first tea bushes (possibly imported from Assam) were planted in 1849 by James Taylor on a cleared hill slope just SE of Kandy. It was an attempt at experimenting with a crop which would replace the unfortunate diseased coffee. The experiment paid off and Sri Lanka today is one of the world's leading producers of tea (second only to India), exporting nearly 94% to countries across the world. The bushes now grow from sea-level to the highest slopes, though the lush 'low-grown' variety lacks flavour, colour and aroma which characterise bushes grown above 1,000m. The slow-growing bushes at greater heights produce the best flavour and aroma when handpicked carefully – just two leaves and bud.

The old 'orthodox' method of tea processing, produces the aromatic lighter coloured liquor of the Golden Flowery Orange Pekoe in its most superior grade. The fresh leaves are dried by fans on 'withering troughs' to reduce the moisture content and then rolled and pressed to express the juices which coat the leaves. These are then left to ferment in a controlled humid environment in order to produce the desired aroma. Finally the leaves are dried by passing them through a heated drying chamber and then graded – the unbroken being the best quality, down to the 'fannings' and 'dust'.

The more common 'crushing, tearing, curling' (CTC) method produces tea which gives a much darker liquor. It uses machinery which was invented in Assam in 1930. The process allows the withered leaves to be given a short light roll before engraved metal rollers distort the leaves in a fraction of a second. The whole process can take as little as 18 hrs.

● **Transport**

Train The nearest station is *Nanu Oya*, a short bus ride away. It is too far to walk. Railway Out Agency in town sells tickets. **Colombo**: *Uda Rakamenike*, 16, daily, 0936, 6 hrs; *Podi Menike Exp*, 6, daily, 1244, 7¼ hrs; *Mail*, 46, daily, 2206, 7½ hrs. **Kandy**: *Podi Menike Exp*, 6, daily, 1244, 4¼ hrs.

Road Bus: frequent buses to Badulla and Kandy. 2 CTB buses a day to Colombo (6½ hrs). If you have a car it is perfectly possible to drive from Nuwara to Colombo in a day. The most direct route is the A7 via Ginigathena and Avissawella. It is also possible to take the longer route via Ella, Bandarawela and Ratnapura, travelling round the southern flank of the Central Highlands.

ROUTES To Horton Plains The drive, much of it along poor road, takes about 2 hrs. Take the **A5** out of town on the Badulla Road, past the race course towards the Hakgala Gardens (10 km). This is the market garden area: carrots, bean, brassicas and many other fresh vegetables are grown, much of it for export to the Middle East. Take the road to **Ambewela** at the Warwick tea estate sign. The road condition deteriorates sharply and it is very slow going. Ambewela has the highest railway station in the country. You can see the occasional dairy herd here: the dairy marketed under the Highland Milk brand is also based here. The road, climbing all the time, continues through Pattipola and passes between Mt Totapala (2,359m) and Mt Kirigalpotta (2,393m). Eventually the plains are reached with views of the peaks all around. Keep an eye open for the pyramid shape of Adam's peak in the W looking for all the world like the Paramount Picture's logo.

Horton Plains National Park

Access

(40 km from Nuwara Eliya; *Alt* 2,130m) The island's highest and most isolated plateau forms a part of the **Peak Wilderness Sanctuary**. Entry fee US$10, children US$5 (student reduction possible if you show an identification card) at the rangers hut just below the car park. Make sure that you keep your tickets as they will be asked for at the park entrance (about 100m away!). Best month to visit is Aug.

If you wish to walk, it is best to get to **Ohiya** station, the nearest on public transport, (see Trains below) which has shops selling refreshments, in the early morning. You then follow the 5 km, fairly steep winding track, passing *Anderson Lodge* and reaching *Farr Inn* around mid-day (about 3½ hrs uphill, 2 hrs downhill).

NB Wear stout shoes. It can get cold at night so come prepared.

Background

The Horton Plains which covers 3159.8 ha, was declared a National Park in 1988. There is a mixture of montane temperate forest and wet *patana* grassland. The prominent canopy tree is *Keena* (*Callophylum*) with white flowers cotrasting with the striking red rhododendrons lower down. In some ways this makes them quite like a Scottish moor. In other ways, the gently undulating grassland have an almost savannah-like feel with stunted forest on the hill tops. There is widespread concern in Sri Lanka about the condition of the forest which appears to be slowly dying. Blame seems to be attached to the many water irrigation schemes which are allegedly changing the climate.

Wildlife

The bleak and windswept area harbours many wild animals (though no longer the elephant or leopard); you should see plenty of sambhur (sambar) and some toque macaques, Purple-faced leaf monkeys, bear monkeys and horned lizards. There is a rich variety of hill birds (including the Dusky blue flycatcher, Sri Lanka white-eyed arrenga, Yellow-eared bulbul) and a good range of butterflies. People have been disappointed by the lack of wildlife – particularly birds. The best bet is to look out for bear monkey although these are not easy to see in the trees which are quite heavily leafed and also are covered in wispy ferns.

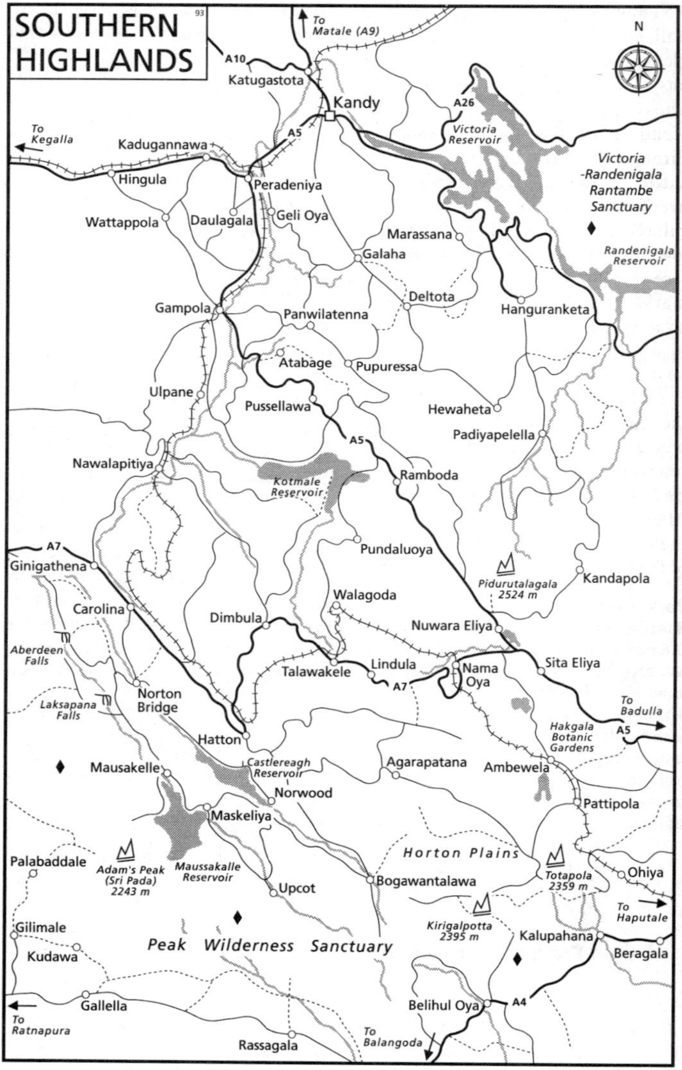

Viewing
Jeep tracks allow you to visit the Plains as a day excursion (see Transport below) but it is worth spending a night there. Unfortunately, the Plains are often covered in mist. **Warning** If misty keep to the footpaths as a number of people go missing each year.

World's End Most people will take the well-trod path to World's End, a

4.5 km bridle path from *Farr Inn*. The walk takes about 40 mins, and is quite pleasant, crossing a small stream with lots of croaking frogs before passing across the grassland and then descending a few hundred metres through the forest. You first come to Little World's End, a mere 260m cliff, overlooking a ravine (more a wide valley) with a tiny village 700m below. You can look along the sheer cliff face to the big green rock which marks (Big) World's End about 1 km away which has a spectacular precipice with a 1,050m drop. This is best visited early in the morning.

On a clear day, you can apparently see the coast, but more realistically, it is the blue-green lake of the Samanala Wewa reservoir project. Once at Big World's End, take the small path up the hill. After only a few yards, there is a split in the rock which gives an excellent view of the valley below.

Park information

● Accommodation

D *Farr Inn Rest House* (CHC), just to the NW of the car park (10 km from Pattipola railway station), T Colombo 323501, F 422732, 5 double and 3 single rm (US$15) with hot shower, clean and comfortable, the restaurant (clock has a funny chime) is a good place to stop for a drink, non-residents have to pay a small fee to use the toilet! beautiful surroundings at 2,100m.

There are various park bungalows (bring provisions and sleeping bag): ***New Buttuwa***, US$25; ***Anderson Lodge***, 3 km before *Farr Inn* from Ohiya, sleeps 6 people (US$20); ***Wana Nivahana*** dorms, (US$5).

Camping: fees are US$5. Reservations, Department of Wildlife Conservation, T 687347, nr river close to *Farr Inn*, rec.

● Transport

Train If you want to walk it is best to travel to Ohiya station (on the Colombo-Badulla line). *Udarata Menike*, daily, dep Ella, 0652, 1¾ hrs; dep Bandarawela, 0724, 1¼ hrs; dep Haputale, 0755, 40 mins. You can do a day-trip if you plan to travel towards Colombo via Nanu Oya, the Night *Mail* dep Ohiya, 2047, arr Colombo 0540 (about Rs 40 for 3rd class).

Road Access by 4WD from Nuwara Eliya through Mahagastota and Hakgala or via Talawakelle, Agrapathna and Dayagama Estate or Haputale, Welimada and Boralanda. From Nuwara Eliya, about 1½ hrs by road.

ROUTES Horton Plains to Bandarawela From the Plains, a track winds down quite steeply through the Udeirva/Ohiya estate through wooded slopes (where you might see bear monkeys). At Borlanda, the track joins the B805. A turn to the S allows approach to Bandarawela along the **A4** through Haptule. Alternatively, the road to the N to Welimada joins the B810 which passes through pleasant countryside. You can sometimes see resin being collected from pine trees. There is a large school (St Thomas College) in a very attractive location at Gurutwala, just outside Welimada.

KANDY TO NUWARA ELIYA VIA HATTON AND TALAWAKELE

The most scenically beautiful route up into the hills runs through the great tea estates of the Hatton-Dikoya region to the popular holiday resort for Sri Lankans at Nuwara Eliya. As far as Hatton it follows the upper reaches of the Mahaweli Ganga towards its source near Hatton. This route is also followed by the train, which despite its snail-like pace offers a really relaxing alternative to the road journey.

ROUTES The **A5** goes S from Peradeniya to **Gampola** where the B43 branches to the right for Nawalapitiya and the **Ginigathena Pass** (38 km) where it joins the A7 which comes up from Avissawella in the low country. There are magnificent views at the top, although they are often obscured by cloud, for the pass is in one of the wettest areas of Sri Lanka. From here on the road runs through tea country. Ginigathena is a small bazaar for the tea estates and their workers. The A7 winds up to **Watawala** (10 km); nearby the **Carolina Falls** are spectacular in the wet season. The A7 follows the left bank of the Mahaweli Ganga up to Hatton (12 km). **Note** This route can be quite slow. The alternative from Nawalapitiya (B41) to Dimbula and A7 to Hatton was very poor in 1995 and even slower, occasionally allowing only 10 km/hour.

Hatton

Hatton (*STD Code* 0512) is one of the major centres of Sri Lanka's tea industry, and the base from which most pilgrims and tourists trek to the top of Adam's Peak. Hatton lacks suitable places to stay or eat. The only reason to stay a night here would be before or after climbing Adam's Peak.

• **Accommodation** **D** *Lanka Inn Tourist Rest*, 47/6 Dunbar Rd, 1 km from railway, T 647, 11 rm (Rs 460), restaurant, bar; **D-E** *Hatton Rest House* is poor, 6 dirty rm (Rs 400), not rec; **E** *Ajantha*, just across railway tracks (sign on road when entering town from A7), poor rooms (Rs 300), not rec. At **Dikoya**: **C** *Brown's Upper Glencairn Guest House*, 3 km S of Hatton among tea plantations, T 348, 6 rm in colonial estate bungalow, with view of Adam's Peak.

• **Transport Road** The car journey from Nuwara Eliya or Kandy takes at least 3 hrs as the surface is poor.

Adam's Peak

(*Alt* 2,260m) A steep footpath leads to the peak sacred to Buddhists, Hindus and Muslims which is one of Sri Lanka's main centres of pilgrimage. The object of pilgrimage on the summit is the giant footprint – of the Buddha, of Adam or Siva – covered by a huge stone slab, in which has been carved another print. Local Buddhist tradition promises any woman who succeeds in climbing by this route that she will be re-born in the next life as a man.

Buses run the tortuously winding route from Hatton to **Maskeliya** (20 km; *Alt* 1,280m) and on to Dalhousie. By car it takes about an hour, going through some of the most productive tea growing areas towards **Norwood**. Keep to the Maskeliya road up the Pass before Norwood. The air is already strikingly fresh, and the higher road is lined with tropical ferns. The bus journey takes about 2 hrs to Dalhousie.

Dalhousie is where the climb itself starts. There are tea shops in town and you can pick up some food for the climb. **Accommodation** There are only a few small guest houses incl **D** *Green House*, with 3 basic but clean rooms with shared bath, friendly owners and excellent home cooking and lots of it.

The climb to the top from Maskeliya takes about 3 hrs. The path is clearly marked throughout, beginning fairly easily but rapidly become steeper. Most people do the walk by moonlight, arriving in time to see the dawn when the conical peak, only 50m sq, forms an extraordinary shadow across the plains to the W. It is completely safe, even the steepest parts being protected, and steps and chains provided where necessary. The route is ancient – **Marco Polo** commented on the chains provided for pilgrims in the 13th century. An alternative route, much steeper and more difficult, comes up from the Ratnapura side. **NB** It is very cold on top of the peak until well after sunrise. It is essential to take warm clothing, as well as some food and drink.

ROUTES From Hatton the road crosses the railway line and winds up through the tea estates of **Dimbula** to **Talawakele** (10 km). For much of the way it is above 2,000m, though it drops slightly between Dimbula and Talawakele. In Talawakele, Sri Lanka's Tea Research Institute (sometimes open to visitors) has played a major role in improving Sri Lanka's tea production. From Talawakele to Nuwara Eliya the road runs through country in the rainshadow of hills to the SW and the NE, the range halving the total rainfall. A right turn after Talawakele in Lindula leads up a beautiful mountain road to **Agrapatana**, but the **A7** continues through Nanu Oya, and finally down into Nuwara Eliya.

Nuwara Eliya to Badulla, Ella and Haputale

A very pleasant circular route from Nuwara Eliya gives excellent views of the SE Highlands. It makes a very pleasant day tour, although there are also some comfortable and very attractive places to stay if you do not want to rush. From Badulla it is possible to go E across the Dry Zone to Arugam Bay or Batticaloa, and from Ella two roads go S, the A23 goes to Hambantota, and the A4/B53 to Ruhunu-Yala National Park and Kataragama. These are thus in comfortable reach of a 2 or 3 days excursion from Kandy or Nuwara Eliya.

From Nuwara Eliya the A5 goes SE across Wilson's Plains then E to Badulla. Just past the **Hakgala Gardens**, 10 km (see page 185) is a superb view SE across the hills of Bandarawela and over the baked plains of the E coastlands. The road drops rapidly through to **Welimada** on the Uma Oya River.

Istripura caves, N of Welimada, a pot-holers delight, are reached by a path from Parangama, which is 10 km along the road N from Welimada. The maze of damp caves hold a large lake.

ROUTES From Welimada, a right turn (the B51) leads to Bandarawela (see page 196), past terraced fields of paddy and across occasional streams. At **Hali-Ela**, the **A5** goes to Badulla. This area is already in the rainshadow of the hills to the W, sheltered from the SW monsoon and much drier than Nuwara Eliya. Rubber plantations cover some of the slopes before Badulla.

Badulla

(45 km; *Alt* 675m; *STD Code* 055) The capital of Uva Province, it is one of the oldest towns in Sri Lanka though there are no traces of the earlier settlement. The Portuguese once occupied it but set the town on fire before leaving.

The town is surrounded by paddy fields along the banks of the river Gallanda Oya which has an ancient wooden bridge with an unusual tiled roof, see page 196. It has an old fort against a backcloth of mountains and a small lake.

The **Muthiyangana Vihare** attributed to Devanampiya Tissa, the first Buddhist convert on the island, is thought to have a 2,000-year-old ancient core. The Hindu **Kataragama Devale** is also on the site of an earlier temple; note the plaster-on-wood statues and wooden pillars of the 'throne room'. There is also a revered **Bo tree**.

At one time Badulla was an extremely active social centre for planters, with a race course, golf, tennis and cricket clubs, long since fallen into disuse. The park was once a small botanic garden.

Notice the little stone grey Methodist church on the left; Major Rogers, an elephant hunter who died from a lightning strike is believed to have been buried in the cemetery. The clock tower celebrates the opening of a garment makingfactorybyPresidentPramadesa.

Excursions

Duhinda Falls The road out of town lined with many stalls selling lime, rapidly descends before reaching the 6 km away.

There is a small car park on a bend in the road about 2 km from the falls which takes about 25 mins (you may have to pay for the car to be guarded). Buses also stop here. The path to the falls is across the road from the car park; it is quite rough and steep in places, so take care and wear suitable shoes. The valley at this point is also quite narrow which can make it very hot (humidity is also very high, near the falls) if you have come down from the highlands.

Numerous stalls sell cold drinks, herbs etc at the start of the walk and along it; some even have tables and seats. As the falls are very popular with Sri Lankans, foreign travellers are not hassled too much.

Shortly after the beginning of the path you can see the lower falls (more of a cascade really), quite a long way down in the valley below. These are only about 15m in height and much broader than the main falls. A ledge about 10m from the top makes for a spectacular 'spurt' when the river is running high. At the main falls, the river plunges in two stages about 60m through a V in the rock which causes a misty haze (*duhind*) which gives the falls its name. There are granite cliffs on either side and a large pool at the bottom. It is quite spectacular and well worth the effort. Here there is also a large, kidney shaped observation platform where concrete tables and benches have been constructed to give a pleasant picnic spot. Beware though as it can be very busy at times.

Local festivals

Jul: *Kataragama festival* with fire-walking, is held at the Devale.
Sep: *Esala Perehera* at Muthiyangana Temple when Veddas participate.

Local information

● Accommodation

D *Eagle's Nest*, 159 Lower St, T 2501; **D** *New Tourist Inn*, Falls Rd, pleasant with nice garden overlooking the stream); **D** *Rest House* in town centre, is good value; **D** *Tourist Resort*, 97 Duhinda Rd, towards the waterfall, good value; **D-E** *Duhinda Falls Inn*, 35/11-1/1 Bandaranayake Maw 1.5 km from city centre, signposted from bus and railway station with mountain view, T 3028, F 2718, 20 rm (Rs 250-600), ground flr cheaper, restaurant, bar, exchange, car/cycle hire, visits to tea gardens.

Budget hotel: **E** *Riverside Holiday Inn*, 27 Lower King St, 8 mins walk from railway station, T 2090, 15 rm, restaurant, but no river here!

Paying guests: local families take in guests and offer good home cooking. Some rec: 5/2 Malla Gastenne, not far from Railway and Bus Stand and 28 Passara Rd, well kept with a garden.

● Transport

Local Car hire: from *Sugimal Fast Foods*, opp Muthiyangane Vihare, T 3028.

Train To **Colombo** via Demodara, Ella, Bandarawela, Haputale, Ohiya: *Udarata Menike*, 16, daily, 0555, 9¾ hrs; *Podi Menike Exp*, 6, daily, 0850, 11¼ hrs; *Mail*, 46, daily, 1745, 12 hrs. **Kandy**: *Podi Menike Exp*, 6, daily, 0850, 8 hrs.

Road Bus: frequent buses to Nuwara Eliya (2 hrs); also to Bandarawela. Occasional buses to the E coast.

Ella, Bandarawela and Haputale

Retracing your route along the **A5** to **Hali-Ela**, the **A16** turns S to **Demodara**; this is also tea country and there is a tea factory here. The road then reaches the beautiful gap town of Ella.

ROUTES To reach Ella from Bandarawela keep on the A16. After 7 km turn right. At this junction the road to Badulla goes straight on (20 km). Alternatively, it is a pleasant walk along the railway line; there are only a few trains and the route is well used by local people.

Ella

(13 km; *STD Code* 057) A traveller writes, "The view through the Ella gap was probably the best in the entire island. It was quite early and the isolated hills on the plain popped up like islands in the mist." Most visitors go to the *Rest House* garden to get the best view.

6.5 km S from Ella is the Rawana Ella Falls, while closer to the *Rest House* is the vast Rawana Ella cave which is associated with the *Ramayana* story; according to legend it is where the demon king of Lanka, Ravana, imprisoned Rama's wife Sita.

Rawana Ella Cave The cave in the massive **Ella Rock** which can be seen from the *Rest House*, to the right of the Ella Gap, is of particular interest to palaeontologists. The small upside-down teardrop entrance scarcely lets light in. It is filled by water from an underground stream which has hindered exploration but excavations here unearthed prehistoric remains of human skeletons and tools dating from 8000 to 2500 BC. The skeleton is believed to belong to *Homo Sapiens Balangodensis*. According to Deraniyagala, the finds show evidence of a culture superior to that of the present-day Veddas.

Walk downhill beyond the *Ella Rest House* for 10 mins up to the road bridge then branch up the track to the right which climbs (good views) to a rock monastery where a young monk will happily show you the temple and hope for a few rupees' donation. There is often someone who will be happy to accompany you up a very difficult path to the cave; the guide usually does not expect any payment.

Rawana Ella Falls Return to the main road by the bridge and continue downhill for 1½ hrs (6.5 km) to the falls. The road is not too busy so it is a pleasant walk with views over fire-affected forest/savanna of the small **Rawana Ella Wildlife Sanctuary** and onwards to the plains to the SE. The Falls are a popular site but are comparatively small and a disappointment to many – 'they are right on the road. You can scramble up the rocks for a little way but the stream is not very nice; the whole area is rather dirty'.

Bambaragama Restaurant sells snacks which are very expensive – and can often get warm – 'cold' drinks at the bottom. There are frequent buses back to Ella (Rs 4).

• **Accommodation** **C** *Ella Gap Tourist Inn*, nr *Rest House*, T/F 2628, 5 clean rm (Rs 850) some with bath, good restaurant, bar, river bathing, friendly; **D** *Lizzie Villa Guest House*, off station road, rooms with shared bath in a peaceful garden, friendly owners, rec; **D** *Rest House* (CHC), overlooking Ella Gap, 1 km S from railway station, T 2636, reservations T Colombo 323501, F 422732, 6 large rm with hot water (2 upper ones have best views, US$15), rooms and dining room rather shabby but bathrooms modernized, very comfortable, attractive terrace verandah and garden with superb views from its position high above the plains, outdoor restaurant, bar, very popular especially during wedding season so book rooms in advance, friendly management, highly rec, stop for a meal if not staying; **D** *Rock View Guest House*, T 2661, good hill-top position nr *Rest House* but is ruined by dirty rooms (Rs 400-500), unfriendly management; also owned by same family, the more expensive, **D** *Tea Garden Holiday Inn*, right on top of the hill (park vehicle at *Rock View*), T 2915, good, fairly clean rooms with hot water (Rs 750) with views second only to the *Rest House* but not very private due to surrounding dining area, sadly a place with great potential in a charming position let down by unsatisfactory management, travellers in 1995 found "when booking by phone you may be promised a room here only to find that they are full on your arrival and you are transferred to a shed-like room at *Rock View* instead!"

• **Places to eat** *Ella Gap Tourist Inn*, unimpressive surroundings, expensive but tasty food, smallish servings but can be topped up; *Rest House* serves reasonable food, excellent setting and views.

• **Shopping** Shops on the main street nr the *Rest House* are overpriced; walk up the street and pay half the price for water and provisions.

• **Transport Train** To **Colombo**: *Udarata Menike*, 16, daily, 0652, 8¾ hrs; *Podi Menike Exp*, 6, daily, 0947, 10½ hrs; *Mail*, 46, daily, 1844, 11 hrs. **Kandy**: *Podi Menike Exp*, 6, daily, 1022, 6¼. **Road** From Ella to Bandarawela by car takes about 45 mins.

ROUTES From Ella the **A23** runs due S to Wellawaya. Wellawaya is an important crossroads on the **A4**, the main road connecting the SW and SE coasts and the Central Highlands with the S coast at Hambantota. A road has recently been opened from Migahawela due S to Yala National Park and Kataragama. It is not shown on all maps, but is a well-made and relatively quick route.

Wellawaya (*STD Code* 055) Wild elephants can be seen from the bus, around this area; ask in town for directions. The turn off for the **Buduruvagala** rock carvings of the Mahayana Buddhist period is 7 km, along the Tissa road; the 4 km dry-weather jeep-track leads to the massive rock which is to the left of the track. Of the seven rock-cut figures, the 16m high Buddha in the centre is flanked by *Avalokitesvaras* and Tara; some find these a little disappointing. **Accommodation C** *Saranga Holiday Inn*, 37 Old Ella Rd, T 4891, with some a/c rooms; **D** *Rest House*, 50m N of Haldummulla-Moneragala-Pottuvil Rd, 2 good rm.

Bandarawela

(*Alt* 1,230m; *STD Code* 057) The rain shadow of the Central Highlands gives Bandarawela a drier SW monsoon than the hills immediately to the W. It is perhaps most renowned for tea and for fruit production.

Bandarawela is a straggling town, with nothing much of interest to see; really a long wide road sloping quite steeply with lots of shops lining each side. It has a bustling market-town feel and is a good place for picking up supplies. It is, however, pleasantly small, with a reputation for a very good climate and is a good base for walks and for exploring the Uva basin.

Excursions Bindunuwewa nearby has an Ayurvedic herbal treatment centre which travellers visit for excercise routines and herbal massages. **D** *Himalie*, Badulla Rd, T 2362, in a tea estate 3 km from town (8 km from Ella), T/F 2362, 7 comfortable rm with bath, restaurant.

Bogoda Cave Temple Taking the Badulla road out of town, shortly after the *Queens Hotel* (3 km), you pass the **Dowa** temple squeezed between the road and the stream in the bottom of the valley. The Bogoda temple, a short distance away, is near the attractive old wooden bridge across the Gallanda Oya which is constructed without nails (the original claimed to date from to the 1st century BC); it has an unusual patterned-tiled roof in the Kandyan style.

Dunhinda Falls (see page 194 takes about 1 hr. Take the A16 along the valley. It is a fairly steady descent with the valley slowly widening and paddy fields becoming more apparent. The railway line hugs the contours on the opposite side of the valley.

• **Accommodation B** *Bandarawela Hotel*, 14 Welimada Rd, on a hill overlooking the main street nr Cargill's supermarket at the top end of town, T 2501, Reservations

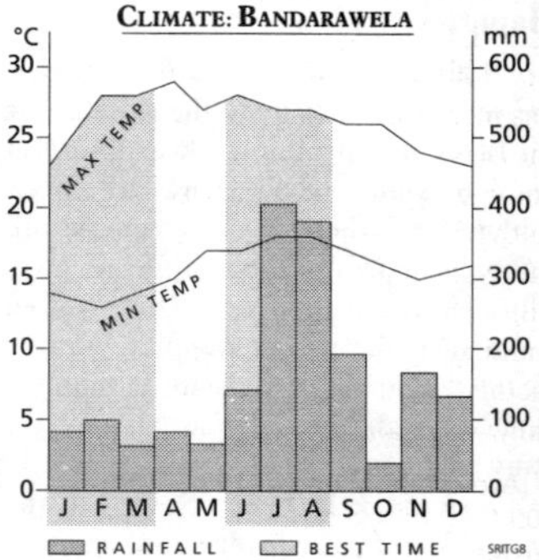

T/F Colombo 433755, 35 rm (US$36), once an old tea planters club, built 1893, renovated retaining period furniture, rooms are large and are built around a central courtyard (look for the tortoises), fairly comfortable public rooms, restaurant passable but rather old-fashioned (still has brown Windsor soup on the menu!), good gardens, particularly pleasant to sit out in, very popular with tour groups; **B** *Orient*, 10 Dharmapala Maw, 500m from railway station, T/F 2407, 50 rm (US$30), huge white barracks-like building; **C** *Queens* formerly *Madhu*, Badulla Rd, 3 km E of town, T/F 2806, 30 rm (US$23), services incl ayurvedic herbal care centre; **C** *Rest House*, nr *Orient Hotel*, 9 large rm, restaurant, pleasant location, views of waterfall, good value; **D** *Ideal Resort*, Welimada Rd, 2 km N of centre, T 2476, 6 rm in a tea plantation bungalow, restaurant, bar, large garden; the pleasant **D** *Ventnor Guest House* is also on the main road.

• **Banks & money changers** Peoples Bank changes up to US$200 only; **Seylan Bank** is very efficient.

• **Transport Train** To **Colombo**: *Udarata Menike*, 16, daily, 0724, 8 hrs; *Podi Menike Exp*, 6, daily, 1020, 9¾ hrs; *Mail*, 46, daily, 1912, 10½ hrs. **Kandy**: *Podi Menike Exp*, 6, daily, 1020, 6¼ hrs. **Road** To **Ella** by car takes 45 mins on a good road (A16); watch out for sign to branch right about 10 km from Bandarawela. **Bus**: frequent service to Haputale, Badulla and Ella. Nuwara Eliya direct bus takes just over 1 hr.

ROUTES From Bandarawela the road crosses the railway line and climbs before descending into Haputale.

Haputale

(*Alt* 1,400m; *STD Code* 057) Haputale has magnificent views of the dawn over the Low Country to the E. On a clear day you can see the salt pans at Hambantota to the S, and the horizon is the sea. To the N in magnificent contrast are the hills. The monastery on the hill is worth walking up to. If you wish to visit a tea factory, most managers are willing to show you around if you ask.

• **Accommodation** **C** *New Rest House*, 100 Bandarawela Rd (road between private bus stands, 1 km centre), T 8099, 6 rm with bath, simple but comfortable with very good food and bar, very pleasant garden, rec; **D** *Old Rest House*, nr railway station in town centre, 5 rm, noisy, not very clean with smelly toilets; **F** *Bawa Guest House*, uphill off Temple Rd, about 1.5 km from railway station T 8021, some rooms with bath, good rice and curry, friendly owners who press you to eat more and more!

• **Places to eat** No real restaurant here but you can buy rotties and snacks in food stalls. The *Bakery* at the private bus station does a good cup of hot milk tea.

• **Transport Train** Services to Colombo and Kandy. **Road Bus**: separate bus stands for CTB and private buses. Services to Wellawaya and Matara.

ROUTES From Haputale the **A16** goes W to Beragala (10 km) where it joins the **A4**. This has some of the most rugged scenery in Sri Lanka. Black rocks tower above the road as it goes towards Belihuloya (see page 147). Much of the route is very windy, not steep but with many blind bends. The A4 continues W to Ratnapura or E to Koslande, past the Diyaluma waterfall (170m) to Wellawaya (see above).

Diyaluma Falls Should you wish to see a waterfall without having to walk, the easiest way is to take this diversion off the A4 near Wellawaya. The minor road to the falls which winds through rubber plantations can be found just before the sign for the New Resthouse in Haputale. The Diyaluma are not as spectacular as the Dunhinda falls mainly because the stream is much smaller. They descend in two stages over a huge convex outcrop. It is quite peaceful here and although there are no official places for picnics, there are several large rocks to sit on. Beware of the monkeys though! You can buy warm drinks at a store nearby.

ROUTES At Wellawaye you can either take the **A23** N to Ella and Nuwara Eliya, or the **A2** S to Hambantota, or the **A4/B53** to Ruhunu-Yala and Kataragama. If you wish to return direct to Nuwara Eliya the B48 goes directly through Boralanda and Nawela and Welimada, where it rejoins the **A5** to Nuwara Eliya.

KANDY TO THE CULTURAL TRIANGLE

The most famous cultural and archaeological sites in Sri Lanka can easily be visited in a short tour from Kandy. The development of a new road network accompanying the huge irrigation and colonization plans of the Mahaweli Ganga scheme in the Dry Zone to the NE of the highlands has opened up the possibility of making a circular tour. The route described below follows a clockwise direction, returning from Polonnaruwa to Kandy by the new and fast road through the Mahaweli Ganga Project area via Mahiyangana, but the journey can equally well be undertaken the other way round.

If you are really pressed for time it is possible to visit Dambulla, Sigiriya and Polonnaruwa by car and to return to Kandy in 1 day, though it makes a very long day. It is best to allow at least 3 days to see all the major sites and to enjoy some of the magnificent scenery in comfort.

Road to Dambulla

A very attractive road, the **A9**, runs from Kandy N to Nalanda and Dambulla. It passes through spice gardens (some of which are open to the public) and plantations of coffee, cocoa and rubber around the small town of Matale.

Matale

(24 km; *STD Code* 066) **Accommodation** *Home Seas*, decent rooms, restaurant, modern and very clean, rec. Also *Rest House* opp the Post Office, T 2299, 5 rm, and a *Tourist Guest House*, 149 Nagolla Rd, T 2259, 10 rm. There is a Bank of Ceylon in town.

Aluvihare

3 km N of Matale Aluvihare has the renovated ruins of an ancient rock temple. In the 1st-2nd century BC, the site was associated with King Vattagamani Abhaya (103-77 BC). The *Mahavansa* (Buddhist chronicle of the island) was inscribed here in Pali. The original manuscript, inscribed on palm leaf manuscripts prepared by 500 monks, was destroyed in the mid-19th century, and replacements are still being inscribed today. With the expectation of a contribution to the temple (for which you are given a receipt) you are shown the technique of writing on palmyra palm.

Aluvihare is very quiet and may be a welcome alternative to the nearby Dambulla cave temple for those jaded by the tourist route. Four of the 10 caves have ancient inscriptions; there are frescoes (some vivid illustrations of punishment doled out to sinners) and impressive painted reclining Buddhas. The stupa on top of the rock just beyond the cave temples gives fine views of the Dry Zone plains and pine covered mountains.

Nalanda

49 km from Kandy, 1 km off the main road, Nalanda has a small *gedige* (Buddha image-house built with stone slabs) originally dating from the 7th-10th centuries. The reconstructed temple stands

Palm Leaf Manuscripts

The palmyra palm strips were prepared for manuscripts by drying, boiling and drying again and then flattened and coated with shell. A stylus was used for inscribing; held stationary while the leaf was moved to produce the lettering or illustration (the rounded shape of some South Asian scripts was a result of this technology). The inscribed grooves would then be rubbed with soot or powdered charcoal while colour was added with a brush. The leaves would then be stacked and sometimes strung together and sometimes 'bound' between decorative wooded 'covers'.

by a reservoir. Some tantric carvings have been found in the structure which combines Hindu and Buddhist (both Mahayana and Theravada) features. It is the only extant Sri Lankan *gedige* built in the architectural style of the 7th century Pallava shore temples at Mamallapuram near Madras, India. There is a *Rest House* with 6 rm.

ROUTES The **A9** continues to Dambulla (an area known for its mangoes), where there are famous rock caves and temples, only 15 km from the magnificent and dramatic site of Sigiriya.

Dambulla

(*STD Code* 066) Dambulla is sited on a gigantic granite outcrop which towers more than 160m above the surrounding land. The rock is more than 1.5 km around its base and the summit is at an altitude of 550m. The caves were the refuge of King Valagam Bahu (Vattagamani Abhaya) when he was in exile for 14 years. When he returned to the throne at Anuradhapura in the 1st century BC, he had a magnificent rock temple built at Dambulla. The caves have been repaired and repainted several times in the 11th, 12th and 18th centuries.

The caves have a mixture of religious and secular painting and sculpture. There are several reclining Buddhas, including the 15m long sculpture of the dying Buddha in Cave 1. The frescoes on the walls and ceilings date from the 15th-18th centuries; the ceiling frescoes show scenes from the Buddha's life and Sinhalese history. Cave 2 is the largest and most impressive, containing over 150 statues, illustrating the Mahayana influences on Buddhism at the time through introducing Hindu deities such as Vishnu and Ganesh.

Entry

Open 0600-1100; 1400-1900. The entrances to the caves are about 1.5 km S of the clocktower at the junction of the A roads. Visitors in 1995 failed to find any sign of a ticket office. The site is covered by the 'Cultural Triangle Permit', see page 21. **NB** Bags, shoes (and sometimes, hats) are not allowed into the complex; they can all be left with the 'shoe keepers'; they will also 'hire out' a *lungi* (sarong) to anyone wearing shorts so get this from the same person otherwise you will be tipping repeatedly. Alternatively, wear trousers or a longish skirt. It is helpful to have a torch. Guides are available; in fact, it is difficult to dodge the guides as they stand in the temple doorway. You can feel rather pressurized to pay various people providing services (guide, shoe keeper, sa-

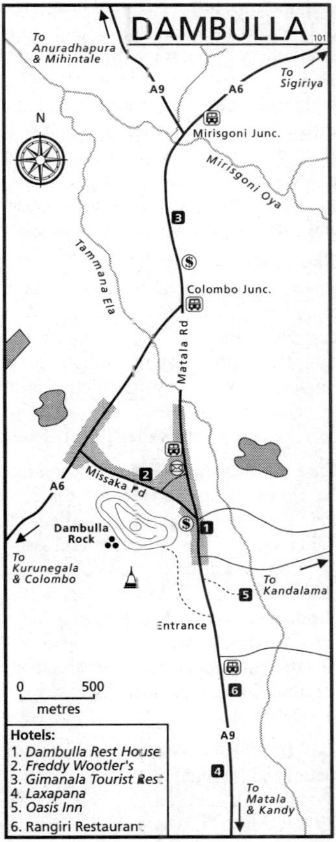

rong provider) and also make a donation to the temple.

There is little evidence of monks who are housed in monasteries in the valley below (where there is a monks' school). Excellent views of Sigiriya in the distance. Good booklet in English and German Rs 250.

Further reading

Golden rock temple of Dambulla by A Seneviratna, Sri Lanka Central Cultural Fund, 1983.

Approach

From the car park, it can be a hot and tiring climb. It is quite steep – first, almost 100m across the bare granite and then there are about 200 steps in a series of 18 terraces – some longer and steeper than others. It is not too difficult to get to the top but try to avoid the heat in the middle of the day (it is best visited in the early morning). The caves are about half way up the hill and now form part of a temple complex. There are panoramic views from the top of surrounding jungle and lakes, and of Sigiriya, 19 km away.

The Caves

There are five caves, although it is really more like an enormous overhang. Monastic buildings have been built in front, complete with cloisters, and these in turn overlook a courtyard which is used for ceremonial purposes and has a wonderful view over the valley floor below.

Cave 1 (**Devaraja-Viharaya**) contains the huge lying *Parinirvana* Buddha which is 14m long and is carved out of solid rock. The frescoes behind the Arahat Ananda (a disciple) are said to be the oldest in the site. Devaraja refers to the Hindu god Vishnu. The deity may have been installed here in the Kandyan period though some believe it is older than the Buddha images; there is a Vishnu temple attached.

Cave II (**Maharaja-Viharaya**, about 24 sq metres and 7m high) was named after the two kings whose images are here. To the left as you enter is a wooden painted statue of Vattagamini Abhaya (Valagambahu) who founded the temple here. The principal Buddha statue facing the entrance is in the *Abhaya mudra*, under a makara torana or 'dragon arch'. The cave has about 1,500 paintings of the Buddha – almost as though the monks had tried to wallpaper the cave. The paintings of his life (near the corner to the right) are also interesting – you can see his parents holding him as a baby, various pictures of him meditating (counted in weeks, eg cobra hood indicates the sixth week): some have him surrounded by demons, others with cobras and another shows him being offered food by merchants. The other historical scenes are also interesting with the battle between Dutthagamenu and Elara particularly graphic – the decisive moment when the defeated falls to the ground, head first from an elephant. You will notice that some paintings clearly show other older ones underneath.

Here in the right hand corner, you can see the holy pot which is never empty – the water collected drips into a bucket which sits in a wooden fenced rectangle and is used for sacred rituals by the monks.

Cave III (**Maha Alut Viharaya**: about 30 sq metres and 18m high) was rebuilt in the 18th century, which has about 60 images (some under 'dragon arches') and more paintings of thousands of the seated Buddha on the ceiling. This cave was a former storeroom and the frescoes are in the Kandyan style.

Cave IV (**Pascima Viharaya** or 'western' cave) is the smallest and was the westernmost; it had the fifth cave constructed later to its W. It contains about 10 images. Unfortunately the stupa here was damaged by thieves who came in search of Queen Somawathie's jewels. One image in particular, at the back of the cave, has had to be restored; unfortunately it is now painted in a very strong yellow which jars with the rest of the cave.

Cave V (Devana Alut Viharaya), is the newest and was once used as a storeroom. The images here are built of brick and plaster and in addition to the Buddha figures, also includes the Hindu deities, Vishnu, Kataragama and Bandara (a local god).

Some of the other subsidiary caves which were occupied by monks contain ancient inscriptions in Brahmi.

Excursions

Aukana, W of the Kalawewa Tank, is best visited early in the morning. There is a remarkable 12m high free-standing statue of the Buddha carved out of a single rock which is now protected by a brick-built shelter in the style of an image house. It has been ascribed to King Dhatusena (459-477) who was responsible for the building of several tanks including the one here. However, JC Harle dates it to 8th/9th century by the stylized quality of the face. *Getting there*: direct buses run from Dambulla. From the A6, turn off E at Kekirawa and continue for about 10 km on the minor road that skirts the N and along the causeway on the W side of the tank and then travel 4 km to the W to Aukana.

Sasseruwa, about 13 km E of Aukana, has an ancient monastery site with over 100 cave cells, remains of stupas, moonstones and inscriptions, dating back to the 2nd century BC. Here too, there is a similar standing Buddha framed by the dark rock, but not quite as impressive in workmanship. It was possibly carved at the same time as the Aukana, although some believe it to be a later copy. Its location, halfway up a rocky hillside requires climbing nearly 300 steps. *Getting there*: the road from Aukana continues to the site via Negampaha; the surface is poor.

Local information

● Accommodation

A *Kandalama*, 30 mins drive from Sigiriya, T 8303, 162 plush a/c rm (US$70) in resort style complex with restaurants, pools, views of lake and rock.

C *Gimanala Tourist Rest*, 754 Anuradhapura Rd, 1 km N of Colombo Junc, T 8364, F 8317, 10 comfortable a/c rm (US$16), restaurant, friendly.

D *Dambulla Rest House* (CHC), 1 km N of entrance to the site, T 8299, 4 large rm with bath (US$9), good restaurant, bar, exchange, pleasant verandah overlooking garden, good value, rec; **D** *Freddy Wootler's Holiday Inn*, 62 Missaka Rd, clean rooms with bath, fan and net, restaurant; **D** *Laxapana*, Matala Rd, 500m S of site entrance, T 8303, 5 rm with fan (Rs 450) in simple family guest house, Sri Lankan meals any time of day.

E-F *Oasis Inn*, lane E off A9, 500m N of the site entrance, Matala Rd, very basic rooms and dorm, canteen

Several families take in guests along the main Matala Rd.

● Places to eat

Rangiri, 44th mile post, Matale Rd, excellent family-run 'rice and curry' restaurant just down the road from the caves, rec.

● Banks & money changers

Bank of Ceylon, Kandy-Jaffna Rd (A9).

● Useful addresses

Petrol Station Kandy-Jaffna Rd (A9).

● Transport

Road Bus: most long-distance buses stop at Colombo Junc, about 2.5 km N of the cave site; local buses run to the site entrance, as do Kandy buses. Regular services from Colombo (takes 4 hrs), Anuradhapura, Kandy and Polonnaruwa (about 2½ hrs each) and frequent to/from Sigiriya (30 mins).

The road to Anuradhapura & Mihintale

From **Dambulla** the **A9** to Anuradhapura (65 km) forks left at Mirisgoni Junction. It passes through Kekirawa near the large Kalawewa tank where you can see the magnificent Buddha colossus at Aukana (see above).

ROUTES The A9 has a good surface and is reasonably quiet. It crosses the flat plain, interspersed by occasional boulders of granite breaking the surface, with rice fields occasionally appearing as pockets of bright green in the widespread forest, before entering Anuradhapura on the **A13**.

ANURADHAPURA AND MIHINTALE

Anuradhapura

Anuradhapura is Sri Lanka's most sacred town. From origins as a settlement in the 6th century BC, it was made capital in 377 BC by King Pandukhabhaya (437-367 BC) who started the great irrigation works on which it depended, and named it after the constellation Anuradha. Although the city has remained a symbol of Sinhalese regal power and of Buddhist orthodoxy its period as a centre of real political power had ended by the 12th century AD though for 500 years before that it had suffered widely fluctuating fortunes. By the 19th century it was completely deserted. 'Re-discovered' in the early 19th century by Ralph Backhaus, archaeological research, excavation and restoration have been going on ever since. The new town was started in the 1950s.

At its height Anuradhapura may have stretched 25 km. Its ruins and monuments today are widely scattered, which makes a thorough tour time consuming, but it more than repays the effort.

The first era of religious building followed the conversion of **King Devanampiya Tissa** (r 250-210 BC). In his 40 year reign these included the Thuparama Dagoba, Issurumuniyagala, and the Maha Vihara with the Sri Maha Bodhi and the Brazen Palace. A branch of the **Bodhi tree** (see below) under which the Buddha was believed to have gained his enlightenment was brought from India and successfully transplanted. It is one of the holiest Buddhist sites in the world.

Anuradhapura remained a capital city until the 9th century AD, when it reached its peak of power and vigour. After the 13th century it almost entirely disappeared, the irrigation works on which it had depended falling into total disuse, and its political functions taken over first by Polonnaruwa, and then by capitals to the S. The earliest restoration work began in 1872, and has continued ever since. The town is now the headquarters of the Sri Lanka Archaeological Survey.

Places of interest
The site covers a large area and the places of interest are scattered widely; one of the most enjoyable ways of seeing them is by bicycle but you may need a compass! Many guest houses can provide cycles or arrange car hire. Since there are a lot of minor tracks that lead off the main roads it is not always easy to follow the map; you may find a guide helpful.

Entry The **Ticket office** (and the Archaeological Museum) is just N of the *Tissawewa Rest House*. Combined 'permit' for the triangle of ancient sites (US$30), or for the single site (US$12) are available (see page 107). **NB** The Cultural Triangle Permit does not cover all places within this site, eg here the Sri Maha Bodhi and Issurumuniya temple charge Rs 25 each.

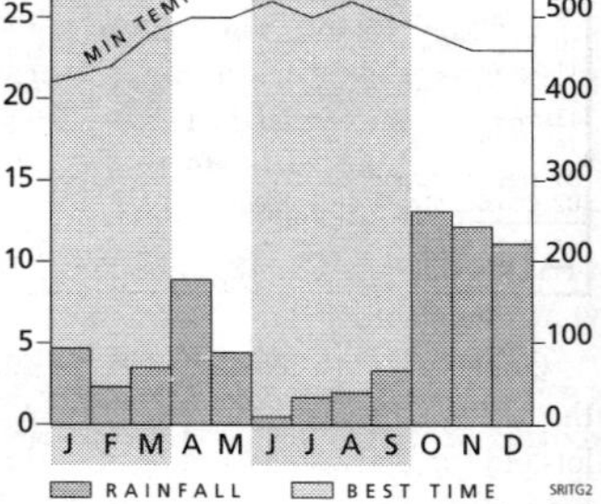

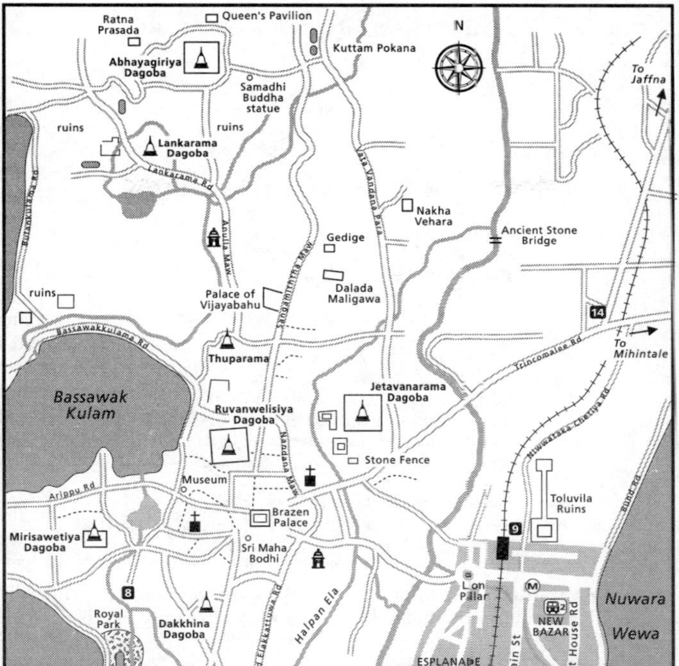

Guides about Rs 300 for 3-4 hrs; ask at the Ticket Office or Museum. There are lots of little drink stalls around; the ones near the dagobas are more expensive.

The Archaeological Museum (see below) is central to the site and makes a good starting point for a tour. Immediately to its W is the Basawak Kulam

DUTTHAGAMENU: BATTLE WITH ELARA

A.L. Basham gives a flavour of the Mahavansa's account of the battle between Putthagamenu and Elara's forces:

The city had three moats, And was guarded by a high wall.
Its gate was covered with iron, Hard for foes to shatter.
The elephant knelt on his knees, and battering with his tusks
stone and mortar and brick, he attacked the iron gate.
The Tamils from the watch-tower, threw missiles of every kind,
balls of red hot iron and vessels of molten pitch.
Down fell the molten pitch upon Kandula's back.
In anguish of pain he fled and plunged in a pool of water.
"This is no drinking bout!"cried Gothaimbara.
"Go, batter the iron gate! Batter down the gate!!"
In his pride the best of tuskers took heart and trumpeted loud.
He reared up out of the water and stood on the bank defiant.
The elephant-doctor washed away the pitch, and put on balm.
The King mounted the elephant and rubbed his brow with his hand.
'Dear Kandula, I'll make you the lord of all Ceylon!' he said,
and the beast was cheered, and was fed with the best fodder.
He was covered with a cloth, and he was armoured well
with armour for his back of seven-fold buffalo hide.
On the armour was placed a skin soaked in oil.
Then, trumpeting like thunder, he came on, fearless of danger.
He pierced the door with his tusks. With his feet he trampled the threshold.
And the gate and the lintel crashed loudly to earth.

Tank, the oldest artificial lake in the city, built by King Pandukabhaya in the 4th century BC.

Ruvanwelisiya Dagoba is opposite the museum. It was begun by King Dutthagamenu (Dutugemunu) to house relics; priests from all over India were recorded as being present at the enshrinement of the relics in 140 BC. A huge dagoba, it is surrounded by the remains of lots of buildings. You can see the columns often no more than 500 cm in height dotted around in the grass underneath huge rain trees where monkeys play. The dome is 80m in diameter at its base and 53m high. A small passage leads to the relic chamber. At the cardinal points are four 'chapels' which were reconstructed in 1873, when renovation started. The restoration has flattened the shape of the dome, and some of the painting is of questionable style, but it remains a remarkably striking monument. Today, you may find watching the dagoba being 'white washed' – an interesting spectacle.

Mirisawetiya Dagoba (originally from the 2nd century BC) is near the *Tissawewa Rest House*, 1 km to the SW. It was completely rebuilt during the reign of King Kasyapa V in 930 AD. Surrounded by the ruins of monasteries on three sides, there are some superb sculptures of Dhyani Buddhas in the shrines of its chapels. Renovation work on the dagoba started in 1979 with support from Unesco. To the S is the **Tissawewa** lake (150 ha) built by King Devanampiya Tissa. You can either go S along the tank *bund* or round by the road to the Royal Park and Issurumuniyagala.

Issurumuniyagala This small group of striking black rocks is one of the most attractive and peaceful places in town. It also has some outstanding sculpture. The temple, carved out of solid rock, houses a large statue of the seated Buddha. On the terraces outside is a small square pool; there are also some beautifully carved elephants, showing great individual character. Note also, the carvings beside the main entrance just above the water level.

Gleaming White Bells

Dagobas are one of the striking features of the land. They are everywhere and range in size from tiny village structures to the enormous monuments at Ruvanwelisiya at Anuradhapura and Maheseya at Mihintale. Even in nature the stone of the canonball tree fruit is a perfectly formed white dagoba.

There are of course many reasons why they stand out in a landscape – partly for their position, partly their size but mostly for their colour – a dazzling white. Most are beautifully maintained and are often repainted before important festivals.

It is no easy job to paint a large dagoba. A lime whitewash is used. Elaborate bamboo scaffolding cocoons the spire linked to the base by rickety bamboo ladders. Bamboo is ideal as it can be bent to conform to the shape of the dome and the lightness makes the ladders easily moveable. A team of about five painters assembles on the ladder which is about 20m in height. Four men are deployed with ropes attached at the top and midpoints to give it some form of stability. At each stage, a painter is responsible for about 3m of the surface in height, and an arm's width. The topmost 1.5m of the painter's patch is covered first. Then he takes three steps down the ladder to cover the bottom 1.5m. Once completed, the bamboo structure is moved an arm's width round and the whole process starts again.

The end result is a gleaming white bell standing out majestically against the green of the countryside and the blue of the sky. Sadly not all the dagobas have yet been restored, their red brick or plain plastered suface still dull in comparison with those that have been returned to their original condition.

Museum to the left of entrance. Entry Rs 25. Some of the best sculptures in Anuradhapura, found here, are now housed in the small museum, including a horse's head on the shoulders of a man, the superbly executed '*Kapila*'. Perhaps the most famous of the sculptures is 'the lovers'.

King Elara's tomb From Issurumuniyagala return E to the road and back towards the centre, passing after 1 km, the tomb also known as **Dakkhina dagoba** (Southern dagoba). The Chola Tamil king had captured Anuradhapura in 205 BC, setting up a Tamil Kingdom which lasted over 40 years. Sinhalese kingdoms in the S eventually rose against him, and he was killed in a single-handed duel by King Dutthagamenu, who gave him full battle honours.

Sri Maha Bodhi tree 800m to the N is one of Sri Lanka's most sacred sites. The 'Bo' ('Bodhi') tree or Pipal (*Ficus religiosa*) was planted as a cutting brought from India by Mahinda's sister, the **Princess Sanghamitta**, at some point after 236 BC. Guardians have kept uninterrupted watch over the tree ever since. There are other Bo trees around the Sri Maha Bodhi which stands on the highest terrace. In Apr a large number of pilgrims arrive to make offerings during the *Snana Puja*, and to bathe the tree with milk. Every 12th year the ceremony is particularly auspicious.

A broad, paved path leads from the point you leave your shoes. It is shaded by a tent like structure – tasselled ropes crossing the path coloured yellow, blue, red, white and orange. Groups of drummers in the courtyard may approach visitors and demand payment for performing. You can only see the top of the Bo tree which is supported by an elaborate metal structure and is surrounded by brass railings which are bedecked with colourful prayer flags and smaller strips of cloth which pilgrims tie in expectation of prayers being answered.

Brazen Palace Immediately opposite is the Brazen Palace which is combined with this site; you have to take the

Gateway leading to the Sacred Tree, Anuradhapura
Illustrated by Rev W Urwick in 1885

eastern gate and walk out over a moon stone. The name refers to its now-disappeared roof, reputedly made of bronze. It is the most remarkable of many monastic buildings scattered across the site. Described in the *Mahavansa* as having nine storeys, there are 600 pillars laid out over an area 70m sq. The pillars, just under 4m high, supported the first floor. You need imagination to visualize the scale of the building as it may have been as there is no hint of its structural style or decoration. The walls between the pillars were made of brick while the upper floors were wooden. Built by Dutthagamenu, it was the heart of the monastic life of the city, the **Maha Vihara**. Much of what is visible today is the reconstruction of King Parakramabahu I in the last quarter of the 11th century, making use of the remnants of former buildings.

Nuwarawewa The road E between the Brazen Palace and the Bo tree goes to the new town, the railway station and the largest of Anuradhapura's artificial lakes (1,000 ha) completed about 20 BC. Going E from the Brazen Palace (along the Mihintale/Trincomalee Rd), a left fork after 800m goes N to the ruined Jetavanarama Dagoba. Along the Malwatu Oya, N of the road are ruins of ancient stone bridges with pillars and slabs – these may have been used as elephant crossings.

Jetavanarama Dagoba was named after the first Buddhist monastery (names of the Jetavanarama and Abhayagiriya dagobas are sometimes reversed). The largest dagoba in Anuradhapura (considered by some to be the highest in the world) it is also being renovated with help from Unesco. Started by King Mahasena (AD 275-292), the paved platform on which it stands covers more than 3 ha and it has a diameter of over 100m. In 1860 Emerson Tennet, in his book *Ceylon*, calculated that it had enough bricks to build a 3m high brick wall 25 cm thick from London to Edinburgh, equal to the distance from the southern tip of Sri Lanka to Jaffna and back down the coast to Trincomalee! Its massive scale was designed in a competitive spirit to rival the orthodox Maha Vihara.

Thuparama Continuing N from the Jetavanarama Dagoba, turn left at the crossroads to the site's oldest dagoba to house the right collar-bone of the Buddha. Built by Devanampiya, the 19m high dagoba has retained its beautiful bell shape, despite restoration work. It is surrounded by concentric circles of graceful granite monolithic pillars of a Vatadage which was added in the 7th century, possibly originally designed to support an over-arching thatched cover. It is a centre of active pilgrimage, decorated with flags and lights. Immediately to its NE was the original **Dalada Maligawa** where the Tooth Relic was first enshrined when it was brought to Ceylon in AD 313. Fa Hien gave a vivid description of its display, but only the stone columns remain.

Samadhi Buddha The road N (Sanghamitta Maw) goes 1.5 km through the site of the 11th century palace of **Vijayabahu I** to the superb statue of the serene Buddha with an expression depicting 'extinction of feeling and compassion'; some think the expression changes as the sun's light moves across it. Roofed to protect it from the weather, it probably dates from the 4th century AC. It is one of the more active religious sites it is adorned with lotus buds and payer flags.

Kuttan-Pokuna Across the Vatavandana Para, a little to the N, you turn right for the two ponds – recently restored 8th and 9th century ritual baths with steps from each side descending to the water. They were probably for the use of the monastery or for the university nearby. Though called 'twin' ponds, one is over 10m longer than the other. You can see the underground water supply channel at one end of the second bath.

Abhayagiriya Dagoba is left from the crossroads. It is 400m round and was supposedly 135m high in its original form (part of the pinnacle has disappeared); it is now about 110m high. Built in 88 BC by Vattagamani (and later restored by Parakramabahu I in the 12th century), it has two splendid sculpted *dwarapalas* (guardians) at the threshold. The dagoba and its associated monastery were built in an attempt to weaken the political hold of the Hinayana Buddhists and to give shelter to monks of the Mahayana school. It was considered an important seat of Buddhist learning and the Chinese traveller/monk Fa Hien visiting it in the 5th century noted that there were 5,000 monks in residence.

Ratna Prasada To the W of the Abhayagiriya Dagoba are the ruins of the monastery. The area had once been the 'undersirable' outskirts of Anuradhapura where the cremation grounds were sited. In protest against the King's rule, an ascetic community of monks set up a *tapovana* community of which this is an architectural example. Though they lived an austere life, the buildings here were superbly crafted and curiously, contained elaborately carved lavatories (examples in the Archaelogical Museum)! This type of monastery typically had two pavilions connected by a stone bridge within a high-walled enclosure which contained a pond. The main entrance was from the E, with a porch above the entrance. Here the Ratna Prasada did not remain a peaceful haven but was the scene of bloody massacres when a rebellious group took refuge with the monks and were subsequently beheaded by the King's men; their turn to have their heads roll in the dust followed another bloody revolt. The nearby **Mahasena Palace** has a particularly fine carved stone tablet and one of the most beautifully carved moonstones, see page 73, though the protective railing surrounding it makes photography difficult.

You can return to the Museums by taking the Lankarama Rd to the S.

Museums

Archaeological Museum in the old colonial headquarters. Open 0800-1700 (closed Tues). An excellent small museum, with a large collection including some beautiful pieces of sculpture and finds from Mihintale. Well laid out, occasional informative labels and some fascinating exhibits. Statues from several sites, moonstones (see note in introduction), implements, and outside in the garden, beautifully sculpted guardstones and meticulously designed latrines. Separate latrine plinths were used for urinals, solid waste and bidets. Under each immaculately carved platform was a succession of pots containing sand, charcoal and limestone to purify the waste. Mr KS Pereira is very knowledgeable and will act as your guide (a small payment, eg Rs 100, is gratefully received).

Folk Museum reflects rural life in the N Central Province with a large collection of vessels used by villagers in Rajarata.

Local festivals

Apr: *Snana piya* at Sri Maha Bodhi.

Jun: at the full moon in *Poson*, the introduction of Buddhism to Sri Lanka is celebrated with huge processions when many pilgrims visit the town.

Local information

Accommodation

There are 2 main clusters of hotels – along Rowing Club Rd and the junction with Harishchandra Mawatha, and along Freeman Maw. Both are some distance from the railway and the new bus station (Freeman Maw is further S and more remote) but are often full in season. At the top end you can choose between a conventional hotel or a *Rest House* with character. Alternatively opt for the new *Rest House* in Mihintale, see page 209.

B *Miridya*, Rowing Club Rd, T 2112, F 2519, 40 rm, some a/c, some with view over Lake Nuwarawewa, Rs 1,600 (more for extra bed, bath tub), 4-bed rooms good value, restaurant, bar, exchange, entertainment, small book/souvenir shop, lake fishing, pleasant atmosphere and attractive gardens, the most comfortable hotel in Anuradhapura, popular with package tourists.

C *Nuwarawewa Rest House*, New Town, T 2565 (Reserve direct or T Colombo 583133/5, F 587613), nr New Town, on the edge of the lake in attractive garden, 60 a/c rm (US$38), restaurant serves good mild curries (ask for a selection), evening meals European but curries to order, bar, exchange, shop, entertainment, clean pool, friendly and helpful staff though some visitors found it a "dull environment"; slightly cheaper **C *Tissawewa Rest House***, nr tank, T 2299, F 3265, Reservations (see above), 25 comfortable, clean rm (some small, some suites), 7 a/c (US$25-30), formerly the *Grand Hotel* undergoing refurbishing, the charming colonial house with some period furniture (and interesting eccentricities on the 1st flr terrace), beautifully situated in a secluded parkland with lots of monkeys, good restaurant (within the religious area hence no alcohol served), restaurant food can sometimes be bland rice and curry but complaints produce excellent results, great string hoppers for breakfast (must order night before), exchange, bike hire (Rs 60/half day) all guests may use *Nuwarawewa's* clean pool – ask at *Tissawewa* reception, towels supplied, excellent, rec, good value so often heavily booked, only drawback is the sometimes excessively tip-seeking nature of the staff; **C-D *Rajarata***, Rowing Club Rd, re-building in progress in 1995.

D *Ashok*, 20 Rowing Club Rd, T 2753, 20 spacious rm (Rs 700), 2 a/c some with view of tank, bathroom rather dated, no hot water, functional restaurant with TV, lacks ambiance (meals about Rs 220), popular especially for wedding parties, helpful manager; **D *Chanika***, 388/25 Harishchandra Maw, down an alley, T 2535, 5 rm in an old house, 1 a/c (Rs 500-750), not rec as most (particularly unmodernized bathrooms) are in a poor state, 20-rm extension planned which may be a great improvement; **D *Cottage Tourist Rest House*** 388/38 Harishchandra Maw, T 5363, 5 rm, small but very good value (Rs 550); **D *Kondamalie Guest House***, 388/42 Harishchandra Maw, T 2029, 7 rm, 1 a/c (Rs 500-600), good verandah restaurant, warmly rec; **D *Randiya***, Rowing Club Rd, 10 rm, 2 a/c with bath and TV (Rs 750), restaurant (pricey); **D *Shalini Tourist Inn***, 41/388 Harishchandra Maw, T 2425, opp Water Tower Stage 1, 7 clean rm in modern house, some with hot water (Rs 450-650), good food, well kept, keen owner, bike hire, highly rec.

Budget hotels: have rooms with shared facilities but may have some rooms with attached shower room and toilet. **E *Indra Inn***, 745 Freeman Maw, along a lane S, 1 km from New Bus Stand, 3 clean rm; **E *Railway Retiring Rooms***, 10 good-sized rm (Rs 300) upstairs, bathrooms have seen better days but an option at the cheap end, only 1 train at night, so quite quiet, security-conscious pleasant caretaker, rooms available for non-passengers; **E *Swan***, 310/1 Harishchandra Mawatha, on Bank Site, T 2058, 5 rm which are often let to long-term guests, good Chinese restaurant; **E-F *Shanti Guest House***, 891 Mailagas Junc, Freeman Maw, T 2515, 1.5 km from New Bus Stand, 4 km railway (about Rs 30 and 60 respectively by 3-wheeler/taxi) or phone on arrival for free taxi, 14 rm (Rs 150-350), will arrange tours to Mihintale (Rs 400) and to see wild elephants (Rs 800/group), also car/bike hire, basic but friendly, and one of the cheapest, popular; **F *Youth Hostel***, Travellers' Hotel, 15 Jafna Junc, has 15 beds.

Places to eat

Varied choice of menu at the following hotels: *Miridya* and the 2 *Rest Houses*, which needs prior notice, offer reasonable food and pleasant seating; no alcohol at *Tissawewa*. *Kondamalie Guest House*, pleasant, open-air seating (take mosquito repellent!), popular with budget travellers.

Chinese: *Swan* upstairs, good food, generous portions, spotlessly clean, reasonable prices.

Cheaper meals at numerous eating places in town – some of these have a couple of rooms to take in guests during the festival season.

● **Banks & money changers**
Some in New Town, nr Bank Site roundabout incl: **Hatton Bank** is on Main St, opp the Police Station; **People's Bank**, open 0900-1600, accepts TCs and sterling but not credit cards for cash, exchange facilities at correct rate, tourists are offered special treatment and transactions can be completed in about 10 mins even when the bank is very busy.

● **Transport**
Local Hire: most guesthouses and hotels in the New Town will arrange cycle hire (about Rs 125/day), and sometimes, motorbike (Rs 300), car hire (Rs 400). 3-wheelers from station to Bank Site charge about Rs 25 and to Freeman Maw hotels, Rs 60; from Museum to Bank Site Rs 60-70; from Bus station to Freeman Maw, Rs 30, and to Bank Site, about Rs 50. **Bus**: frequent service between Old and New Bus Stands.

Train Colombo: *Rajarata Rajini*, 86, daily, 0505, 4½ hrs; *Yaldevi*, 78, daily, 1428, 4¼ hrs; 868, daily, 1540, 5 hrs. **Jaffna**: *Yaldevi*, 77, daily, 0945, 5 hrs; *91 Mail*, daily, 0045, 6 hrs. **Talaimannar**: 463, daily, 1335, 5¼ hrs; *97 Night Mail*, daily, 0112, 4 hrs. **NB** Services to Jaffna and Talaimannar may be disrupted.

Road From Dambulla, the road surface is good and there is usually little traffic. **Bus**: several to **Colombo** (6½ hrs) and **Kandy** (5 hrs) from Old Bus Stand. **Mihintale** has a frequent service; **Trincomalee** a daily service. In normal times the journey to **Jaffna** is 6 hrs. **NB** The service is currently completely unreliable.

ROUTES Take the **A12** out of Anuradhapura to Mihintale.

Mihintale

11 km E of Anuradhapura, Mihintale (Mahinda's hill) is revered as the place where Mahinda converted King Devanampiya Tissa to Buddhism in 243 BC, thereby enabling Buddhism to spread to the whole island. It is a beautiful site. The legend tells how King Tissa was chasing a stag during a hunting expedition. The stag reached Mihintale and fled up the hillside followed by the King until he reached a place surrounded by hills, where he was astonished to find a man. It was Mahinda, Asoka's son, who had come to preach the Buddha's teachings.

In the cool of the evening, it is certainly worth walking the short distance to the sanctuary. You can see the huge dagoba from miles around. As well as being important historically, it is an important religious site. It is well worth visiting not least because it is largely bypassed by tourists.

Local festivals
Jun: *Poson* at full-moon in Jun is of particularly importance to Buddhists who commemorate the arrival of Buddhism on the island. The width of the steps indicate the large number of pilgrims who visited the sacred site on special occasions in the past. Today tens of thousands flock to climb to the sacred spot, chanting as they go: *Buddham saranam gachchaami; Dhammam saranam gachchaami; Sangam saranam gachchaami*, meaning "In the Buddha I seek refuge, In Dhamma I seek refuge, In the Sangha I seek refuge".

The hilltop sacred site is close to the Anuradhapura-Trincomalee Rd. At the junction with the village road there are statues of six of the principle characters of the site. The minor road leading to the site has ruins of a **Hospital** with a stone tank for oil and herbal baths on the right and evidence of a quincunx **vihara** to the left. There is a small **Museum** nearby which has erratic opening times.

Approach There are about 1,840 granite steps to the top but they are very shallow and it is much less of a climb than it first looks. About half the steps can be avoided if you have your own transport, by driving around the back of the lower car park. An old road leads to flat area at the refectory level. There are drinks kiosks near the car park. **Entry** Open 0600-1800. You don't need a guide for this site; allow 1½-2 hrs for the visit.

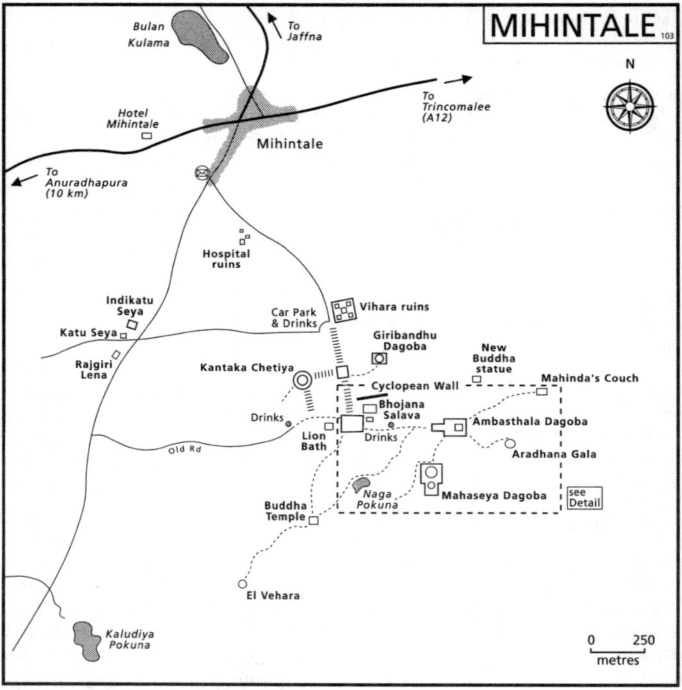

The climb starts gently, rising in a broad stairway of 350 steps shaded by frangipani trees which lead to the first platform. Further steps to the right take you up to an open area with Kantaka Chetiya.

Kantaka Chetiya, the earliest *stupa* here. A board at this point states that it was built by King Lajji Tissa at the improbably early date of 424-434 BC, more than 200 years before Buddhism was brought to Sri Lanka. Excavated in 1932-35, it had been severely damaged. Over 130m in circumferance, today it is only about 12m high compared with its original height of perhaps 30m. There is some fine carving: note the beautiful sculptures at the four cardinal points – geese, dwarves, and a variety of animals – and several rock cells around it.

The second terrace Returning to the first platform, steeper steps lead to a large refectory terrace. As you climb up you can see the impressive outer cyclopean wall of the complex (it takes under 10 mins from the car park, at a gentle pace).

As an alternative to the steps to get to the refectory level, take a faint footpath to the left between the second and third flights. This crosses an open grassy area. Walk to the end and you will see the lake, green with algae. A path to the left takes you towards the **Giribandhu Chetiya Kiri Vehara**. Largely ruined and grassed over on the N side, it is not really worth a visit. You can look down on the lower car park and the quincunx. To the right, the path approaches the refectory from the rear and you pass a massive stone trough.

MIHINTALE SACRED CENTRE

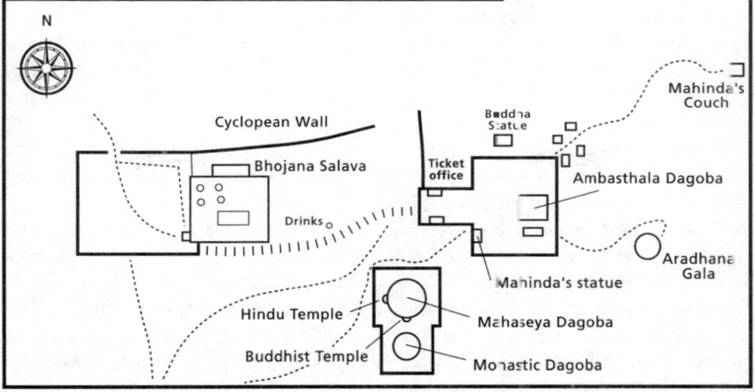

The Refectory Immediately on the left is the Relic House and the rectangular **Bhojana Salava** (Monks' refectory). There is a stone aqueduct and a trough which may have been used for storing water.

The square **Chapter House**/'Conversation Hall' with signs of 48 pillars and a 'throne' platform, immediately to the N, is where the monks and lay members met. This has the bases of a series of evenly spaced small brick dagobas. At the entrance, stone slabs covered in 10th century inscriptions on granite give detailed rules governing the sacred site.

The flat grassy terrace which can also be approached by car from the S up the old paved road or steps down from the Kantaka Chetiya, is dotted with trees and the outlines of three small shrines.

The **Sinha Pokuna** (Lion Bath) to the S of the terrace is about 2m sq and 1.8m deep and has excellent carvings in the form of a frieze around the bottom of the tank, of elephants, lions and warriors. The finest, however, is the 2m high rampant lion to the W whose mouth forms the spout.Water was gathered in the tank by channelling and feeding it through the small mystic gargoyle similar to the one that can be seen at Sigiriya.

The main path up to the Ambasthala Dagoba up the long flight of steps, starts by the 'Conversation Hall' in the Square.

After a 5-min climb a path leads off to the right, round the hllside. Take this and walk through cool forest to the **Naga Pokuna** (Snake Pond) with a five-headed cobra carving which you can still make out. It is a 40m pool carved out of solid rock which stored water for the monastery and, some believe, where King Tissa would have bathed. At one end is a very small tank, now without water; apparently this was where the Queen would bathe. It is a peaceful and beautiful place which you might like to visit after climbing to the sacred centre of Mihintale, which is another 2 mins climb.

Ambasthala Dagoba Straight ahead at the heart of the complex is the the 'mango tree' dagoba, the holiest part of the site, built at the traditional meeting place of King Tissa and Ashoka's son Mahinda. Foreigners are charged Rs 50 entry fee and shoes must be removed. The monk in his office makes frequent loud-speaker announcements for donations from pilgrims – these donations have funded the erection of a large Buddha statue overlooking the central area, in 1991. The bronze Buddhas are gifts from Thailand.

The **Sela Cetiya** (rock stupa) at the site of the original mango tree has a replica of the Buddha's footprint. It is quite small and is surrounded by a double circle of crowned pillars – there is a gilt railing covered in prayer flags and with a scattering of pilgrims' coins.

A path leads out of the NE corner of the compound between a small cluster of monks' houses down a rough boulder track to **Mahinda's cave**, less than 10 mins walk away. A stall selling local herbal and forest product remedies (including 'a cure for arrack!') is sometimes set up halfway to the cave which is formed out of an extraordinary boulder, hollowed out underneath to create a narrow platform at the very end of a ridge above the plain below. From the stone 'couch', known as Mahinda's bed, there are superb views to the N across the tanks and forested plains of the Dry Zone. You have to retrace your steps to the Ambasthala compound.

From the NW corner of the compound a path with rudimentary steps cut in the bare granite rock leads to the summit of the **Aradhana Gala** (Meditation Rock). It is a very steep climb, and if you have no socks, very hot on the feet; a strong railing makes access quite secure. There is nothing much to see on the rock but there are superb views from the top, especially across the compound to the Mahaseya Dagoba, which is at the same height.

Mahaseya dagoba A short flight of steep steps from the SW corner of the compound, just beyond a small temple with a modern portrayal of Mahinda meeting King Tissa at the mango tree, leads up to the summit (310m) with the Mahaseya Dagoba. According to legend this was built on the orders of King Tissa as a reliquary for a lock of the Buddha's hair or for relics of Mahinda. The renovated dagoba which dominates the skyline, commands superb views back towards Anuradhapura to the SW. Another monk will ask for donations here (anything above Rs 100 is recorded in a book).

On the S side of the main dagoba is a smaller brick dagoba while abutting it on its S side is a small Buddhist temple. To the W side is a Hindu temple with modern painted images of four Hindu deities, Ganesh, Saman, Vishnu and Kataragama.

After collecting your shoes, look out for a rock inscription (showing the allocation of land in the area). Immediately below this and opposite a lime-washed building is a small path which leads to the Naga Pokuna, mentioned above.

Local information

● Accommodation

B-C *Hotel Mihintale*, Anuradhapura Rd, nr crossroads, 10 km from Anuradhapura, 1 km from the sacred site, T 025 6599, 10 well-furnished a/c rm, (US$20-30), good-value 4-bed family rm ($36), to be extended by 40 rm and swimming pool (completion due end 1995), good, reasonably-priced open-sided restaurant (meals about Rs 100), pleasant atmosphere, excellent value, no credit cards or TCs.

ROUTES An A road runs E to the coast at Trincomalee but due to the uncertain political situation this is not often used. Buses were running in the daytime in mid-1995, but drivers are extremely reluctant to take the road until the political climate improves.

ROUTES **Habarana & Sigiriya to Polonnaruwa** From Mihintale the **A9** goes S to rejoin the Kandy-Jaffna road and continues S as far as Maradankadawala. The **A11** turns left and passes the ancient site of Ritigala to join the **A6** (Kurunegala-Trincomalee road) at Habarana.

Ritigala

The marked Ritigala hills (*Alt* 810m) can be seen clearly to the N from the road; the 8 km track up to it leaves the A11 at the village of Galapitagala.

The forest hermitage complex (see page 82), where Brahmi inscriptions in the caves date the site from the 3rd-2nd century BC was occupied by *Pan-*

sakulika monks. The structures found here include the typical double-platforms joined by bridges, stone columns, pavements, bathing ponds and monks' cells.

Habarana

(24 km; *STD Code* 066) Habarana is an important crossroads, though apart from a scattering of hotels and rest houses and its accessibility has little to recommend it. It is the quality of the accommodation and the central location which make this an excellent place to stay if you are travelling by car and groups also often spend 1 night here. There is an attractive Buddhist temple with excellent paintings. Behind the tank next to the temple is a rock with superb views from the top, over the forest to Sigiriya.

• **Accommodation A** *The Lodge*, T 8321, F Colombo 447087, 150 tastefully decorated rm in bungalows (US$70-80), excellent facilities and grounds, good service, highly rec; **B** *Village Habarana*, T 8316, F Colombo 447087, 106 cottages (US$45-55), extensive gardens, excellent food; **D** ***Habarana Rest House*** (CHC), Polonnaruwa Crossroads, T 8355, Reservations, T Colombo 323501, F 422732, 4 rm ($7), simple, clean, reasonable food (meal Rs 200), good value.

ROUTES Continue S along the **A9** and turn left at Inamaluwa to see the rock fort at Sigiriya, 11 km. The road from Mihintale has a good surface, the journey takes about 1½ hrs.

SIGIRIYA

(*STD Code* 066) The rewards of Sigiriya (pronounced See-gee-ree-ya) justify the steep climb. There are stunning views. Very early morning is beautiful – the site still very quiet until 0730, but the late afternoon light is better for the frescoes. In addition to the rock fortress, there are extensive grounds at the base and the whole is enclosed by an outer moat which contains water. UNESCO workers are busy with conservation of the site.

The small **museum** and the temple at the base, are free. There is the **Mapagala Rock** with evidence of dressed stone work, a dagoba and other ruins on the roadside just over a km away. The **Pidurangala Royal Cave Temple** Buddhist Meditation centre (1.5 km) is signposted from the car park. The cave on the rock Pidurangala where there had been an ancient monastery still has a stupa with a 10th century reclining Buddha and an inscription dating from the 1st century BC. These, and other finds of early settlement in RamaKale nearby point at the ancient nature of the spot chosen by Kasyapa for his palace fortress. The water gardens and moat are a delight, not least because they afford the visitor more room to move around before you arrive at the crush to climb the rock.

Entry

The Gate to the site opens at 0600 but the ticket office only opens around 0700; if you wish to make an early start (avoiding groups which start arriving by 0800) buy your ticket on the previous day if you arrive in time. US$7 (may be reduced for students with ID). Cultural Triangle Tickets to all three sites including Sigiriya, US$30, see page 73. Allow 2 hrs for a visit. There can be long queues on public holidays and the rock can be very crowded from mid-morning. **NB** Women are advised to wear shorts or trousers as the strong wind plays havoc with skirts much to the entertainment of local lads! **Warning** Visitors suffering from a fear of heights are advised not to attempt the climb. Young children may find the final ascent rather frightening. Not suitable for the frail or unfit.

Further reading

Sigiriya, by RH De Silva, Ceylon, Department of Archaeology, 1971.

Guides

There are about 65 licensed guides here so competition is fierce; it is worth getting one. Charge, about Rs 300 per 2 hrs.

Carry your drink if you want to avoid paying an excessive price at the kiosk half way up. Refreshments are available at the *Rest House* nearby; it is a good place to stop for breakfast after an early morning visit to the site.

Background

The vast flat-topped 200m high **Lion Rock** (*Sinha-Giri*) stands starkly above the surrounding countryside of the central forest with magnificent views over the Dry Zone and S to the Central Highlands. It was an exceptional natural site for a fortress, taking its name because lions were believed to occupy the caves. Hieroglyphs suggest that it was occupied by humans from very early times, long before the fortress was built.The royal citadel (477-495 AD) was surrounded by an impressive wall and a double moat; the city had the Palace and quarters for the ordinary people who built the royal pavilions, pools and fortifications. The top of the rock has a surface area of 1.5 ha built on the precipitous edge.

When the citadel ceased to be a palace, it was inhabited by monks until 1155, and then abandoned. It was rediscovered by archaeologists in 1828. The Mahavansa records that King Kasyapa, having killed his father to gain the

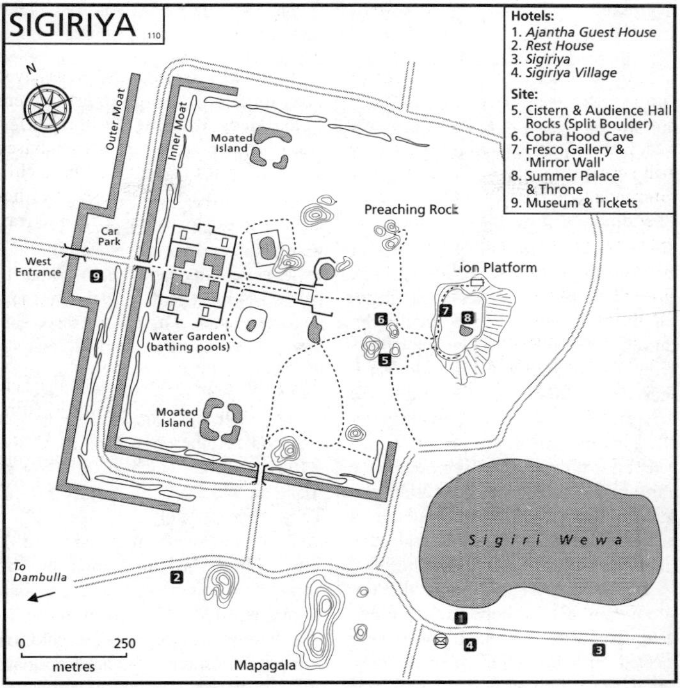

throne, lived in terror that his half-brother, who had taken refuge in India, would return to kill him. He did come back, after 18 years, to find that Kasyapa had built a combination of pleasure palace and massive fortress. Kasyapa came down from the hill to face his half brother's army on elephant back. Mistakenly thinking he had been abandoned, he killed himself with his dagger.

At Sigiriya, Kasyapa intended to reproduce on earth the legendary palace of *Kubera*, the God of Wealth, and so had it decorated lavishly with impressive gardens, cisterns and ponds. Excavations have revealed surface and underground drainage systems. For the famous frescoes he gathered together the best artists of his day.

Water, a scarce commodity in the Dry Zone, was conserved and diverted cleverly through pipes and rock-cut channels to provide bathing pools for the palace above and enhance the gardens below with pools and fountains. It is thought that on the islands in the two pools in the water garden near the entrance, stood pavilions, while the shallow marble pools reflected the changing patterns of the clouds.

Apart from the exceptional frescoes, it is worth noting that the entire site was built over a period of 7 years and effectively abandoned after 18 years. The engineering skills required for the water and fountain gardens as well as lifting water by a series of bamboo lifts to the top of the rock, were remarkable for the time.

Approach

At the western approach to the rock are the 5th century **water gardens**, being restored by the Central Cultural Fund sponsored by UNESCO, with walks, pavilions, ponds and fountains which are gravity fed from the moats as they were 1,500 years ago. You can see the secret changing room doors!

A straight path leads through the group of four fountain gardens with small water jets (originally 5th century), some with pretty lotuses attracting a number of water birds. Finally the flower garden with flower beds and flowering trees including *Azedirachta Indica* (bearing red flowers and flat seed pods), *Cassia Siamea* and yellow-flowered *Nerium Oleander*. To the right as you walk up to the rock is a **miniature water garden**. The whole area (including the moat and drive) is immaculate. It is difficult to visualize the winter palace as there are no visible foundations.

The Rock It is easy to forget that the site was in fact developed as a massive defensive fortress. Lookout points were located on ledges clinging to the rock and as you climb up you will see there is a massive rock, close to the Guard House, wedged with stone supports which could be knocked out to enable it to crash on the enemy far below.

Base of the rock Before reaching the steps the path goes through the boulder garden where clusters of rocks, including the **Preaching rock** with 'seats', are marked with rows of notches and occasional 'gashes'. These may have been used for decorating the area with lamps during festivals.

To the right at the start of the climb, under a natural overhang is the **Cobra Hood** rock which has a drip ledge inscription in Brahmi script dating from the 2nd century BC. The floor and ceiling have lime plaster, the latter is decorated with paintings and floral patterns. A headless Buddha statue is placed horizontally; it is thought to have been a monk's cell originally.

The **Cistern** and the **Audience Hall** rocks are parts of a single massive boulder which had split, and half of which had fallen away; the exposed flat surface had a 'throne' at one end and came to be called the Audience Hall while the upper part of the standing half, retained the rectangular cistern.

The climb begins in earnest with steps leading through the Elephant Gate on well-maintained brick-lined stairways and up to the second checkpoint immediately below the gallery containing the frescoes.

Steps then lead up to the **Fresco gallery**, painted under an overhanging rock and reached by a spiral staircase which was made in 1938. Be patient: the steps are not really adequate for the numbers visiting at certain times of the day. Of the 500 or so frescoes, which vie with those in Ajanta in Western India, only 21 remain. They are remarkably well preserved, as they are sheltered from the elements in a niche. In the style of Ajanta, the first drawing was done on wet plaster and then painted with red, yellow, green and black. The figures are 'portraits' of celestial nymphs and attendants above clouds – offering flowers, scattering petals or bathing. Here, guides are keen to point out the girl with three hands and another with three nipples. Some paintings were destroyed by a madman in 1967 and you can see pictures of this in the small museum. Half the murals were undergoing restoration and were inaccessible to visitors in 1995.

The **Mirror Wall** Immediately beyond the foot of the spiral staircase the path is protected on the outer side by the 3m high, highly polished plaster wall believed to have been coated with lime, egg white and wild honey. After 15 centuries it still has a reflective sheen. Visitors and pilgrims between (mostly 7th and 11th century) wrote verses in Sinhalese – 'graffiti' prompted by the frescoes and by verses written by previous visitors. Some, today, find this section a little disappointing. It is also difficult to stop and look at the graffiti because of the pressure of people when the rock is 'busy'.

The **Lion Terrace** marks the halfway point of the climb where there is welcome shade and welcome cool drinks (expensive at Rs 50). The wire cage is apparently to protect people from wild bees. You can see their nests under the metal staircase.

Final stairway The main path takes you to the top of the rock up the steep W and N sides.The final stage of the ascent on the N ledge leads through the giant plaster-covered brick paws of the lion (the remainder of the animal has disappeared); the size of the paws gives some clue to the height of the lion's head. It is worth studying the remaining climb to the summit. You can clearly see the outline of small steps cut into the granite. The king was apparently scared of heights so these steps would also have been enclosed by a 3m high mirror wall. Here was the lion's gate after which the place is named: *Si* (shortened form of lion) *Giriya* (throat). The stairway of 25 flights is mostly on iron steps with a small guard rail and is steep (particularly in one place where a small flight resemble a ships ladder!); small children can find this quite frightening.

At the top are the ruins of the **Summer Palace** – the foundations reveal the likely size which appears very small especially when compared with the size of the stone throne underneath it. There was the granite throne, dancing terraces, a small pool fed by rain water, drinking water tanks, sleeping quarters of the concubines, a small flower garden and precariously positioned platforms for guards. If you walk to the sign on the W, there is a very good birds-eye view of the winter palace and its surrounding moat. Retrace your steps to the second checkpoint. Just below this, the path splits to the left from where you can get a view of the king's audience chamber and his anteroom. Once again, there is a huge throne in a semicircle where his advisors would sit – justice was swift and often brutal. Immediately below the audience chamber was another granite slab: this was the place of execution. Again to the left is the antechamber which was cooled by a tank of water cut into the rock above the ceiling. It too would have been covered in frescoes. Much of the construction is in brick, faced with lime plaster but there are sections built with limestone slabs which would have been carried up. The upper structures which have disappeared were probably wooden.

Finally you exit through the cobra gate – a huge, overhanging rock. All around this area you can see steps cut into the rock for soldiers to guard the palace. The King apparently feared attack not only from his half-brother but also from enemies within his palace.

Museums

The small Archaeological Museum has been rather badly neglected and is not particularly impressive.

Local information

● Accommodation

The best two are 1 km away. They are very comfortable with restaurants, games, shops and pools.

A *Sigiriya*, 600m beyond entrance to rock, T 8311, F 025 4501, started as a small guest house it now has 80 well decorated rm, few a/c, comfortable rooms arranged around 2 terraces (US$60), likely to leak in heavy rain, food reasonable: good Sri Lankan buffet, in a picturesque location set against the rock, large pleasant garden, attractive wooded setting, range of activities, reasonably good cultural shows (would be better with commentary), seasonal discounts, good pool (though a bit over-chlorinated; non-residents pay Rs 150); **A** *Sigiriya Village*, T 8216 or Colombo 688421, F Colombo 699226, 120 rm with terraces (US$70), good (but pricey) open-sided restaurants (own seasonal vegetables from garden, meat and eggs), 26 acre site, beautifully planted with labelled trees, in thoughtfully-landscaped site with theme clusters of cottages, each with its own colour scheme and accessories (eg 'Rice' – yellow/green scheme with baskets for lampshades etc, rice growing in the garden, typical stooks, tree-house for farmers to scare away animals at night), elephant rides (min 20 people/1 hr), cultural shows, friendly and efficient management catering mainly for large tour groups, ideal for triangle visit. Both hotel pools are open to non-residents for a fee.

C *Sigiriya Rest House* (CHC), T 8324, very nr entrance to monument, 15 clean, simple rm, 2 a/c (US$20), pleasant dining area and terrace, Sri Lankan meals rather bland and over-priced (Rs 300), breakfast after climbing Sigiriya early in the morning better value (Rs 150), quite friendly service although accounting suspect (no receipt given for some items), watch your bill.

Guest houses: **D-E** *Apsara* 3 km N of site is popular with backpackers; **E** *Nilmini Guest House* on the road S, 2 rm, 1 with bath, good food; **F** *Ajantha Guest House*, nr the rock, 5 basic rm (Rs 300-350) reported dirty (1995) indifferent service, eager to sell souvenirs.

● Shopping

There are shops selling bottled water and film but no restaurants other than very basic 'hopper' shops.

● Useful addresses

Tourist Police: Sigiriya Village, Hotel Rd.

● Transport

Air Lionair flies to Sigirya and uses the Air Force strip nr the rock; flies Colombo-Sigiriya Fri, returns Mon, one-way Rs 2,500. It is possible to fly to Trincomalee or elsewhere on a round trip.

Train Inter-city to Dambulla from **Colombo**, a/c, Rs 300; taxi from there to Sigiriya.

Road The journey by car from **Colombo** takes about 3 hrs and from Kandy about 2½ hrs, the latter on a good surface between Matale and Dambulla; you might stop at a spice garden on the way or at Aluvihare just N of Matale (see page 198). **Bus**: non-stop from **Colombo** to Dambulla (3 hrs, Rs 100); then hourly local buses to Sigiriya (30 mins) or 3-wheeler/taxi, Rs 300; daily bus between **Kandy** and Dambulla or Matale and connections to Sigiriya (total 3½-4 hrs); fewer in the afternoon. From Kandy, direct bus daily to Sigiriya.

ROUTES Take the **A11** E from Habarana which skirts the Minneriya-Giritale sanctuary. Stands of gum trees line the road in the valley bottom, with low forest clad hills.

Minneriya-Giritale sanctuary

(*STD Code* 027) 26 km from Polonnaruwa is King Mahasena's magnificent Minneriya Tank (4th century AD), covering 3,000 ha. At the end of the dry season there is little evidence of the Tank which gets covered in weeds. However, you may spot some wildlife along the road, eg giant monitor lizards, or, if you are lucky, see Ceylon Fish-Owl and the large White-bellied Sea-Eagle hovering over the water. At the N end of the tank the *Anusha Curio Factory* has carvings and masks, where many tour buses stop. A further 12 km away is the **Giritale** Tank (7th century AD).

● Accommodation Two upmarket hotels overlook the lake in beautiful settings, and can make a convenient base for Polonnaruwa: **A** *Royal Lotus* with fine views over the Giritale Tank, 56 comfortable a/c rm (US$50), 8 cottages, T 6316 or Colombo 448850, F 448849, good food; **B** *Giritale Hotel*, high above the tank, T/F 6311, 42 rm, most a/c (US$38), superb views from restaurant and terrace, good facilities; **C-D** *Woodside Tour Inn*, on the left, Polonnaruwa Rd, with good clean rooms with fan and net, restaurant serves satisfying meals; **D** *Himalee*, on the right on Polonnaruwa Rd, T 6257, 15 simple rm, helpful staff, pleasant guest house; **E** *Minneriya Inn*, Patapilikanda Rd, simple rooms.

● Transport Road Frequent bus service to Polonnaruwa.

ROUTES Polonnaruwa is another 13 km E along the **A11**.

POLONNARUWA

(*STD Code* 027) The Sinhalese kings of Anuradhapura in 369 AC used Polonnaruwa as their residence but it did not rank as a capital until the 8th century. The Cholas destroyed the Sinhalese Kingdom at the beginning of the 11th century, and taking control of most of the island, they established their capital at Polonnaruwa. In 1056 King Vijayabahu I defeated the Cholas, setting up his own capital in the city. It remained a vibrant centre of Sinhalese culture under his successors, notably Parakramabahu I (1153-1186) who maintained very close ties with India, importing architects and engineers, and Nissankamalla (1187-1196). The rectangular shaped city was enclosed by three concentric walls, and was made attractive with parks and gardens. After them the kingdom went into terminal decline and the city was finally abandoned in 1288, after the tank embankment was breached.

Many of the remains are in an excellent state of repair though several of the residential buildings remain to be excavated. The restoration at the site is by the UNESCO sponsored Central Cultural Fund.

Polonnaruwa owes much of its glory to the artistic conception of King Parakramabahu I who planned the whole as an expression and statement of imperial power. In its imperial intentions, and the brevity of its existence, it may be compared to the great Mughal emperor Akbar's city of Fatehpur Sikri, near Agra. Its great artificial lake provided cooling breezes through the city, water for irrigation and at the same time, defence along its entire W flank. The bund is over 14 km long and 12m high, and the tank irrigates over 90 sq km of paddy fields. Fed by a 40 km long canal and a link from the Giritale tank, it was named after its imperial designer, the Parakrama Samudra (Topa Wewa). Today it attracts numerous water birds, including cormorants and pelicans.

Places of interest

Allow a day to get some impression of this ancient site. You can cover part of the tour by taxi and part on foot. If you are staying at the lakeside *Rest House*, or one of the hotels nearby you can start the tour by going 1.5 km S towards the village.

Entry The Ticket office is near the approach road to the *Rest House*. Cultural Triangle Permit, combined tickets to all important sites available ($30, only worhtwhile if visiting all), single ticket, US$12 (child 5-12, Rs 295); student discount was not available in 1995. Open 0600-1800. The main entrance is now only by the Rest House Group and there is a one-way route N through sacred site; generally quite well signed. Allow about 3 hrs. For guides, ask at the ticket office.

The **Southern Group** You will first see the giant 3.5m high **statue** of a bearded figure, now believed to be **King Parakramabahu** himself, looking away from the city he restored, holding in his hand the palm leaf manuscript of the 'Book of Law' (some suggest it represents 'the burden of royalty' in the shape of a rope. To its S is the now restored **Potha Gul Vihara**, a circular *gedige* type building which is circular (instead of being corbelled from two sides), with four small solid *dagobas*. It has been renovated, and inside a circular rooms with 5m thick walls is thought to have housed a library.

The **Rest House Group** Nissankamalla's 'New' Palace close to the water's edge with its royal Baths just outside the wall, is a short distance from the *Rest House*. They are sadly in a poor state of repair. Further along, the Council Chamber had the stone Lion throne (now housed in the Colombo National

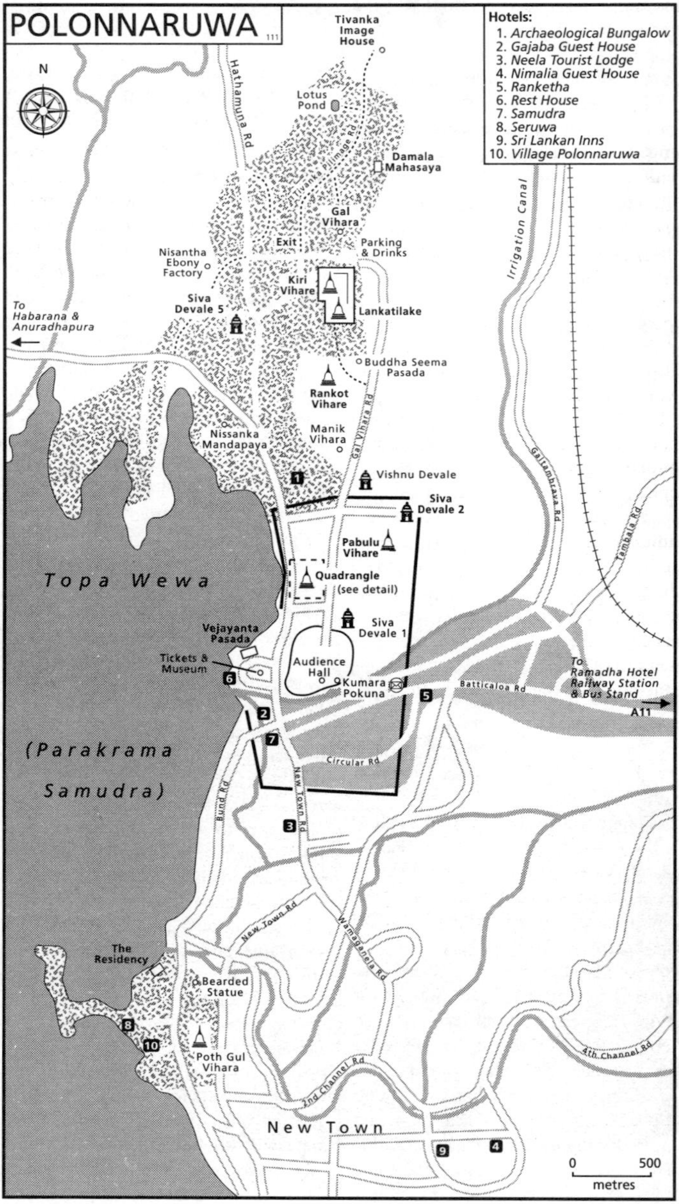
POLONNARUWA
N
Hotels:
1. Archaeological Bungalow
2. Gajaba Guest House
3. Neela Tourist Lodge
4. Nimalia Guest House
5. Ranketha
6. Rest House
7. Samudra
8. Seruwa
9. Sri Lankan Inns
10. Village Polonnaruwa
Tivanka Image House
Lotus Pond
Damala Mahasaya
Gal Vihara
Exit
Parking & Drinks
Nisantha Ebony Factory
Kiri Vihare
Lankatilake
Siva Devale 5
To Habarana & Anuradhapura
Buddha Seema Pasada
Rankot Vihare
Nissanka Mandapaya
Manik Vihara
Vishnu Devale
Siva Devale 2
Pabulu Vihare
Quadrangle (see detail)
Topa Wewa
(Parakrama Samudra)
Siva Devale 1
Vejayanta Pasada
Tickets & Museum
Audience Hall
Kumara Pokuna
To Ramadha Hotel Railway Station & Bus Stand
A11
Batticaloa Rd
Hathamuna Rd
Tivanka Pilimage Rd
Gal Vihara Rd
Irrigation Canal
Galtambrava Rd
Tambala Rd
Circular Rd
New Town Rd
Bund Rd
Wamaganela Rd
The Residency
Bearded Statue
Poth Gul Vihara
4th Channel Rd
2nd Channel Rd
New Town
0 500 metres

Museum). Towards the mound which remains above flood water are the ruins of the King's summer house which was decorated with wall paintings.

Taking the path to the E from the *Rest House*, you cross the road to **King Parakramabahu's Palace** (Vejayanta Pasada). It is described in the Chronicles as originally having had seven storeys and 1,000 rooms, but much of it was of wood and most of it was destroyed by fire. The large central hall on the ground floor (31m x 13m) had 30 columns which supported the roof; you can see the holes for the beams in the 3m thick brick walls. It has porticos on the E and W and a wide stairway.

The Audience Hall and the Council Chamber are immediately to the E. The **Council Chamber** has superb friezes of elephants, lions and dwarves, which follow the entire exterior of the base. The **Audience Hall** has four rows of 10 sculpted columns. Inscriptions on the columns indicate the seating order in the council chamber, from the King at the head to the record keepers and representatives of the business community at the opposite end. Nearby, to the SE, is the **Kumara Pokuna** (Prince's Bath), restored in the 1930s. It was formerly flanked by two lion statues. You can still see one of the spouts where the water is channelled through the open jaws of a crocodile.

The Ancient City The '**Quadrangle**' is immediately to the N of the Citadel covering a huge walled area. The structures are comparitively modest in size but are carved in fine detail. To the E of the entrance is the **Siva Devale I**, a Hindu Temple (one of the many Siva and Vishnu temples here) built in about 1200 AC which has lost its brick roof. An example of the Dravidian Indian architectural style, it shows exceptional stone carving, and the fine bronze statues discovered in the ruins have been transferred to the Colombo Museum. **NB** This is still regarded as a sanctuary and shoes have to be removed.

The **Vatadage** ('hall of the relic') near the entrance is a circular building with a dagoba on concentric terraces with sculptured railings, the largest with a diameter of 18m. A superbly planned and executed 12th century masterpiece attributed to Nissankamalla

Moonstone

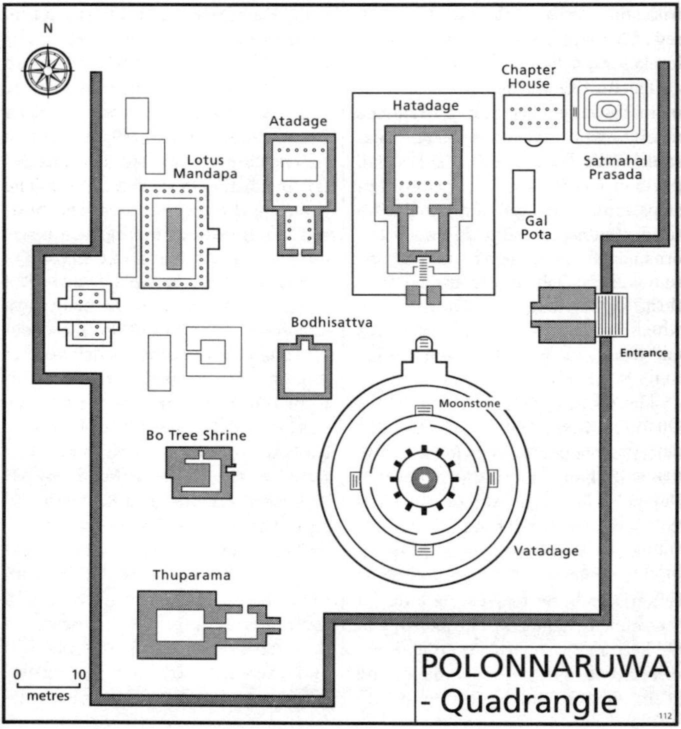

(1187-1196), the Vatadage has modest proportions but remarkably graceful lines. It was almost certainly intended to house the Tooth Relic. There are impressive guardstones at the entrances of the second terrace; the *moonstone* to the N entrance of the top terrace is superb. The dagoba at the centre has four Buddhas (some damaged) with a later stone screen.

The **Hatadage** (also known as the Atadaga – 'house of eight relics') is opposite (N) 'built in 60 Sinhalese hrs' which made up a day. With extraordinary *moonstones* at its entrance (see page 73), the sanctuary was built by **Nissankamalla** and is also referred to as the **Temple of the Tooth**, since the relic may have been placed here for a time. See the Buddha statue here framed by three solid doorways, and then look back at one of the Buddha statues in the Vatadage, again beautifully framed by the doorways.

Gal Pota To the E of the Hatadage is 'Book of Stone' which is to the side of the path and can easily be missed. According to the inscription it weighs 25 tons, and was brought over 90 km from Mihintale. It is in the form of a palm leaf measuring over 9m by 1.2m, over 60 cm thick in places, with Sinhalese inscriptions praising the works of the King Nissankamalla including his conquests in India. The **Chapter House** nearby dates from the 7th century. The ziggurat-like **Satmahal Prasada** (originally 7-'storeyed') in the NE corner, decorated with stucco figures, has lost its top 'storey'. The 9m sq base decreases at each level as in Cambodian *prasats*.

The **Bo Tree shrine** is to the W of the main Vatadage. The **Lotus Mandapa** nearby was built by **King Nissankamalla** for a dagoba. This small pavilion has remains of a stone seat, steps and a stone fence imitating a latticed wooden railing with posts. The ornamental stone pillars which surround the dagoba are in the form of thrice-bent lotus buds on stalks, a design which has become one of Sri Lanka's emblem. A statue of a **Bodhisattva** is to its S.

The **Thuparama**, in the S of the Quadrangle is a small *gedige* which was developed as a fusion of Indian and Sinhalese Buddhist architecture. This has the only surviving vaulted dome of its type and houses a number of Buddha statues. It has very thick plaster-covered brick walls with a staircase embedded in them, now usually locked.

The **Hindu temples** belong to different periods. If you walk past the **Pabulu Vihare**, a squat stupa up to the N wall of the ancient city, you come to one of the earliest temples with Tamil inscriptions, **Siva Devala 2**. Built of stone by the Indian Cholas in a style they were developing in Tamil Nadu (as at Thanjavur) but using brick rather than stone. Another group of scattered monuments is further N. To the left of the path is the **Rankot Vihara**, the fourth largest dagoba on the island with a height of 55m, built by **Nissankamalla** in the 12th century. Note the perfection of the spire and the clarity of the statues round the drum.

Alahana Parivena (Royal Cremation Ground) was set aside by **Parakramabahu** and is worth exploring. The UNESCO restoration project is concentrated in this area. The large *gedige* **Lankatilaka** ('ornament of Lanka') or Jetavanarama (see Anuradhapura above) the image house with a Buddha statue had five storeys. It has walls which are 4m thick and still stand 17m high, although the roof has crumbled. The design illustrates the development in thinking which underlay the massive building, for it marks a turning away from the abstract form of the dagoba to a much more personalized faith in the Buddha in human form. The building is essentially a shrine, built to focus the attention of worshippers on the 18m high statue of the Buddha at the end of the nave. Though built of brick and covered in stucco, the overall design of the building shows strong Tamil influence. The exterior bas relief sculpture, most of which is in very impressive, sheds light on contemporary architectural styles.

Queen **Subhadra** is believed to have built the 'milk white' **Kiri Vihara** next to it, so named because of its unspoilt white plasterwork when it was first discovered. It remains the best preserved of the island's unrestored dagobas; the plasterwork is intact although the whitewash is only visible in place, eg around the relic box. In addition this separate group also has the *mandapa* with carved columns and a Hall, just S of the Lankatilaka. There are excellent views from the Chapter House which has the foundations only just visible.

The **Gal Vihara** (Cave of the Spirits of Knowledge) is a short walk from the car park in front the Kiri Vihara alongside a small tank. It is rightly regarded as one of the foremost attractions of Sri Lanka and has great significance to Buddhists. It forms a part of Parakramabahu's monastery where a gigantic Buddha seated on a pedestal under a canopy, was carved out of an 8m high rock. On either side of the rock shrine are further vast carvings of a seated Buddha and a 14m recumbent Buddha in Parinirvana rather than death, indicated by the way the higher foot is shown slightly withdrawn. The grain of the rock is beautiful as is the expression. Near the head of the reclining figure of the *Parinirvana* Buddha, the 7m standing image with folded arms was once believed to be his grieving disciple Ananda but is now thought to be of the Buddha himself. The foundation courses of the brick buildings which originally enclosed the sculptures, are visible. There are drink stalls nearby.

Northern monuments A path continues N to rejoin the road. The **Lotus Pond** a little further along, is a small bathing pool with five concentric circles of eight petals which form the steps down into the water.

The road ends at the **Tivanka Image House** (pilimage) where the Buddha image is in the unusual 'thrice bent' posture (shoulder, waist and knee) associated with a female figure, possibly emphasising his gentle aspect. This is the largest brick-built shrine here, now substantially renovated. There are remarkable frescoes inside depicting scenes from the *Jatakas*, though not as fine as those in Sigiriya. Under the 13th century frescoes, even earlier original paintings have been discovered. The carvings on the outside of the building are excellent with delightful carvings of dwarves on the plinth.

The image house actually has a double skin and for a small tip the guardian will unlock a door about half way inside the building. You can then walk between the outer and inner walls. The passage is lit from windows high up in the wall. It is an excellent way of seeing the corbel building technique.

Museums

Archaeological Museum near the *Rest House* is small but interesting.

Local information

● Accommodation

C *Rest House* (CHC), by the Parakrama Samudra, T 2299, reservations T Colombo 323501, F 422732, 10 rm, 5 a/c (US$15), built when Queen Elizabeth II visited Sri Lanka in the 1950s now rather old-fashioned and requiring refurbishment, well located for visiting the site with superb views over lake, restaurant, bar, exchange, boating, fishing, still on the tourist route but sadly rooms are not well maintained, travellers in 1995 reported dirty rooms and toilets, poor food, slow service and unenthusiastic (sometimes unfriendly) reception, however, in Aug 1995, some found the Queen's room good value.

D *Seruwa* (CHC), T 2411, Reservations, T Colombo 323501, F 422732, 40 lake-facing comfortable a/c rm (US$15), Reservations, T 323501, F 422732, some with bath, restaurant; **D** *Village Polonnaruwa*, was *Amalian Nivas*, T 2405, reservations T/F Colombo 541199, 36 cleanish, fairly comfortable a/c rm (Rs 960), 3 family cottages, expensive restaurant (no choice out-of-season). Both have a bar, exchange, boating, use of pool. **D** *Nimalia Guest House*, 2nd Channel Rd, good restaurant; nearby **D** *Sri Lankan Inns*, 2nd Channel Rd, T 2403, 17 rm with baths around a court, scrupulously clean, good restaurant, rec. Some of the less expensive hotels are nr the New Town, some distance from the site, so you need transport. You can get a bus from the railway station or the Old Town bus stop to the New Town and take the path signposted beyond the Statue, for a km to the E.

Two hotels nr the Poth Gul Vihara by the lakeside further S provide better accommodation but lack character. 3 km from old town hence transport essential; bikes for hire.

Budget hotels: nearer the centre of the Old City are cheaper hotels with rooms with or without bath. **E** *Archaeological Bungalow* by Lakeside has 2 rm; **E** *Gajaba Guest House* nr Lake, Kuruppu Gardens, T 2392, 15 rm with bath, restaurant, garden; the small **E** *Neela Tourist Lodge* has 5 rm; **F** *Free Tourist Resort* is simple with a reasonable restaurant; **F** *Samudra* nr Lake is basic. Towards the Railway Station and Bus Stop, on the Batticaloa Rd, are a couple of simple hotels which have rooms with baths. **E** *Ramadha*, Batticaloa Rd, Kaduruwela (750m railway and bus stations, 4 km from site), T 2022, 20 rm (Rs 450), restaurant, bike/car hire, paddy fields behind; **E** *Ranketha*, Batticaloa Rd, T 2080, some rooms with a/c in a small family guest house, good restaurant, pretty garden.

● Places to eat

If you are in the Old Town, the *Ranketha* offers the best food.

● Shopping

Nishantha Ebony Factory, No 3, 26th Post, Hathamuna Rd, expects tourists to call where craftsmen can be seen carving, large stock on sale but make sure you bargain hard though.

● Transport

Train The Railway Station is 4 km W of the Old Town on the Batticaloa Rd. **Colombo**: *Udaya Devi*, 80, daily, 1225, 6 hrs; *Mail*, 94, daily, 2147, 8 hrs.

Road From Anuradhapura, the surface deteriorates from Habarana; the route passes through some relatively unspoilt Dry Zone forest. **Bus**: the out-of-town Bus Stop is nr the railway station. Several buses daily to Colombo (6 hrs), via Dambulla (2 hrs); minibuses to/from Anuradhapura (3 hrs), Kandy (4 hrs), Sigiriya and Batticaloa.

To Kandy via Mahiyangana

This is a quiet road with a good surface and beautiful scenery, only 15 km longer than the route via Dambulla.

ROUTES The **A11** through Polonnaruwa crosses the Mahaweli Ganga on a road/rail bridge. The road to Mahiyangana (via Siripura) is signed to the right. There is a good chance of seeing elephants feeding near the road.

The road turns back towards the hills with one of Sri Lanka's most recent reserves, **Wasgomuwa National Park** to the right. Entrance in 1995 was only via Handungamuwa (the new entrance is ready near Polonnaruwa, but awaits a bridge). Call the Wildlife Department first (T 433012); there is some pricey accommodation in the park. There is a belt of woodland on both sides of the river but otherwise the vegetation consists of grass, scrub and low bushes.

The **Maduru Oya National Park** is to the left. It was designated a National Park in 1983 to protect the catchment of the reservoirs in its neighbourhood and also to conserve the natural habitat of the large marsh elephant which is found particularly in the Mahaweli floodplain. Deer, sambhur and the rarer leopard or bear are present, in addition to a large number of bird species.

The area to the E of Mahiyangana is one of the few areas left where **Veddas**, the original inhabitants of Sri Lanka are found. They live on the edge of the Maduru Oya National Park and have rights to hunt in the National Park and can sell the meat to local people. Their numbers are shrinking and travellers are requested not to seek them out.

ROUTES There are wonderful views of spectacular mountains of central Sri Lanka in the distance and rice fields and forest in foreground before the A26 turns right into Mahiyangana town.

Mahiyangana

(*STD Code* 055) This is a bustling town with a long history. In legend it is associated with a visit by the Buddha, and the new temple which the late Premadasa had built to resemble the famous Buddhist temple at Bodhgaya in Bihar, India.

The centre is busy with a bazar with shops of all kinds; curiously even a dealer in elephant tusks! The Mahaweli Ganga Project has added to the town's importance and there are obvious signs of prosperity in the modern office buildings.

Mahiyangana Dagoba 500m S from the main Kandy Rd is of special importance since the Buddha was supposed to have visited the spot and preached to the tribal people. Unfortunately it is not so well kept as those in the N, possibly because it is slightly out of the way now that the E coast cannot be visited. The area though is very attractive – the park with the dagoba in it is well kept and is overlooked by the hills on the far bank of the Mahaweli.

Excursions

Sorabora Wewa, is just on the outskirts of Mahiyangana on the road to Bibile. According to legend a giant is said to have created the dam. You will probably have to ask someone to find the road for you. You can see two enormous

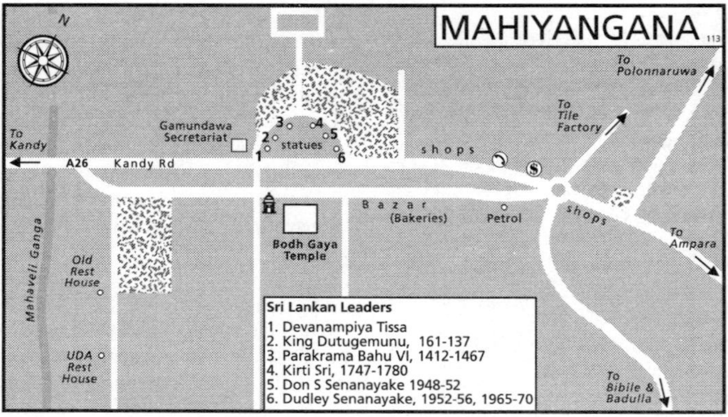

outcrops (the Sorabora Gate) through which the run off from the lake is channelled.

Local information

● Accommodation

D *Rest House* (UDA), W of Clocktower Junc, 1 km S of the A26, T 7099, 10 rm with bath, 2 a/c (Rs 500-1,200), restaurant serving good food (meals Rs 150), rooms are large but not of a particularly good standard, nice position overlooking the river, pleasant garden, quiet (the river is dangerous for bathing; 1 person was drowned in 1994).

A smaller **F** *Rest House*, closer to the main road, 3 rm at the back, meals in dining room, fairly clean, basic but good value for the price. Ask the bus to drop you at the *Old Rest House* stop for both rest houses.

● Places to eat

Best at the *UDA Rest House*. Small food stalls and 'bakeries' in the bazar.

● Banks & money changers

People's Bank, opp the New Temple, where, with special treatment for foreign visitors you can get exchange against TCs within 15 mins.

● Transport

Road Bus: buses to/from Kandy, several between 0500 and 1530; to Kandy takes 3 hrs, from Kandy about 2¾ hrs, Rs 21.

ROUTES There are two main possible routes to Kandy from Mahiyangana. The shortest is the traditional route, the **A26**. The slightly longer and less frequented route (which has its own minor alternative) crosses two of the new major dams in the Mahaweli Irrigation Project and runs through the still-wild landscape of the Central Highlands' forests.

The main route to Kandy

The A26 passes through several small hamlets – Udadumbara (46 km) Hunnagiriya (40m) and Teledeniya (23 km). There are superb views of the Victoria Lake, created in the late 1970s as part of the British Aid sponsored Mahaweli Project.

It runs W through Pallewatta and Hasalaka (with an entrance to the National Park awaiting completion of a bridge over the Mahaweli Ganga) into the hills before climbing through a series of 18 hairpin bends between 62 and 57 km from Kandy. This road is often described locally as Sri Lanka's most dangerous road. For anyone familiar with mountain roads in the Himalaya the relatively gentle climb and forested slopes present little sense of hazard, but buses often take the bends too fast for safety. There are spectacular views across the plains of the Dry Zone, newly irrigated by the Mahaweli Ganga Project. Do not forget to stop near the top to look back on the glistening Mahaweli crossing the plains below.

Approaching Kandy the road passes the dolomite quarries of Rajooda and the Kandy Free Trade Zone before crossing to the W bank of the Mahaweli Ganga. The roads in and out of Kandy can all be very congested, particularly at festival times.

Alternative route to Kandy

ROUTES From Mahiyangana there are two pleasant alternatives to the **A26** which go through the **Randenigala Sanctuary**. The slightly shorter route crosses the Mahaweli Ganga at Mahiyangana and then goes due S to Weragantota immediately after crossing the river. The road climbs to the S side of the Randenigala Reservoir, then crosses the Victoria Dam to rejoin the **A26** about 20 km from Kandy. **NB** There is no fuel available on this route.

To take the second alternative, nearing completion in 1995, you have to take the B road out of Mahiyangana to the SE to Pangarammana, then join the new road which also climbs to the S edge of the Randenigala Reservoir.

The irrigation development has created an area of intensive rice production. During the *maha* harvest (Apr-May) you will come across farmers winnowing the stalks being constructed into quite large circular walls. The road also offers a perfect example of Sri Lankan life. Water is so important that it is very rare indeed to travel without seeing people washing clothes and themselves in rivers, streams or other water courses.

After passing through Minipe, the road follows the 30 km long Minipe Right Bank Canal, then slowly starts to rise. It crosses the river at the base of the Randenigala Reservoir Dam, which straddles the last gorge before the Mahaweli Ganga plunges to the plains. Its crest is 485m long and 94m high. The road then winds spectacularly around the southern side of the upper lake. This is wild country and elephants can often be seen roaming along the shores of the lake. Notice too the 'contour lines' on the lake side as the water level drops during the dry season. The road continues to climb over a small pass – you see paddy fields in the valley below. Once over the pass you can see the Victoria Dam. There are a couple of vantage points from which you can take photographs. Over 120m high, the dam is a massive structure, even bigger than the Randenigala Dam. There is a restaurant and look out place on the dam's N side. Not surprisingly both dams are quite heavily guarded and there are several checkpoints.

THE EASTERN PROVINCE

CONTENTS

Eastern Province (North)	229
Trincomalee	229
Beaches North of Trincomalee	232
Trincomalee to Mihintale and Anuradhapura	233
Trincomalee to Habarana	233
Eastern Province (South)	235
Trincomalee to Batticaloa	235
Batticaloa to Badulla and the Central Highlands	235
Batticaloa to Arugam Bay and Nuwara Eliya	236

MAPS

Trincomalee	230
Trincomalee Area	232
Eastern Province (South)	235
Pottuvil and Arugam Bay	237

INTRODUCTION

The Eastern Province is located entirely in the Dry Zone. Comparatively sparsely populated, the coastline is dotted with fishing hamlets along the lagoon fringed shore. Inland are some of Sri Lanka's largest wildlife parks, soon to be joined together in a corridor which it is hoped will allow elephants free passage right across the region. But the dry interior has also seen some of Sri Lanka's most ambitious re-colonisation projects, including the 1950s Gal Oya scheme.

In the early 1980s the coastal fringe from Batticaloa through Trincomalee to Kuchchaveli was designated one of Sri Lanka's five Tourist Development Zones. It was hoped to capitalize on the superb beaches and underwater opportunities of diving and snorkelling, and on the distinct climatic regime which makes Jun to Aug the best season, just when the Wet Zone beaches of the SW are being lashed by the SW monsoon. However, since 1983 the Eastern Province, with the strategically important port of Trincomalee and Batticaloa its largest towns, has been devastatingly affected by the civil war. Many of the large hotels completed before 1983 have been unoccupied since, and some have become derelict. They will not be restored until peace is securely established again. Only the western region of Uva is still readily and safely accessible, including the hill towns of Badulla District. These are most accessible from Nuwara Eliya and are described above (see page 77).

In Trincomalee Tamil speakers comprise over 60% of the total population, roughly evenly divided between Hindus and Muslims. Tamil Hindus make up 60% of the population in Batticaloa District, and Tamil speaking Muslims – the 'Moors' – make up a further 20%. Further S in Ampara District, the Tamil speaking population also comprises about 60% of the total, but here it is the Muslims who form the largest single group, comprising about 40% of the total.

The civil war has made it impossible to travel freely in much of the eastern region and many coastal areas remain dangerous. Trincomalee has been open to visitors periodically in 1995, but Batticaloa and other coastal towns have not been safe.

EASTERN PROVINCE (NORTH)

Trincomalee

(*STD Code* 026) The main points of interest in Trincomalee today are the harbour and Fort Frederick. At any one point it is only possible see sections of the magnificent Bay which gives Trinco its reputation as one of the finest natural harbours in the world.

In the 1770s the future Lord Nelson described it as 'the best harbour in the world', and it remains an outstandingly well-sheltered deep port with an area of more than 80 sq km. The harbour has often been fiercely contested, and it was a crucial naval base for the British during WW2.

The town itself is a remarkable exception to the typical pattern of colonial ports which, once established, became the focal points for political and economic development of their entire regions. In India – Madras, Calcutta and Bombay, each in turn owed their origin to colonial development and succeeded in re-orienting the geography and economy of their entire regions. However, Trincomalee was established as a colonial port purely for its wider strategic potential, the finest natural harbour in Asia, dominating the vital navigation lanes between Europe and Asia, especially significant from the late 19th century when steam power saw a massive increase in the size and draught of naval ships. Trincomalee was home to the South East Asia Command of the British Navy during the Second World War, and its bombing by the Japanese in 1942 was seen as a major threat to the Allies lifeline to Australasia and the Pacific.

Desite the port's global strategic importance it had virtually no impact on its immediate hinterland. Barren and thinly populated, the region around the city saw no development, and economically Trincomalee District remained one of Sri Lanka's most backward regions. The town itself has never been very important, but that reflects its location in Sri Lanka's dry NE region, where the interior has been difficult to cultivate and malaria-infested for centuries. Only today, with the completion of the Victoria Dam and the re-settlement scheme of colonizers using irrigation from the Mahaweli Ganga Project, is the area inland developing into an important agricultural region.

However, it is also torn by political strife. The civil war since 1983 destroyed the tourism which offered one of the few opportunities for increasing revenue, and the possibility of a return to peace remains the best hope of stimulating significant economic development in its hinterland. Future development is wholly dependent on a permanent improvement in the political situation, which in late 1995 remained an unpredictable prospect. The town had miserable connections by narrow and badly surfaced road to the rest of the country and only a skeleton train and bus service.

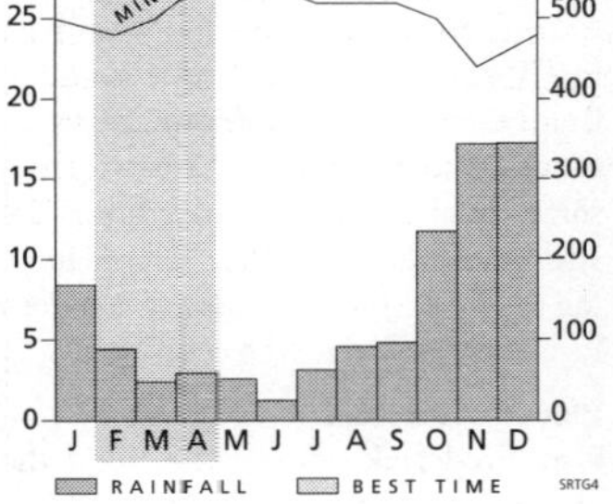

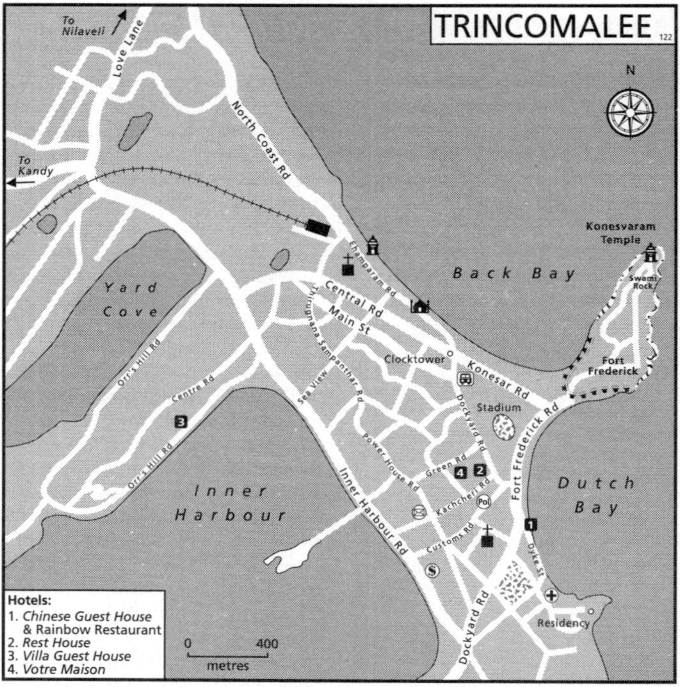

The main **town** is built on a fairly narrow piece (perhaps 700m wide) of land between Back Bay and the inner harbour. The town itself holds little of interest and is rather depressing. Nearer the centre, there is a thriving shopping area. Small single-storey shops selling all sorts of goods, as well as several pawn brokers, line Central St. Many shops are Muslim run (a mosque is halfway up on the W side of the street). The N end of Central St is more residential. Ravages of the civil war, however, are evident – some homes have clearly been destroyed, while the Mother Teresa Home for the Destitute on Colombo Rd does its share to alleviate the condition.

Places of interest

Fort Frederick Bear left around the Stadium near the bus stand to reach the Fort. This is still an active army base but visitors may enter to go up to the Swami Rock and the Hindu temple built on the cliffs high above the sea. The magnificent harbour gave 'Trinco' a huge strategic importance; it was fought over many times. The Fort was originally built by the Portuguese who destroyed the original and ancient Siva temple. The gatehouse dates from 1676; outside are two cannons, a howitzer and a mortar. Inside, apart from Wellesley house (closed to visitors) you can see some classic British Army colonial buildings (the design seems to have been used in all tropical locations for the British army) and the parade ground. Part of the area has been given over to a deer park. Don't take photos though.

Konesvaram Temple dedicated to Siva (one of five most sacred Saivite

History Of Fort Frederick

1623	Built by Portuguese
1639	Captured by Dutch
1672	Attacked by French
1782	Captured by British (Jan) Recaptured by French (Aug)
1783	Treaty of Paris transferred from French to British and finally Dutch
1795	Captured by British
1800	Duke of Wellington stayed at lodge: missed boat which sank losing all hands
1803	Renamed Fort Frederick after Duke of York
1842	St Stephens Church built
1905	Dismantled
1942	Trincomalee bombed by Japanese
1946	Reservoir completed

sites) stands at the farthest end of the rock in the place of the original. The modern temple has the lingam, believed to be from the original shrine, which was recovered by a diver. Only a couple of stone pillars from the original temple have survived. The new temple is highly decorated and painted. Regular services are held; the one on Fri evening is particularly colourful. A tree on a precarious ledge on the cliff side has typical strips of coloured cloth tied on its branches, left there by devotees in the hope to have their prayers answered.

Go behind the temple to find the so-called 'Lovers Leap' memorial, apparently after the legend according to which the daughter of a Dutch official, Francina van Rhede, threw herself from the rock after her lover sailed away. The truth seems to be more prosaic than the fiction, however, for according to government archives she was alive and well when the Dutch memorial was placed here! The memorial stands on an old temple column.

The terrace around the temple offers fine views to the N across Black Bay and the Inner Harbour and from vantage points on the rock cliff, you can sometimes see turtles swimming in the transparent blue-green sea over a 100m below.

St Mary's cemetery is opposite the stadium. On Inner Harbour Rd you get a good impression of this huge harbour with Powder Island just off it. Ferries leave from here for Mutur on the far side of the bay.

Other buildings of interest, eg Admiralty House, the British Dockyard are not open to visitors. There is little left of the British naval days apart from picturesque names on the map: Marble Bay, Sweat Bay, Yard Cove, Deadman's Cove, Powder and Sober Islands. French Pass marks the passage where the French fleet escaped.

Museum

The Archaelogical Museum has some Buddhist finds from the coast.

On the N outskirts of town, at **Sampalthivu** is the **British War Cemetery** just before the road crosses the Uppveli creek. A number were killed as a result of the Japanese air raid on the harbour in 1942. HMS Hermes was sunk off Kalkudah and Passekudah, just S of Trinco. However, the island was a recuperation centre and many more died as a result of their wounds. Princess Anne planted a tree here in Mar 1995.

The cemetery was damaged by bombing during Sri Lanka's civil war in the late 1980s; the damaged headstones have now been replaced and the garden is beautifully maintained in the tradition of Commonwealth War cemeteries. It has great sentimental value for many in Britain whose families were stationed at the naval base. The custodian has a register of the graves and will show the visitor some interesting documents relating to Trincomalee.

Local information

● Accommodation

Some hotels have closed due to the uncertain political climate

A *Seven Islands*, Orrs Hill Rd, has closed, the old Naval Officers' Club now has most of the surrounding land taken over by the Naval Base.

C *Villa Guest House*, 22 Orr's Hill Rd, opp ICRC, T 22284, rooms with bath.

D-E *Rest House*, corner of Dockyard and Kachcheri rds, next to St Mary's College, with a large banyan tree in front garden, T 22299, 10 rm with bath arranged around small courtyard (Rs 300, Rs 750 a/c), reasonable restaurant, bar, pleasant atmosphere, nr bay.

The modest **E** *Chinese Guest House*, 312 Dyke St, is owned and run by a Chinese family.

F *Railway Retiring Rooms*, 6 rm; **F** *Votre Maison*, 45 Green Rd, backing onto Nelson Cinema, simple rooms but good food.

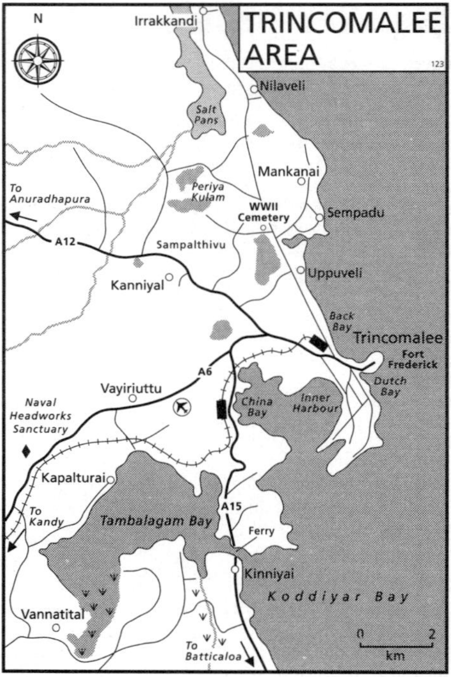

● Places to eat

Some of the hotels serve good sea food specialities. Chinese along Ehamparam Rd, best being *Chinese Eastern* nr the Clock Tower; *Rainbow Hotel*, 322 Dyke St, an open-air restaurant (no longer has accommodation). Fast food, ice creams and cold drinks along Dockyard Rd – *Flora Fountain*, rec. Cheap local food nr the Bus Station.

● Banks & money changers

Bank of Ceylon on Inner Harbour Rd, nr Customs Rd.

● Post & telecommunications

Post Office: corner of Power House Rd and Kachcheri Rd.

● Transport

Air The airport is at China Bay, 10 km SW. Lionair hopes to operate services, depending on the political situation.

Train Colombo (change at Gal Oya): *883*, daily, 0745, 10¾ hrs.

Road Bus: the bus stand is on the edge of McHeyzer stadium. Service daily to Anuradhapura; Colombo, 7 hrs, (fastest is the Intercity bus, dep Colombo 0430, Rs 100, 5¼ hrs); Kandy, 5 hrs, and Polonnaruwa.

Beaches North of Trincomalee

The road from Trincomalee to **Nilaveli** runs inland for much of the way, occasionally close to the lagoon. Several of the hotels closed during the troubles but during 1995, when the area became possible to visit for a time, a few were re-opening.

● **Accommodation** 3 km N of the Trincomalee is the **A** *Club Oceanic*, undergoing complete refurbishment after being closed between 1984-94, 25 rm open in mid-1995 (Rs 600, will rise sharply if peace returns to NE Sri Lanka and refurbishment goes ahead), potentially an excellent site right on the curved bay with a superb sandy beach, wide range of facilities planned incl diving and snorkelling off Pigeon Island (1¼ hrs by boat). 14 km N of town, **D** *Shahira*, set back 200m from sea in a quiet, isolated spot, 17 rm and 10 cabanas with bath (Rs 400-500, a/c Rs 200 extra), now in fair repair, around pleasant shady garden, friendly and helpful staff, good food (particularly seafood), boat to Pigeon Island (about 30 mins), the hotel was spared from destruction as it was occupied by the Indian Peace Keeping

Force. A new hotel is likely to be built between it and the sea when peace returns.

Nilaveli 16 km N of Trincomalee has a palm-fringed, fine 'white'-sand beach.

• **Accommodation** A *Nilaveli Beach Resort*, 20 km Trinco airport, T 026 22071, 80 rm (most a/c rooms Rs 1,000, non-a/c Rs 850, economy rooms with no view Rs 500), attractive hotel with densely-shaded beach-front garden with screw-palms, good pool, pleasant open-sided restaurant serves reasonable meals (about Rs 200), bar quite pricey (lime-soda Rs 70), the hotel was one of the few that have remained open since the troubles began, it has an army post guarding it though the soldiers are not keen to patrol after dark, there were a few groups and individual travellers visiting in 1995 (quite a few people fly from Colombo), other guests were workers at the huge grain silos which are clearly visible across Trinco harbour.

The off-shore **Pigeon Island** which can be reached by boat, has good beaches and snorkelling to view corals and fish; it potentially offers good diving as well. A trip is quite worthwhile. The hotel charges about Rs 600 per boat for six; you can stay as long as you like but there is not much shade. The island is apparantly named after Blue Rock pigeons which are found here; their eggs are prized and many Sri Lankans come here to try and find them.

Trincomalee to Mihintale and Anuradhapura

The direct route along the **A12** to Anuradhapura and Mihintale runs WSW across the Dry Zone. Few people use this route which was closed for long periods during the civil war and which during 1995 some still feared to be unsafe. However, buses travel regularly during daylight hours, and although police checks were relatively frequent over the first 50 km, the journey from Mihintale (inspite of the occasionally poor surface) is at least 1 hr shorter than the more widely used alternative via Habarana.

The route itself runs through one of Sri Lanka's least populated regions. Abandoned irrigation tanks and marshy ground are interspersed by forest and occasional fields of paddy land. Once the low range of hills just inland of the coast is left behind most of the route crosses the flat plain, broken by a few isolated granite blocks.

Trincomalee to Habarana

The **A6** goes SW to Habarana, passing Kantalai. From Trincomalee the road passes through the heart of the Dry Zone and shifting '*chena*' cultivation across the gently sloping plain to **Habarana** (85 km). Irrigated rice is interspersed with extensive tracts of mixed jungle, including teak, bamboo and eucalyptus.

ROUTES The journey along the **A6** is not very pleasant. Since the outbreak of the civil war it has frequently been interrupted by many checkpoints, both police and army. In 1995, the road surface was very poor until just NE of Habarana, and there were few places suitable for travellers to stop along the 85 km route. The road may also be subject to a dusk to dawn curfew. There has been obvious clearance of bush on each side of the road to provide a clear firing zone for military bunkers.

For the first 20 km the road is narrow and the surface very poor. There are, however, some attractive areas such as the Devils Bends around the Kandurukanda peak and as the countryside changes when the road passes through pleasant forested hills. In the last part of the route the landscape has a more 'domesticated' feel, with fruit trees, coconut, mango, tamarind and palmyra palms. It is possible to visit the Minneriya-Giritale Sanctuary, just off this route (see page 218).

Kantalai (Kantale) has fuel and a few shops. It is the centre of a very intensive farming area made possible from the irrigation provided by the huge Kantalai Tank, originally dating from the 7th century, which provides water to extensive rice fields to the SE of the main road. The restored tank bund (retaining dam) was breached in 1987 with hundreds killed. Kantalai is also the Headquarters for the 2nd Battalion Sri Lanka National Guard. There is a highly reputed Rest House in a beautiful position by the Lake, particularly appreciated by those with an interest in waterbirds, but in the present political situation visitors cannot stay. In 1995, there was not much evidence of the Somawathie National Park which comes quite close to the road for a few kilometres just before the Kantalai Tank, nor of the Naval Headworks Sanctuary.

EASTERN PROVINCE (SOUTH)

Trincomalee to Batticaloa

The A15 hugs the E coast all the way S to Batticaloa, sometimes between the sea itself and shallow lagoons and with numerous ferries. This coastal road was devastated by a cyclone in 1978, and the damage to housing is still visible. It is a desolate journey. During the present civil war it is completely inaccessible to tourists.

Batticaloa

This old Dutch town is called the 'town of tamarinds' by its predominantly Tamil population. The Dutch fortified the town in 1602, the remains of which can be seen near the present day *Resthouse*, but today it is famous for its **singing fish**, heard in the middle of the lagoon on still nights. The centre of the lagoon bridge is reputed to be the best place for listening to the extraordinary resonating sounds.

• **Accommodation** In 1995 the only suitable one for travellers was **C** *Lake View Inn*, 22 Mudaliyar St, T 065 2593, 3 rm, restaurant with good seafood, rec. The following may be available: nr the Dutch Fort on Arugam Bay side, the rebuilt **D** *Resthouse*; **E** *Sunshine Inn*, 118 Bar Rd, on the other side of the railway track from the station, clean, in a pleasant garden; **F** *Railway Retiring Rooms*, T 065 2271, 8 rm. 5 km from town, at the end of the bus route are: **E** *Beach House Guesthouse*, Bar Rd, nr Lighthouse, quiet, good food; and **E** *East Winds*, next door.

Warning Batticaloa has been the centre of repeated violent fighting between the Tamil Tigers and the Army. Check locally whether it is possible and safe to go.

Batticaloa to Badulla and the Central Highlands

The route from Batticaloa to Badulla leaves the coastal lagoons and goes due SW across the heart of the Dry Zone long the A5 for 70 km to the junction with the A26. This then climbs low outliers of the

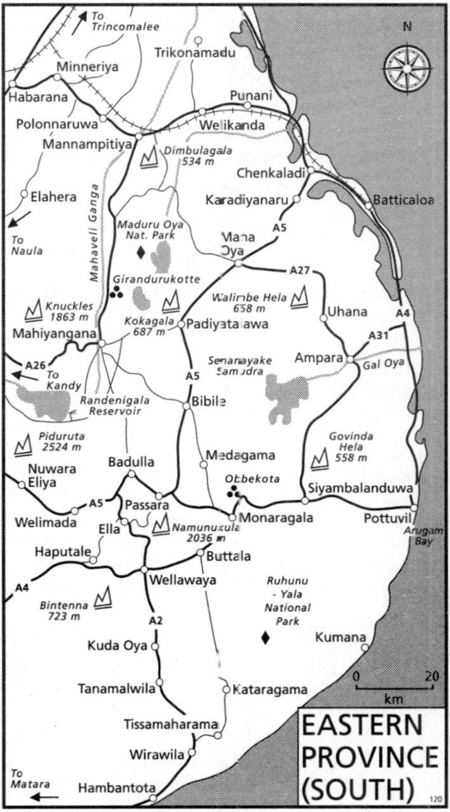

Central Highlands before droping down again to Mahiyangana on the banks of the Mahaweli Ganga. The road then climbs through the Highlands to Kandy.

The A15 leaves Batticaloa to the NW, running 10 km to its junction with the A5 at Chenkaladi. The A5 then goes SW across the Dry Zone through Maha Oya. 35 km beyond Maha Oya the road passes SE of the 687m hill Kokagala before being joined by the A26 to Waywatta. This is the shortest route into the Central Highlands, going via Mahiyangana. For alternative routes from Mahiyangana to Kandy, see page 226.

An alternative route to the Central Highlands continues S down the A5 through Bibile and climbs steeply to Lunugala and Tennugewatta. The A5 continues to Badulla.

Batticaloa to Arugam Bay and Nuwara Eliya

The coastal route S of Batticaloa is no easier than that to Trincomalee. A succession of tiny fishing hamlets line the coast, but the A4 has had little work on it for years and it runs through an area subject to periodic violence.

ROUTES At Karativu the A31 goes inland to Ampara, a district headquarters. A minor road then goes to **Inginiyagala** where you can stay to visit the Gal Oya National Park early in the morning. **Accommodation A** *Inginiyagala Safari Inn*, superbly situated, T 063 2499 or in Colombo T 91805, 22 comfortable rm, restaurant, 10 mins walk brings you to the lake, picturesque at sunset, the hotel will organize tours into the Park.

Gal Oya National Park

Background The National Park was established in early 1950s around the huge lake, Senanayaka Samudra which was created when a dam was built across the Gal Oya. It covers 540 sq km of rolling country most of which is covered in tall grass (*illuk* and *mana*) with a sizeable area of dry evergreen forest which escaped being submerged. The Veddas lived in the forests; certain areas of the park still harbour medicinal herbs and plants which are believed to have been planted centuries ago.

Wildlife The park is famous for its elephants and a variety of water birds which are attracted by the lake. Best visited in the early morning for watching elephants and white buffaloes which come down to the lake, the crocodiles in the water and the birds including the White-bellied Sea-Eagle (*Haliaeetus leucogaster*). You can take motor-boat tours on the lake, lasting 2-3 hrs.

- **Accommodation** A simple ***Lodge*** outside the park at Ekgal Oya, 20 km which has 3 rm, elephants may be seen nearby.

ROUTES From the Gal Oya National Park you can rejoin the A25 which runs S past the 558m hill known as Westminster Abbey to the E of the road. It joins the A4 at Siyambalamduwa.

If you do not wish to visit the Gal Oya National Park you can continue S from Karativu on the **A4** towards Pottuvil and Arugam Bay.

Arugam Bay

(15 km passing through Pottuvil) The Bay with its beautiful beach is particularly interesting for not only those keen on watersports (it has excellent surf), and underwater photography but also offers exciting possibilities for divers keen to explore wrecked ships. The lagoon here attracts water birds; take a sailing boat at dawn and dusk. You can visit old temple ruins by walking over the dunes.

Although Arugam Bay itself has not seen political violence in recent years the surrounding area is not free from trouble. In 1995 the Special Task Force was based in this area hence there are barbed wire fences and machine guns in evidence; curfew was enforced from 1800-0800. It was possible to hire a bicycle and go S as far as **Panama**. **Warning** Do not to go further S because of military activity.

• **Accommodation** Large number of moderately priced simple hotels, cabanas and beach cottages to choose from; the cheaper places S of the bridge. **C** ***Stardust Beach Hotel***, just on S edge of mouth of lagoon, 3 km S of Pottuvil in a superb location between the sea, 20 well-appointed, thatched bungalows, good restaurant, bar, laundry, Danish owned, attentive service, highly rec, arranges trips to Yala East National Park (20 km), cycle hire available; **D** ***Resthouse***, on the beach, 3 rm, restaurant, pleasant and comfortable; **F** ***Arugam Bay Hilton***, has double rooms without bath for Rs 200 and a good restaurant, popular with budget travellers.

In normal political circumstances the coastal road S of Arugam Bay takes you to Kumana (40 km) via Okanda in a 4WD.

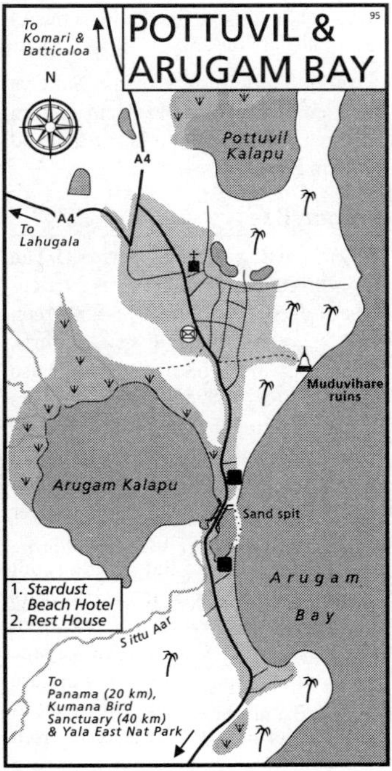

Kumana Bird Sanctuary or Yala East National Park

Kumana, to the NE of the larger Yala National Park, is visited for its resident and migratory aquatic birds including flamingoes, ibis, herons, pheasants, particularly impressive in May and Jun when many nest in the mangrove swamps. You may see the endemic Red-faced malkoha or the Blue magpie in the forested areas.

Herds of elephants can be spotted, although leopards and bears are more elusive.

• **Accommodation** There are 2 simple **F** *Bungalows* at Tunmulla and Okanda, with warden/cook, bring your bedding and food. Reservations: Wildlife Conservation Department, 82 Rajamalwatta Rd, Battaramulla, T 433012.

ROUTES From Pottuvil the A4 runs due W to Monaragala. 12 km W of Pottuvil is the small national park at Lahugala which is good for watching birds and elephants.

Lahugala National Park

Background The 15 sq km sanctuary (20 km) was established in 1980 and is open throughout the year. **NB** The area has been politically unstable from time to time. The park, lying between Gal Oya and Ruhunu-Yala is part of the government's endeavour to provide a connected parkland 'corridor' for the elephant poulation to move freely across the southeastern part of the island.

Wildlife The Lahugala (Mahawewa) and Kitulana tanks here attract numerous species of water birds. It is also a very good spot to see the large elephant herds, sometimes numbering over a hundred, especially in the dry season (Aug-Oct) when they come down to the water. They are attracted by the *beru* grass that grows in the shallow tanks and the best time to watch them is in the late afternoon. The Climbing Perch (*Anabas testudineus*) fish is believed to slither across from the Mahawewa to Kitulana when the former

ELEPHANTS

Elephants are both the most striking of the mammals and the most economically important, for there are many areas where they are put to work. The Asian elephant (*elephas maximas*), smaller than the African, is the world's second largest land mammal. Compared to the African elephant, the male rarely reaches a height of over 3m; it also has smaller ears. Other distinguishing features include the rounded shape of the back and the smooth trunk with a single 'finger' at the end. Unlike the African, the female is often tuskless or bears small ones called *tushes*, and even the male is sometimes tuskless (makhnas). The Lahugala National Park is the best place for viewing elephants. The Mahaweli basin has the larger marsh elephant. There is a plan to create an elephant 'corridor' of contiguous national parks and sanctuaries in the south east of the island in order that they may move freely over a large area as needed, throughout the year.

Ceylon elephants illustrated by Rev W Urwick in1885

runs dry! You might also catch sight of the colourful Ceylon blue magpie (*Cissa ornata*) or the Red-faced malkoha (*Phaenicophaeus pyrrhocephalus*) in the woodland near the tanks.

• **Accommodation** Report at the ***Park Lodge*** on the edge of the park on arrival; there are some rooms for overnight stay.

ROUTES A few kilometres on, to the S of the main road is **Magul Maha Vihara** – ruins in a jungle setting of a vatadage and a dagoba with impressive *moonstones* and guardstones.

It is a relatively short drive from Pottuvil to Monaragala. Just beyond the small town and district headquarters the A22 goes W to Tennugewatta and into the Hills, while the A4 goes to Ratnapura. From Buttala it is an easy drive either to Yala Park and the S coast.

JAFFNA AND THE NORTHERN PROVINCE

Contents

Jaffna 240

Maps

Northern Province 240

Introduction

The Jaffna Peninsula and the offshore islands have a highly distinctive physical environment, deriving from the combination of its limestone geology, Dry Zone rainfall pattern and centuries of Tamil Hindu culture. Since 1983 it has been impossible for visitors to go freely either to the town of Jaffna or its surrounding villages. By some accounts the town has been devastated by economic collapse and military bombardment, and while much of the Peninsula was back in Sri Lankan army hands by mid-1995 it remained far from clear whether peace would be restored in the near future.

Jaffna's proximity to India ensured that when Tamil settlers came to Sri Lanka as much as 2,000 years ago Jaffna was one of their earliest homes. Over the centuries they built a wholly distinctive culture. Despite the unsuitability of much of the thin red soil for agriculture, Tamil cultivators developed techniques of well irrigation which capitalized on the reserves of groundwater held in the limestone, making intensive rice cultivation the basis of a successful economy. Diversity was provided by coconut and palyra palms, tobacco and a wide range of other crops, but the Tamil population was also in a real sense international in its outlook. It maintained trading links with the Tamil regions across the Palk Straits but also with South East Asia. From the mid-19th Century Jaffna Tamils took up the educational opportunities which came with an extended period of British rule, and rapidly became numerically dominant in a range of Government services and jobs both inside and outside Sri Lanka.

The ability to cope with the harsh environment of the Peninsula and their specific adaptation to its own regional character isolated the Jaffna Tamil community just as much as cultural distinctiveness from the regions to the S. The colonial period widened the geographical divide between the peninsula and the economically productive areas of southern Sri Lanka. In addition to the disasters that had overtaken the complex irrigation works of the Dry Zone after the 13th Century, the northern part of the Dry Zone around

Climate: Jaffna

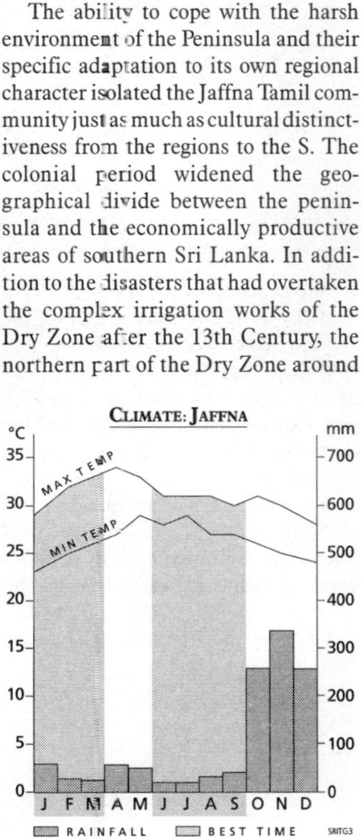

Vavuniya, known as the Wanni, was laid waste by a succession of wars with the Dutch and the British, contributing to its present character as an almost uninhabited wasteland. Through the 19th and 20th centuries the Wanni had the reputation of being one of the poorest areas of the island. The routes from Jaffna town to the rest of the island have to cross through the Wanni. The main road S goes through Vavuniya to Anuradhapura, following the route of the railway line (currently closed). One road runs E to Trincomalee, while another goes SW to Mannar and Talaimannar, formerly the port for crossings to India.

Jaffna

(49 km; *Pop* 120,000) **NB** In the absence of authentic and up to date information it has been decided not to publish a guide section to Jaffna and the northern Peninsula until the next edition of this Handbook.

THE MALDIVES

Dhivehi Jumhuriyya, the Republic of the Maldives (pronounced 'a' as in all, 'i' as in give) is the smallest member state of the UN. It comprises a group of islands stretching over 823 km N to S and nearly 130 km from E to W approximately 650 km SW of the S tip of India. Of the 1,190 coral islands, many of which are no more than sandbanks, only 202 are inhabited. Over 70 have been turned into tourist resorts, scattered around five central atolls of N and S Male, Ari, Lhaviyani and Vaavu plus Gan which has a tourist resort.

As recently as 1969 a United Nations report stated that the Maldives were unsuitable for the development of tourism because they were too wet and had insufficient infrastructure. If you have the chance to look out of the window as the plane comes in to land at the modern international airport of Hulule, built by linking two small coral islands close to the capital Male, you may well be stunned not only at the almost luminous blue of the sea and coastline but at the thought that today anyone could imagine these tiny islands unsuitable for tourism. Indeed, in 1995 the Maldives had made tourism their most important single earner of foreign exchange, building holiday resorts with a full range of facilities, making it possible to enjoy the extraordinarily distinctive beauties of coral islands in the Indian Ocean.

Development has taken place rapidly in the last 25 years, but the Maldives Government has been at pains to protect both its cultural heritage and its island environment. The expansion of tourism to a widening range of the hundreds of uninhabited atolls has been carefully controlled, to good effect. It is now looking to take advantage of its strategic location in the heart of the Indian Ocean by turning its southern outpost of Gan, where the British had left a large airport used to service its forces in South East Asia, into a major international airport as a stopover for flights between Africa, Asia and Australasia.

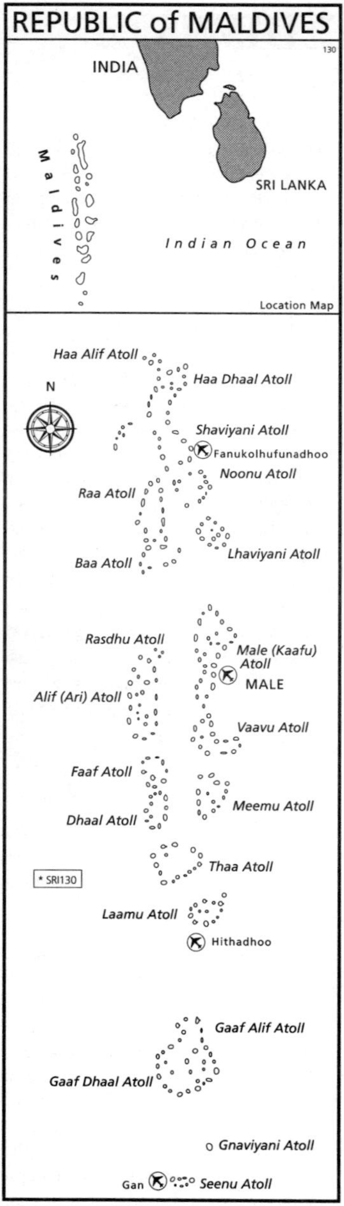

OFFICIAL NAME Divehi Jumhuriya (Republic of Maldives)

CAPITAL Male

NATIONAL FLAG Green rectangle with a red border; a white crescent in the centre.

EMBLEM Coconut palm, crescent and star, two crossed national flags and the title of the state.

OFFICIAL LANGUAGE Dhivehi

OFFICIAL RELIGION Islam

NATIONAL ANTHEM "Qawmee mi ekuveri kan mathee thibegen kureeme salaam" (In National Unity we salute our nation).

KEY STATISTICS *Population*: 225,000 (1996 estimate); 48.5% women; *Urban*: 30% (Malé 61,000); *Rural*: 70%. *Religion*: Islam (Sunni) 100%. *Pop growth rate*: (1991) 3.2%. *Birth rate*: 39/1,000. *Death rate*: 9/1,000. *Infant mortality rate*: 56/1,000. *Life expectancy*: 67 years. *GDP per capita*: (World Bank) US$500. *Real GDP per capita*: (UN) US$1,200. *Literacy*: 92%. *Chief foreign exchange earnings as % of GDP*: Tourism 25% ($28mn); Fisheries 24% ($27mn).

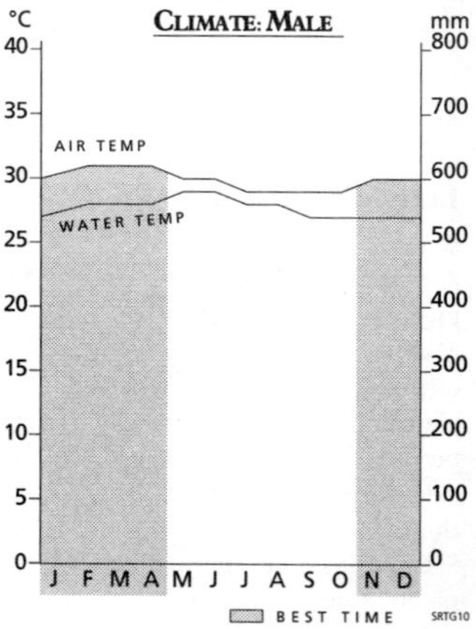

INFORMATION FOR VISITORS

Contents

Before travelling	243
Entry requirements	243
When to go	244
Health	244
Money	244
Getting there	244
Air; Boat; Customs	
On arrival	245
Airport information; Clothing; Conduct; Hours of business; Official time; Restrictions; Security; Shopping; Voltage; Weights and measures	
Where to stay	246
Food and drink	247
Getting around	247
Air, Boat	
Communications	248
Postal services; Telephone services	
Entertainment	248
Newspapers	
Holidays and festivals	249
Further reading	249

Before travelling

Entry requirements

● Visas

All tourists holding a full passport are given a 30 days permit to enter the Maldives free of charge (no photo required). Indians, Pakistanis, Bangladeshis and Italians are given staying permits for 30 days on arrival. The stay can be extended for a nominal fee, though you must prove you have at least $10 a day. An international certificate of inoculation against yellow fever is required if coming from or through an infected country. Tourists must carry US$10 minimum per day of stay except those travelling with a tour company or coming on recruitment to an Agency.

● Representations overseas

Honorary Consuls and trade representatives: Austria: G Wiedler, 1190 Wien, Weimarerstrasse 104, T 345273, F 043222. Belgium: FE Drion, rue de Vignes 16, 1020 Brussels, T 4781426, F 4785682; Egypt: Md AAA Daem, 16 Ahmed Omar Rd, 4th Flr, Flat 7, El-Helmeya-El Adida, Cairo, T 391052, F 94062; France: Dr JP Laboureau, Zone Artisanale, 5 rue de Lafontaine, 21560 Arc sur Tille, T 80372660, F 80372661; Germany: G Muecke, Immanuel Kant Str Be 16, D-6380 Bad Homburg, T 69066789, F 69692102; Hong Kong: BN Harelela, 201-5 Kowloon Centre, 29-39 Ashley Rd, Kowloon, T 3762114, F 37662366; India: AS Nathani, 202 Sethi Bhavan, 7 Rajendra Place, N Delhi 110000, T 5718590, F 5725991 and Nathan Rd, Vidyavihar, Bombay 400086, T 22515111, F 225146311; Italy: M Giacoma, via Calderini 68/D, INT 800196, Rome, T 519115 F 534115; Japan: H Shimuzu, Chiyoda Bldg 1-2, 2 Chome, Marunochi, Chiyodaku, Tokyo, T 32115463, F 32116921; Pakistan: AS Tapal, PO Box 51, Karachi, T 737945, F 737817; Saudi Arabia: HE Sh Md Saleh Bahareth, PO Box 404, Jeddah 21411, T 6423666; Singapore: Trade Representative, 10 Anson Rd, 18-12 International Plaza, Singapore 0207, T 225 8955, F 224 6050; Switzerland: MA Odermatt, Gerechtigkeitsgasse, 23 8002, Zurich, T 2028448, F 2027505; UK: Trade Representative, Adam Hassan, 22 Nottingham

Place, London W1M 2FB, T 0171 224 2135, F 0171 224 2157.

● Tourist offices overseas

Japan: Mr T Asakura, 3-32-13 Horikiri, Katsushika-ku, Tokyo 124, T 6924455, F 6913785; Norway: H Hussain Afeef, Stubbratan 20, 1352 Kolsas, T 02137221; Sweden: S Ericsson, Heimdalsvagen 5 A, S-756 52 Uppsala; UK: Toni de Laroque – The Maldive Lady, 3 Esher House, 11 Edith Terrace, London SW10 0TH, T 0171 352 2246, F 0171 351 3382.

● Specialist tour operators

UK: *Maldive Travel*, 3 Esher House, 11 Edith Terrace, London SW10 0TH, T 0171 352 2246, F 0171 351 3382. This is the only specialist company in the UK for the Maldives who also handle ground arrangements.

When to go

● Best time to visit

There is no really unsuitable time to visit. Jan-Feb are the driest and the best period, but it can rain heavily at any time. End of May-Jun and Nov are likely to be most showery although these showers are not persistent. The High Season (Nov-Apr) is mostly dry with occasional showers and calm seas. On a few islands higher rates also apply in Aug, though this probably reflects European holiday periods rather than climatic conditions in the Maldives themselves. The Low Season (May-Oct) has higher humidity, more rain (though not prolonged) and rough seas.

Health

Health care is far from comprehensive in the Maldives and facilities are basic. Maldivians themselves have to go abroad for any specialist treatment. Come prepared with reasonable precautions. Know your blood group and be properly insured, as good health care is not cheap. Take a high protection factor suntan lotion, wear a straw hat and a T-shirt for the first few days to avoid over-exposure. Avoid sunburn when snorkelling. See Health section in the introduction.

Money

● Currency

The unit of currency is the Ruffiyaa divided into 100 Laari. Notes are in denominations of 100, 50, 20, 10, 5 and 2 Rufiyaa. Coins are in denominations of 1 Rufiya, 50, 20, 10 and 5 Laari.

● Exchange

The law requires all transactions to be conducted in Maldivian currency. Most banks, shops and tourist resorts will convert foreign currency, American dollars being the commonest.

Unauthorized dealing Do not convert your currency with an unauthorized dealer. Keep your exchange receipts as you may need them when you re-convert any Maldivian currency when you depart. There is no restriction on the amount of foreign currency that visitors may bring in or take out.

● Travellers cheques and credit cards

Hotels are authorized to accept foreign currency, TCs and credit cards; US$ TCs are preferred. Among credit cards, most common are American Express, Visa, Master Card, Diners and Euro Card. Some shops accept TCs or foreign currency, and give change in dollars.

Getting there

Air

Most tourists arrive by air at Male International Airport on Hulule Island. The airport departure tax is US$10 (payable only in dollars).

● From India

Indian Airlines operate 5 flights a week from **Trivandrum** (Mon, Tues, Thur, Fri, Sat), but they are extremely heavily booked. Depart Trivandrum, 1430; depart Male, 1610 (40 mins), fare US$62.

It is often necessary to make a reservation 4 weeks in advance to obtain an OK ticket. Waiting lists are long, but it is sometimes possible to fly even if well down the waiting list. The only travel agent who has direct links with the Maldives in Trivandrum is *Aries Travels*, Ayswarya Building, Press Rd, Trivandrum 695001, T 65417.

● From Sri Lanka
Air Lanka at least one flight daily from Colombo to Male.

● From UK
From London: Air Lanka from Heathrow via Colombo. Britannia (charter) operated by Kuoni, Gatwick/Heathrow via Dubai. Emirates Airlines from Gatwick/Heathrow via Dubai. Qatar Air from Gatwick via Doha Fri, return Sun. Singapore Airlines from Heathrow (via Singapore).

● From Asia and Africa
From Colombo: Air Lanka. From Dubai: Emirates Airlines. From Karachi: Pakistan International. From Kathmandu: Royal Nepal Airlines.

● From Europe
Scheduled airlines From Rome: Alitalia. From Amsterdam, Brussels, Paris, Singapore, Vienna: Singapore Airlines.

Charter airlines From Dusseldorf, Munich: LTU/LTS. From Dusseldorf, Frankfurt, Munich: Condor. From Vienna: Lauda Air, Austrian Airlines. From Copenhagen, Stockholm, Helsinki and Greece: Sterling Airways. From Milan, Zurich: Balair.

Boat

It is very unusual for foreign tourists to arrive by sea but if you are in Colombo in Sri Lanka or in Tuticorin in Tamil Nadu, India, you may wish to enquire from shipping agents whether they will allow passengers on their cargo boats.

Customs

● Prohibited items
Any alcohol carried by passengers will be kept at the airport (resorts are well-stocked). It can be reclaimed on departure. You are also not allowed to bring in drugs, pork products, pornographic magazines (including *Playboy*) or videos. Landing cards have to be completed on board the plane before arrival, and it is necessary to state where you will be staying.

On arrival

● Airport information
The airport on Hulule island is 15 mins boat ride to the N of Male. There is a bank at the airport; it is worth changing money immediately, as banks on Male are only open in the mornings. A travel agent is available at the airport on arrival. A boat jetty lies directly outside the airport exit and help is available to carry bags if required. The boat fare to Male from the airport is US$5, and taxi fares on Male are up to US$3. Fares to other islands depend on distance. See map for details.

● Clothing
Light cottons are best. Nudity is forbidden and tourists visiting inhabited islands should be clothed modestly. The Department of Tourism advises 'Minimum dress – Men: T-shirts and shorts, but jeans or long trousers are preferable. Women: T-shirts, blouses or shirts and skirts or adequate shorts which cover the thighs, made of non-seethrough or diaphanous material; a piece of cloth simply wrapped around the torso is not acceptable or indeed permitted'. Sun hat and beach shoes are essential. Bring all toiletry requirements; plenty of shampoo to counteract hard water!

● Conduct
Courtesy and social customs are similar to Sri Lanka, see page 20.

● **Hours of business**

Most offices are open from Sat to Thur, although banks are also open on Sun. **Banks**: 0900-1300. **Government offices**: 0730-1330. **Shops**: are open daily 0600-2300, some remaining closed on Fri morning. During the day shops and restaurants close their doors for 15 mins a few times a day when there are calls to prayer. If you are in a café or restaurant, you are not expected to leave but can carry on eating.

● **Official time**

5 hrs ahead of GMT.

● **Restrictions**

Nudity is banned. You may not pick up shells or coral and spear fishing is prohibited. Turtles are now protected in the Maldives; no shop may sell turtle-shell ornaments.

● **Security**

Crime is virtually unknown on the islands.

● **Shopping**

Opportunities for shopping are extremely limited. Local sea shells and some coral are available, but most other goods for sale have been imported, largely from India, Sri Lanka and South East Asia. The range is generally narrow, the quality rather mediocre and the price comparatively high, but it is possible to find attractive items reasonably priced.

● **Voltage**

Islands generate their own electricity at 240 volts.

● **Weights and measures**

Metric.

Where to stay

If you do not have accommodation fixed, ask for assistance at the Airport Tourist Information Unit before completing customs formalities. Unfortunately, because of the practice of 'over-booking' to ensure maximum take-up, some visitors may find they have to be found alternative accommodation on arrival.

Hotel and guest house accommodation on Male is limited. During the season book well in advance. Private rooms in Male can cost less than US$10 but are not well advertised, so ask around. There are over 70 outlying resort islands, most of which are small with self-contained communities and it will take you 15-30 mins to walk around most of these. The accommodation is mainly in single storey units – 'bungalows', rooms in 2-storey chalets, or in 'rondavels' (round thatched houses) with modern conveniences; attractive 'water-bungalows' with immediate access to the sea are on stilts. Many resorts offer a/c rooms, have open-air restaurants and bars, a gift shop, and a few have discos and other entertainment. Do not expect a television (though a few offer videos) and telephone in every room and newspapers daily! The islands have beautiful, pollution free beaches and a wealth of watersports; several have diving schools.

The hotel categories are based on the price in US$ per day sharing a double room on an island resort in the Low Season (this often includes half or full board). **AL** US$200 and over; **A** US$150-200; **B** US$100-150; **C** US$70-100; **D** up to US$70. See also page 265. In comfort, facilities and sophistication, however, they don't compare with what is expected in similarly priced hotels in western seaside resorts and you may be surprised by the sand floors in some of the hotels public areas.

Toilets These are flush WCs in hotels and resorts but there are few public toilets suitable for foreign visitors on Male. The better cafés and restaurants (eg *Seagull*) and the newest shopping centres (eg STO, Orchid Magu, Chandanee Magu End) provide them.

Water supply This can be erratic and different from what you are accustomed to. In resorts, 'Island water' is sea water pumped and filtered and remains slightly salty. It is adequate for showers and washing but you will find it quite hard. Some resorts have desalination plants or rain water reservoirs while a few provide fresh water. Some resorts only supply unheated water although this does not create a problem as it is usually luke-warm. During the peak season and dry periods the supply of fresh water and rain water may be restricted.

Food and drink

● Food

Local and continental cuisine is available, often heavily dependent on freshly caught fish (*mas*) and a variety of sea food, with occasional buffets and barbecues organized for guests. You may expect some Sri Lankan food too. Here too, freshly grated coconut forms a typical ingredient and chillis are added for spicing up most dishes.

Unlike some other tropical resorts, the islands produce very little by way of fruit and vegetables, although the coconut (*kurumba*) palm thrives and there are some bananas (*donkeo*), mangoes (*don ambu*), breadfruit (*bambukeyo*) and pawpaws (*falor*).

The Maldivians usually eat rice (*bai*), sometimes unleavened bread similar to an Indian *roti* or *chapati* (*roshi*) with a fish dish, accompanied by pickles. Fish comes in different forms: curried (*mas riha*), fried (*teluli mas*), smoked (*valo mas*) or as a soup (*garudia*). Meat and chicken are only eaten on special occasions.

Male cafés serve *hors d'oeuvre* (short eats) which are snacks offered on a plate; restaurants serve more substantial snacks: *roshi* and dry curried fish or meals of fish curry and rice. Some hotel restaurants offer Continental and Far Eastern dishes. On resort islands, buffet breakfasts with a large choice, are common. There is usually a choice of restaurats serving western and eastern cuisine as well as bars, snack bars and coffee-shops.

● Drink

Drinking water quality on Male has been improved significantly in the last few years but foreigners are advised to drink mineral water to be on the safe side.

Tea for the Maldivians, is invariably with milk and sugar already added (*sa*) and milk (*kiru*) which too is often served sweetened. If you prefer your tea unsweetened ask for *hakuru naala sa* and for black tea *kiri naala sa*.

Soft drinks can be fresh-pressed fruit juice (about Rs 10-15) often prepared on ordering, or bottled. Local bottled drinks are manufactured under licence and include soda water and Coke; others are imported.

Alcohol is readily available for visitors on tourist islands. **NB** It is not available in Male or allowed on board when you are in a boat. You may not import it or offer it to Maldivian nationals. The local toddy *raa*, can be an acquired taste, which is drunk after the juice from the palm has been left to ferment, but freshly tapped is considered delicious by those who don't wish to take alcohol.

Getting around

There is no centralized transport between the islands.

Air

Air Maldives operates domestic flights to two southern and one northern atoll.

● Helicopters

Hummingbird Helicopters, MHA Bldg, 4th Flr, 1 Orchid Magu, Male, T 325708, F 323161, operate from the helipad at the Hulule airport. Their prices do not include transfers to Hulule from resorts. Options include: 'flips' which are 15 mins sightseeing flights which capture the magic of the local reefs US$49/pp); 'Sunrise Picnic' – 15 mins flight to a locally inhabited island in the S Male Atoll, short transfer to Sunrise island to enjoy beach and lagoon and a barbecue lunch; 'Robinson Crusoe Picnic' – away-day excursion with a 25 mins flight to an uninhabited island on the Ari atoll and includes lunch or beach barbecue, diving and snorkelling (US$149/pp). Pick-ups may be arranged when a resort has a landing site.

Airport-resort transfers are available; contact at airport Main Arrivals behind the Tourist Information desk.

● Maldivian airtaxis

Maldivian Airtaxis (float planes and helicopter) operate inter-island services by Twin Otter (for 18) and Cesna 208 Caravan (for 9) including island-hopping, excursions and Male shopping. Their airport transfer takes about 20-35 mins; boat-transfer time is 3-5 hrs for distant resorts. Contact at airport, T 315201, F 315203.

Seagull Helicopters and Superspeed (a large hovercraft) also operate between islands.

Boat

Dhonis, the local boats, are the commonest form of transport which average about 13 km per hour. Dhonis and speedboats are available for hire. Tourist resorts have their own boats and the transfer charges appear above (in US$).

Communications

● Postal services

The Post (Office) Shop in Male, is on Chandanee Magu, just N of Majeedee Magu junction on the 1st Flr. Open 0815-1145, 1330-1830, closed Fri; collections at 0830 and 1300. Cost of postcards by air to anywhere, Rf7; aerogrammes, Rf5; air letters (up to 20g), Rf8 for Asia, Rf10 for rest of the world (Express to UK, Rf255, and a few others).

Post Office counter, also at the airport departure lounge and new agency counters at other points in Male (Island resorts are responsible for transporting mail to Male).

● Telephone services

International telephone, telefax, telex and telegraph services are available 24 hrs. The private telecommunications company is Dhiraagu, 19 Meduziyaaraiy Magu, nr Chandanee Magu, opp the Islamic Centre in Male; open 0730-2000 daily, except Fri and holidays, 0800-1800.

Telephones International calls are handled by operator at 190 (the number for Directory enquiries). Phonecards may be bought from Dhiraagu, the post office and some shops; Rf20 for local, Rf200/Rf500 for overseas calls. The cardphone booths are at the airport and in Male; they are painted blue and grey. Some shops permit you to use their telephones for a small charge.

Fax Bureau Fax, Dhiraagu Bldg, provides facilities for sending and receiving fax messages. Handling charge, Rf20 plus cost/page, eg Rf60 for India; Rf90 for UK. Resorts have fax facilities which guests may request to use; charge may be 'per page' or 'per minute' of call.

Telegrams May be sent from Dhiraagu; per word charge, SAARC, Rf2; UK Rf3; Africa, Europe, Middle East, Rf4; Australia, USA Rf4.50.

Entertainment

● Newspapers

The one Male daily, the '*Haveeru*', carries a section in English. Entertainments are also advertised in English. Fortnightly English '*News Bulletin*' published locally. Some weekly international news magazines are also available at the Male bookshops. Hotels do not usually provide newspapers in guest rooms.

Holidays and festivals

Fri are holidays.

1 Jan: New Year's Day.
5 Feb: Martyr's Day commemorating the death of Sultan Ali VI in 1558.
26-27 Jul: Independence Day marking the end of British Protection.
29-30 Aug: National Day.
3 Nov: Victory Day, marking defeat of the Sri Lankan mercenaries in 1988.
11-12 Nov: Republic Day commemorating the 2nd Republic, 1968. Huravee Day marks the defeat of the Malabar Indians in 1752.
10 Dec: Fishermen's Day.

In addition, **Muslim** festivals are observed (dates vary according to the lunar calendar): beginning of Ramadan; Eid-ul-Fitr; Haj Day; Eid-ul-Adah; Islamic New Year; Prophet Mohammed's Birthday. See also, page 32.

Further reading

Anderson, Charles & Hafiz, Ahmad; *Common Reef Fishes of the Maldive Islands*; 1987; 72 fishes with photographs, aimed at snorkellers. *Living reefs of the Maldives*; 1991; more depth, helpful for divers, well-illustrated, both from Male, Novelty Printers. Bell, HCP; *The Maldive Islands*; 1940. Reprinted Male, 1985. Hooper, Neil, *Let's visit Maldives*; London, Macmillan, 1988; a brief general introduction but not a practical guide. Ellis, Royston; *Guide to Maldives*; Chalfont St Peter, Bradt, 1995; the latest, with plenty of information for the first-time traveller. Deptartment of Information and Broadcasting; *Maldives, a historical overview*; Male, 1986. Maloney, Clarence; *People of the Maldive Islands*; Madras, Orient Longmans, 1980. Reynolds, CHB; *Maldives* (World Bibliographical Series); Oxford, Clio P, 1993; an invaluable bibliography for anyone wishing to study any aspect of the nation of islands. Webb, Paul A; *Maldives – people and environment*; Bangkok, Media Transasia, 1988; a good introduction, covering people, flora and fauna.

MALDIVES: LAND, CULTURE AND HISTORY

LAND AND LIFE

Contents

Geography	250
Climate	250
Flora and fauna	251

Geography

The tiny islands are grouped around the fringes of shallow lagoons, collectively known by the Maldivian word which has entered the English language, **atoll**. Huvadhu atoll in the S is the world's largest true atoll, enclosing a lagoon area of 2240 sq km. In regions with the greatest depth, the sea is 200 fathoms deep; the islands themselves are rarely more than 2.5m above sea level. There are 19 administrative groups of atolls each named after a letter of the **Dhivehi** alphabet.

The approach by air is dramatic. A line of white waves indicates the reefs nearing but often not breaking the surface. Inside, are the aquamarine and turquoise shallows, with the coral clearly visible beneath, and then tiny patches of islands.

The formation of the atolls

The 1,600 km long island chain of which the Maldives are a part, stretching from the Laccadives in the N to the Chagos Archipelago in the S, are on the western edge of the Indian plate. The Indian plate broke away from its former neighbours, southern Africa and Antarctica, about 65 million years ago and started moving steadily, and quite rapidly, northwards. There is still uncertainty about the geological origins of the ridge on which the Maldives' coral islands have grown, but it is one of the remarkable submarine features of the Indian Ocean Sea floor, possibly associated with now extinct volcanic activity and running to the W of and approximately parallel with the Western Ghats in India, but stretching well S of the Equator. The surface of the highest points of the ridge has provided an ideal home for coral, which has produced the distinctive character of the Maldives' scattered tiny islands, whose total surface area amounts to just under 300 sq km compared with the area of just under 90,000 sq km of territorial seas.

Soil

The thin (15 cm) surface covering of dark sandy humus contains some parent coral rock making it very alkaline. The sandstone layer underneath gives way to a layer of sand which retains a lens of fresh-water on many islands which can be tapped by shallow wells. However, agricultural soils are extremely restricted, covering no more than 31 sq km, or 10% of its total land area.

Climate

Temperatures

The Maldives' climate reflects its equatorial oceanic position; the islands have no winter nor real summer season. Temperatures remain almost the same throughout the year, remaining between 25.7°C and 30.4°C. Minor variations reflect differences in cloud cover more than the apparent movement of the sun. Water temperatures are similarly equable and high.

Rainfall

Rainfall is spread throughout the year with an annual average of 1,950 mm. Like Sri Lanka the Maldives do experience the wind reversal characteristic of the monsoon. However, because the islands lie across the Equator the monsoons are not as pronounced as in the rest of South Asia, even though the two monsoon periods are the same. The SW monsoon (May-Oct) brings rain while the NE Monsoon (Nov-Apr) is marked by stronger but drier winds. The islands are situated in the doldrums, too far S to be affected by cyclones. The tidal range usually remains below a metre.

Flora and fauna

Most islands, including the uninhabited ones, have a substantial cover of tall coconut palms, screw pines, salt-resistant bushy plants and breadfruit. On some of the inhabited islands. Fruit and vegetables including mangoes, papayas, sweet potatoes, pumpkins and bananas as well as cereals are grown.

Though the island lacks land-based fauna, the coral reefs harbour a rich variety of tropical reef fish. Big fish include tunas, sharks, barracudas, manta rays and bonitos. Groupers and red snappers are fairly easily caught.

CULTURE

Contents

People	252
Language	252
Religion	253

People

The Maldivian people are descended from Aryan, Dravidian, Arab and Negro ancestors. The original population may have been Dravidians from S India followed by Indo-Aryan settlers from India and Sri Lanka and by 500 AD Buddhists dominated the islands; archaeologists have found remains of temples and stupas in some atolls. Research by Clarence Maloney in the 1970s demonstrated the importance of the 'underlaying layer' of the Tamil population, including the presence of Tamil in names, poetry, dance and religious belief.

Despite S Indian contacts, it seems probable that the majority of Dhivehis themselves came from Sri Lanka, but other streams of migration included South East Asia and Gujarat. There are records of trading ships from Gujarat making contact with Sri Lanka as early as the 5th century BC, and it is likely that Gujarati sailors also found their way to the Maldives. The Indonesians, who travelled right across the Indian Ocean to settle in Madagascar, left in the Maldives both physical and cultural evidence of their presence, such as sweet potatoes and taro.

Language

Dhivehi, the Maldivian language, is related to an old form of Sinhala from Sri Lanka which belongs to a North-Western Indian branch of the Indo-Aryan group. However, it incorporates important elements of early Tamil onto which the Sinhala was grafted, and today the vocabulary includes words of virtually every language used by sailors who have stopped for any length of time in the islands.

The Maldivian script shows a particularly interesting mixture of cultural traditions and influences. Sinhala and Tamil scripts both derived ultimately from Brahmi, the sript used by the Buddhist Emperor Asoka in the 3rd century BC. The earliest known form of Dhivehi script – *Evala Akuru* – was very similar to the Sinhala script of Sri Lanka, but by the 14th century AD a modified form had evolved, *Dives Akuru*, which was used from the 14th to the 19th centuries.

The arrival of Islam did not lead to an immediate change in script, but after the departure of the Portuguese the modern Dhivehi script, *Tana*, was invented, bringing together important features of Arabic and Indian scripts. In

"The Koimala Connection"

Maloney illustrates the importance of the Tamil and Malayalam connection with the Maldives through the story of the epic *Koimala*, which describes how a prince, Koimala, brought his whole royal family from India to a northern atoll and then settled in Male, which he made his capital. The word *koi* is derived from the Malayalam *koya*, which means son of the prince, and Maloney points to the presence of a high caste group in the Lakshadweep Islands called Koimala. This is just one strand of the evidence linking the early culture and pre-Muslim peoples of the Maldives with South India.

common with Arabic it is written from right to left. Its use continues widely despite the pervasive influence of Roman script and in particular English.

Religion

From the mid-7th century Arab traders landed on Maldivian islands when sailing back from Malacca and China and although the Berber Abul Barakaath (see Medhu Ziayarath below) is remembered as the bringer of Islam to the country, the long association with Arab sailors, going back before the foundation of Islam, paved the way for its adoption. In 1153 the ruler Sultan Mohammed ibn Abdullah (King Dovemi Kalaminja) was converted to Islam and declared it the religion of his kingdom. He was subsequently followed by the whole population. The commonly held myth explains the origins of the king's conversion in the power over the djinns of the sea demonstrated by Abu Barakaath Yousuf Al Barbary, a trader and holy man from Morocco. These terrifying spirits had long played a central part in the islanders' religious beliefs and ritual in a belief system called *fandita*, which Maloney suggests comes from very similar Indian systems of belief. Customs which are designed to control such spritis and powers common in India and Sri Lanka, including the tying of charms around the neck, continue to be practised in the Maldives, but with the additional Islamic touch that marks which look like Arabic are now engraved on the charms. For more about Islam, see page 67.

Although Islamic law is enshrined in the constitution social practice has some distinctive Maldivian characteristics. Patterns of marriage and divorce appear to reflect some of the different cultural streams which have influenced the islands, the Dravidian, the N Indian and the Arab. Maloney has described how rules relating to cousin marriage for example reflect both S and N Indian traditions.

One of the most striking features of the Maldives social organisation is the frequency and ease of marriage and divorce. In the 1970s there were reported to be 85 divorces for every 100 marriages, and many men and women married each other several times. Clarence Maloney has described the system: "By Islamic law as interpreted in the Maldives, the same man and woman can marry three times, after which they must marry other partners, and then they are free to marry each other another three times. An official notification limited the number maximum to three such cycles, or nine marriages for the same couple. But by giving a gift to charity even this could be relaxed, so some couples have remarried many times more than that. Traditionally there was an element of pride, even piety, in a man having had many marriages. Some individuals claim to have had 40 to 80 marriages".

HISTORY

Contents

Early history	254
The Sultanate	254
A Republic	255

Early history

Recording of history in the Maldives only began with the arrival of Islam in the 12th century but prior to that the islands were referred to by many outsiders. They are mentioned in Sinhala Buddhist texts, including the Dipavansa, the earliest Sinhala epic, and Clarence Maloney suggests that the islands may have been occupied by people from Kerala in the 1st century AD. Indeed, he has argued that the islands were originally settled from Sri Lanka. Greek writers in the 1st century AD and the Alexandrian Pappus in the 4th century referred to the Maldives, and the 6th and 7th century Pallavas from Tamil Nadu also conquered the islands, so it is not surprising that there is clear evidence of Buddhist and Hindu influences in the islands before the arrival of Islam.

The islands were part of the Arab trading network which connected the Arabian peninsula with the SW coast of India and with the Far East from Roman times onwards. The first reference to them in Arab literature dates from about 900 AD when Suleiman the Merchant gave a description. Despite Arab Muslim contact, however, the islands remained Buddhist, though in 1017 they were conquered by the empire building Chola king of Tamil Nadu Rajaraja Chola. It was only in 1153 that the islanders abandoned their version of Theravada Buddhism they had brought with them from Sri Lanka and followed their king in converting to Islam. Contact with the western world, both Islamic and Christian, continued. Marco Polo visited in the middle of the 13th century while the great Arab traveller and scholar Ibn Battuta acted as the islands' legal advisor between 1343-46.

The whole archipelago was originally probably referred to as the Lakshadweeps (100,000 islands). It also included at least the southern Minicoy Island of the present group, which was ruled from Male up to the 18th century and with which it has strong cultural and linguistic links, though it is now a part of India.

The islands might be thought to have had limited attractions to traders on their way between the ports of the Persian Gulf, Red Sea or East Africa and SW India, Sri Lanka and South East Asia. Shelter and the possibility of fresh water supplies, albeit limited, must have been a part of the attraction, but the islanders also appear quickly to have realized the value of their cowrie shells as a traded commodity. With very limited potential for growing food the Maldivian islanders were exporting cowries at an early stage in exchange for vital foodstuffs, especially from India, sea shells which then entered into world trade as a form of money as well as with religious, social and medicinal values beyond the imagining of their original exporters.

The Sultanate

From their conversion to Islam the Maldives remained an independent country with a sultanate until the mid 16th century. The Portuguese arrived in Male in 1513 and with the consent of the Sultan built a fort there. However, in 1558 they invaded and killed the Sultan, but then only ruled for 15½ years, when in 1573 they were driven out by

Muhammad Takarufanu. In the 17th century the Dutch considered the islands a protectorate while they ruled over Sri Lanka, though in practical terms Dutch influence was negligible. Then the Malabari Moplas from S India attacked Male in 1752 and remained in power for the brief period of 3 months and 20 days. The country was liberated by the founder of the Huraagé Dynasty which ruled the islands until the Maldives became a Republic over 200 years later.

The Maldives became a British Protectorate in 1887 though the country in effect remained a sultanate. In 1953 an attempt to found a Republic failed after 7 months and the sultanate returned (though in name only in the latter years). The country enjoyed British defence protection until independence on 26 July 1965 with the British keeping the island of Gan under lease as an RAF base until 1978 when they prematurely terminated the lease.

A Republic

As an independent state the Maldives joined the United Nations in Sep 1965. 3 years later, after a referendum, the Sultanate was abolished and country was declared a Republic on 1 April 1968. Ibrahim Nasir (who had held the post of Prime Minister since 1958 and had negotiated independent status) was elected President of the new republic on 11 November 1968.

MODERN MALDIVES

CONTENTS

Government	256
Economy	257

Government

The President is the Head of State and Chief Executive, nominated by the Citizens' Majlis and elected by a public referendum, for a 5-year term. The Majlis (Parliament) comprises 48 members (two elected from each atoll and eight nominated by the President); there is no party system. Ibrahim Nasir, the first President resigned in 1978, succeeded by Maumoon Abdul Gayoom.

Recent developments

The Maldives joined the Commonwealth in 1982 and is also a member of the principal international financial institutions. 20th century modernisation has been making an impact on the Maldivians since the 1960; changes have also been brought about particularly by developing the tourist atolls. The young population (47% under 15 years) however, is no longer guaranteed a job on finishing high school, giving rise to some frustration and discontent. There have been occasional attempts at overthrowing the present government; in Nov 1988 a coup attempt had to be crushed with Indian help, and in 1993 President Gayoom was challenged for the Presidency by his brother-in-law Iliyas Ibrahim in the election held among the country's 49 MPs.

President Gayoom himself has stressed that now so many Maldivians are receiving higher education and are changing their way of life he wishes to introduce much wider forms of democracy. In an interview quoted in the Far Eastern Economic Review President Gayoom was quoted as saying "We have a lot of young and educated people who have been abroad and seen other political systems at work, and they would very much like to see a more open sort of system in which there could be a number of candidates, and then the people can choose whomever they want. I think that is going to be a very good change and I want to put it into practice". He has now established committees to review the Constitution.

Foreign relations

The Maldives Government maintained a policy of strict non-alignment between the superpowers during the Cold War and tried to keep on very good terms with all its immediate neighbours. It has particularly strong links with Sri Lanka as it is the source of a high proportion of the labour used both in construction work and in the tourist industry. However, it also sees India as a vital friend, and called on the help of the Indian Navy in Nov 1988 when an abortive coup threatened the Government. The Maldives is an active member of the South Asian Association for Regional Co-operation (SAARC).

The Maldives also plays a part in international agencies, being particularly active in promoting the interests of small states. There is a strong lobby suggesting that 'global warming' through environmental change can pose a serious threat to its own low-lying islands. The high tidal swell in 1987 which caused severe damage to the airport island and Male brought the issue to the forefront. Figures quoted in 1990 by the Inter Governmental Panel on Climate Change claim that if conditions remain unchanged, the sea level may rise by 1m by the year 2100. While this figure is hotly disputed by some scientists, international concern is unabated.

Economy

The Maldivians depended heavily on trade in the past, exchanging fish, coconut products, ambergrise and cowries (which was used as currency on the subcontinent and beyond), for grain (particularly rice) and cloth. Today fishing and coconut growing remain major activities, although tourism has come to rival their importance as earners of foreign exchange.

Agriculture

Natural constraints such as poor, alkaline soil which retains some coral rock with low water-retentive quality, the scarcity of fresh-water, and the unfavourable climate, leaves only 10% of the land area on these small islands suitable for agriculture. Maldivians depend on the wet SW monsoon between May and Oct as the principal source of rain-water supplemented by a small amount of fresh-water available underground. In spite of this, cash crops are increasingly common.

Coconut palm is the chief crop, its products, especially the wood, being used for boat-building and construction. This is followed by breadfruit, mango, papaya, lime and banana among tropical fruit, as well as some vegetables and chilli, which is in great demand. The government is trying to improve conditions by limiting pest damage, improving seed varieties and distribution of seeds, encouraging new ventures, eg bee-keeping (which could also increase crop yields), poultry farming (for meat and eggs which have to be imported in large quantities) and growing cereals other than rice, and also through education.

Tourism

Since the the building of the first resort in 1972 tourism has transformed the economy, and now contributes over 20% to the GDP, employing 5% of the workforce. It is the largest earner of foreign exchange (60%) and there are now over 9,000 rooms. Europeans form the largest group of tourists (led by the Germans and Italians) while tourist numbers from Japan and Australia are growing very fast. In 1995 over 220,000 tourists visited the islands. This sector has enabled some enterprising Maldivians to become rich overnight; they lease uninhabited islands from the government for a nominal rent and re-lease these to foreign developers who pay large sums to turn them into resorts.

Fishing

Fishing has remained the traditional occupation of the islands for centuries; today's exports are canned (particularly Tuna), frozen and salted, and trade is mainly with the Far East and Europe. The vessel mechanisation programme since 1974 has greatly increased yields. Fishing employs 25% of the workforce and is the second largest contributor of foreign exchange.

Another 25% (mostly women) are occupied in the traditional boatbuilding, mat-weaving, rope-making and craft industries. In the modern sector fish canning and garment lead the export oriented group. Major trading partners include UK, USA, Sri Lanka, Thailand, Germany, Singapore, Japan, the Netherlands and Hong Kong.

Shipping

From the mid-1960s upto the early 80s the National Ship Management Ltd handled enough trade to become a significant source of foreign exchange. However, the decline in world trade has resulted in the industry being forced to shrink considerably to remain economic.

Communication

The Satellite Earth Station on Villingili island provides the country with international direct dialling telephones, telex and fax services. Between the atolls communication is through HF transceivers although UHF and VHF telephones are in use between many islands.

MALE

Contents

Male	
Places of interest	259
Museums	261
Parks	261
Local information	261
Island Resorts	265
Choosing an island	265
Resort categories and transfer from airport	265
Entertainment and sport	266
Resorts	268

Maps

Male	260
Ari Atoll	266
Kaafu Atoll	266

The capital, Male is in one of the central atolls of the archipelago. It covers about 3 sq km and houses one quarter of the nation's population. You can walk from one end of the island to the other in 20 mins, including finding all the major streets and restaurants, or cover it by motor bike in under 5 mins. Overcrowding in the tiny capital has resulted in a temporary solution; the shallow waters within the western and southern reefs have been reclaimed to increase the area by a third.

(*Pop* 56,000) Male is the only island on which it is possible to stay quite cheaply, but it is not a place for a long visit. There are no beaches (it is now almost completely built up), and it is easily possible to see the sights of interest in a couple of days.

Though the resident population is small, Male also has a floating population of many thousands from the atolls who come to carry out business, buy and sell products and to receive medical treatment not available on the other islands. Government and private schools also attract large numbers of pupils although each inhabited island has a government school.

Male is divided into four wards: Heneveiru (NE) with the finer houses, the residential area of Maafannu (NW and W) with some guest houses, and the smaller two, Galolhu (centre and SW) and Machchangolhi (C and SE). The Inner Harbour with the jetties to the N is enclosed by a coral stone breakwater which was first built between 1620 and 1648. Over the last few years, a long string large concrete 'tetrapods' have been used for a similar purpose. The Outer Harbour beyond the breakwater demarcated by three neighbouring islands is used for shipping; ocean going vessels anchor there, the cargo being transported by small towed boats to and from the new wharf near Male Customs.

Places of interest

Most of Male's sights can be seen in a day; they are clustered to the N of the island. **Grand Friday Mosque** (Masjid-al-Sultan Mohamed Thakurufaan Al-A'z'am), three storeys high, is the country's largest and is the **Islamic Centre** with a library and conference hall. Named after the national hero who defeated the Portuguese in 1573, it was completed in 1984. The prayer hall with its large gold coloured dome, decorated with beautiful woodcarving and Arabic calligraphy, can accommodate about 5,000 worshippers. The minaret is over 40m high. Non-Muslim visitors are welcome from 0900-1700 except at prayer times. Late morning and mid-afternoon are suitable times. Visitors must dress modestly, remove their shoes and wash their feet before entering.

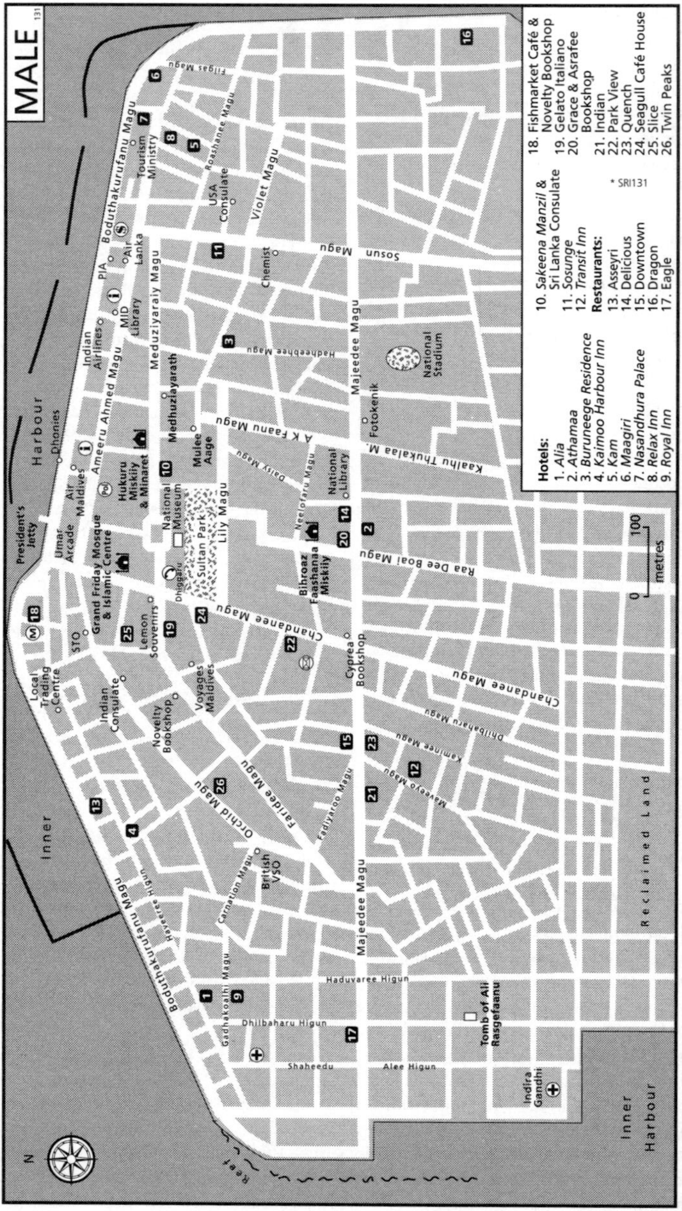
MALE
Hotels:
1. *Alia*
2. *Athamaa*
3. *Buruneege Residence*
4. *Kaimoo Harbour Inn*
5. *Kam*
6. *Maagiri*
7. *Nasandhura Palace*
8. *Relax Inn*
9. *Royal Inn*
10. *Sakeena Manzil* & Sri Lanka Consulate
11. *Sosunge*
12. *Transit Inn*
Restaurants:
13. Asseyri
14. Delicious
15. Downtown
16. Dragon
17. Eagle
18. Fishmarket Café & Novelty Bookshop
19. Gelato Italiano
20. Grace & Asrafee Bookshop
21. Indian
22. Park View
23. Quench
24. Seagull Café House
25. Slice
26. Twin Peaks
* SRI131
0 100 metres
Harbour
Inner
Inner Harbour
Reclaimed Land
Reef
Boduthakurufanu Magu
Majeedee Magu
Chandanee Magu
Sosun Magu
Violet Magu
Orchid Magu
Faridee Magu
Lily Magu
Ameeru Ahmed Magu
Meduziyaraiy Magu
Raa Dee Boai Magu
Kaalhu Thukalaa M.
A K Faanu Magu
Hadheebee Magu
Roashanee Magu
Filgas Magu
Daisy Magu
Neelofaru Magu
Dhilbaharu Magu
Kaminee Magu
Maveeyo Magu
Fadiyaroo Magu
Carnation Magu
Gadhakoalhi Magu
Haveeree Higun
Haduvaree Higun
Dhilbaharu Higun
Shaheedu
Alee Higun
Tourism Ministry
USA Consulate
Chemist
PIA
Air Lanka
MID Library
Indian Airlines
Dhonies
Air Maldives
Hukuru Miskiiy & Minaret
Medhuziayarath
Mulee Aage
National Museum
Sultan Park
Dhiggaru
President's Jatty
Umar Arcade
Grand Friday Mosque & Islamic Centre
Lemon Souvenirs
STO
Local Trading Centre
Indian Consulate
Novelty Bookshop
Voyages Maldives
Cyprea Bookshop
Bihroaz Faashanaa Miskiiy
National Library
Fotokenik
National Stadium
British VSO
Tomb of Ali Rasgefaanu
Indira Gandhi
N

Hukuru Miskiiy, the old Friday Mosque on Meduziyaraiy Magu, had the foundation stone laid in 1656 during the reign of Sultan Ibrahim Iskandhar. Built of stone, it has the tombs of Sultan Ibrahim Iskandhar and the royal family who reigned after him as well as other famous Maldivians. Verses of the Koran and an account of the conversion of the Maldivian people to Islam are carved on the walls. To prevent further deterioration of the coral stone structure, the western end has been protected from the sun by rather ugly corrugated iron sheets. **Munnaaru**, the white minaret at its gate was built 1675, inspired by Mecca after the King's visit and was originally used for calling the people to prayer.

Medhu Ziayarath opposite the old mosque, a shrine commemorating the Moroccon Abul Barakaath-al Barbarie who is believed to have brought Islam to the Maldives in 1153; some believe it was Yusuf Shamsuddin of Tabriz. **Mulee-Aage** (c1913) The official residence of the President is nearby. Built by Sultan Shamsuddeen III for his son and heir, it shows colonial rather than Islamic architectural influence. The Sultan however, was deposed and his family never used it. Used as government offices for many years, it was subsequently altered and enlarged; since the Maldives was declared a Republic in 1953 it has become the Presidential Palace.

Markets The colourful vegetable, fruit and firewood markets on H Boduthakurufanu Magu are worth visiting. The Fish Market is particularly busy in the late afternoon/early evening when the fishermen return.

Local industries On the outlying islands boat building and fishing continue to be the most important means of gaining a livelihood while coir production provides some employment. Attempts are being made to diversify with small scale textile printing and lace making for the tourist market.

Museums

The **National Museum** is behind the Islamic Centre Allow an hour. Open 0900-1140, 1500-1740. Entry Rf5, children under 12 Rf2. Attractively housed in one of Male's older wooden 2-storey houses, it includes collections of early sculptures, mainly in coral, some in wood, probably of the pre-Islamic Buddhist period in the Maldives. Some wooden boards show examples of early Dhivehi script. Dates of most of the early artefacts are uncertain, and are broadly listed as 11th century. More recent exhibits include royal memorabilia (furniture, clothes, transport such as palanquins, and arms); coins from the time of the first Sultan (Mohamad Imaadudin) in 1620, up to recent and contemporary items such as two motorbikes hit by bullets during the Nov 1988 coup attempt.

Parks

Sultan Park The space occupied by the Sultan's Palace complex which was demolished when the Maldives became a Republic for the second time in 1968 was declared a public park; the huge iron gate at the main entrance has been retained. The only surviving building houses the National Museum.

Local information

● Accommodation

All the accommodation on Male is simple, the most expensive charging about US$100 per room in high season. Some hotels have a/c rooms but there are also guest house rooms with fan and attached shower, and inexpensive rooms in private homes which usually do not provide meals. Several are 'Govt Registered', charging between US$15-30 per night. Most are small (less than 10 rooms), with a very limited range of services, but those listed here are clean and good value.

Alia, 32 M Haveeree Higun, western end, T 322080, F 322197, 18 rm, some a/c with bath, restaurant, bar, fresh water, not very quiet owing to location; *Athamaa*, Majeedee

Magu, E of junc with Chandanee Magu, T 323249, modern rooms with bath (hot water), restaurant downstairs; ***Kam***, H Roanuge, Meheli Goalhi, T 320612, F 320614, is the newest hotel in the capital (1995), 31 a/c rm with TV, phone, 4th flr restaurant with a good choice, coffee-shop, small swimming pool (only one in Male); ***Nasandhura Palace***, H Boduthakurufanu Magu, E end, T 323380, F 320822, 31 rm, some a/c with bath (fresh water), phone and satellite TV, restaurant (*Trends* rec), bar, rather dull and dated; ***Relax Inn***, Ameeru Ahmed Magu, Henveiru, nr *Kam*, T 314531, F 314533, a modern, tall (6-storey) hotel with smallish rooms with bath, phone, TV, good *Ground Six* restaurant; ***Sosunge***, Sosun Magu, few blocks from H Boduthakurufanu Magu, T 323025, 4 rm, former government guesthouse, one of the more expensive hotels in town.

Smaller hotels and guesthouses (with attached baths): ***Buruneege Residence***, Heethafiniva Magu, T 322870, 9 good rm, mostly a/c, good value in pleasant house; ***Kaimoo Harbour Inn***, Haveeree Higun, Maifaanu, T/F 323241, 4 rm with bath, good Chinese restaurant open all day (Fri from 1300); ***Maagiri***, Roashanee Magu, nr H Boduthakurufanu Magu, E end, T 322576, F 328787, small, friendly; ***Nivikoa***, Chandanee Magu, T 322942, 7 rm, rec; ***Royal Inn***, Izhadeenu Magu, T 320573, F 320574, nr *Alia*, 5 a/c rm with phone, good value; ***Transit Inn***, Maveeyo Magu, T 320420, F 326606.

The following are conveniently situated fairly close to the shops, sights and restaurants. Ask around for private rooms (some under US$10) in the Tel office area. One opp crossing with small red plate (US$25), others around Kosheege (US$15). ***Sakeena Manzil***, Meduziyaraiy Magu, T 323281, meals available, but crowded rooms, you may be woken early by the call to prayer from nearby mosque.

● Places to eat

Several are nr the junction of Chandanee and Majeedee Magus; menus are limited. Several are open all day except on Fri when they may open in the evening.

Downtown, Majeedee Magu, good food, friendly atmosphere, popular; ***Dragon*** Chinese, on the E side, is bit out of the way; ***Eagle Restaurant*** is close to the *Male Tour Inn*; ***Grace***, Majeedee Magu, serves inexpensive Sri Lankan; ***Indian Restaurant***, Majeedee Magu (Fun World), lacks ambiance but has reasonably priced curries; ***Park View***, nr Post Shop, Chandanee Magu; ***Twin Peaks*** on Orchid Magu is quite expensive but rec.

Cafés: open early and close late. A plate of savoury 'short eats' and sweet snacks are put on the table to have with a drink of tea or sweetened milk. You pay for what you eat. More substantial snacks are served in many. ***Delicious***, Majeedee Magu, for tea and snacks. On H Boduthakurufanu Magu, nr the harbour, are the popular: ***Fishmarket Café*** above the busy fish market and the ***Asseyri*** to its W, where you get good snacks while you watch the harbour activities from the 1st flr; ***Quench***, Majeedee Magu, has tables outside or under a thatch, Indian, continental and American fastfood style menu; ***Slice***, is a snack bar off Famudheyi Magu, nr the Grand Friday Mosque.

Ice cream parlours: some serve soft drinks, coffee in addition to ice creams. Among the upmarket ones: ***Gelato Italiano***, nr the corner of Chandanee Magu and Faridee Magu, has a good variety; ***Seagull Café House***, a little further S on Chandanee Magu, is more than an ice cream counter, the open-sided café in the garden does good, mildly spiced evening meals (up to 2200), in pleasant surroundings.

● Bars

Tourist hotels serve a full range of alcoholic drinks.

Soft drinks: there are shops clustered just behind H Boduthakurufanu Magu where the boats from the airport and other islands berth. Soft drinks are twice as expensive immediately around the jetties as they are in the small local stores just a little further inland.

● Airline offices

Scheduled: **Air Lanka**, Ameeru Ahmed Magu, T 323459; **Air Maldives**, Maldives Air Services Ltd, H Boduthakurufanu Magu, T 322436; **Alitalia**, c/o Air Maldives, T 322436; **Emirates Air**, H Boduthakurufanu Magu, T 325675; **Indian Airlines**, Sifaa, H Boduthakurufanu Magu, T 323003; **Pakistan International**, 4 Luxwood, 1 H Boduthakurufanu Magu, T 323532; **Royal Nepal Airlines**, c/o Air Maldives, H Boduthakurufanu Magu, T 322436; **Singapore Airlines**, 2nd Flat, MHA Bldg, T 320777.

Charter: **Air 2000**, **Air Europe**, **Belair**, **Sterling Airways**, c/o Voyages Maldives, 2 Faridee Magu, T 323617; **Balkan**, **Tarom**,

ZAS, Maldives Air Services Ltd, H Boduthakurufanu Magu, T 322436; **Condor**, c/o Universal Travel Department, 18 H Boduthakurufanu Magu, T 323116; **Lauda Air**, c/o Fantasy Travels, Faridee Magu, T 324668; **LTU/LTS**, Orchid Magu, c/o Faihu Agency, H Maaleythila, T 323202.

● Banks & money changers

Open 0900-1300, Sun-Thur. They are the only authorized money changers. **Bank of Ceylon**, Alia Building, Ground Flr, Orchid Magu; **Bank of Credit** and **Commerce and Habib Bank** on Chandanee Magu; **Bank of Maldives**, **Maldives Monetary Authority** and **State Bank of India** on H Boduthakurufanu Magu.

● Embassies & consulates

Most European countries have their embassy and consular staff based in Sri Lanka. Their telephone numbers are given in the Sri Lanka section (see page 105). In an emergency they should be contacted by telephone, which can be done readily from Male and from some other islands.

High commissions: **India**, Maafannu Aage, T 323015, F 324778; **Pakistan**, 2 Moonimaage, T 323024, F 321823; **Sri Lanka**, Sakeena Manzil, T 322845.

Honorary consuls & others: **Bangladesh**, c/o Universal Enterprises, T 323080; **France**, 27 Chandanee Magu, T 320258, F 322516; **Denmark**, **Norway**, **Sweden**: 25 H Boduthakurufanu Magu, T 3222451, F 323523; **UK**, c/o Dhiraagu, PO Box 2082, T 322802, F 325704; **USA**, Violet Magu, T 321981.

● Entertainment

See under 'Island Resorts' below.

● Hospitals & medical services

Central Hospital, Sosun Magu, Henveira, T 322400; new *Indira Gandhi Hospital*.

● Libraries

The Library is on Majeedee Magu, open daily, 1330-1700, 1930-2100, closed Fri. ***MID***, the private library on Ameeru Ahmed Magu, belonging to the Didi family which has some good reference books and books about the islands. Open daily 1400-2200, 1730-2000 during Ramazan. Monthly subscription and deposit.

● Post & telecommunications

Post: Post Shop (with poste restante), 1st Flr, Chandanee Magu, nr *Park View* restaurant. Open 0815-1145, 1330-1800, closed Fri. Counter at airport Departure Lounge and agency post offices at several points in Malle.

Telecommunications: Dhigaaru Telecommunications Office, nr corner of Chandanee and Meduziyaraiy Magus, daily, 0800-2000, for telegrams, fax, IDD calls. See also page 248 for details.

● Shopping

Open daily except Fri, 0800-2300. The shopping streets are 5 mins walk from the wharf. It is best to browse before buying and ignore the advice of local 'guides'. **NB** Turtles are now protected in the Maldives; no shop may sell turtle-shell ornaments. ***STO Shopping Centre***, Orchid Magu, by the Presidential Palace with a bank and toilets. ***Lemon Souvenir Shop***, Chandanee Magu, sells jewellery made from tortoise shell, mother of pearl, and red and black coral, colourful T-shirts and books and postcards. The ***Crafts Market*** is worth visiting. ***Asrafee***, Orchid Magu.

Bookshops: *Cyprea* and *Novelty Bookshop*, Faridee Magu sell books and postcards.

Duty free: the duty free shopping complex is in ***Umar Shopping Arcade***, Chandanee Magu, which stock electrical goods, watches and cosmetics etc. The Airport ***Duty free*** shop is small but well stocked and competitively priced. **NB** Take your passport with you.

Photography: ***Fototeknik, Fotogenic*** and ***Centofoto*** are on Majeedee Magu.

● Sports

See under 'Island Resorts' below.

● Tour companies & travel agents

A selection of internal travel, cruises and accommodation on the islands: ***Cyprea***, 25 H Boduthakurufanu Magu, T 322451, F 323523; ***Galena Maldives***, H Buruneege, T 324743, F 324465; ***Safari Tours***, Chandanee Magu, Male 20-02, T 323524, F 322516, offers a choice from a group of small islands designed for those keen on watersports; ***Sun Travel and Tours***, Manaage, Machchangolhi, Maaveyo Magu, T 325975, F 320419, they offer resort holidays and 'diving and cruising safaris' which usually stop at an island for the night; ***Treasure Island Enterprise***, agents for American Express, 8 H Boduthakurufanu Magu, PO Box 2009, T 322165, F 322798, they organize diving holidays on 3 resorts with special diving bases (Full Moon Island, Maayafushi and Bathala) and other island holidays; ***Voyages Maldives***, PO Box 2019, 2 Faridee Magu, T 323019, F 325336, they offer special 'Divers' Dream' min 8 days, 'Sailing Safaris' min 8 days, 'Adventure Sailing' or simply a beach holiday; ***ZSS Hotels and Travel Service***, 5 Fiyaathoshi Goalhi, Henveiru, also offer similar special packages.

● Tourist offices

Department of Information & Broadcasting, F/3 Huravee Bldg, Ameeru Ahmed Magu, T 323836, F 326211; **Information Unit** at the airport; **Ministry of Tourism**, F/2 Ghazee Building, Ameeru Ahmed Magu, T 323224.

● Useful addresses

Chambers of Commerce: Ministry of Trade and Industries, F/1 Ghazee Building, Ameeru Ahmed Magu, T 323668.

● Useful telephone numbers

Ambulance: T 102.
Fire: T 118.
Police: T 119.

● Transport

Local The usual mode of transport on Male is bicycles. However, all sightseeing and shopping areas are within walking distance and although taxis are available, you are not likely to need one except perhaps when you arrive and leave Male. **Taxi**: taxis can be contacted by phone; it is best to agree the fare in advance – Rf15-20 (Rf5/piece of luggage). ***Dialcab***, T 323132, Kulee Dhuveli, T 322122, and others. **Transport from airport** *Dhonis* are available to the jetty on the water front. (For the airport, *dhonies* wait at E end opp Emirates office on H Boduthakurufanu Magu.)

ISLAND RESORTS

The resort islands are scattered around a few atolls – most are on N and S Male(Kaafuatoll) where only nine out of the 81 islands are inhabited and Ari or Alif atoll where 18 of the 76 islands are inhabited. There are also resorts on Baa, Lhaviyani, Rasdhu Atoll, Vaavu Atoll and one on Gan. Travel agents and tour operators offer packages to the Maldives either flying direct to the islands for 2-4 weeks or as an extension to a holiday in India or Sri Lanka. You can choose to visit two or more islands.

Choosing an island

Choosing an island can be difficult when virtually all offer the promise of excellent sand and sun with plenty of watersports and diving. Size is an indicator with the most exclusive islands having as few as seven upmarket units while the larger complexes may have over 150 rooms. You might prefer one offering plenty of entertainment and a disco or one that promises peace and privacy. Some are more geared to young families with small children, others to the sophisticated. Some are 'no shoes, no news' with sand floors and a more informal atmosphere.

You can sometimes get an idea of the physical nature of the island from its name – the Dhivehi word for island is *du* or *fushi* which are usually established with thicker vegetation. A *finolhu* suggests a sandy strip with young vegetation which is progressively gaining in size. Some islands are within easy reach of others (with or without a transfer) thus providing variety. Some have shallow lagoons, attractive house reefs, exciting wrecks etc to suit snorkellers or divers; some may be better for swimming, others for windsurfing.

Some island resorts openly attract certain nationalities; you can also get a feel for the clientele by the foreign companies that predominantly operate in certain countries, and sometimes from the type of specialist restaurants.

Distance from Male can also be important for those who want a quick transfer by boat with the chance to visit Male, instead of a 3-hr journey on an occasionally choppy sea (or sometimes the option of an expensive air transfer).

Resort categories and transfer from airport

Resorts offer comfortable to fairly simple rooms, with fans or a/c, with attached bathrooms with hot and cold fresh water or desalinated water for showers (occasionally bath tubs). See Water supply on page 247. Some resorts charge luxury hotel prices but should not be expected to provide facilities or service of international class, city hotels. Most resorts offer good watersports and diving facilities; some offer some of these free.

Categories

Some islands charge a High Season rate in Aug; normally the higher rate applies from Nov-Apr and the Low Season is May-Oct. Price category based on average charged per day for a double room in Low Season, often with half or full board (High Season price increase can vary from 10-50%): **AL** US$200 and over; **A** US$150-200; **B** US$100-150; **C** US$70-100; **D** up to US$70.

Transfer

The transfer cost (payable in US$) is for return travel between the airport and the resort either by local *dhoni* boat, speed boat or by seaplane or helicopter for the distant resorts. Sometimes it is necessary to change to a *dhoni* from one of the

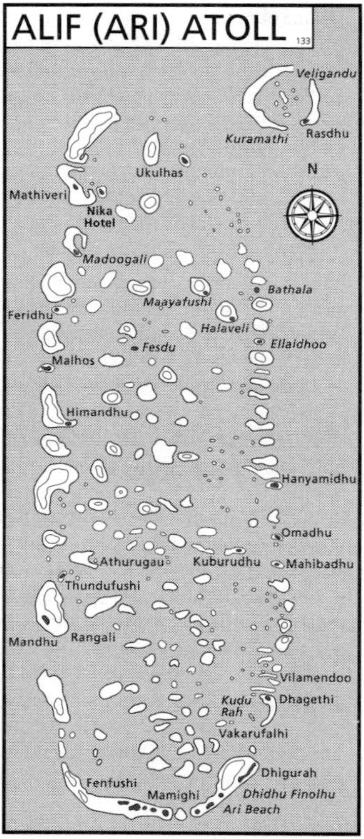

other means of transport, when you get close to your resort island (you are advised to wear sensible shoes while travelling). See Transport above for transport from airport to Male.

Travel between islands can be fairly expensive. Most travellers with pre-booked holidays are met by a resort representative at the airport. Others may phone resort to enquire about transfer arrangements.

NB Resorts on Ari atoll and others a long way away are not possible to reach in the dark (after about 1830). Late arrivals have to spend a night in Male since the boat ride takes 3-4 hrs. Those catching early morning flights out of the Maldives similarly must arrive in Male the night before. There are no inter-island flights at night.

Entertainment and sports

Entertainment

Some resorts have live bands and/or discos, beach barbecues (sometimes at night) and 'local' dances. It is government policy to keep holiday islands separate from the settled islands; indigenous cultural activities or entertainments are 'put on' for the tourists, in resorts.

Sports

'On land' usually includes tennis, football and volleyball. Some islands have provision for indoor games and a few a billiard table.

Watersports

Scuba diving, snorkelling, fishing (night fishing, which is not usually for big game fish), wind surfing, waterskiing, parasailing, sailing are all available on various islands. Big fame fishing is possible from a number of islands with a club on Full Moon (Furana).

Diving

Diving can be enjoyed by the beginner and the experienced in the ideal underwater reefs off the islands; wrecks are found near some islands. Expert instruction is available in many resorts; diving school prices vary. All equipment is available including cameras in some resorts; bring your own torch and batteries if you are planning to go out at night and your log book if you have dived before. Scuba diving is safe provided you make sure you have taken professional advice and have all the necessary equipment.

If you are planning to learn to dive on holiday it is best to have at least 14 days at a resort to allow time to join a course. Minimum age for diving, is 12 years. Remember, logbook and certificates can cost an extra US$66 in

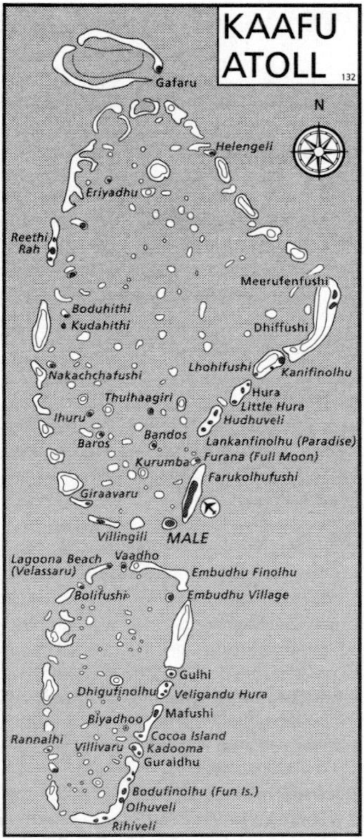

addition to a course fee. To prepare a total beginner for the PADI Open Water course, it is sometimes possible to have a try first in waist-deep water in shallow lagoons. For the qualified diver, '10 dive' or '6-day unlimited diving' options are usually available.

NB Special insurance cover should be taken out by anyone planning to dive.

A rich variety of coral fish plus some big fish, eg tunas, sharks, barracudas, bonitos can be seen from all islands. Manta rays are around in the low season when there is more plankton in the river. Catches of groupers and red snappers when you go fishing are fairly common.

Dhoni Safaris

A few wooden sailing boats have been refurbished and fitted with diesel engines. Others are purpose built 12-15m long 'Dhoni Yachts' with lateen rig, diesel engines and radio. They can take groups of eight with a crew of three or four on trips around the islands. The sleeping accommodation for the tourists is separate but very basic, usually on bunk in saloons. Meals are provided (no alcohol on board); wind surfing, snorkelling and diving equipment is usually taken. Contact Male Travel agents.

Maldive Travel, 3 Esher House, 11 Edith Terrace, London SW10 0TH, T 0171 352 2246, F 0171 351 3382, the only specialist company in the UK for the Maldives, offers 'Magic' tours on a new traditionally built '80 ft' Dhoni boat, twin cabins with shower and WC, comfortable, freedom to choose your pace and destination, all safety precautions. Support boat for diving gear, compressor and to take you ashore. The whole boat for 12 must be chartered for weekly periods.

RESORTS

L-AL *Nika Hotel* (Kuda Folliudhoo), T 450516, F 450577, N end of Ari atoll, is 70 km and 2½ hrs by speed boat or 35 mins by helicopter, from the airport (US$200); helicopter pad is 10 mins boat ride away (late arrivals have to spend a night in a private apartment in Male). 26 very spacious fan-cooled thatched bungalows of unusual design, built partly out of coral and wood, each has a solarium and showers (though no bath) with hot/cold fresh water in private garden, practically private beach. Italian, imaginative continental and eastern dishes, with barbecue and a Maldivian supper twice a week. Very well equipped diving school and all other watersports, and volleyball, badminton and tennis. Strong Italian character. Male, 10 Faridi Magu, T 325087, F 325097. In Italy, contact *Nika Hotel*, 5 Via Albricci, 20122, Milan, Italy, T 02/8077983. Italian run, *Nika* is one of the most exclusive resorts in the Maldives. Small and ideal for honeymoons.

AL *Cocoa Island* or Makunufushi on the E side of the S Male atoll is 30 km from the airport (US$200 by sea), T 343713, F 441919. Expensive, with eye-catching design, the 8 cottages are built of striking white coral with high thatched roofs lined with palm leaves and sand flr. Raised sleeping area is upstairs. Restaurant and bar have a good reputation. **NB** No hot or fresh water. Wind surfing, diving, catamaran, fishing and waterskiing. Male T/F 322326. Stronger on exclusivity than comfort.

AL *Kudahithi* A tiny island on the W side of N Male atoll, transfer by boat (US$75). A tiny island with exclusive accommodation for the select in 7 luxury bungalows. Watersports on Bodhuhithi nearby.

AL *Olhuveli View*, in SE of the S Male atoll, 36 km from the airport, transfer by boat (US$70), T 441957, F 445942. An upmarket resort with accommodation spread around in 125 rm in green-roofed bungalows, incl 13 floating suites on stilts accessed by wooden walkways over the sea. All mod-cons incl a/c, TV, video for movies, choice of restaurants. Most watersports, housereef, diving. Male, T 342788, F 345942; Singapore, T 223 2157, F 223 1673; Tokyo, T 327 19754, F 3275 0480.

AL *Rhiveli Beach Resort* (Mahaana Elhi Huraa) is on the S side of the S Male atoll about 40 km from Male (US$135), T/F 443731, 46 rm. A 500m long silver sand resort with Island of Birds and Rising Sun Island within easy reach. French owned with particularly good restaurant and bar. Free watersports includes wind surfing, sailing, waterskiing and tennis. Package incl 2-day cruise around nearby islands. Male T 323767, F 322964. Quietly attractive.

A *Athurugau* to the SW of Ari atoll, 20 mins by seaplane, US$240 (30 mins by helicopter, 2½ hrs by speedboat), T 450508, F 450574. 42 large rm in tiled cottages, heated fresh water, a/c in pretty palm covered island. Meals incl, entertainment laid on, plenty of watersports and PADI diving school. *Voyages Maldives*, T/F 324435.

A *Banyan Tree Island* formerly **Vabbinfaru**, 17 km NW of the airport in the N Male atoll is about 20 mins by speedboat (US$50), T 443147, F 443843. Small resort with 48 spacious thatched rondavels with fans, desalinated water, private gardens and terrace. Good food with a choice of restaurants, indoor games and a variety of watersports (some free), night diving, PADI dive school. Male T 323369, F 324752. Popular with Australians and Italians.

A *Bandos Island Resort* S of the N Male atoll, 9 km from the airport; transfer 45 mins by local boat or 20 mins by speedboat (US$40), T 443310, F 443877. One of the larger tourist islands from which you can cross to uninhabited and attractive Kuda Bandos nearby but do not swim across as currents are strong. 223 comfortable rooms with terrace, recently upgraded, half a/c, with terraces and heated spring water showers (some suites with bath). A/c restaurant, bar, 24-hr open-air coffee shop and aquarium. Swimming pool and sports complex (squash, gym, sauna) and indoor games. Excellent watersports and diving school (suitable for beginners and advanced), large decompression chamber, new medical centre. Male, *Dhirham Travels*, T 323369, F 324752. Larger island, good for families with young children (kindergarten, babysitting).

B *Digufinolhu Tourist Resort*, transfer time 1¼ hrs by speed boat (US$55), T 443599, F 443886. 50 a/c semi-detached bungalows and 10 new a/c 2-storey sea-facing units with patio. Hot/cold fresh water showers/bath tubs, coffee shop, beach BBQ, small shop. Dive School (PADI), good wind surfing, sailing in beautiful lagoon, day/night fishing but have to travel on day trips to find coral. Friendly, family island. Shares facilities with Veligandu Huraa, which is connected by bridge. Male T/F 327058. Good for swimming and windsurfing, ideal for families.

A ***Full Moon Island*** (Furana) Just N of Male, nr the airport and reached in 25 mins (US$20), T 443878, F 443879. Larger island with white sandy beaches (1½ hrs to walk around) with banyan trees and plenty of birds. There is a large lagoon and you can also visit a nearby fishing village or deserted islands. 65 rm in water bungalows on stilts, plus 92 rm in 2-storey blocks of 4, all sea facing with balcony, heated fresh water to bath or shower. Restaurants (incl Mediterranean and Thai), barbecue terrace deck extending onto sea open at night, disco, piano bar and coffee shop. Fresh water pool, business centre, gym, tennis, diving school (located on the eastern outer reef, diving waters are 15 mins away). The large lagoon offers plenty of scope for wind surfing, sailing and waterskiing. It is one of the few with a Big Game Fishing Club; night fishing excursions possible. Male, *Universal Enterprise*, T 322971, F 322678. Modern luxury resort with interesting architecture, lively.

A ***Kuda Rah Island Resort*** SE of Ari atoll, 84 km from the airport, 30 mins helicopter transfer (helipads on nearby islands), 10 mins by dhoni boat (US$50) or speedboat; transfer by seaplane (20 mins, US$85) optional, T 450549, F 450550. A small uncrowded island with plenty of vegetation, a virgin reef and ample white sand. 30 spacious a/c bungalows and 5 water-bungalows with steps down to the sea, bath tubs, hot/cold fresh water, private garden. Imaginative cuisine, disco, doctor and infirmary, billiards. Snorkelling, wind surfing, day/night fishing, canoeing, sailing, PADI diving (all equipment incl in price). Male T 325847, F 322335. Rather characterless but functional modern concrete buildings.

A ***Kurumba Village*** (Vihamana Fushi) Maldive's first resort island on N Male atoll, now fully modernized. Small island only 3 km from airport, 20 mins transfer by boat (US$20), T 443234, F 443885. 169 comfortable rooms in single/double storey bungalows or deluxe cottages, set apart from the main reception area. All have a/c and heated fresh water to bath/shower. Four restaurants (Indian, Chinese, continental), regular entertainment, fresh water pools and tennis. Full range of watersports, dive centre (about US$25 for single dives), conference centre and modern business facilities. Male, Universal Enterprises, T 322971, F 322678. Not as idyllic as far-off islands since you can see Male, popular with business clients.

A ***Laguna Beach Resort***, previously Velassaru is on the northern tip of the S Male atoll, only 10 km from the airport (US$40), 40 mins transfer by motor boat, T/F 343041. 115 comfortable a/c rm, some in individual tiled bungalows, others in groups of 4, phones, heated fresh water for bath/ shower. Choice of 5 excellent restaurants (incl Italian, Chinese), disco, fresh water pool, gym, flood-lit tennis, beach barbecue All facilities incl diving school, wind surfing, parasailing and night fishing. Male, *Universal Enterprise*, T 322971, F 322678. Elegant palm-covered up market resort, sporty cosmopolitan guest list.

A ***Thundufushi*** to the SW of Ari atoll, 20 mins by seaplane, US$240, (30 mins by helicopter, 2½ hrs by speedboat), T 450583, F 450515, 42 large a/c rm in tiled cottages, heated fresh water. Meals included, entertainment laid on, plenty of watersports and PADI diving school. Italian management. Male T/F 324435. An 'all-found' resort incl unlimited cigarettes and alcohol, popular with Italians and British.

A ***Soneva*** New luxury resort, SW of Male in the Baa atoll, 3 hrs by speedboat, 35 mins by helicopter, on one of the larger (1.5 km long, 450 wide) and greener islands. 42 well-furnished rm, some with 4-posters, bath and shower (desalinated water), set along the beach but taking advantage of the natural greenery. Restaurants, bar, dive school, watersports (some free), island hopping and excursions organized. One of the newest resorts.

B ***Alimatha*** on Vaavu Atoll, 2 hrs by boat (US$80), 35 mins by sea plane. A palm-covered island, 70 a/c bungalows (some inter-connecting for families) with hot freshwater showers, restaurant, disco, live band. Dive school with decompression chamber, underwater photography school, good fishing (day and night), incl big game, especially merlins. Excellent diving and windsurfing, large lagoon good for beginners.

B ***Biyadhoo Island Resort***, 29 km from the airport in the S Male atoll, close to Cocoa Island, transfer 1 hr by speedboat (US$65),

T 447171, F 447272. 96 comfortable a/c rooms on 2 storeys with heated fresh water showers and patio/balcony. A/c restaurant and bar, weekly barbecue, disco, local and Indian folk evenings. Virtually every kind of watersport including parasailing; night fishing catches can be barbecue. 'Nautico' watersports centre, PADI diving and decompression chamber. Two housereefs for shore diving with 5 passages each on this and Villivaru. Speedboats and dhonis available for trip to Male or helipad for helicopter 'flips'. Male T 324699, F 327014. Wide ranging facilities, Indian management.

B *Boduhithi Coral Isle*, 27 km from airport on the W side of N Male atoll, transfer by boat (US$70). 87 a/c bungalows, 4 over water, watersports, indoor games.

B *Embudhu Finolhu* NE of S Male atoll, 11 km from airport, transfer by boat (US$33), T 444451, F 445925. The long, narrow island has little natural shade but plenty is provided by the attractive lagoon. 42 rm, the original pairs of rather grey rooms with steps down to lagoon, but since the Indian Taj group has expanded it since 1994, 16 new cottages have been added. Good food in restaurant, some watersports, diving, relaxed atmosphere. Taj Maldives, 10 Medhuziyaaraiy Magu, T 317530, F 320336.

B *Farukolhufushi* in the N Male atoll, immediately N of the airport so a quick transfer but on the flight path, T 343021. French run, typical Club Med resort which is one of the largest – guests must stay minimum of a week. 152 rm, no a/c. No day-trippers allowed. The large thatched restaurant serves good food. Usual watersports but no water skiing. Club Med resort.

B *Fun Island Resort*, (Bodu Finolhu) is on the E reef of the S Male atoll, 40 km from the airport, about 3 hrs by boat (US$75), 45 mins by dhoni speedboat, T 444558, F 443958. A very small island which may feel a little overcrowded but has a shallow lagoon making it possible to walk across to 2 tiny neighbouring uninhabited islands at low tide. 100 comfortable rm in blocks of 2/3/4, all a/c, with verandah, and shower/ bath with hot/cold desalinated water. Comfortable open-sided restaurant, bar and coffee shop with an attractive terrace overhanging the lagoon. Disco and weekly cultural shows ('boduberu') in season, recreation complex, new photo lab and clinic. Diving, wind surfing, snorkelling, fishing and waterskiing. Male, T 324478, F 327845.

B *Holiday Island* (Dhiffushi), on the S Male Atoll, 2 hrs by speedboat, 30 mins by helicopter. 142 luxury beach front rooms with heated 'sweet water', bath tub, colour videos, restaurant for western and oriental cuisine, other usual facilities plus, live band, piano bar, film lab (1-hr developing). Indoor and outdoor, sports including billiards, flood lit tennis, all usual watersports. New in 1995, spacious, colourful, good lagoon for those learning to dive and windsurf.

B *Halaveli Holiday Village*, E Ari Atoll, 55 km from the airport, about 1¾ hrs by speedboad (US$50, one-way). 50 comfortable coral bungalows (US$150, full board), solar-powered water heaters, but 4 cheaper rm, Nos 51-54, with fan only ($80) which are very good value, good food, no disco but good entertainment. The resort has 'kept its 'natural' Maldivian character, simple yet sophisticated'. There is a very good coral reef and sandy beach, free canoe and 2 free excursions by *dhoni* weekly, but guests pay for other watersports. Agents Akiri, H Boduthakurufanu Magu, T 322719, F 323463 for travellers from South Asia; from elsewhere, Grandi Viaggi, Milano, Italy. One with an Italian flavour.

B *Hudhuveli Beach Resort* is a very small island on the N Male atoll 10 km from the airport, about 45 mins by Dhoni (US$30), T 443396, F 443849. 44 units, some rondavels and some terraced bungalows, all thatched and painted white. Restaurant (fresh fish daily), bar and open-air coffee shop. The island claims to be the cleanest in the Maldives, with the best water in the whole atoll and no mosquitos! Diving (either in the inner coral reef or in the outer reef close to larger fish), snorkelling, wind surfing, fishing and waterskiing. Also volleyball, badminton and table tennis. Male, T 322844, F 321026.

B *Ihuru Tourist Resort*, 17 km from the airport, W side of N Male atoll, 16 km from airport, 1 hr transfer by boat (US$44). A very small island, 40 rm, fan-cooled, in simple bungalows with fresh water showers, verandah with Maldivian swing (*undhulhi*), usual watersports, night beech barbecues, offers 'sting ray feeding', on the wall of the housereef (20m).

B *Kanifinolhu Resort* On the E edge of the N Male atoll, 16 km from the airport, transfer, 1½ hrs by boat, 30 mins by speedboat (US$30), T 443152, F 444859. A ¾ km semicircular island with a sheltered lagoon. 106 rooms in semi-detached bungalows, from non-a/c to comfortable luxury a/c suites with balcony or patio. New deluxe rooms, double storied, furnished to high standard. All on the beach side, with fresh water to showers. Restaurant (with à la carte), disco bar, coffee shop, gift shop. Weekly disco and occasional live band. Not too great for swimming but most kinds of watersports incl good diving (PADI), good snorkelling to the S, day and night fishing, also tennis. Male, Cyprea, T 322451, F 323523. Lively – popular with under 35s. Also suitable for families with children. Lagoon ideal for beginners to diving and windsurfing.

B *Nakatchafushi* is on the W side of the N Male atoll, 24 km from the airport and about 1½ hrs boat ride (US$50), 30 mins by speedboat, T 443847, F 442665. This pretty island has Maldivian character. 52 secluded, simply furnished a/c 'rondavels', some with thatch with cane furniture, with heated fresh water for showers or baths. These have been recently refurbished. Small open-air Chinese restaurant, good coffee shop, swimming pool, pleasant (now enlarged) bar deck over water, dance flr for parties. All kinds of watersports. German diving school. Male T 322971, F 322678. One of the most genuinely 'local' islands.

B *Rangali Island Resort* on the S Ari atoll is 104 km away from the airport, 2½ hrs transfer by boat or 35 mins by helicopter (US$180), T 450629, F 450619. Fairly new, 41 a/c bungalows (some with 3-4 beds), fresh water showers and with verandas to beach. Most watersports, fresh water pool, diving, night fishing, tennis. Rangali Finolhu nearby is a deserted island with its own thatched Maldivian cottage, for honeymooners to spend a day away from the rest! Male T 324701, F 324009. Cosmopolitan, new and well-run resort.

B Rannalhi in the S Male atoll, 40 km from the airport, 45 mins transfer by speedboat. It has an inner housereef and a shallow lagoon. Closed for complete redevelopment.

B *Reethi Rah* on the western edge of N Male atoll, transfer time, 2¼ hrs by boat (US$50), T 441905, F 441906. 50 rm in simple individual cottages and 5 pairs of rooms in water bungalows with a/c, all with thatched roofs and coral walls and heated desalinated water to showers. Simple bars and restaurant, shallow lagoon with wide beach, plenty of watersports, PADI diving. Longish boat journey, simple 'sand-flr' open-air living, good for the sports-loving. Male T 323758, F 328842.

B *Sun Island* on Ari Atoll, new, opening in 1996.

B *Vaadhoo Diving Paradise*, 8 km from the airport, at the N end of the S Male atoll is about 15 mins by speed boat (US$30), T 443976, F 443397. Small island straddling Vadhoo channel, tall palm trees with 24 a/c rm in a 'colonial' style villa and 7 stylish 'Sunset Wing' floating cottages, some with illuminated glass-top table for viewing and feeding the tropical fish and bathrooms with picture windows! Attractive Hut Bar over the water; snorkelling, glass-bottomed boat, night fishing and good diving. Male, T 325844. The floating cottages are classy compared to the simplicity of the rest; popular with the Japanese.

B *Vakarufalhi* on the S Ari Atoll, opened in 1994, transfer, 2 hrs by boat, 25 mins by helicopter. 50 thatched a/c bungalows with hot showers, bath tubs, 'open' toilets in walled gardens. Restaurant (western and oriental), coffee shop, bar. Most sports including PADI diving and night fishing. Small island, good for snorkelling and diving.

B *Veligandu Huraa* (Palm Tree Island) 50 km from the airport in the S Male atoll is about 1¼ hrs by speed boat (US$80), T/F 450519. 63 rm, incl 16 deluxe bungalows, bath tubs, hot fresh water. Restaurants incl Thai, bar, outdoor buffets. Most watersports available. A sophisticated island with a bar (classical music) on the walkway to Digufinolhu island nearby, which has a livelier clientele and occasional disco! A small deserted island between the two. Male, T 322432, F 324009.

B *Veligandu Island* Rasdhu Atoll, 50 km airport, transfer by boat (US$90), T/F 450519. 55 rm, range of sports and night fishing, a/c rooms and bungalows, Male T 322432, F 324009. Good swimming for beginners, long sand bank and shallow lagoon.

B *Villivaru Island Resort*, nr Biyadoo, on the S Male atoll, 29 km from Male, transfer 1 hr by speedboat (US$65), T 447070, F 343742. Smaller than Biyadoo with landscaped gardens. 60 a/c rooms with hot/cold fresh water showers (all water is desalinated), private patios open on to beach. A/c restaurant and bar. Snorkelling and diving. The coral reef harbouring a large variety of fish is approximately 30m offshore and excellent for experienced divers (PADI). Daily ferry service to Biyadoo. Male T 324699, F 327014. The two islands provide good diving and watersports.

B-C *Ari Beach* (was Dhidhu Finolhu) on the SE of Ari atoll, transfer 2½ hrs by speedboat (US$110), 35 mins by helicopter, 30 mins by seaplane, T 450607, F 450512. 120 simple but comfortable rm in Maldivian style thatched huts, some a/c, mostly unheated fresh water showers. Less visited than those nearer Male, good beaches, plenty of vegetation and shallow lagoon, diving. Male T 321930, F 327355. Far from Male and bright lights, deliberately more back-to-nature, newer resort with good watersports, attracts Italian guests.

B-C ***Dhiggiri***, 48 km from airport on Vaavu atoll, transfer, 2 hrs by boat (US$80), 35 mins by sea plane. 70 a/c rm with hot showers, incl 20 round water bungalows with sun deck and steps down to the sea, open air restaurant, small bar. Watersports includes big game fishing off Alimatha nearby (10 mins). Guests are take their litter (bottles, batteries etc) back home! Small and informal, a 'primitive' resort with plenty of local flavour.

B-C ***Ellaidhoo*** 56 km from airport on E side of Ari atoll transfer by boat (US$80). 50 rm under thatch roofs. Plenty of space and greenery, an island for the sportsman (grass pitch) but also a serious diver's island.

B-C ***Kuramathi Tourist Island***, Rashdu Atoll, on the N fringe of the Ari atoll 60 km W of Male, transfer time about 2 hrs by speed boat (US$100), 30 mins by helicopter, T 450527, F 450556. One of the larger islands, attractive for diving and snorkelling. The N tip is occupied by the **B** ***Blue Lagoon Club***, with its own private pier. 50 comfortable units with hot/cold desalinated water. The 20 thatched cottages on the E side, built on stilts, are reached by walkways; private terrace with steps down to water. The Lagoon restaurant (with à la carte) and terrace bar. At low tide it is possible to walk a long distance out beyond the N tip – take care not to get stranded! The **C** ***Kuramathi Village*** in the SE corner of the island is less expensive. 122 a/c units, some thatched round houses. Restaurant, bar and coffee shop are all open-sided. Live entertainment weekly and discos on other evenings. The **C** ***Cottage Club*** is the third centre. Watersports include snorkelling, diving (with a dive shop) and wind surfing school and day/night fishing. You may see hammerhead sharks nearby. Also tennis and archery. Male, *Universal Enterprise*, T 322971, F 322678. A large island with plenty of green and birdlife.

B-C *Lily Beach* (Huvahendhu) in the S Ari atoll, 550m by 100m, 35 mins by helicoper plus 30 mins boat ride from heli pad. 68 beach front bundgalows, desalinated hot water; 16 on water bungalows have private sun deck, bath tub, small garden, usual facilities with spacious public areas. Diving (Ocean Pro, Swiss) offering PADI courses, windsurfing. Good sporting facilities on a small island.

B-C *Vilamendhu* on the S Ari Atoll, opened in Nov 1994. 100 a/c rm with private terrace, hot water to showers opening onto small garden, restaurant with choice of western and oriental dishes. A large island by Maldivian standards with ample use of local cadjun thatching. Usual outdoor and watersports including PADI diving.

C *Baros* Oval shaped, small island 16 km from the airport on the N Male atoll, 1 hr by boat (US$40), T 442672, F 443497. 56 upgraded a/c rm wiith verandah close to the water, and 12 new luxury water-bungalows on stilts with steps down to lagoon, all with fresh water heated showers. One of the oldest, popular with British tourists. Restaurants (incl new *Asian Garden*), bar, new beach coffee-shop and barbecue area, small gift shop and dive shop. Good housereef on one side – the coral and fish make diving and snorkelling particularly interesting for beginners, while wind surfing on the lagoon on the other side, and waterskiing are also excellent friendly. Male, *Universal Enterprises*, T 322971, F 322678. Ideal for families, good introduction to snorkelling and diving, friendly atmosphere.

C ***Bathala Island Resort*** is a small island on the NE edge of the Ari atoll about 85 km and 2½ hrs by boat from the airport (US$150 or US$190 by air), T 450587, F 450558. Sri Lankan managed. The island is completely encircled by the reef, the inner reef being only 30m from the waters' edge. 37 round bungalows have pointed palm thatch roofs, some deluxe with a/c. Simply furnished with hard water outdoor showers in private walled gardens. Restaurant (fish caught daily) and small bar are open-sided. Watersports include catamaran, waterskiing and wind surfing (currents can be strong), expert diving instruction. A 'Treasure Island Enterprise'. Male T 323323, F 324628. Small and informal resort popular with the young.

B/C ***Lhohifushi Tourist Resort*** on the E of N Male atoll, 18 km from the airport, 1 hr by boat (US$30), T 441909, F 441908. It is a smaller quieter island surrounded by a lagoon and has a house reef. The resort with pretty, lush vegetation, is unsophisticated and has attempted to retain Maldivian character in its buildings with flower-filled gardens. 105 rm, some a/c simply furnished, with small verandahs, have island water to showers. Choice of restaurants and bar/lounge, open-air coffee shop with balcony overhanging the sea. Swimming pool and most sports incl diving. Male, T 323378, F 324783.

C ***Maayafushi Tourist Resort*** On NE fringe of the Ari atoll 65 km W of Male, transfer by air, (US$150). T 450588, F 450568. 60 small thatched units in rows with terraces with showers. Restaurant serving hot/cold buffets and bar. Expert diving instruction (the house reef is only 70m away); boats to farther reefs twice daily. For non-divers there is a large lagoon for snorkelling, wind surfing, water skiing, parasailing and sailing. Visits to other islands possible. A 'Treasure Island Enterprise' resort popular with under 35s. Male T 320097, F 326658.

C ***Ocean Reef Club*** has opened on Gan; the transfer by air costs US$160. Offers snorkelling, diving, tennis. Phoenix Hotels and Resorts in Male will book rooms, T 323181, F 325499.

C ***Paradise Island*** (Lankan finolhu) in the N Male Atoll, 12 km from the airport, 20 mins by speedboat. 103 beach front delux rm and 27 over water with private balconies, all with open air toilets, gardens, colour video, phone. Flood lit tennis, swimming pool, diving and windsurfing.

D ***Embudhu Village***, NE of S Male atoll, 10 km from the airport, 25 mins by boat,(US$30, T 444776, F 442673. 124 rm some a/c, mostly simple and functional ones in stark buildings with metal roofs, others on waterside, better but noisy from machines. Restaurant, sand bar, snorkelling, wind surfing, dive school (shark feeding!), 28m deep house reef but strong currents. *Kaimoo Travels*, Male, T 322212, F 320614.

D ***Eriyadhu Island Resort*** is 29 km NW of Male and 3 hrs by local boat (US$50), T 444487, F 445925. One of the cheaper resort islands, quite informal, with 46 sea-facing rooms (some family rooms for 4), in simple, white-washed bungalows with fans and fresh water. Restaurant and water bar with bar deck. Wide stretch of beach, shaded, pretty lagoon and good housereef. Diving (Swiss sub-aqua), snorkelling, wind surfing, day/night fishing and volleyball. Male T 326483, F 326482.

D ***Helengeli Tourist Village*** in the far N of the N Male atoll, is about 50 km from the airport (US$75). T/F 444615. Small resort, 30 rm with salt water showers. Limited watersports; good coral reef so convenient for snorkelling and unlimited diving (reasonable charges). Male T 325587, F 325625.

D ***Kuredu*** is one the Lhaviyani atoll, 130 km from the airport, transfers by speedboat (US$100) or air (US$200), T 230337, F 230332. At the cheap end of the market, one of the larger islands with a variety of vegetation, with the two long beach sides lined with 150 chalets, catering for the young who don't mind the campstyle atmosphere. Uninhabited island visit possible, usual watersports, plenty of underwater life in inner and outer reef, diving is the main attraction. Male, T 321751, F 326544.

D ***Meerufenfushi Island Resort*** or 'sweet water island' is to the NE of the N Male atoll, T 443157, F 445946. 40 km from the airport, transfer time is 2½ hrs by boat (US$50). One of the larger island resorts with a large lagoon – pleasant and green in the centre, with coral sand beach and only islands on the horizon. You can swim to Fishman Island 100m away (take towel and shirt). 164 non-a/c very simply furnished rooms in single storey blocks with unheated island water showers. Restaurant (midday coffee shop meal US$6), open-sided bar, good value. Diving, expensive compared to some others (eg US$50 for single, certification US$500), usual watersports with sailboarding popular on the lagoon. Friendly service.Rec for sight-seeing – a roundtrip from Male costs about US$45. Male T 324910, F 324711. Long boat journey, modest resort for those seeking a simple life, rec as best in the lower-price group, gaining in popularity with the British.

GLOSSARY

Words in *italics* are common elements of words, often making up part of a place name

A

aarti (arati) Hindu worship with lamps

abhaya mudra Buddhist symbolic posture, signifiying protection. The forearm is raised, the palm of the hand facing outward, fingers together

ahimsa non-harming, non-violence

ambulatory processional path

amla/amalaka circular ribbed pattern (based on a gourd) at the top of a temple tower

Ananda the Buddha's chief disciple

anda lit 'egg', spherical part of the stupa

antechamber chamber in front of the sanctuary

apse semi-circular plan, as in apse of a church

arama monastery (as in Tissamaharama)

architrave horizontal beam across posts or gateways

Arjuna Hero of the Mahabharata, to whom Krishna delivered the Bhagavad Gita

arrack spirit distilled from palm sap

aru river (Tamil)

Aryans lit 'noble' (Sanskrit); prehistoric peoples who settled in Persia and N India

asana a seat or throne

ashram hermitage or retreat

Avalokiteshwara Lord who looks down; Bodhisattva, the Compassionate

avatara 'descent'; incarnation of a divinity, usually Vishnu's incarnations

B

banamaduwa monastic pulpit

Bandaras sub-caste of the Goyigama caste, part of the Sinhalese aristocracy

bas-relief carving of low projection

basement lower part of walls, usually adorned with decorated mouldings

bazar market

begum Muslim princess; Muslim woman's courtesy title

beru elephant grass

Bhagavad-Gita Song of the Lord; section of the Mahabharata in which Krishna preaches a sermon to Arjuna explaining the Hindu ways of knowledge, duty and devotion

bhikku Buddhist monk

bhumi 'earth'; refers to a horizontal moulding of a shikhara

bhumisparasa mudra earth-witnessing Buddha mudra

Bo-tree *Ficus religiosa*, large spreading tree associated with the Buddha

Bodhisattva Enlightened One, destined to become Buddha

Brahma Universal self-existing power; Creator in the Hindu Triad. Often represented in art, with four heads

Brahman (Brahmin) highest Hindu (and Jain) caste of priests

Brahmanism ancient Indian religion, precursor of modern Hinduism and Buddhism

Buddha The Enlightened One; founder of Buddhism who is worshipped as god by certain sects

bund an embankment; a causeway

Burghers Sri Lankans of mixed Dutch-Sinhalese descent

C

cantonment large planned military or civil area in town

capital upper part of a column or pilaster

catamaran log raft, logs (*maram*) tied (*kattu*) together (Tamil)

cave temple rock-cut shrine or monastery

chakra sacred Buddhist wheel of the law; also Vishnu's discus used as a weapon

chapati unleavened Indian bread cooked on a griddle

chena shifting cultivation (Sri Lanka)

Chera early and medieval Kerala kingdom (India)

chhatra, chatta honorific umbrella; a pavilion (Buddhist)

Chola early and medieval Tamil kingdom (India)

choli blouse

circumambulation clockwise movement around a stupa or shrine while worshipping

cloister passage usually around an open square

coir coconut fibre used for making rope and mats

copra dried sections of coconut flesh, used for oil

corbel horizontal block supporting a vertical structure or covering an opening

cornice horizontal band at the top of a wall

crore 10 million

Culavansa Historical sequel to Mahavansa, the first part dating from 13th century, later extended to 16th century

D

dagoba stupa (Sinhalese)

dan (a) gift

darshan (darshana) viewing of a deity

Dasara (dassara/dussehra/dassehra) 10 day Hindu festival (Sep-Oct)

devala temple or shrine (Buddhist or Hindu)

Devi Goddess; later, the Supreme Goddess; Siva's consort, Parvati

dhal (daal) lentil 'soup'

dharma (dhamma) Hindu and Buddhist concepts of moral and religious duty

dharmachakra wheel of 'moral' law (Buddhist)

dhoti loose loincloth worn by Indian men

dhyana meditation

dhyani mudra meditation posture of the Buddha, cupped hands rest in the lap

distributary river that flows away from main channel, usually in deltas

Diwali festival of lights (Sep-Oct) usually marks the end of the rainy season

Dravidian languages – Tamil, Telugu, Kannada and Malayalam and peoples mainly from S India

Durava caste of toddy tappers

Durga principal goddess of the Shakti cult; riding on a tiger and armed with the weapons of all the gods, she slays the demon (Mahisha)

dvarpala doorkeeper

E

eave overhang that shelters a porch or verandah

eri tank (Tamil)

F

finial emblem at the summit of a stupa, tower, dome, or at the end of a parapet; generally in the form of a tier of umbrella-like motifs, or a pot

frieze horizontal band of figures or decorative designs

G

gable end of an angled roof

garbhagriha literally 'womb-chamber'; a temple sanctuary

gedige arched Buddhist image house built of stone slabs and brick

gopura towered gateway in S Indian temples

Goyigama landowning and cultivating caste among Sinhalese Buddhists

H

Haj (Hajj) annual Muslim pilgrimage to Mecca (Haji, one who has performed the Haj)

hakim judge; a physician (usually Muslim)

Hanuman Monkey hero of the Ramayana; devotee of Rama; bringer of success to armies

Hari Vishnu Harihara, Vishnu- Siva as a single divinity

harmika the finial of a stupa in the form of a pedestal where the shaft of the honorific umbrella was set

Hasan the murdered eldest son of Ali, commemorated at Muharram

Hena washermen caste

horst block mountain

howdah seat on elephant's back, sometimes canopied

Hussain the second murdered son of Ali, commemorated at Muharram

I

illam lens of gem-bearing coarse river gravel

imam Muslim religious leader in a mosque

Indra King of the gods; God of rain; guardian of the East

Isvara Lord (Sanskrit)

J

jaggery brown sugar, made from the sap of a variety of palm

jataka stories Buddhist accounts of the previous lives of the Buddha

jelebi snack prepared by frying circles of batter and soaking in syrup

JVP Janatha Vimukhti Peramuna (People's Liberation Army) – violent revolutionary political movment in Sinhalese areas of Sri Lanka in 1970s and 1980s

K

kachchan dessicating hot wind

kadu forest (Tamil)

kalapuwa salty lagoon

Kali lit 'black'; terrifying form of the goddess Durga, wearing a necklace of skulls/heads

kalyanmandapa (Tamil) hall with columns, used for the symbolic marriage ceremony of the temple deity

kapok the silk cotton tree

kapurala officiating priest in a shrine (devala)

karandua replica of the Tooth Relic casket, dagoba-shaped

Karavas fishing caste, many converted to Roman Catholicism

karma present consequences of past lives; impurity resulting from past misdeeds

Kataragama the Hindu god of war Skanda

Kartikkeya/Kartik Son of Siva, God of war. Also known as Skanda or Subrahmanyam

katcheri (cutchery, Kachcheri) public office or court

khondalite crudely grained basalt

kolam small lake (Tamil); masked dance drama (Sinhalese)

kovil temple (Tamil)

kitul fish-tailed sago palm, whose sap is used for jaggery

kotkarella dagoba spire

Krishna 8th incarnation of Vishnu; the mischievious child, the cowherd (Gopala, Govinda) playing with gopis; the charioteer of Arjuna in the Mahabharata epic (see above)

Kubera Chief of the yakshas; keeper of the treasures of the earth, Guardian of the North

kulam tank or pond (Tamil)

L

laddu round sweet snack

lakh 100,000

Lakshmana younger brother of Rama in the Ramayana

Lakshmi Goddess of wealth and good fortune, associated with the lotus; consort of Vishnu

lattice screen of cross laths: perforated

lena cave, usually a rock-cut sanctuary

lingam (linga) Siva as the phallic emblem

Lokeshwar 'Lord of the World', Avalokiteshwara to Buddhists and of Siva to Hindus

LTTE Liberation Tigers of Tamil Eelam, or "The Tigers", force rebelling against Sri Lankan Government in North and East

lungi wrap-around loin cloth

M

madrassa Islamic theological school or college

maha great; in Sri Lanka, the main rice crop

Mahabodhi Great Enlightenment of Buddha

Mahadeva lit 'Great Lord'; Siva

maharaja great king; maharajkumar, crown prince

maharani great queen

Mahavansa Literally "Great dynasty" or "Great Chronicle", the epic history from Vijaya, the legendary founder of Sri Lanka, to King Mahasena, d AC 303 a major source on early history and legend

Mahayana The Greater Vehicle; form of Buddhism practised in East Asia, Tibet and Nepal

Mahesha (Maheshvara) Great Lord; Siva

mahout elephant driver/keeper

mahseer large freshwater fish, carp found especially in Himalayan rivers

Maitreya the future Buddha

makara crocodile-shaped mythical creature

malai hill (Tamil)

mandapa columned hall preceding the sanctuary in a Jain or Hindu temple

mandir temple

mantra sacred chant for meditation by Hindus and Buddhists

Mara Tempter, who sent his daughters (and soldiers) to disturb the Buddha's meditation

marg 'path', wide roadway

maya illusion

Minakshi lit 'fish-eyed'; Parvati worshipped at Madurai, India

Mohammad 'the praised'; The Prophet; founder of Islam

moksha salvation, enlightenment; lit 'release'

moonstone the semi-circular stone step before a shrine carved with symbolic animals and plants

mudra symbolic hand gesture and posture associated with the Buddha

Muharram period of mourning in remembrance of Hasan and Hussain, two murdered sons of Ali

N

Naga (nagi/nagini) Snake deity; associated with fertility and protection

Nandi a bull, Siva's vehicle and a symbol of fertility

Narayana Vishnu as the creator of life

Nataraja Siva, Lord of the cosmic dance

Natha worshipped by Mahayana Buddhists as the bodhisattva Maitreya

navagraha nine planets, represented usually on the lintel or architrave of the front door of a temple

navaratri lit '9 nights'; name of the Dasara festival

niche wall recess containing a sculpted image or emblem, mostly framed by a pair of pilasters

nirvana enlightenment; (lit 'extinguished')

nritya pure dance

O

ola palm manuscripts (Sri Lanka)

oriel projecting window

oya seasonal river

P

pada foot or base

paddy rice in the husk

padma lotus flower Padmasana, lotus seat; posture of meditating figures

pagoda tall structure in several stories

Pali language of Buddhist scriptures

pankah (punkha) fan, formerly pulled by a cord

pansukulika Buddhist sect dwelling in forest hermitages

parapet wall extending above the roof

Parinirvana (parinibbana) the Buddha's state prior to nirvana, shown usually as a reclining figure

Parvati daughter of the Mountain; Siva's consort, sometimes serene, sometimes fearful

pilimage Buddhist image house

potgul library

pradakshina patha processional passage or ambulatory

puja ritual offerings to the gods; worship (Hindu)

pujari worshipper; one who performs puja (Hindu)

punya karma merit earned through actions and religious devotion (Buddhist)

R

raj rule or government

raja king, ruler (variations include rao rawal); prefix 'maha' means great

Rama Seventh incarnation of Vishnu; hero of the Ramayana epic

Ramayana ancient Sanskrit epic – the story of Rama

Randalas sub-caste of the Goyigama caste, part of the Sinhalese aristocracy

Ravana Demon king of Lanka; kidnapper of Sita, killed by Rama in the battle of the Ramayana

rickshaw 3-wheeled bicycle-powered (or 2-wheeled hand-powered) vehicle to transport passengers

Rig Veda (Rg) oldest and most sacred of the Vedas

rupee unit of currency in India, Pakistan, Nepal, and Sri Lanka

S

sagar lake; reservoir

Saiva (Shaiva) the cult of Siva

sal hall

sal hardwood tree of the lower slopes of Himalayan foothills

salaam greeting (Muslim); lit 'peace'

samadhi funerary memorial, like a temple but enshrining an image of the deceased; meditation state

samsara eternal transmigration of the soul

samudra sea, or large artificial lake

sangarama monastery

sangha ascetic order founded by Buddha

Saraswati wife of Brahma and goddess of knowledge; usually seated on a swan, holding a veena

Shakti Energy; female divinity often associated with Siva; also a name of the cult

shaman doctor/priest, using magic

Shankara Siva

sharia corpus of Muslim theological law

singh (sinha) lion; also Rajput caste name adopted by Sikhs

Sita Rama's wife, heroine of the Ramayana epic. Worshipped by Hindus, esp in Janakpur, India, her legendary birthplace

Siva The Destroyer among Hindu gods; often worshipped as a lingam or phallic symbol

Sivaratri lit 'Siva's night'; festival (Feb-Mar) dedicated to Siva

Skanda the Hindu god of war

sri (shri) honorific title, often used for 'Mr'; repeated as sign of great respect

stucco plasterwork

stupa hemispheric funerary mound; principal votive monument in a Buddhist religious complex

Subrahmanya Skanda, one of Siva's sons; Kartikkeya in S India

sudra lowest of the Hindu castes

svami (swami) holy man; also used as a suffix for temple deities

svastika (swastika) auspicious Hindu/ Buddhist emblem

T

tale tank (Sinhalese)

tank lake created for irrigation

Tara historically a Nepalese princess, now worshipped by Buddhists and Hindus, particularly in Nepal

thali S and W Indian vegetarian meal

torana gateway with two posts linked by architraves

tottam garden (Tamil)

Trimurti Triad of Hindu divinities, Brahma, Vishnu and Siva

U

Upanishads ancient Sanskrit philosophical texts, part of the Vedas

ur village (Tamil)

V

Valmiki sage, author of the Ramayana epic

varam village (Tamil)

varna 'colour'; social division of Hindus into Brahmin, Kshatriya, Vaishya and Sudra

Varuna Guardian of the West, accompanied by Makara (see above)

vatadage literally circular relic house, protective pillard and roofed outer cover for dagoba

Veda (Vedic) oldest known religious texts; include hymns to Agni, Indra and Varuna, adopted as Hindu deities

vel Skanda's trident

Vellala Tamil Hindu farming caste

verandah enlarged porch in front of a hall

vihara Buddhist or Jain monastery with cells opening off a central court

villu small lake (Sri Lanka)

Vishnu a principal Hindu deity; creator and preserver of universal order; appears in 10 incarnations (Dashavatara)

vitarka mudra Buddhist posture of discourse, the fingers raised

W

Wesak Commemoration day of the Buddha's birth, enlightenment and death

wewa tank or lake (Sinhalese)

Y

yala summer rice crop (Sri Lanka)

yoga school of philosophy concentrating on different mental and physical disciplines (yogi, a practitioner)

yoni female genital symbol, associated with the worship of the Siva Linga (phallus)

Index

NB items in *italic* indicate that the entry is in the coloured Sri Lanka Wildlife Guide in the middle of this Handbook. Those numbers in bold identicate an accompanying map. (M) indicates Maldives and (SL) Sri Lanka.

A

Abhayagiriya Dagoba 207
accommodation (M) 246
accommodation, Male 261
acknowledgements 39
Adam's Peak 144, ***192***
agriculture (M) 257
ahimsa 61
Ahungalla 115
AIDS 41
air travel (M) 244
air-conditioning 25
airport (M) 245
alcohol (M) 247
alcohol (SL) 30
Alif atoll, Isl (M) 265
Alimatha, Isl (M) 269
Aluthgama 114
Aluvihare 198
Ambalangoda 116
Ambalantota 132
Ambepussa 150
Angelfish W22
Animals W2
Anuradhapura 202, **203**
appearance 20
architecture
  Buddhist 73
  Hindu 74
Ari Beach, Isl (M) 265, 266, ***272***
arrival in Sri Lanka 19
art and architecture, booklist 36
Arugam Bay 236, **237**
Asiastic
  Elephant W2
  Wild Buffalo W2
Athurugau, Isl (M) 268
atoll 250
Aukana 201
Avissawella 141
Avocado Pear W18
Ayurvedic medicine 168

B

Baa atoll, Isl (M) 265, 269
Babbler
  Black-headed W12
  White-headed W6
Baddegama 118
Badulla 193
Bakr-Id 36
Balangoda 81, 146
Bamboo W20
Banana W14
Bandaranaike SWRD 149
Bandarawela 196
Bandos, Isl (M) 268
Banyan Tree, Isl (M) 268
Banyan W20
Barking Deer W2
Baros, Isl (M) 272
Bathala, Isl (M) 272
Batticaloa 235
Battulu Oya, Riv 164
Bawa, Bevis 115
Bawa, Geoffrey 99
Baya Weaver W6
Bear, Sloth W2
Bee-eater, Little W8
before travelling (SL) 40
Belihuloya 147
Bellan Bendi Pelessa 147
Bentota 114
Beruwela 113
Bhagavata Purana 79
bhakti 79
bhikkus 82
Bindunuwewa 196
Birds W6
  booklist 38
  Sanctuaries 133, 135
  watching 132, 133
Biyadhoo, Isl (M) 269
Black-headed Babbler W12
Blue Rock Dove W6
Blue Surgeon W22
Boar, Wild W2
Bodhi tree 57, 205
Bodhisattvas 53
Bodu Finolhu, Isl (M) 270
Boduhithi, Isl (M) 270
Bogambara, Lak 171
booklist
  art and architecture 36
  birds 38
  flora and fauna 38
  language 37
  literature 37
  Maldives 249
  maps 38
  natural history 38
  religion 37
  Sri Lanka 36
  travel 37
  wildlife 38
Bougainvillea W18
Brahminy Kite W6
Brazen Palace 205
Brief Garden, nr Bentota 115
Buddha, The ***53***, 63
Buddhism 53
  caste 66
  cosmology 56
  Hinayana 53
  Mahayana 53
  Sri Lankan 55
  Vajrayana 54
Buddhist
  architecture 73
  practice 56
Budugala 146
Buduruvagala 196

Buffalo
  Asiatic Wild *W2*
  water *W2*
Bulbul
  Red-vented ***W6***
  Yellow-eared ***W12***
Bundala, Npk 133, 135
Burghers 82

C

Cadjugama 150
Canna Lily ***W18***
cannon ball tree 51
canoes, outrigger 159
Cashew Nut ***W18***, 150
Cattle Egret ***W8***
caves, prehistoric 146, ***195***
Central province **169**
cemetery, WW2 231
Ceylon Grackle ***W12***
Ceylon Ironwood ***W14***
Ceylon Lorikeet ***W12***
Ceylon National Congress 87
changing money (M) 244
checklist
  general 18
  health 18
Chilaw 164
children, travelling with (SL) 31
Chital ***W2***
Cholas 77
Christianity 69
Cocoa Island, Isl (M) 268
Coconut Palm ***W20***
Colombo 93, **94**
  Bambalapitiya **103**
  Galle Face and Beira lake **99**
  Fortand Pettah **97**
  Kollupitiya **102**
Common Langur ***W5***
Common Mongoose ***W5***
Common Myna ***W6***
Coral
  Orange Tube ***W22***
  Soft ***W22***
  Staghorn ***W22***
cosmology, Buddhist 56
cowries ***W22***
Crocodile
  Estuarine ***W13***
  Marsh ***W13***
  Mugger ***W13***
  Saltwater ***W13***
Crow, House ***W6***
Culavansa 82

D

Dalada Maligawa 175, 206
Dalhousie 192
Dalugama 157
Dambulla **199**
Deepavali 36
Deer
  Barking ***W2***
  Spotted ***W2***
Demodara 194
Demon Dances 116
departure tax (SL) 20
Devanampiya Tissa 55, 83
Devil Dances 116, ***127***
dharma 60
Dhiffushi, Isl (M) 270
Dhiggiri, Isl (M) 272
Dhivehi 250, 252
dhonis (M) 248
diarrhoea 43
Digufinolhu, Isl (M) 268
Dikoya 192
Dikwella 130
Dimbula 193
diving (M) 266
Diyainna 147
Diyaluma Falls 197
Dodanduwa 120
Dondra 130
Dove
  Blue Rock ***W6***
  Spotted ***W6***
Dravida 77
drink (M) 247
drinking water (M) 247
Drongo ***W8***
Drongo, Racquet-tailed ***W8***
Duhinda Falls 194
Dumbara Hills 178
Durga 65
Duruthu Perahera 98
Dusky Blue Flycatcher ***W12***
Dutch, The 86

E

Eastern province **235**
economy (M) 257
Egret
  Cattle ***W8***
  Little ***W8***
Elara, King 205
Elephant Bath 177
Elephant
  Asiastic Elephant *W2*
  marsh 225, 238
Ella 195
Ellaidhoo, Isl (M) 272
Embekke Devalaya 177
Embilipitiya 147
Embudhu Finolhu, Isl (M) 270
Embudhu Village, Isl (M) 273
Encephalitis 41
entertainment (M) 248, 266
entertainment (SL) 32
Eriyadhu, Isl (M) 273
Esala Perahera, Kandy 178
Estuarine ***W13***
Eucalyptus ***W18***
exchange (M) 244

F

Farukolhufushi, Isl (M) 270
Fax (M) 248
festivals (M) 249
festivals (SL)
  Id-ul-Fitr 36
  Id-ul-Zuha 36
  Muslim 69
  poya days 58
fire-walking 138
fishing (M) 257
Fish-tail Palm ***W20***
Five-striped Palm Squirrel ***W5***
flag, Sri Lankan 47
Flowering plants ***W18***
Flowering trees ***W14***
Flycatcher Dusky Blue ***W12***
Flycatcher Paradise ***W8***
Flying Fox ***W5***
food (M) 247
food (SL) 26
foreign currency (SL) 19
Frangipani ***W18***
Fruit trees ***W14***
Full Moon Isl (M) 269
Fun Island Resort (M) 270
Further information (SL) 45

G

Gadaladeniya Temple 177
Gal Oya, Npk 236
Gal Vihara 223
Galle 120, **121**
Gampola 183, 192
Gan 255
Gan, Isl (M) 273

Ganesh 65
Ganga, Riv 77
Gayoom, Maumoon Abdul 256
Getting around (SL) 30
Ginigathena, Pas 141, 192
Giritale 218
Gopurams 77
government (M) 256
***Grackle* W12**
***Grackle, Ceylon* W12**
***Grey Tit* W12**
guardstones 74
***Gul Mohur* W14**
***Gum Tree* W18**

H

Habarana 213
Hakgala Gardens 186, 193
Halaveli, Isl (M) 270
Haldummulla 147
Hali-Ela 193, 194
Hambantota 133, **134**
Handagiriya 147
***Hanuman Langur* W5**
Hanuman 64
Hanwella 141
Haputale 197
Hatton 192
health (SL) 40
  AIDS 41
  diarrhoea 43
  heat stroke 45
  heat 42
  Hepatitis A 41
  immunization 40
  inoculation 40
  insect pests 25
  leeches 145
  Malaria 41
  medicines 45
  Meningitis 41
  Polio 40
  rabies ***41***, 45
  snake bites 44
  stomach upsets 43
  sunburn 45
  tetanus 40
  typhoid 40
  vaccinations 40
health (M) 244
Helengeli, Isl (M) 273
helicopters (M) 247
Heneratgoda 149
herbal cures 168
***Hibiscus* W18**
Hikkaduwa **117, 118**
***Hill Myna* W12**
Hinayana cosmology 56
Hinayana 53
Hindu sects 64
Hindu temple architecture 74
Hinduism 59
history (M) 254
Holiday Island, Isl (M) 270
holidays (M) 249
holidays (SL) 32
Homo Sapiens Balangodensis
  147, ***195***
Horana 142
***Hornbill, Malabar Pied* W8**
Horton Plains, Npk 189
hotel categories (SL) 24
hotel, resort, prices (M) 265
hotels (M) 246
hotels, Male 261
***House Crow* W6**
***House Sparrow* W6**
Hudhuveli, Isl (M) 270
Hulule 245
Hummanaya 130
Hungama 132
Huvahendhu, Isl (M) 272

I

Id-ul-Fitr 36
Id-ul-Zuha 36
Ihuru, Isl (M) 270
Imperial (Emperor)
  ***Angelfish* W22**
Induruwa 115
industries (M) 261
Infectious Hepatitis (jaundice)
  41
Information for Visitors (SL) 15
Inginiyagala 236
insects 42
Islam, Sri Lanka 67
island resorts, Maldives 268
Issurumuniyagala 204
Istripura Caves 193

J

***Jacana, Pheasant-tailed* W12**
***Jacaranda* W14**
Ja-ela 157
Jaffna 240
***Jakfruit* W14**
Jambudvipa 74
Jati 66
Jayawardenepura 98
Jetavanarama Dagoba 206
Jetavanarama 223
JVP 88

K

Kaafu atoll, Isl (M) 265, 266
Kaduwela 141
Kala Oya 165
Kalametiya Bird Sanctuary 132
Kali 65
Kalpitiya 165
Kalutara 113
Kandy 170, **173**
Kandyan Kingdom 84
Kanifinolhu, Isl (M) 270
Kantalai 233
Karambagala 133
karma 60
Kasyapa, King 214
Kataragama 65, 138
Katugastota 177
Kegalla 151
***King Coconut* W20**
Kingfisher, White-breasted
  W6
Kiriberiya 142
Kirinda 136
Kirti Sri 171
Kite
  ***Brahminy* W6**
  ***Pariah* W6**
Kitulgala 141
Knuckles Range 178
Kogalla 127
Kosgoda 115
Kotte 98
Krishna 63
Kubera 215
Kuda Rah, Isl (M) 269
Kudahithi, Isl (M) 268
Kumana Bird Sanctuary 237
Kuragala Cave 146
Kuramathi, Isl (M) 272
Kuredu, Isl (M) 273
Kurumba, Isl (M) 269
Kurunegala **154, 155**
Kuruwita 142

L

Labookellie Tea Estate 183
Laguna Beach Resort 269
Lahugala National Park, Npk
  237

lakes 48
Lakshmi 64
language (M) 252
language (SL) 79
language, booklist 37
Langur
Common W5
Hanuman W5
Purple-faced W2
Lankan finolhu, Isl (M) 273
Lankatilaka Viharaya, Kandy 177
Lankatilaka 223
Lapwing, Red-wattled W8
Layard's Parakeet W12
Leather-back Turtle W23
Leopard W2
Lhaviyani atoll, Isl (M) 265, 273
Lhohifushi, Isl (M) 272
Liberation Tigers of Tamil Eelam (LTTE) 88
Lily Beach, Isl (M) 272
Lily
Canna W18
Water W18
Linga 65
literature, booklist 37
Little Bee-eater W8
Little Egret W8
Long-nosed Butterfly Fish W22
Lorikeet, Ceylon W12

M

Maayafushi, Isl (M) 273
Macaque, Tocque W5
Madampe 146, 164
Madungala 132
Maduru Oya National Park, Npk 225
Maduwanwela 147
Magpie-robin W6
Mahapelessa 133
Mahara 149
Mahavansa 82
Mahaweli Ganga, Riv 177
Mahayana 53
Mahinda 209
Mahiyangana 225, **226**
Maho 156
Maitreya 55
Malabar Pied Hornbill W8
Malala Lagoon 133
malaria 44
MALDIVES 260
accommodation 246
agriculture 257
air travel 244
airport 245
alcohol 247
changing money 244
climate 250
clothing 245
communication 258
conduct 245
crime 246
culture 252
currency 244
customs 245
customs, social 245
diving 266
drink 247
drinking water 247
economy 257
entertainment 248, 266
exchange 244
Fax 248
festivals 249
fishing 257
government 256
health 244
helicopters 247
history 254
holidays 249
hotels 246
island resorts 268
language 252
money 244
opening times 246
overseas representations 243
people 252
phones 248
places of interest 259
prices, resorts 265
rainfall 251
religion 253
representations 243
resort categories 265
resort islands 268
shipping 257
shopping 246
specialist tour operators 244
telephones 248
temperatures 250
toilets 246
tourism 257
tourist offices overseas 244
transfer to resorts 265
travel to Maldives 244
travel, internal 247
travellers cheques 244
visas 243
voltage 246
water supply 246
watersports 266
wildlife 251
Male atolls, Isl (M) 265
MALE 259, 260
mandala 74
Mango W14
manuscripts, palm 198
maps 38
Maradanmaduwa 165
Marawila 164
Marsh Crocodile W13
marsh elephant 225
Maskeliya 192
Matale 198
Matara 128, **129**
Md Takarufanu 255
medicines 45
Meerufenfushi, Isl (M) 273
Meetiyagoda 116
Meningitis 41
Mihintale 209, **210, 211**
Minneriya-Giritale, Npk 218
Mirisawetiya Dagoba 204
Mirissa 128
Money Cowrie W22
money (M) 244
Mongoose, Common W5
Monitor W13
Moonstones 73, 116
Moors 82
Moplas 255
Moratuwa 113
Mt Lavinia **112**
Mt Meru 74
Mugger W13
Mulgirigala 131
Munneswaram 164
Muntjac W2
Murex W22
museums (M) 261
Muslim
beliefs 67
calendar 69
festivals 69
Sects 68
Myna
Common W6
Myna W12
Mythology 63, 76

N

Nakatchafushi, Isl (M) 271
Nalanda 198
Nandin 65
Nanophrys frogs 51
Nasir, Ibrahim 256
national anthem 47
national festivals (SL) 32
national holidays (SL) 32
National Parks **52**
- Bundala 133, 135
- Gal Oya 236
- Horton Plains 189
- Kalametiya Bird Sanctuary 132
- Kumana Bird Sanctuary 237
- Lahugala 237
- Maduru Oya 225
- Minneriya-Giritale 218
- Peak Wilderness 146, 189
- Ruhunu 139
- Sinharaja Biosphere 144
- Somawathie 234
- Uda Walawe 148
- Wasgomuwa 225
- Wilpattu 165
- Wirawila Wewa 135
- Yala East 237
- Yala 139

Nattarampota 178
natural history, booklist 38
Negombo 157, **158, 160**
newspapers (SL) 32
Nika, Is 268
Nissankamalla, King 100
Nissankamalla, King 219, 223
Nittambuwa 150
Nochchiyagama 166
North Central province **169**
Northern provinces 240
Nuwara Eliya 184, **185**

O

Ocean Reef Club, Isl (M) 273
Ohiya 189
Olhuveli, Isl (M) 268
opening times (M) 246
Orchids W18
oruva 159
overseas representations, Maldives 243

P

Painted Stork W8
Palk Straits 47
palm manuscripts 198
Panadura 142
Panama 237
Pandiyas 77
Panther W2
Papaya W14
Paradise Flycatcher W8
Parakeet
- ***Layard's W12***
- ***Rose-ringed W8***

Parakrama Samudra, Lak 219
Parakramabahu, King 84, 219
Pariah Kite W6
Parvati 65
Pasyala 150
Peafowl W8
Peak Wilderness Sanctuary, Npk 146, 189
Pedro, Mt, Mnt 187
Peepal W20
Pelican, Spot-billed W8
people (M) 252
Peradeniya **151**
Perahera, Kandy 178
personal security 22
Pettah, Colombo 96
Pheasant-tailed Jacana W12
phones (M) 248
Pidurangala 214
Pidurutalagala, Mnt 187
Pigeon Island 233
pilgrimage 76
Pineapples W20
Pinnawela Elephant Orphanage 150
Pitcher Plant W18
places of interest (M) 259
Polhena **129**
police 21, 22
Polio 40
Polonnaruwa 219, **220, 222**
Portuguese 86
postal services (SL) 32
Pottuvil **237**
poya days 58
prayer flags 205
prehistory 146, **195**
price of accommodation (SL) 24
prices, resorts (M) 265
puja 61
Purple-faced Langur W2
Pussellawa 183
Puttalam 164

R

rabies ***41***, 45
Racquet-tailed Drongo W8
radio 32
railway retiring rooms 25
Rain Tree W18
rainfall (SL) 49
rainfall (M) 251
Raja Maha Vihara 98
Rajaraja I 84
Rajarata 83
Rama 64
Ramadan 69
Ramayana 64, 138
Ramboda 183
Ranagala 148
Rangali, Isl 271
Ranna 132
Rannalhi, Isl (M) 271
Rasdhu atoll, Isl (M) 265, ***271***
Ratnapura 142, **143**
Ravana 138
Rawana (Ravana) Ella Cave 195
reading list 36
- art and architecture 36
- birds 38
- flora and fauna 38
- language 37
- literature 37
- Maldives 249
- maps 38
- natural history 38
- religion 37
- Sri Lanka 36
- travel 37
- wildlife 38

rebirth 60
Red-fin Butterfly Fish W22
Red-vented Bulbul W6
Red-wattled Lapwing W8
Reethi Rah, Isl 271
religion (M) 253
religion, booklist 37
representations, Maldives 243
Reptiles W13
resort categories (M) 265
resort islands, Maldives 268
Rhiveli, Isl (M) 268
Rhododendron W18
rice W20
Ridiyagama 133

Ritigala 212
rivers 48
Rohana 83
Rose-ringed Parakeet W8
rubber W20
Ruhunu, Npk 139
Ruvanwelisiya Dagoba 204

S

Sadhu 59
safaris 267
safety (SL) 22
Sago W20
Sakra 83
sal, Sri Lanka 51
Saltwater Crocodile W13
Samadhi Buddha 206
Sambhur W2
Sampalthivu 231
samsara 60
Sanghamitta, Princess 205
sanni 116
Sapugaskanda 149
Sarasvati 64
Sardinella W22
Sasseruwa 201
Sati 65
Scorpion Fish W22
Sea Fans W22
Sea Urchins W22
Seashore and marine life
- ***Angelfish W22***
- ***Blue Surgeon W22***
- ***cowries W22***
- ***Imperial (Emperor) Angelfish W22***
- ***Leather-back Turtle W23***
- ***Loggerhead Turtles W23***
- ***Long-nosed Butterfly Fish W22***
- ***Money Cowrie W22***
- ***Olive Ridley Turtle W23***
- ***Orange Tube Coral W22***
- ***Red-fin Butterfly Fish W22***
- ***Sardinella W22***
- ***Scorpion Fish W22***
- ***Sea Fans W22***
- ***Sea Urchins W22***
- ***Soft Corals W22***
- ***Spider Conch W22***
- ***Staghorn Coral W22***
- ***Tiger Cowrie W22***

security (SL) 22
Seenigama 117
Senanayake, Dudley 87
shipping (M) 257
shopping (SL) 22
shopping (M) 246
Sigiriya 214, **215**
Sihalam 10
Silk Cotton Tree W14
Sinhala 79
Sinhalese 79
- nationalism 56

Sinharaja Biosphere Reserve, Npk 144
Sinnukgala 148
Sita 138
Situlpahuwa 139
Siva 65
Sivarathri 36
Skanda 65
sloth bear 165
Sloth Bear W2
snake bites 44
Soft Corals W22
soft drinks 26
Somawathie National Park, Npk 234
Soneva, Isl (M) 269
Southern provinces (SL) **110**
Southern Highlands **190**
Sparrow, House W6
specialist tour operators (M) 244
Spider Conch W22
Spot-billed Pelican W8
Spotted Deer W2
Spotted Dove W6
Squrrel Five-striped Palm W5
Sri Jayawardenepura 98
Sri Lanka Freedom Party 88
Sri Lanka 9
- air-conditioning 25
- alcohol 30
- appearance 20
- arrival 19
- Before travelling 15
- before travelling 40
- children, travelling with 31
- climate 49
- Communications 32
- conduct 20
- confidence tricksters 22
- courtesy 20
- credit cards 17
- cuisine 26
- currency regulations 19
- current affairs, booklist 36
- departure tax 20
- entertainment 32
- entry requirements 15
- flag 47
- flora and fauna, booklist 38
- food 26
- foreign currency 19
- further information 45
- further reading 36
- getting around 30
- getting there 18
- health 40
- holidays 32
- hotel categories 24
- information for Visitors 15
- Islam 67
- language 79
- money 16
- national anthem 47
- national festivals 32
- national holidays 32
- newspapers 32
- on arrival 19
- personal security 22
- police 21, 22
- postal services 32
- price of accommodation 24
- radio 32
- railway retiring rooms 25
- rainfall 49, **50**
- safety 22
- security 22
- shopping 22
- soft drinks 26
- telephone services 32
- television 32
- temperatures **50**
- tipping 23
- toilets 26
- transport to Sri Lanka 18
- travel permits 15
- travel 30
- vegetation 51
- visas 15
- What to pay 24
- When to go 16
- Where to stay 24
- wildlife 51

Sri Vikrama Raja Sinha 174
stilt fishing 127
stomach upsets 43
Stork, Painted W8
stupas 73
Sun, Isl (M) 271
sunburn 45
sunnis 68

T

Talawakele 193
Tamarind W14
Tamil 79
Tangalla **129**, 130
tea 91, ***188***
tea W20
tea (M) 247
telephones (SL) 32
telephones (M) 248
television 32
temperatures (SL) 50
temperatures (M) 250
Temple architecture, Hindu 74
Temple of the Tooth
  Kandy 175
  Polonnaruwa 222
tetanus 40
Theravada 53
Thundufushi, Isl (M) 269
Thuparama 206
Tiger Cowrie W22
Tika 131
Timbirimankada 148
tipping 23
Tissa, Devanampiya 55, 202, ***209***
Tissamaharama 135
Tissawewa 136, 204
Tit Grey W12
Tocque Macaque W5
toilets (SL) 26
toilets (M) 246
Tooth relic 156, 170
tourism (M) 257
tourist offices overseas (M) 244
transfer to resorts (M) 265
transport to Sri Lanka 18
travel permits 15
travel to Maldives 244
Travel 30
t booklist 37
  internal (M) 247
travellers cheques (M) 244
Tree
  Bamboo W20
  Banyan W20
  Cashew Nut W18
  Ceylon Ironwood W14
  Coconut Palm W20
  Eucalyptus W18
  Fish-tail Palm W20
  Flowering W14
  Fruit trees W14
  Gul Mohur W14
  Gum W18
  Jacaranda W14
  Jakfruit W14
  King Coconut W20
  Papaya W14
  Peepal W20
  Rain W18
  rubber W20
  Silk Cotton W14
  Tamarind W14
Trees and plants W14
Trincomalee 229, **230, 232**
Turtle 115, 120
  Leather-back W23
  Loggerhead W23
  Olive Ridley W23
typhoid 40

U

Uda Walawe National Park, Npk 148
Udappawa 164
Uggal Kaltota 146
Uma 65
Unawatuna 125, **126**
United National Party 88
Uttaradesa 83
Uva **169**, 193

V

Vaadhoo, Isl (M) 271
Vaavu atoll, Isl (M) 265, 269, 272
Vabbinfaru, Isl (M) 268
vaccinations 40
Vajrayana 54
Vakarufalhi, Isl M 271
Valagam Bahu, King 199
Varaha 63
Varna 66
Vattagamani Abhaya 55
Vedanta 61
Veddas ***81***, 225
vegetation 51
vel 66
Veligandu Huraa, Isl (M) 271
Veligandu, Isl (M) 271
Vellalas 67
Vijayabahu I 84
Vijayanagar 77
Vilamendhu, Isl (M) 272
Villivaru, Isl (M) 271
Vimala Dharma Suriya 170
visas (SL) 15
visas (M) 243
Vishnu 62
Vishnu 63
voltage (M) 246

W

Waikkal 162
walauwas 147
Warakapola 150
Wasgomuwa National Park, Npk 225
Watawela 141, 192
Water Buffalo W2
water cutting 179
Water Lily W18
water supply (M) 246
watersports (M) 266
Wattala 157
Weaver, Baya W6
Weligama **127**
Welimada 193
Wellawaya 196
Werahena 130
Western provinces **110**
What to pay 24
White-breasted Kingfisher W6
White-headed Babbler W6
Wild Boar W2
Wildlife guide to Sri Lanka W1
wildlife 51
wildlife (M) 251
wildlife, booklist 38
Wilpattu, Npk 165
Wirawila Wewa, Npk 135
Wolfendahl Church, Colombo 97
World's End 190
worship
  Buddhism 57
  Christian 70
WW2, cemetery 231

Y

Yala East National Park, Npk 237
Yala, Npk 139
Yapahuwa 156
Yellow-eared Bulbul W12
Yoga 61

WHAT OUR READERS SAY

"A travel guide business that looks set to sweep the world."
The Independent

"Truly excellent guides quite unequalled by competing guides - they have saved their cover price many times over."
J.Hollins, Hampshire

"The most electrifying of all practical travel guides."
Wall Street Journal, USA

"More information - less blah!"
V.Benderoth, Germany

"Superb - you don't need anything else!"
Financial Times, London

"We have used your Thailand & Burma Handbook and have found your recommendations and advice excellent."
M. Jollands, Australia

"Mines of information and free of pretentiousness: make other guidebooks read like Butlins brochures."
Bookshop Review, UK

"We had a wonderful trip and I must say it was due in a very large part to the information in your Handbook."
W.Fischer, USA

"Your guidebooks stand head and shoulders above the competitors."
T Smith, USA